Shunga
Erotic Art in Japan

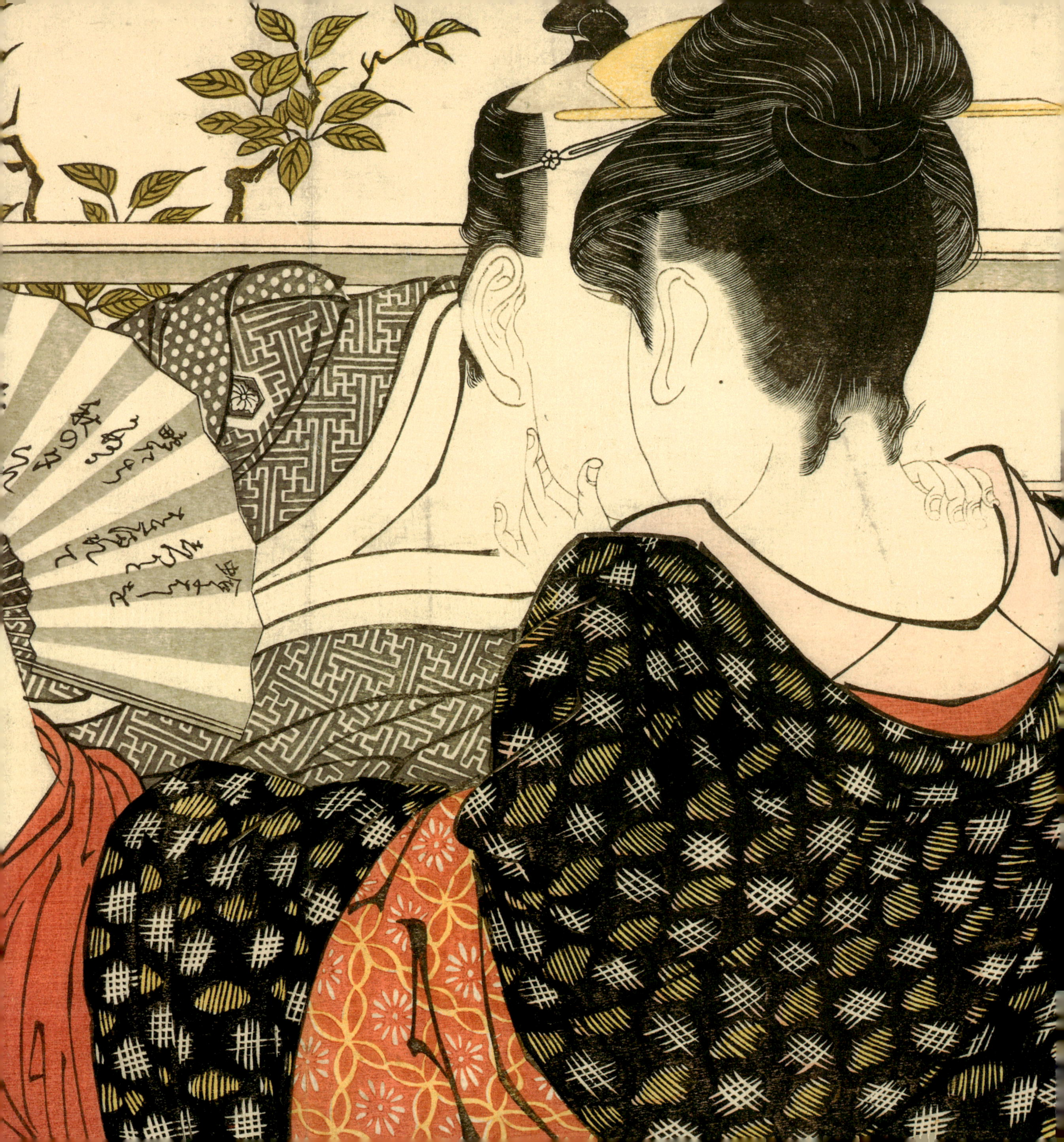

Shunga

EROTIC ART IN JAPAN

ROSINA BUCKLAND

THE BRITISH MUSEUM PRESS

Rosina Buckland has asserted the right to be identified
as the author of this work

First published in 2010 by The British Museum Press
A division of The British Museum Company Ltd
38 Russell Square, London WC1B 3QQ

britishmuseum.org/publishing

Reprinted 2013, 2104

A catalogue record for this book is available from
the British Library

ISBN 978-0-7141-2463-6

Design by Anne Odling-Smee, O-SB Design

Printed in Hong Kong by Printing Express Ltd

The papers used in this book are recyclable products
and the manufacturing processes are expected
to conform to the environmental regulations of the
country of origin.

Frontispiece: Kitagawa Utamaro
***Poem of the Pillow* (*Utamakura*) (detail)**
New Year 1788
Colour woodblock-printed album,
each sheet approx. 25.5 × 37 cm
Caption details pp. 108–9

p. 6: Hishikawa Morohira
Scenes of love-making (detail)
1688–1711
Handscroll painting, ink, colour
and gold on silk, H: 32.6 cm
Caption details p. 71

Contents

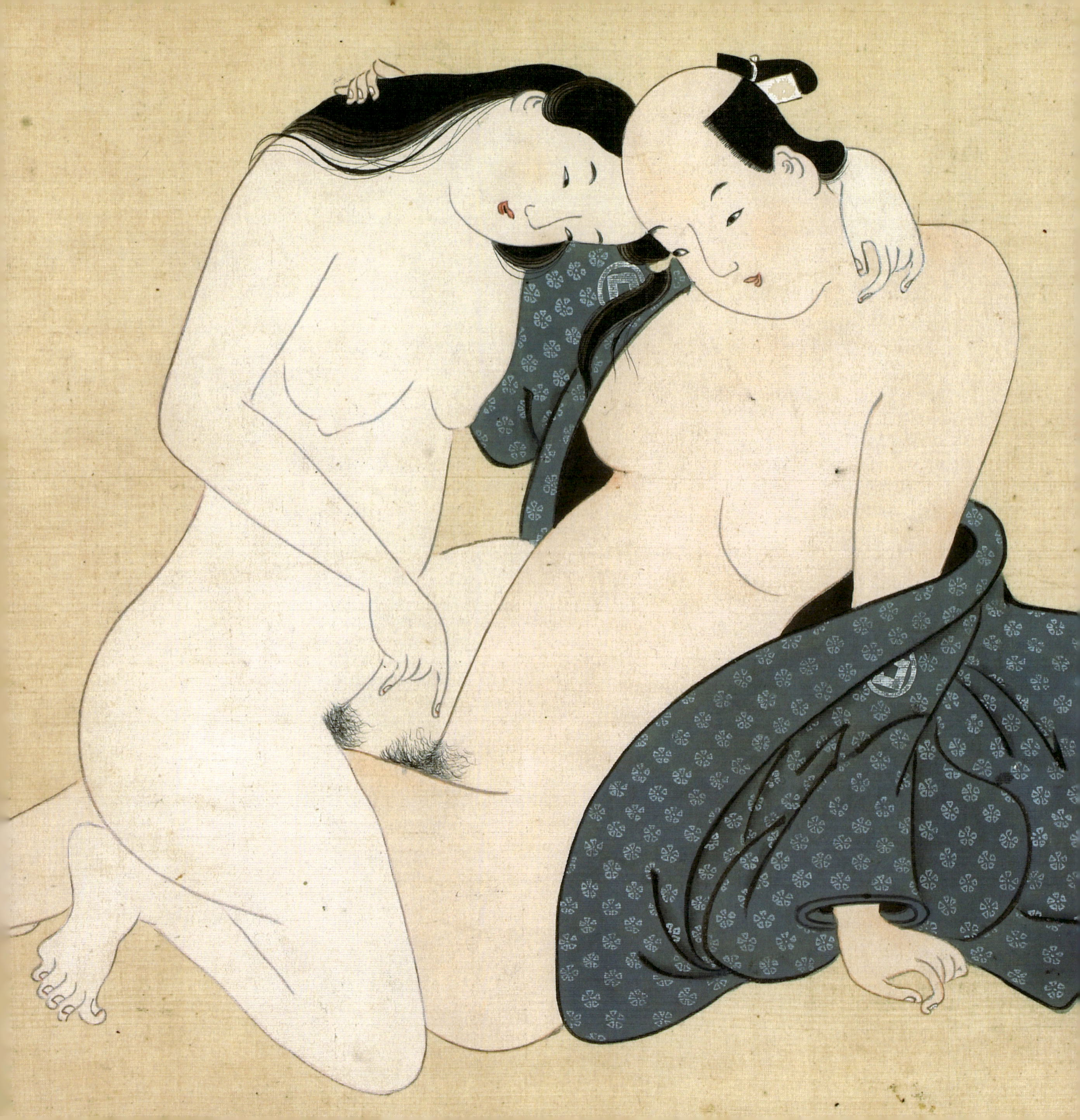

Preface and acknowledgements

Over the course of three centuries, from roughly 1600 to 1900, an extraordinarily large quantity of prints, illustrated books and paintings with erotic or explicitly sexual themes, now known as *shunga*, was produced in Japan. Within the extensive collection of Japanese prints and paintings at the British Museum, there are over 250 erotic works. Attitudes towards such material have varied over the course of the Museum's history, just as they have in the country of their production. Today, however, the works are recognized as constituting some of the masterpieces of this erotic art, not just in Japan, but in the world. This book traces the history of *shunga* production, illustrated with artworks in the British Museum's collection, many previously unpublished.

Sex is an experience shared by the vast majority of mature humans, and its depiction in art might be thought of as universally understandable. However, *shunga* are very much a product of the society and culture which created them, and therefore require a certain amount of 'decoding'. The situation and characters involved in the images are explained here, with translations of the accompanying dialogue. Alongside examples of these remarkable artworks from across the historical range of the collection, this book explains the background of *shunga* production, their functions and general characteristics, as well as the various measures which were taken historically to control their distribution.

I am grateful to colleagues in the Department of Asia, led by Keeper Jan Stuart, for their encouragement and assistance with this project. The opportunity to study this rich subject came to me thanks to Timothy Clark, and I am in his debt for the support and advice he has given throughout. Likewise, Ellis Tinios shared enthusiastically his knowledge and materials, and offered a valuable sounding board. Both kindly read a draft of the book and contributed invaluable comments. My thanks go to Israel Goldman for allowing me to study and reproduce works from his collection, and to Professor Drew Gerstle of the School of Oriental and African Studies, University of London, for inviting me to participate in the larger research project on Japanese erotic art, which will culminate in an exhibition at the British Museum in Spring 2013. In my research I relied greatly on the studies of Hayakawa Monta, who shared generously his time and ideas, showing me the highlights of the *shunga* collection in the International Research Center for Japanese Studies, Kyoto. Ishigami Aki, of Ritsumeikan University, patiently answered my enquiries about the text and interpretation of works. Much of the photography came from the digitization project of the Art Research Center, Ritsumeikan University, led by Professor Akama Ryō. I am also grateful to the British Museum photographers, and the team at the British Museum Press. Lastly, for helping me to understand better a myriad of things, my partner Ian Astley has my thanks, and love.

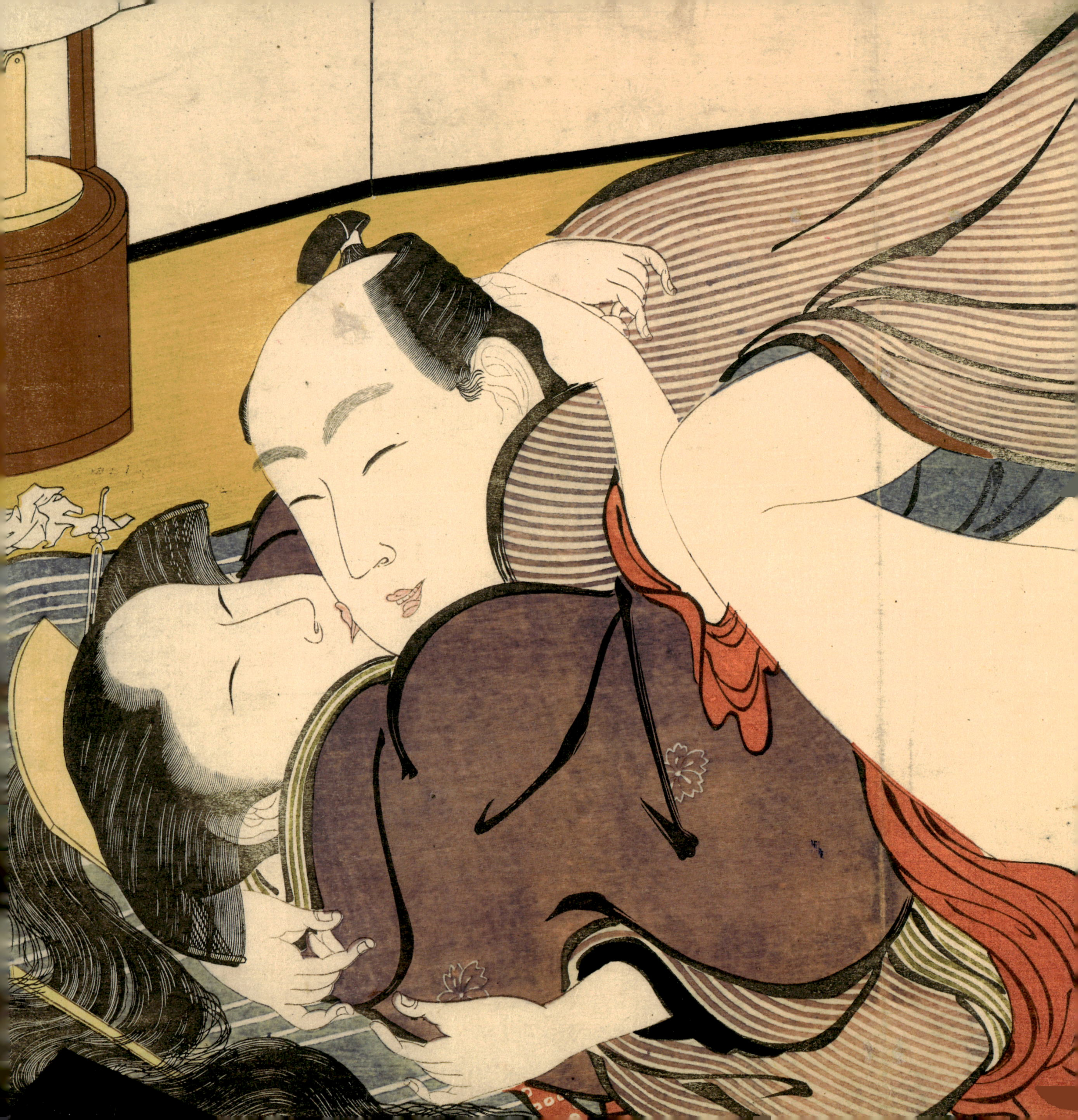

Picturing sex in Japan, 1600–1900

Opposite: Kitagawa Utamaro
***Poem of the Pillow* (*Utamakura*) (detail)**
New Year 1788
Colour woodblock-printed album,
each sheet approx. 25.5 × 37 cm
Caption details p. 10

Right: Kitagawa Utamaro
***Poem of the Pillow* (*Utamakura*)**
New Year 1788
Colour woodblock-printed album,
each sheet approx. 25.5 × 37 cm

Furtive outdoor encounters appear fairly frequently in *shunga*. Here, a man and a woman enjoy a rendezvous in a grove of blossoming cherry trees, all the while keeping an eye out for passers-by. She wears leggings to protect her legs while walking, and a pipe-case and tobacco-pouch hang at his waist, secured by a circular *netsuke* (toggle). The genitals are not visible, but the folds of the robes all converge to create a strong visual focus. This design is from the erotic masterpiece *Poem of the Pillow*, an album by the revered artist Kitagawa Utamaro (see also pp. 117–27).

The term *shunga* refers to a genre of erotic imagery, often explicit and usually beautifully produced, exploring endless variations of love-making, both male-female and same-sex, and extending to scenarios from the realms of fantasy. Images may also depict scenes of flirtation, arousal, foreplay and post-coital relaxation (or exhaustion). The subjects of *shunga* are by and large the ordinary men and women of urban Japan, shown in everyday situations. The settings are as varied as the characters, many encounters taking place in homes (often watched by other people in the house), as well as working environments and out of doors.

Shunga were popular in Japan from the early 1600s to the end of the 1800s. They were just one type of imagery from a large publishing industry that at its height produced tens of thousands of pictures every year. Prints and books were commercial products, and sex was a highly marketable commodity. *Shunga* were available in a range of formats, from expensive, multi-volume books down to small, cheaply priced prints. Approximately 1,200 erotic

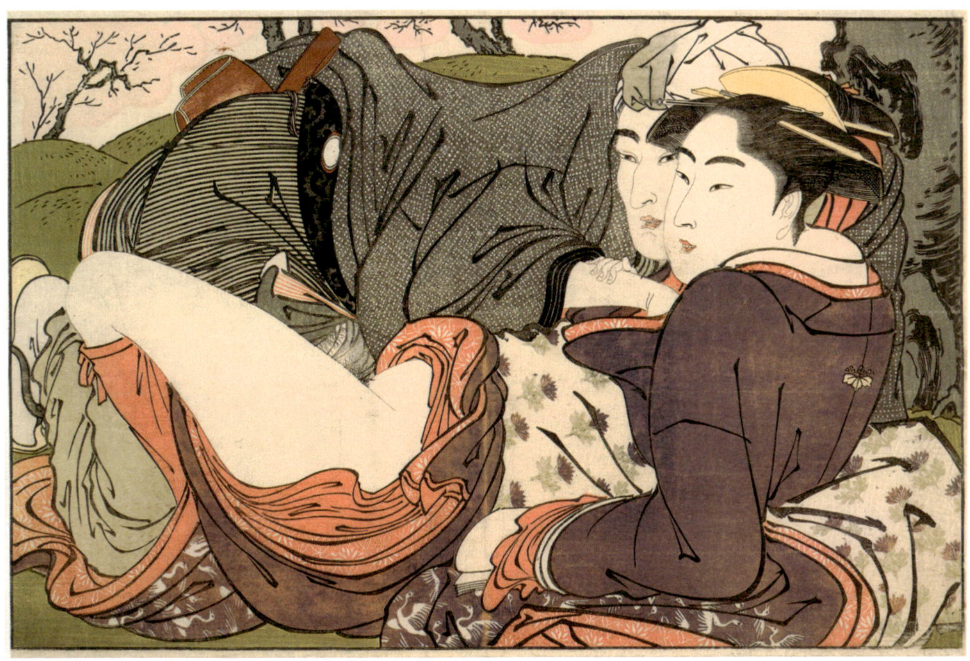

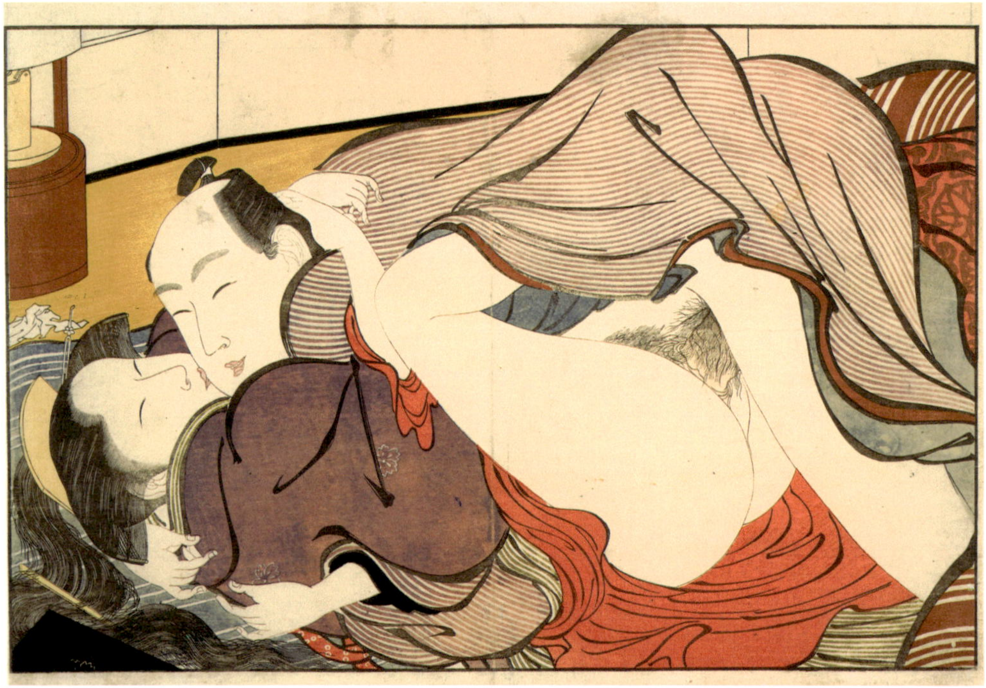

Kitagawa Utamaro
***Poem of the Pillow* (*Utamakura*)**
New Year 1788
Colour woodblock-printed album, each sheet approx. 25.5 × 37 cm

A particular feature of *shunga* is the emphasis on the mutual enjoyment of both man and woman. In this design, again from Utamaro's *Poem of the Pillow*, a couple clasp each other tightly in the privacy of their bedroom at night (indicated by the standing lantern). The man's lips are parted in a smile of pleasure, and the woman presses her lips to his cheek.

illustrated books are known to have survived from 1600 to 1868 (known as the 'Tokugawa period' after the ruling dynasty), but there are certainly many more that have not survived or not yet been recorded by scholars. The majority of such pictures were produced by the woodblock-printing technique, involving a team of print artist, block-cutter and printer, but there were also unique paintings available to wealthier customers.

Some of the most famous artists of the day designed *shunga*. For the majority of print artists and painters working in the popular mode, erotic book illustrations and designs for albums (and sometimes also paintings) were an integral part of their work. Furthermore, the evidence of a manual used by the lineage of painters in service to the government, containing a section on 'Methods for Erotic Pictures', suggests that even official artists needed to know how to paint erotic works for particular commissions from patrons.[1]

Attitudes to sex: Japan and Europe

The vast majority of *shunga* depict ordinary, consensual sexual relations between lovers, husband and wife, or sometimes prostitute and client. Furthermore, the situations represented are often intended to provoke laughter, and the scenes are usually accompanied by descriptive text or in-picture dialogue providing further amusement. *Shunga* are very different in tone from Western 'pornography'. During this period Europe also produced much erotic imagery, but it rarely, if ever, displays the same level of artistic or technical quality as *shunga*. The reason for this lies in the different attitudes towards sex. In pre-modern Japan, sex was considered to be a natural part of human experience, to be explored, enjoyed and celebrated, both for the pleasure it gave and for its positive associations with fertility. There was little sense of shame

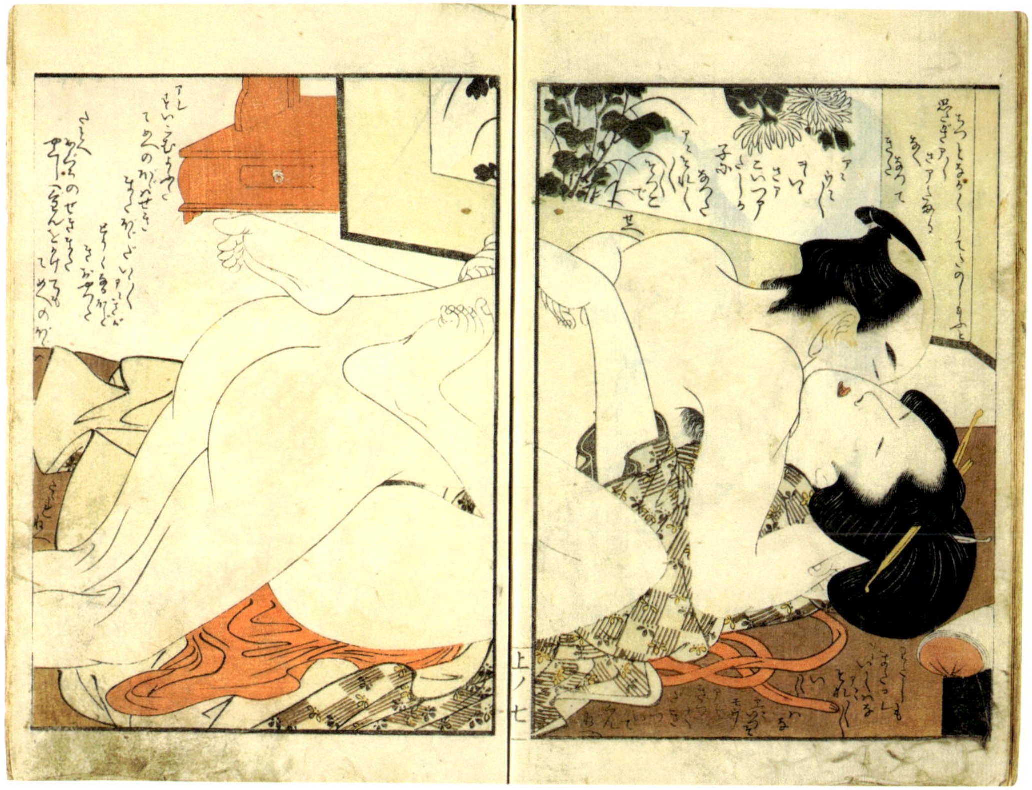

Kitagawa Utamaro
Picture-book: The Laughing Drinker
(*Ehon warai jōgo*)
c. 1803
Colour woodblock-printed book,
20.7 × 15 cm (covers)

Most of the people depicted in *shunga* are ordinary men and women. Here, a young married couple make love enthusiastically in their bedroom. We can listen in on their conversation in the text inscribed on the image. The husband compliments his wife, saying, 'What a great pussy you have – I feel like I'm being sucked right in.' She demands, 'I want to be pleasured much more.'

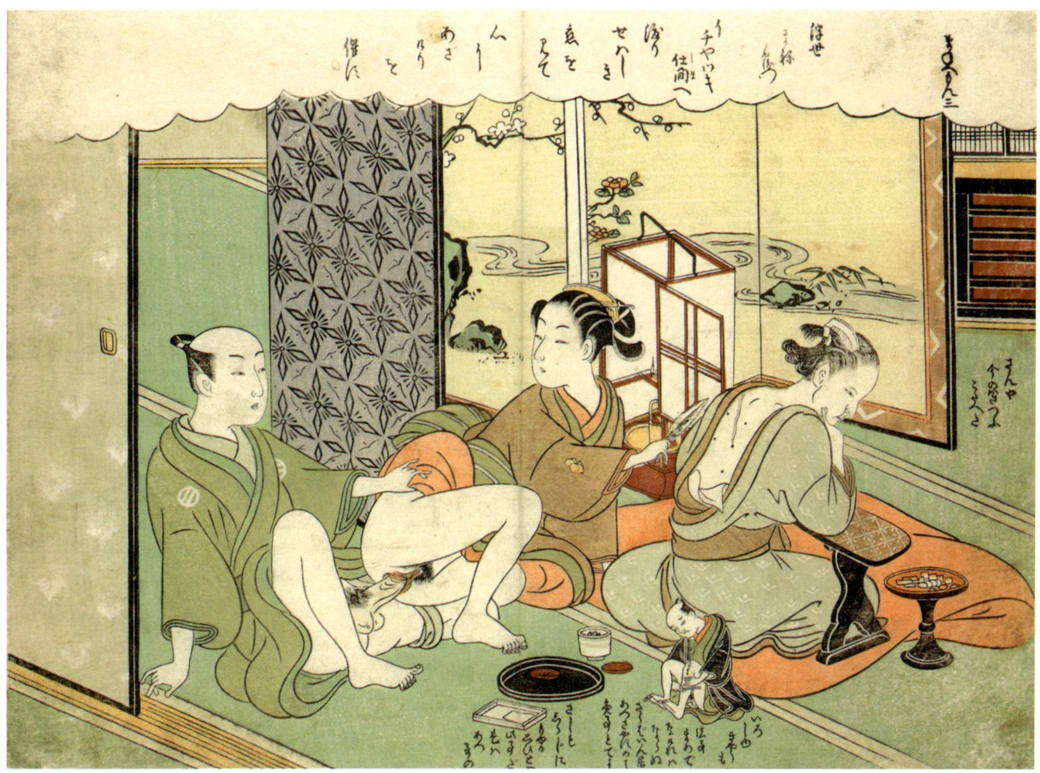

Suzuki Harunobu
Fashionable Lusty Mane'emon
(*Fūryū enshoku Mane'emon*), no. 3
1770
Colour woodblock print,
20.6 × 28.5 cm

In another domestic scene, a wife uses a feather to apply heated moxa (a medicinal herb held to stimulate circulation) to her mother-in-law's back. Her husband, meanwhile, has returned from work and administers his own 'treatment'.

or 'sin' associated with sexual activity or its representation. There was no strict religious or moral code relating to sex: it was instead the rules concerning correct social relations that set the limits on what was permissible.

This relative social acceptance of erotica had its roots in far older attitudes towards sexuality within Japanese society, and the importance of sexual imagery in Japanese culture. An ancient creation myth told of sibling deities, Izanagi and Izanami, who generated the islands of Japan. From prehistoric times there survive stone and clay amulets, wall-carvings and *haniwa* (ceramic figurines placed on tomb mounds) on which the figures' sexual organs are emphasized, or they are shown having sexual intercourse. Phallic worship, with its veneration of the generative power of the penis, and the wider association with fertility and crop harvests, held an important place in the form of worship now known as Shintō, based on animistic beliefs. At many shrines across Japan there are still festivals at which a large phallus is carried in procession. People would make a votive offering of a wooden phallus to petition for help with problems related to sexual performance, fertility or venereal disease. In Buddhism, which originated in India and came to Japan in the sixth century AD, the image of sexual union was used to illustrate cosmic principles. In particular the 'wisdom king' Aizen (literally, 'soaked with passion'), an esoteric Buddhist deity, represented the channelling of sexual energy towards enlightenment.

By contrast, in Europe during the seventeenth to nineteenth centuries sexual desire and activity were closely bound up with Judaeo-Christian beliefs regarding 'original sin' and mankind's fallen state. Depictions of sexual intercourse were subject to moral censure, resulting in a clandestine atmosphere surrounding their production and consumption, which served only to heighten their appeal. Labelled 'pornography', such imagery was regarded as dangerous and subversive, and was thought to demonstrate a preoccupation with depicting 'perversions', or unorthodox sexual practices.

Daikoku
Mid-19th century
Wood, H. 9 cm

The erect phallus suggested fertility and good fortune, as can be seen in its combination with deities who were the objects of widespread, popular worship. Daikoku was one of the seven Gods of Good Fortune and was associated particularly with wealth. He is shown standing on two rice bales (signifying plentiful food), holding a sack and a mallet. When lifted off the bales, this figure reveals a miniature Daikoku within, shaped as a phallus, with his customary flat cap forming the glans. Though undoubtedly designed to provoke humour, the presence of the phallus, both when hidden and revealed, possesses beneficent power.

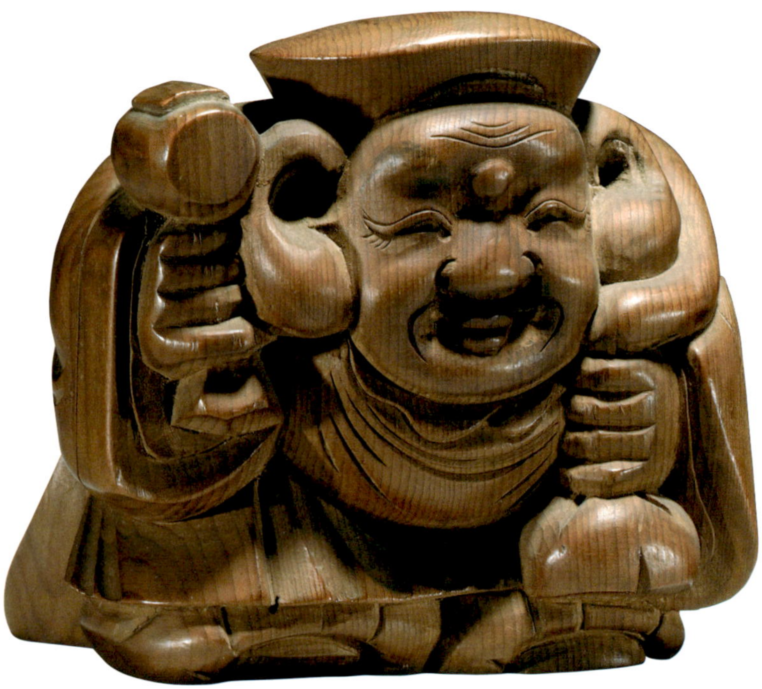

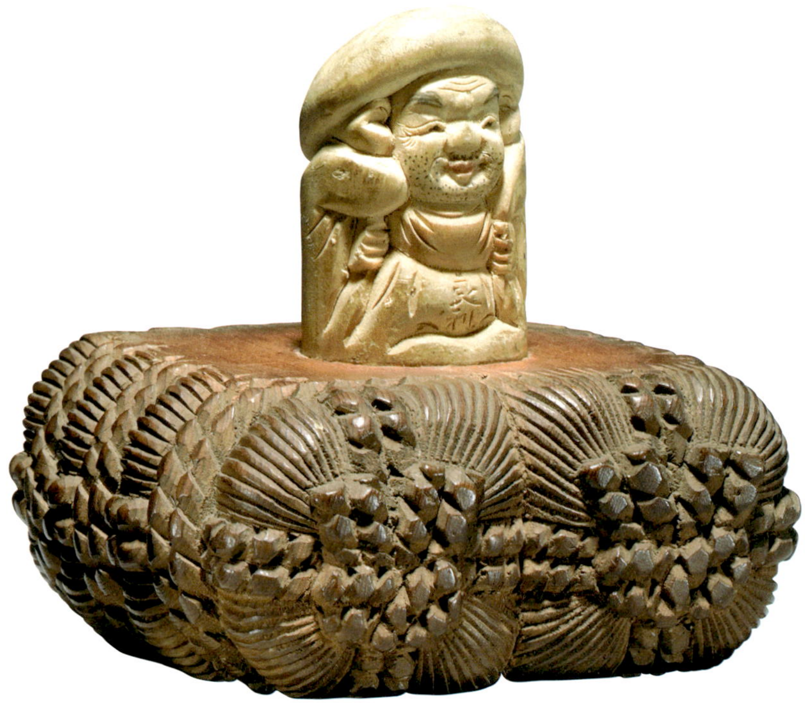

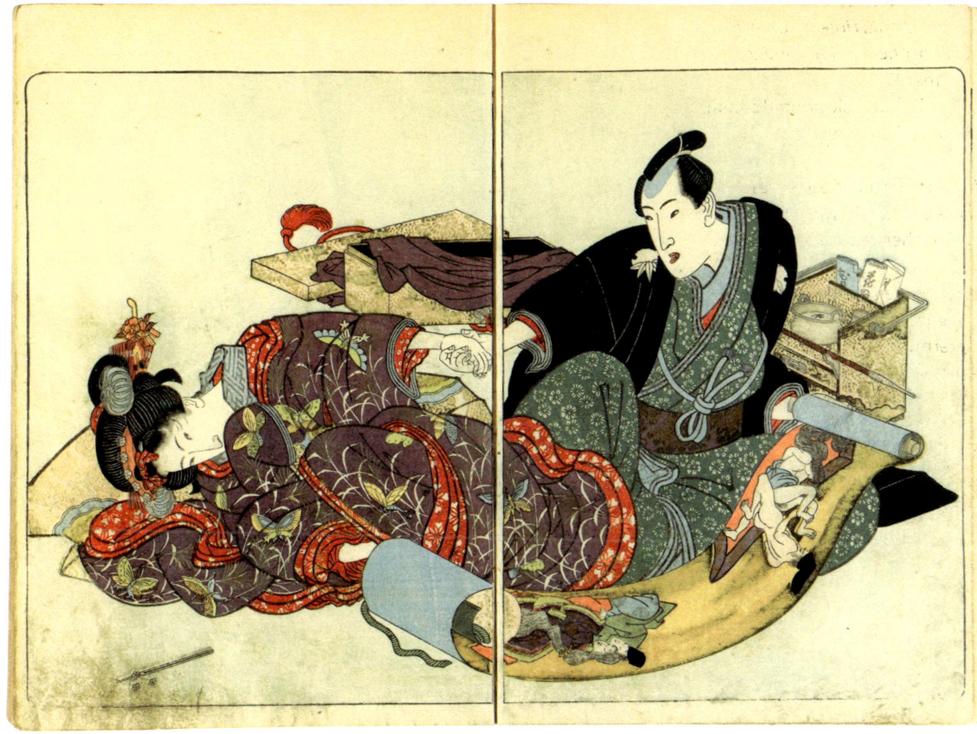

Utagawa Kunisada
***Spring, Summer, Autumn and Winter: Prospects for the Four Seasons* (*Shunka shūtō: Shiki no nagame*), vol. 1**
1827
Colour woodblock-printed book, 25.5 × 18.5 cm (covers)

In a popular conceit a man uses a painted *shunga* handscroll to seduce a woman. She reacts with alarm, but perhaps only for the sake of modesty.

Uses of *shunga*

Erotic pictures in Japan were used by both men and women across the social spectrum for sexual stimulation, as escapism, and as visions of sexual fantasies. The appreciation of *shunga* had many aspects, depending on audience and context. For example, contemporary pictures sometimes show people looking at *shunga*, either a solitary figure or a couple, leading to sexual arousal and intercourse, and they must certainly have served as aids for masturbation for Edo's army of bachelors.[2]

The finest-quality *shunga* were artworks, appreciated for their superior draughtsmanship, composition, use of colour and expressiveness; they were designed by the most prominent artists and produced with deluxe techniques of printing. Like other 'genre' works, they presented scenes of ordinary human life, sparking the viewer's imagination and connecting with their own experiences. That their subject matter dealt with a private area, charged with emotion and physical sensation, obviously heightened their appeal. However, *shunga* are not just pictures of sexual encounters; there are many extra layers of visual enjoyment and meaning, such as the physical settings, the texts printed above the pictures containing narratives or poems, and the dialogue between the lovers. This complex layering of meaning required an alert and well-informed viewer/reader. All these aspects of *shunga* were better appreciated with a companion, and naturally, given the subject, this could lead to the mutual sexual enjoyment of a couple.

Shunga were also used for sex education. Painted handscrolls of erotica were placed in a bride's wedding trousseau for the information they could impart to the sexually

Katsukawa Shunshō
Picture-book: Haikai Album of the Cuckoo **(*Ehon haikai yobuko-dori*)**
New Year 1788
Colour woodblock-printed album,
25.2 × 18.2 cm (covers)

When a courtesan appears in *shunga*, she is usually shown not with a client, but with her secret lover. Here, a high-ranking courtesan and her lover steal moments together at night-time (suggested by the column of a brothel lantern) in a secluded area beside a large water tub. She warns him she can hear people's voices; dawn is breaking and he must leave the quarter before it becomes light.

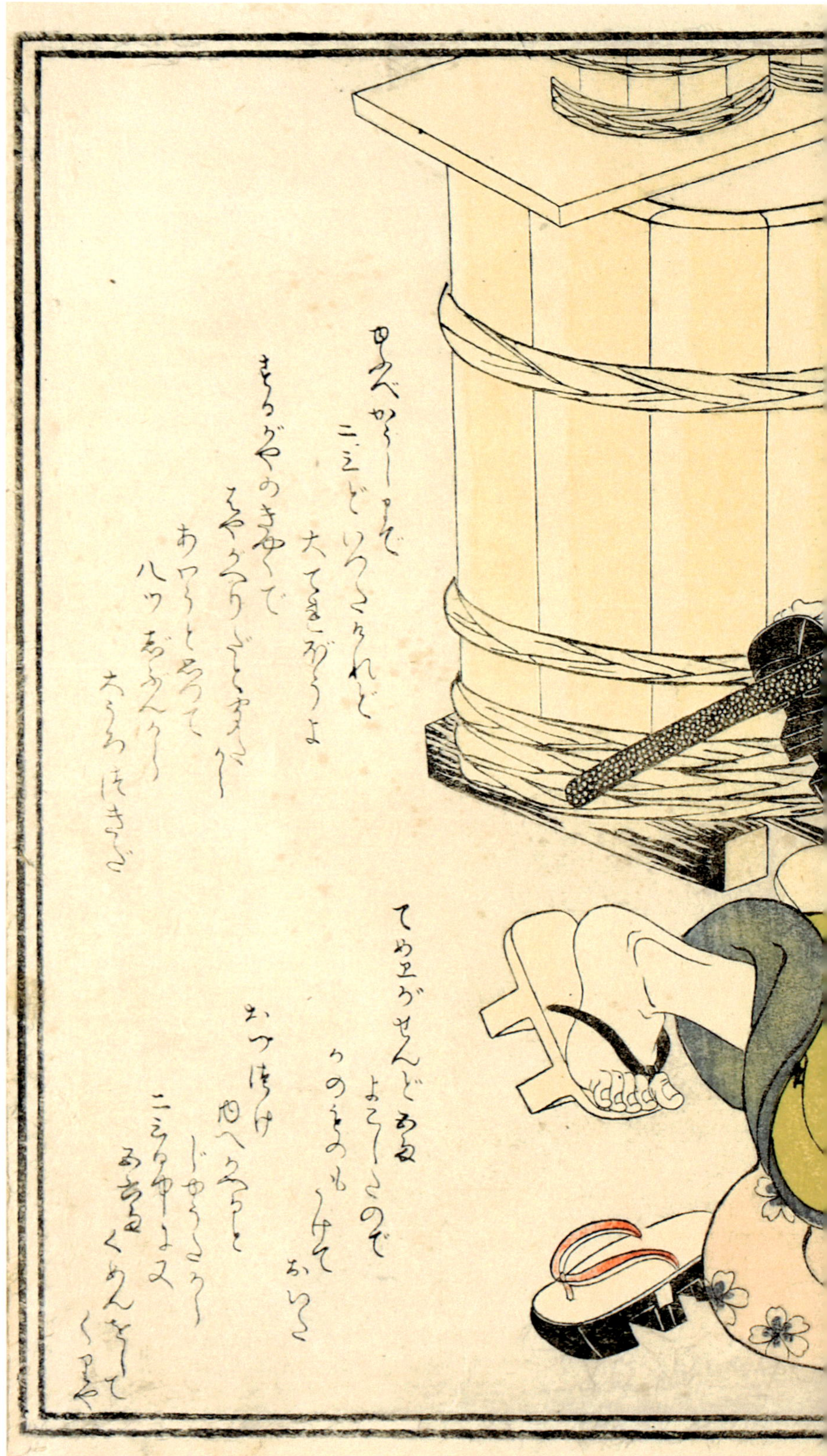

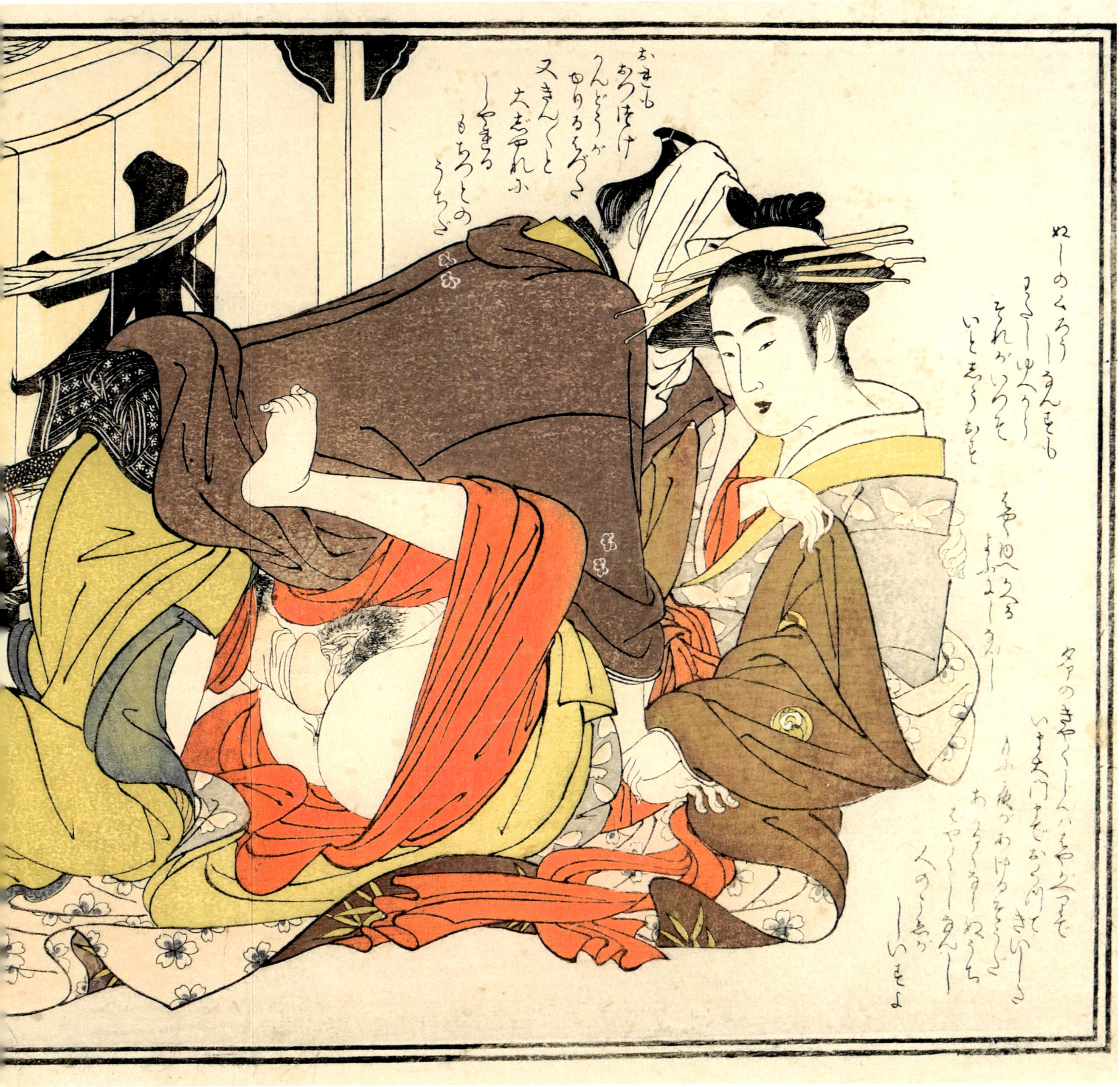

inexperienced woman. Hachisuka Toshiko (1896–1970), a granddaughter of the last shogun, recalled in later life how, at the age of fourteen years, she had been shown a *shunga* handscroll by a senior lady-in-waiting to prepare her for married life.[3] Undoubtedly, the viewing of erotic prints and books by adolescents would likewise have helped the inexperienced understand what lay ahead of them in adult life.

Shunga formats

Shunga were produced in discreet formats, intended for consumption in an intimate setting, so we do not find folding-screen paintings of explicit scenes, and very rarely are there hanging-scroll paintings. The earliest erotica were painted handscrolls produced in the imperial capital, Kyoto, in the twelfth century. Painted on either paper or silk, 20 or 30 centimetres high and up to 10 metres long, they were deluxe works, produced on commission for wealthy customers. They continued to be made until the end of the nineteenth century, and printed imitations were also available. The publication of erotic books in Kyoto began in 1655, quickly followed in Edo five years later. By about 1800 production in the western cities seems to have come largely to an end and nearly all such books were being published in Edo. From the 1680s erotic publications were produced in two formats: bound books and folding albums. The latter allowed for a continuous image across the two pages of an opening without the interruption of the gutter.

Therefore the majority of *shunga* images form part of a larger work. What may appear to be 'prints' most often come from a book or album. Each picture is embedded within a context of other erotic or suggestive scenes, and the sexual act is not presented in isolation, even if there is no continuous narrative linking the scenes. The whole work presents a gamut of erotic experience, usually beginning with an innocent scene of initial attraction, then moving through flirtation to seduction, the throes of passion and finally to post-orgasmic exhaustion.

Terms for erotica in Japan

Erotic pictures of the Tokugawa period are today termed *shunga*. The two characters that make up the word literally mean 'spring pictures', and the common assumption is that this refers to the vitality and energy associated with that season. However, the term is in fact an abbreviation of *shunkyū higa*, meaning 'secret pictures from the Spring Palace', referring to an ancient Chinese belief that the ruler must sleep with twelve women (matching the twelve months of the year) as part of his duty to balance the cosmic forces in the realm (*yin* and *yang*, representing the female and male principles).[4]

Over the centuries of their production and consumption, erotic images were called by various names: during the Heian period (794–1185) *osoku-zu* meant literally 'pictures of [men and women] resting'. In the medieval period, an era of much military strife, warriors are said to have placed erotica inside their armour like amulets, imbuing them with apotropaic powers, and they were called 'victory pictures' (*kachi-e*). In later ages, in a similar protective use, merchants placed them in storehouses to prevent their greatest danger, fires. During the Tokugawa period, a popular term was 'pillow pictures' (*makura-e*), from the associations of the phrase 'placing the pillows together', meaning sexual intercourse. The most common term, however, was 'laughing pictures' (*warai-e*), where *warai* was a euphemism for sexual activity, indicating the close relationship between sex and humour. Books with erotic content were called 'amorous books' (*kōshokubon* or *ehon*, also read *enpon*) and 'pillow books' (*makurabon*). These are now generally referred to by the later term *shunpon*, 'spring books'.

Society and culture in the Tokugawa period

During the period when the works in this book were produced, Japan was ruled by a military government under the control of the Tokugawa clan. With the dynasty's rise to power after a century of civil warfare, a new era of peace and political stability created the conditions for economic and cultural development. There were three main urban centres in Japan (known as the 'three capitals'): Edo (now Tokyo), the seat of government, Kyoto, the imperial capital, and Osaka, the trading centre. Culture and power in the Middle Ages had centred on Kyoto, but the power-base was now deliberately established in the east of the country, far from the intrigues of the court. Edo, once a small fishing village, by 1700 grew to be the most populous city in the world.

Society under the Tokugawa was peaceful but strictly controlled. Government policy was based on Neo-Confucian teachings adopted from China. Accordingly, society was divided into four classes: the samurai who ruled, the farmers who produced, the artisans who crafted

Map of Japan.

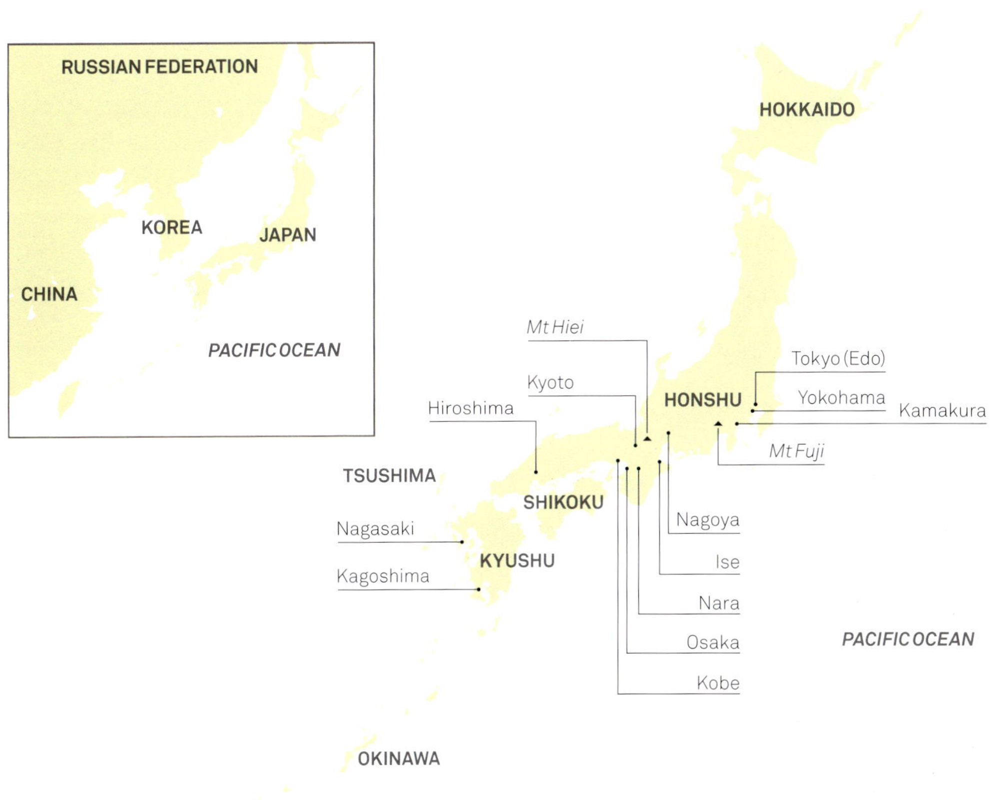

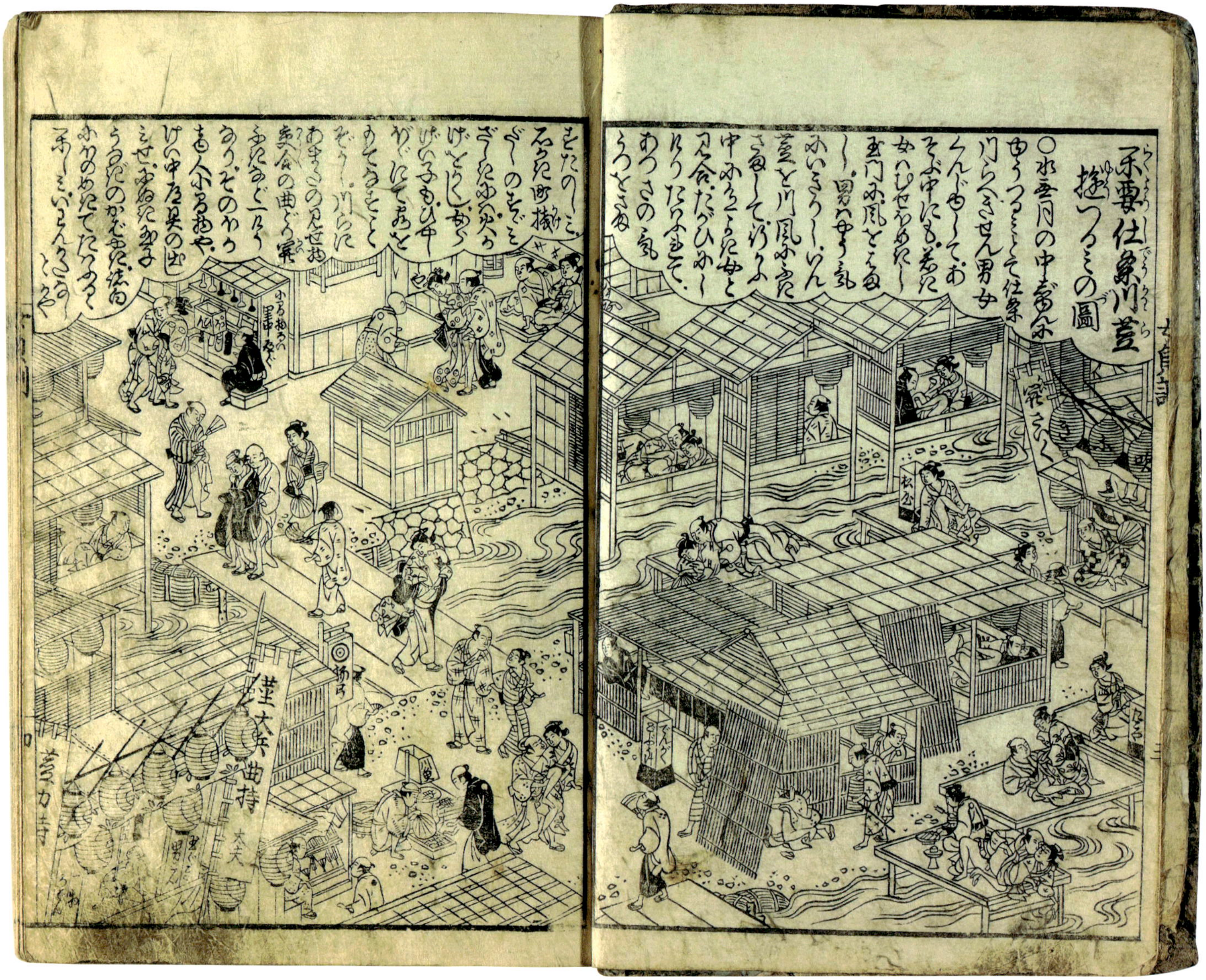

Tsukioka Settei
***Womanly Virtue and a Library on the Private Parts* (*Onna teikin gesho bunko*), vol. 1**
c. 1768
Woodblock-printed book,
26 × 18.5 cm (covers).
Private collection,
Ritsumeikan ARC Database

In this parody of a young woman's conduct manual, Settei gives us bawdy portrayals of Japan's 'three capitals' (see also pp. 84–5). In Kyoto (left), the townspeople, cooling off on a summer evening on the dry riverbed at Shijō-kawara, have coupled off and are becoming amorous. In Osaka (right), the members of the audience at a *kabuki* performance pay little attention to the drama on stage, and are instead busily occupied with pleasuring their companions.

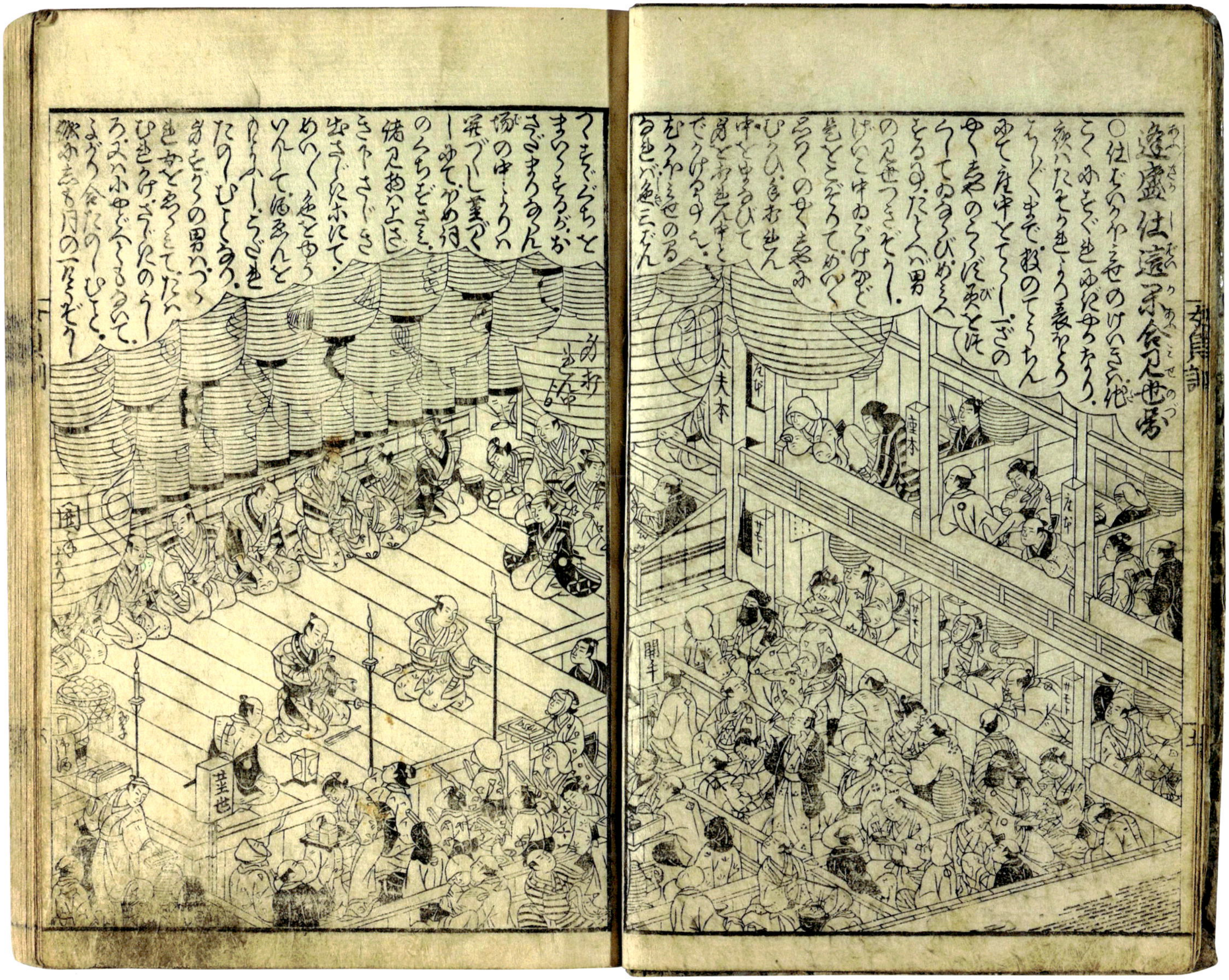

objects, and the merchants who merely sold what others had produced. The urban population other than samurai were known collectively as 'townspeople' (*chōnin*). Certain professions existed outside the official hierarchy, such as actors, entertainers, prostitutes, priests and nuns, likewise those who worked in occupations associated with death (for example, tanning and undertaking). Many were born into these classes, but for townspeople (or sometimes even samurai) to assume a status outside the class hierarchy could allow greater freedom of movement and activity.

The country was divided into approximately 260 domains, each ruled by a hereditary clan headed by a lord (*daimyō*). Uneasy at the wealth and power of some of these lords, who could pose a challenge to Tokugawa rule, the regime required all lords to reside in the shogun's capital in alternate years. They would bring with them a retinue of hundreds of male military retainers (samurai) who had to leave their families behind when in service in Edo. This concentration of men led the author Ihara Saikaku (1642–93) to describe Edo a 'city of bachelors'. Edo contained businesses of every description staffed by a large population of merchants and artisans, which supplied goods and services to the *daimyō* residences and their inhabitants. One of the major service industries was the pleasure quarters, brothel districts providing women as both convivial companions and sexual partners.

During this period, the samurai no longer had to function primarily as a military force, but had instead become more like an army of bureaucrats, collecting taxes and enforcing the laws. They received their stipends as allocations of rice, which they then converted into ready cash. The merchants profited from this situation, but as they were excluded from participation in politics, administration and 'elite' culture (as were even the wealthiest artisans and land-

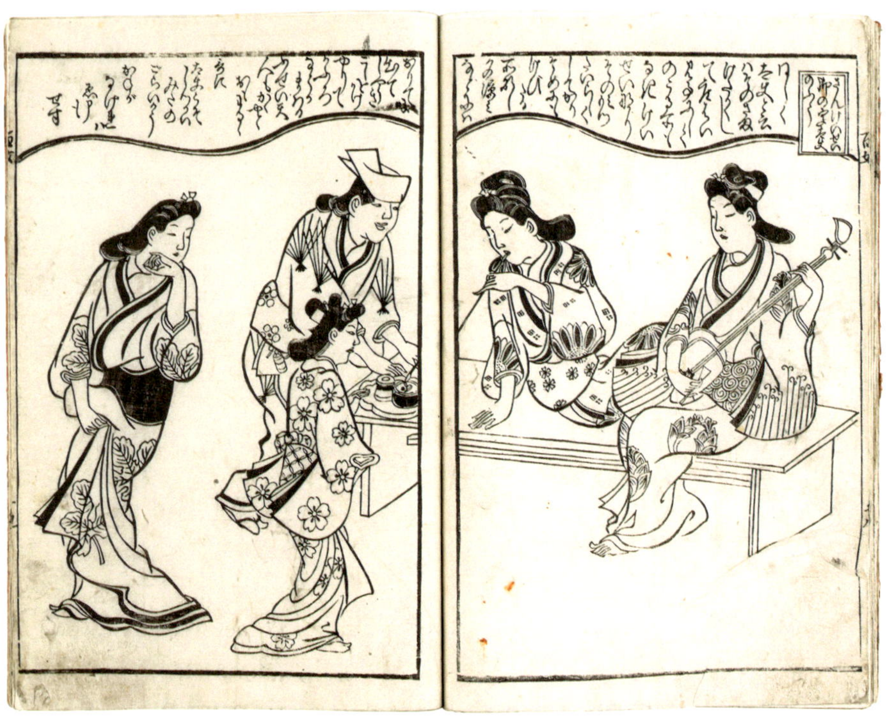

Hishikawa Moronobu
***One Hundred Women of the Floating World* (*Ukiyo hyakunin onna*)**
1681
Woodblock-printed book,
26 × 19 cm (covers)

The production of a book such as this demonstrates that the Japan of the late seventeenth century was a man's world, with women of various classes presented for the appraisal and delectation of male readers. As well as courtesans, townswomen and women engaged in trades and occupations, we find aristocratic ladies in their heavy, multi-layered robes. In this image, entitled 'The Style of the Courtesan Onoji', a group of attractive young women is relaxing around a bench during an outdoor amusement. One strums a *shamisen*, while her companion lights a tobacco pipe from a smoking set prepared by a serving woman.

owners) they developed their own distinct culture, in performance, publications and the company of women in the pleasure quarters. The sophisticated urbanite was proud of his identity as an *Edokko* ('child of Edo'), a playboy who lived for pleasure, earning money only to spend it, heedless of tomorrow. The samurai, too, and sometimes even *daimyō*, were not averse to participating in this vibrant world which presented an alternative to staid Neo-Confucian order and morality.

While moralistic and socially conservative, Neo-Confucian philosophy placed a strong emphasis on education, meaning that a large sector of society was literate, creating substantial demand for reading matter. This fact, together with the concentration of population in the urban centres, efficient communication networks and developments in woodblock printing, all contributed to a boom in publishing. Stories, information and images were now available to a mass audience across the land in the form of popular illustrated books and single-sheet prints.

The harmony of the body politic was easier to maintain when the townspeople were provided with entertainments to absorb their energies. Nevertheless, the government was anxious to police such pleasures and keep them within certain bounds, so the large entertainment industry, which encompassed prostitution, theatres and the publishing industry, was constantly subject to regulations.

Pleasure in Tokugawa Japan

By 1700 Edo had approximately one million inhabitants. All sorts of entertainment could be enjoyed in its streets: showmen, performing animals, itinerant music and dance troupes, acrobats, sideshows and spectacles, as well as sumo wrestling, and various forms of theatrical and musical events in a range of venues. The principal centres of pleasure, however, were the brothel quarters (both licensed and unlicensed) and the *kabuki* theatres. Both were magical spaces of fantasy and make-believe, providing an escape from the mundane routine of life, places where the normal order of things could be overturned and a new world created. Their delights were recognized to be all too brief and fleeting, and they came to be referred to as *ukiyo* ('the floating world'), derived ultimately from a Buddhist term referring to the evanescence of human existence. The economic growth spurred a new artistic movement, producing prints cheaply available to the general populace as well as luxury paintings for private clients. Artists tried to capture the beauties and wonders of these fantasy spheres, and to preserve them for their customers and fans, and the images were called *ukiyo-e*, 'pictures of the floating world'.

Yoshiwara was the only licensed pleasure quarter in Edo. It formed a parallel world with its own particular culture, routine, and rituals. It also functioned as a meeting-place for those involved in the cultural world of Edo: the artists, authors, actors, poets, scholars, samurai, and wealthy merchants and business-owners. The best houses were as much cultural salons as places for sexual encounters.

The quarter comprised just six blocks, housing several hundred businesses where several thousand women were employed as waitresses, singers, dancers and prostitutes. The central street was lined with tea-houses; the brothels themselves were situated on streets

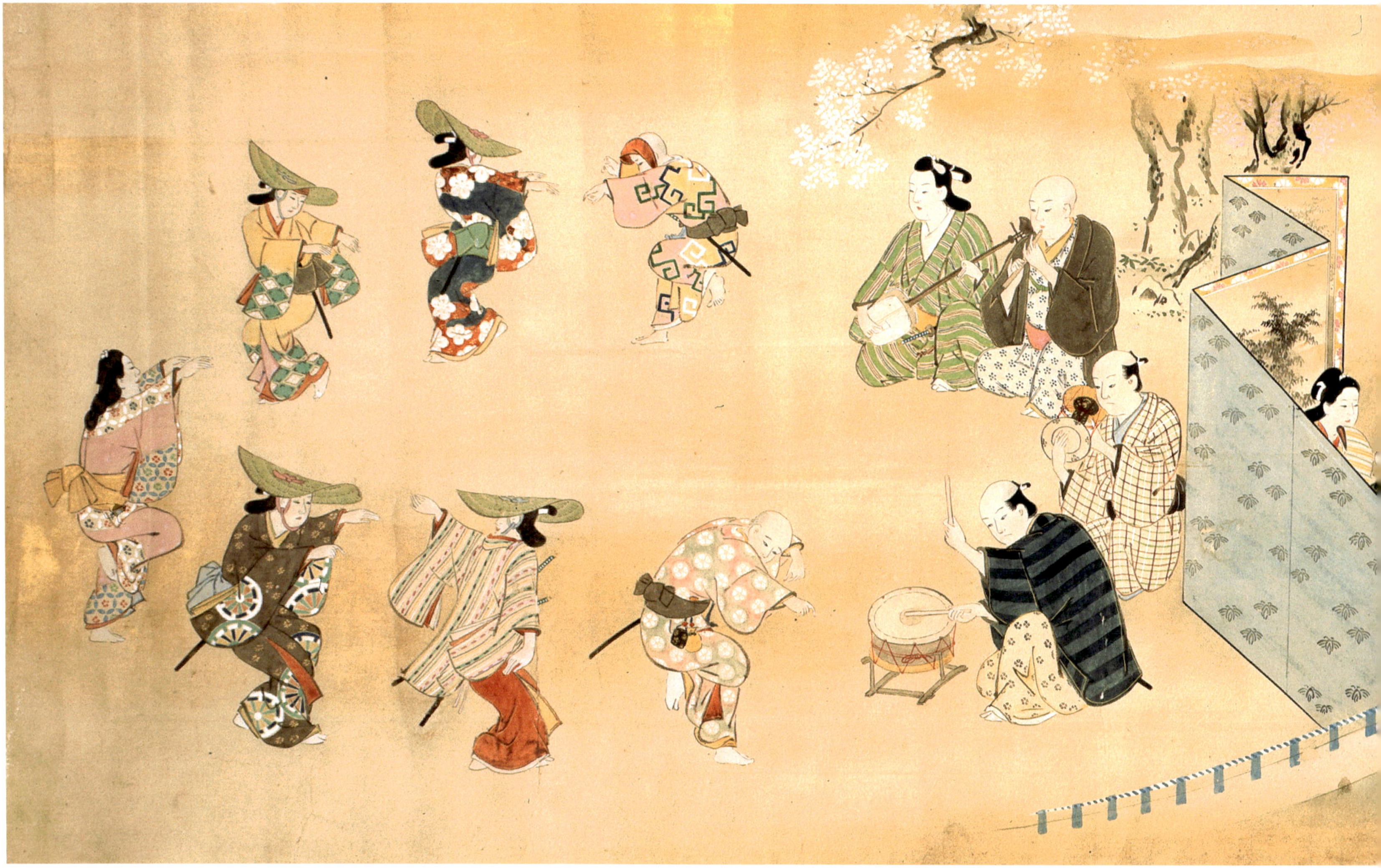

off to the left and right. The tea-houses were the first stop for visitors, and it was here that much of the entertainment and parties took place, the high-ranking courtesans calling there with their retinue of attendants and servants. A visit to one of the brothels, however, was no simple matter. There was an elaborate system of etiquette and correct procedure, involving considerable expenditure – on parties, entertainers, refreshments and particularly gifts – before a customer could be alone with a high-ranking courtesan. Even then, repeated visits and a statement of commitment were required before any sexual relations could begin.

There was a general fascination with life inside the confines of Yoshiwara, and for those who could not afford a visit, vicarious enjoyment of its pleasures was to be had in the form of woodblock prints and illustrated novels. The courtesans were quite literally celebrities, their looks, couture and coiffure endlessly reproduced in prints. The pleasure quarters were for the enjoyment of men, but women were avid consumers of images of the glamorous courtesans. The high-ranking courtesans were not only required to be physically attractive, they also had to be accomplished at the arts of singing, dancing, musical instruments, poetry and calligraphy.

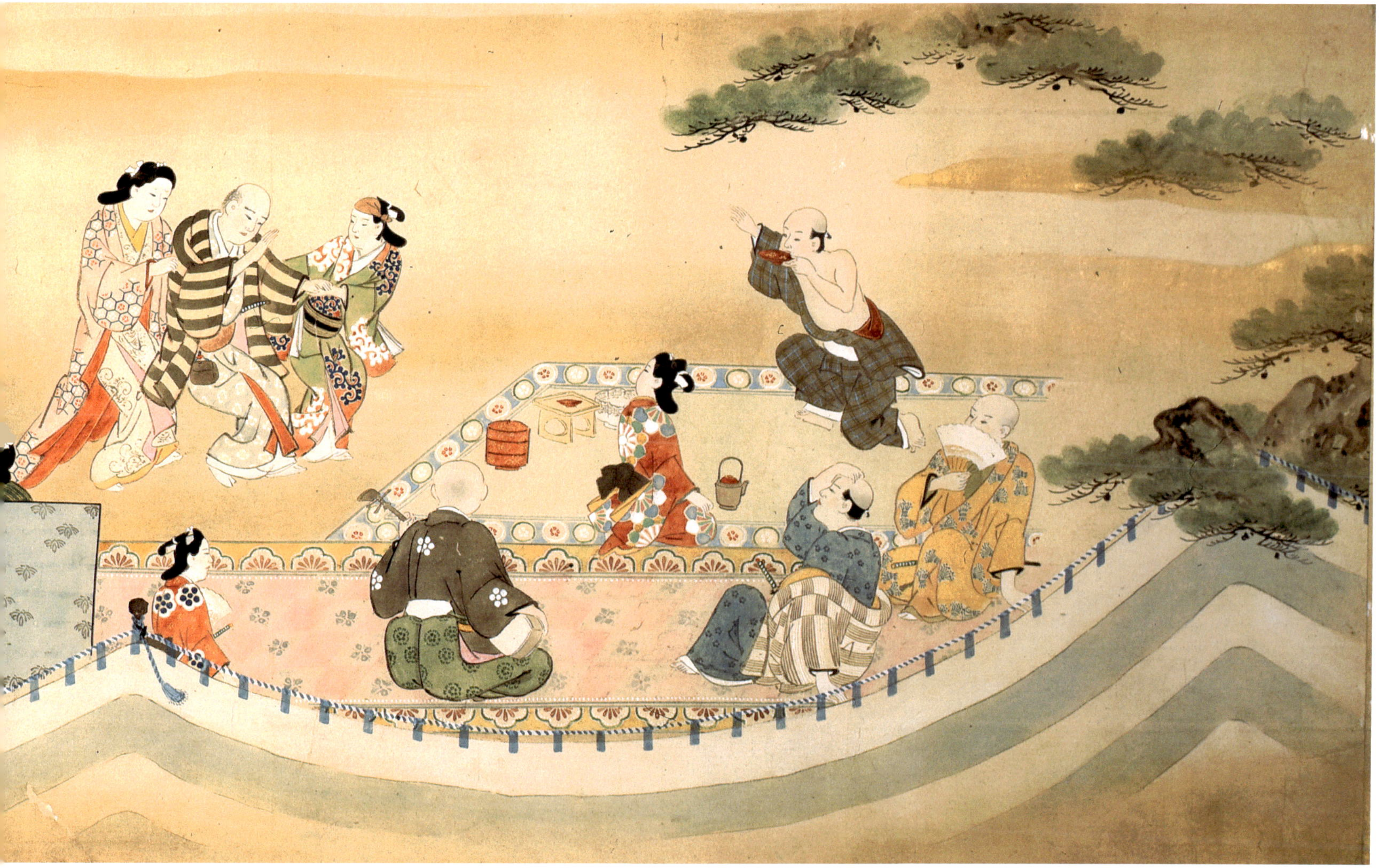

Miyagawa Chōshun
Scenes of Daily Life in Edo
(*Edo fūzoku zukan*) (detail)
1716–36
Handscroll painting, ink and colour on paper, H: 40.1 cm

In springtime then, as now, the people of Edo held parties in the open air beneath the cherry blossoms. On the right, a private picnic area has been set up with mats, a folding screen, musician and *sake*. One man has got up to dance, and another is being helped back towards the group. On the left, people enjoy one of the popular round dances, accompanied by four musicians.

Besides Yoshiwara, there were numerous unlicensed entertainment quarters around Edo. The largest was Fukagawa, to the east of the city across the Sumida River. Here the distinction between courtesans and entertainers (*geisha*) was not as clear-cut, the procedure for selecting a bed-partner was not as convoluted and the women were held to be more natural and straightforward in their manners than their refined and elusive cousins in the so-called 'northern quarter'.

Pictures may present the courtesans in an attractive, glamorous world, but in reality life for the sex-workers in these districts was extremely hard. In Yoshiwara, the women had often been recruited from distant, impoverished rural regions at a young age, and in return for the money paid to their family they were indentured to work for ten years. Women working at the lower, more squalid levels of the hierarchy were prey to violent exploitation. As elsewhere, all prostitutes and their clients were at risk of venereal disease; the clients by choice, but the women through necessity of their trade.

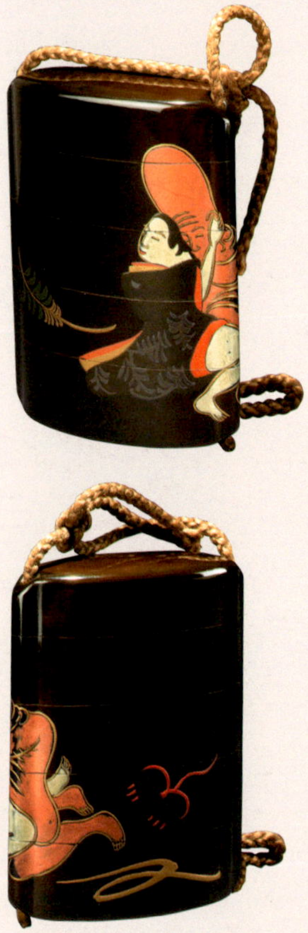

1

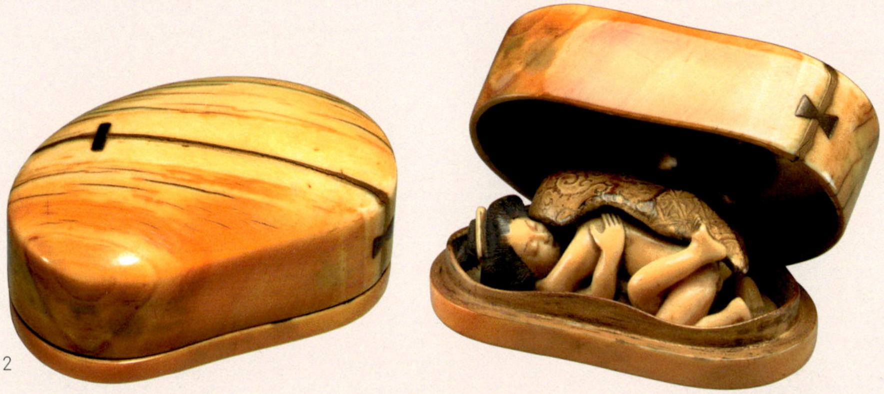

2

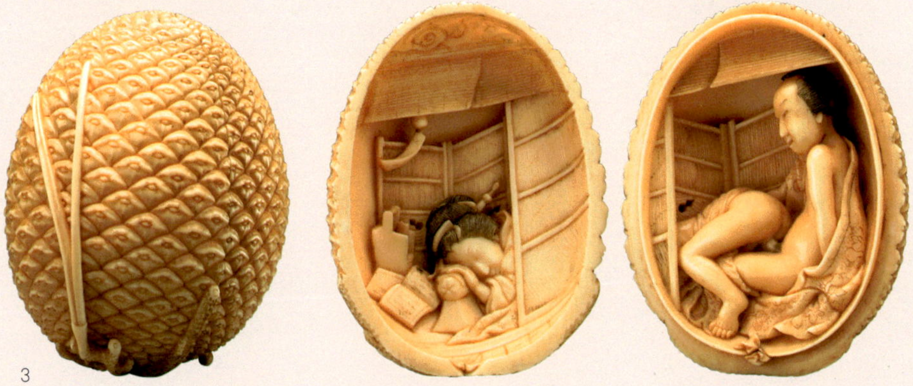

3

Novelty items

Traditional Japanese robes were secured by a sash (*obi*) wound around the waist. Men would suspend from the sash a small, multi-compartment container (*inrō*) made of lacquered wood, with cords running vertically through holes up each side, held together and tightened at the top by a sliding bead (*ojime*). The double cord was passed through the sash; a carved toggle (*netsuke*) at the end stopped the whole ensemble from slipping through. Erotic scenes were not well suited to the visible surfaces of *inrō*, but they do sometimes appear. The *inrō* illustrated here (**1**) presents a woman in an embrace with Fukurokuju, one of the Gods of Good Fortune, identified by his elongated forehead. Only when the case is turned over, however, can it be seen just how intimate the embrace is. The woman looks around, as if aware they are likely to be spied on.

Normally made of wood or ivory, *netsuke* were carved into all manner of shapes, a popular choice being the animals of the calendrical cycle. Erotic themes also had a place here, typically requiring the viewer to examine the *netsuke* in the round. Sometimes they were concealed within innocuous-looking exteriors. This elegant little box of polished ivory (**2**) dates from the late eighteenth century and is signed 'Masanao'. A small gold insert imitates the repairs made to treasured lacquer boxes. Inside, a couple make love under the bedcovers. Though most of the man's body is concealed, the carving of his genitals is anatomically correct.

Other similar pieces were not suitable for use as toggles, but seem rather to have been enjoyed simply as pocket-sized amusements. The exterior of this piece (**3**) is carefully carved from ivory to imitate the texture of a pine cone (complete with foliage strands), but when opened we find a woman who has been disturbed in her reading (perhaps of an erotic novel) by a man who enters her from behind. As with pictorial representations, the setting is depicted in some detail, with plentiful fabrics and objects around the couple. The paper tag of a wind-chime above the woman's head moves in the breeze, suggesting the heat of a summer evening. The potentially awkward transition of her body across the two halves of the piece is cleverly mediated by a bamboo screen.

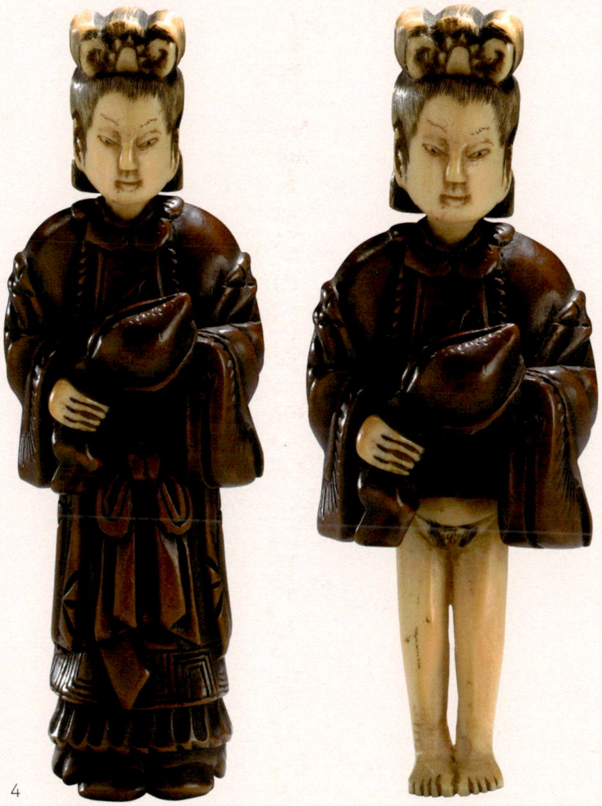

4

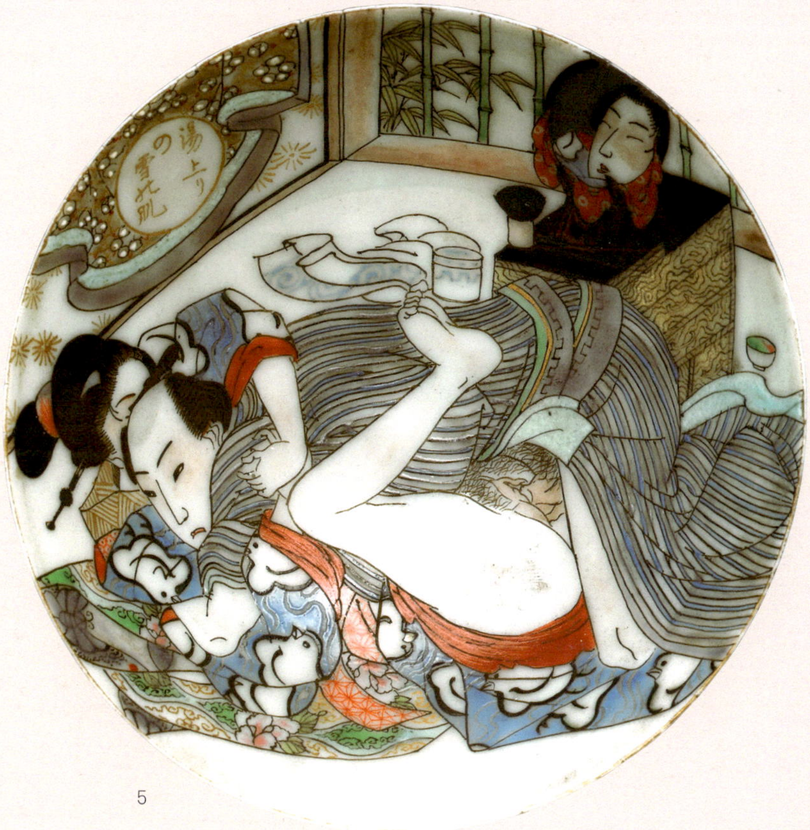

5

The irreverence of sexualizing divine or mythological figures was likely to provoke laughter, as we find with a carving of the Chinese deity Xiwangmu (in Japanese, Seiōbo) (**4**). Her name means 'Queen Mother of the West', and she was believed to live in the western paradise of Kunlunshan. With Chinese coiffure and robes, she holds one of the peaches of immortality which grew there on trees bearing fruit once every three thousand years. Anyone handling the piece, however, would immediately have realized that there was something different about it, as the lower half of her robes slip off to reveal her naked lower body, the genitals and pubic hair delicately coloured. Although the size of a *netsuke*, this seems to have been another small plaything.

Porcelain wares were also decorated with erotic scenes, perhaps for use at parties or entertainments which were likely to lead to sex. The scene on this dish (**5**) is entitled 'Snowy Skin after a Hot Bath' and is probably taken from an as yet unidentified print. It was commonly believed that sexual sensations were heightened just after the woman had taken a hot bath, and such scenes were popular. The man wears a fashionable striped kimono and the woman's robe is decorated with the common motif of plovers over waves. Her toes curl with excitement at the unexpected activity and, although we cannot see her face, the carefully positioned mirror reveals her obvious pleasure.

1. ***Inrō* (medicine case) with Fukurokuju making love to a woman**
19th century
Lacquered wood, L: 7.5 cm

2. **Masanao, *netsuke* box with couple making love inside**
1780–1800
Ivory with gold lacquer, L: 4.8 cm

3. **Ornament in the shape of a pine cone, opening to reveal an erotic scene**
19th century
Ivory, L: 5 cm

4. ***Netsuke* with figure of Seiōbo, opening to reveal naked lower half of body**
1800–50
Wood and ivory, H: 8.7 cm

5. **Dish with design of a couple making love**
1800–50
Enamelled porcelain, Diam: 10 cm

Utagawa Toyoharu
Courtesans in the Tamaya House
1781–5
Six-panel screen painting, ink and colour on paper, 144.1 × 314.6 cm

Life for the courtesans and their attendants could be dull. This painting shows five high-ranking courtesans seated in the 'display room' (*harimise*) of their brothel, surrounded by four pairs of apprentices, dressed in matching robes. This is the quiet period in the middle of the day, with no prospective clients passing by; the women pass the time smoking, playing the *shamisen* and dressing a doll. The emblem of a crane in flight on the lacquer box in front links this scene to a courtesan in the Tamaya brothel, and this name can be half-seen on the entrance curtain at the back. This is a rare surviving example of an *ukiyo-e* screen painting, and must have been an expensive work, specially commissioned by a patron of the Tamaya.

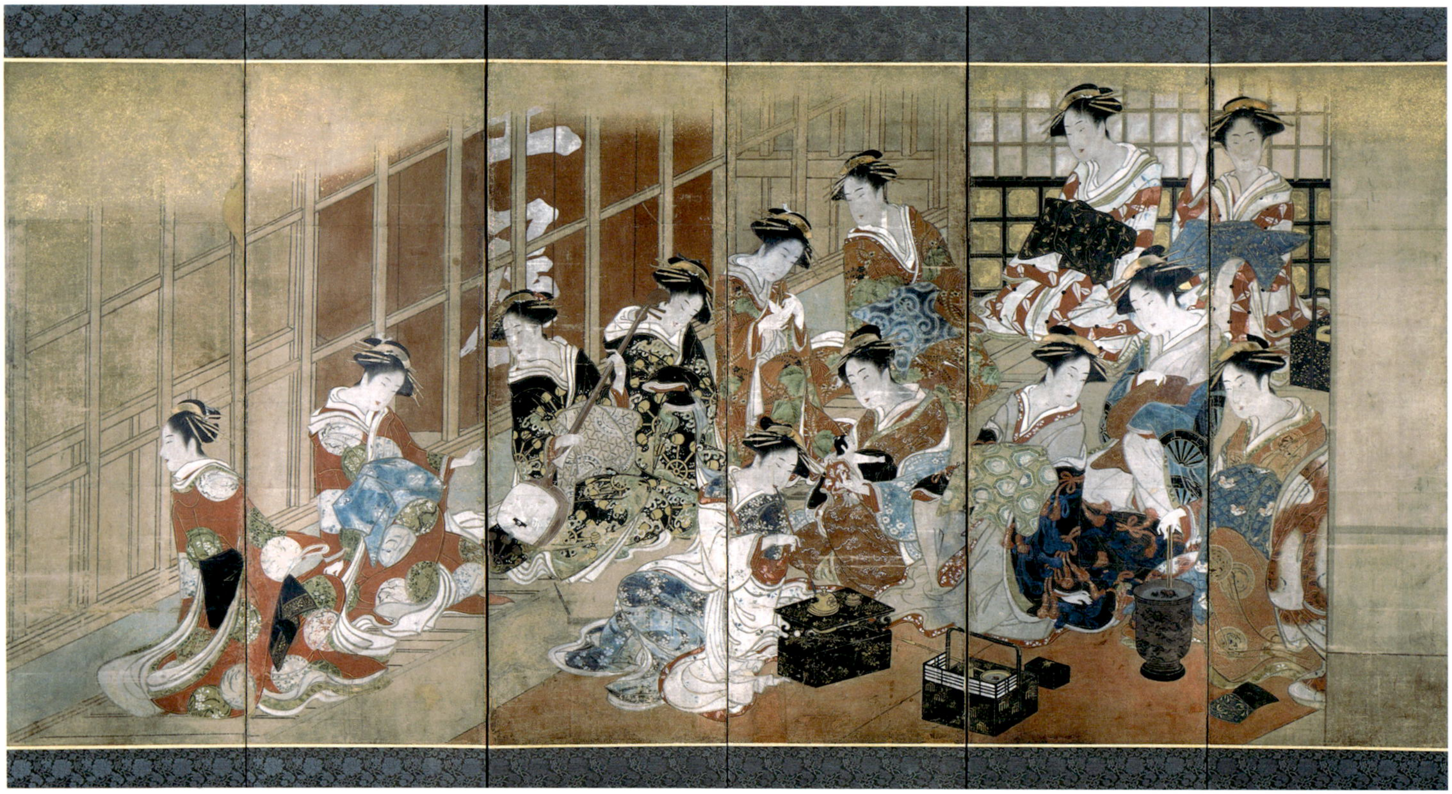

Kitao Masanobu
***Yoshiwara Courtesans Mirrored in their Handwriting: New Matches between Beautiful Women* (*Yoshiwara keisei shin bijin-awase jihitsu kagami*)**
1784
Colour woodblock-printed album, 27.5 × 19 cm (covers)

In this book Masanobu presents courtesans from seven houses in Yoshiwara, paired as if portrayed in a traditional poetry contest, with their Chinese and Japanese poems above. They are shown in various activities at the New Year: parading, reading, playing music, composing poetry and examining presents from patrons. As well as showing the women's appearance and activities, the reader gains an insight into their character from the samples of their actual calligraphy. In this image we see two courtesans of the Chōjiya house. Hinazuru, on the right, wears a robe decorated with flaming Buddhist jewels above surging waves. Behind her, her two young attendants (*kamuro*) wear robes matching hers; one carries a kitten with a bell round its neck, the other carries her mistress's tobacco pipe. On the left, Chōzan has paused from her book, as she reclines at an expensive Chinese lacquer table inlaid with mother-of-pearl. Several cases of books can be seen in the alcove behind. Chōzan's attendant, again in a matching robe of chrysanthemum pattern, blows on the charcoals in the brazier.

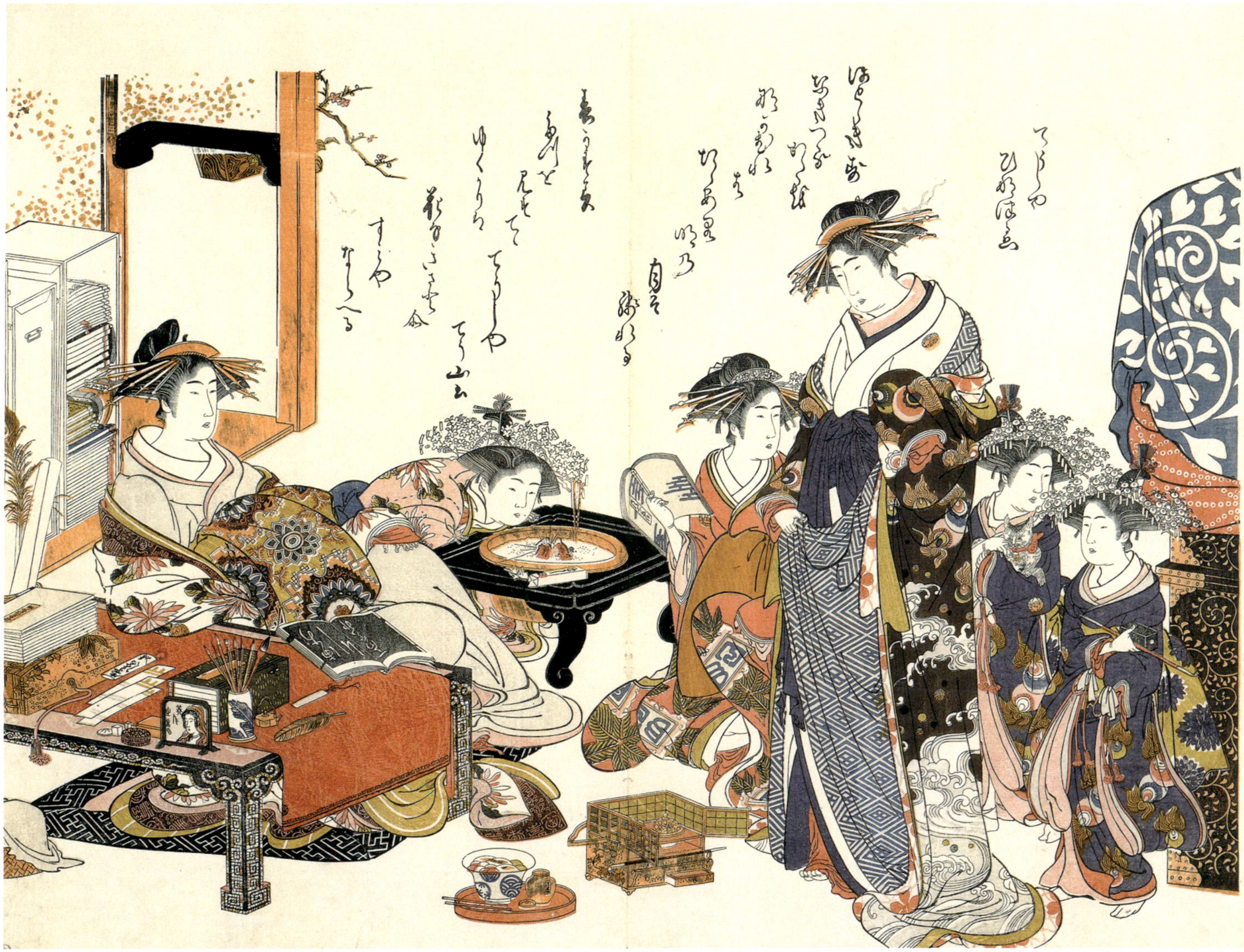

Kitagawa Utamaro
***Picture-book of the Green Houses: Annual Events* (*Seirō ehon: Nenjū gyōji*)**
1804
Colour woodblock-printed book,
22.7 × 15.9 cm (covers)

This two-volume publication is a lavish portrayal of life in a high-class Yoshiwara brothel, depicted by the master artist of beauties, Utamaro, with text by the popular author Jippensha Ikku (1765–1831) and 'crazy verses' by several different poets. The book depicts the various events particular to the quarter throughout the year in a reworking of a classical painting tradition presenting the annual schedule of the court. A sequence of images shows the experience of a customer who stays overnight. Here, we have a view of the private parties for intimate patrons; in one room we see a customer with two companions, to the right a courtesan steadies herself as she steps out of a room and puts on her slippers, and around the corner we see another party with an extravagant display of food in the form of a mythical thousand-year turtle (*minogame*). Labels beside each person indicate who they are. These detailed depictions would have appealed to readers who could never afford such exclusive entertainment.

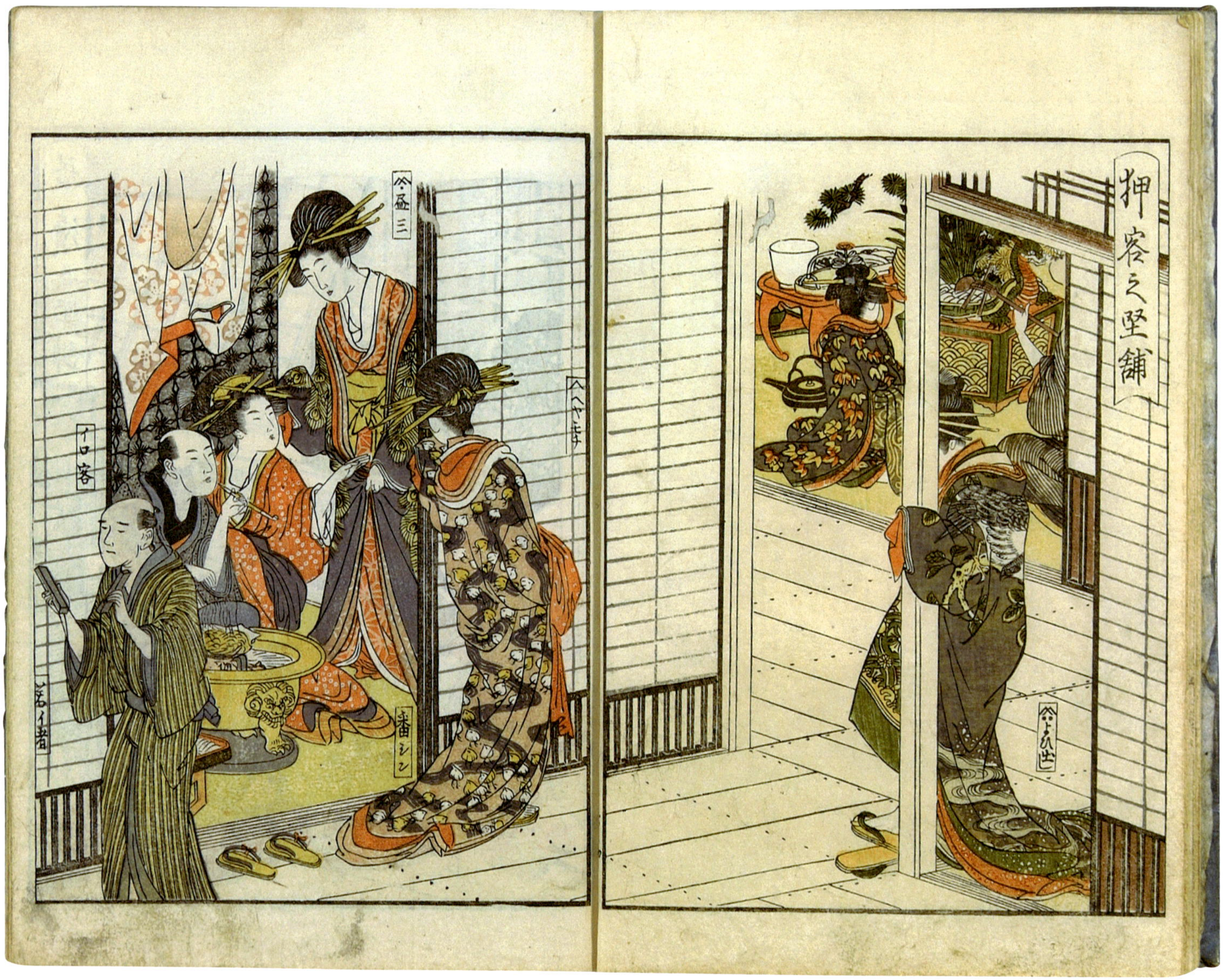

Kitagawa Utamaro
***Picture-book of the Green Houses: Annual Events* (*Seirō ehon: Nenjū gyōji*)**
1804
Colour woodblock-printed book,
22.7 × 15.9 cm (covers)

Even intimate customers who stayed the night had to leave the quarter early in the morning. In this atmospheric view of the upper landing in the murky light before dawn, three customers are being seen off by their courtesans at the top of the staircase; one covers his head ready to conceal his identity. In the corridor behind, another drowsy customer can be seen heading for the toilet.

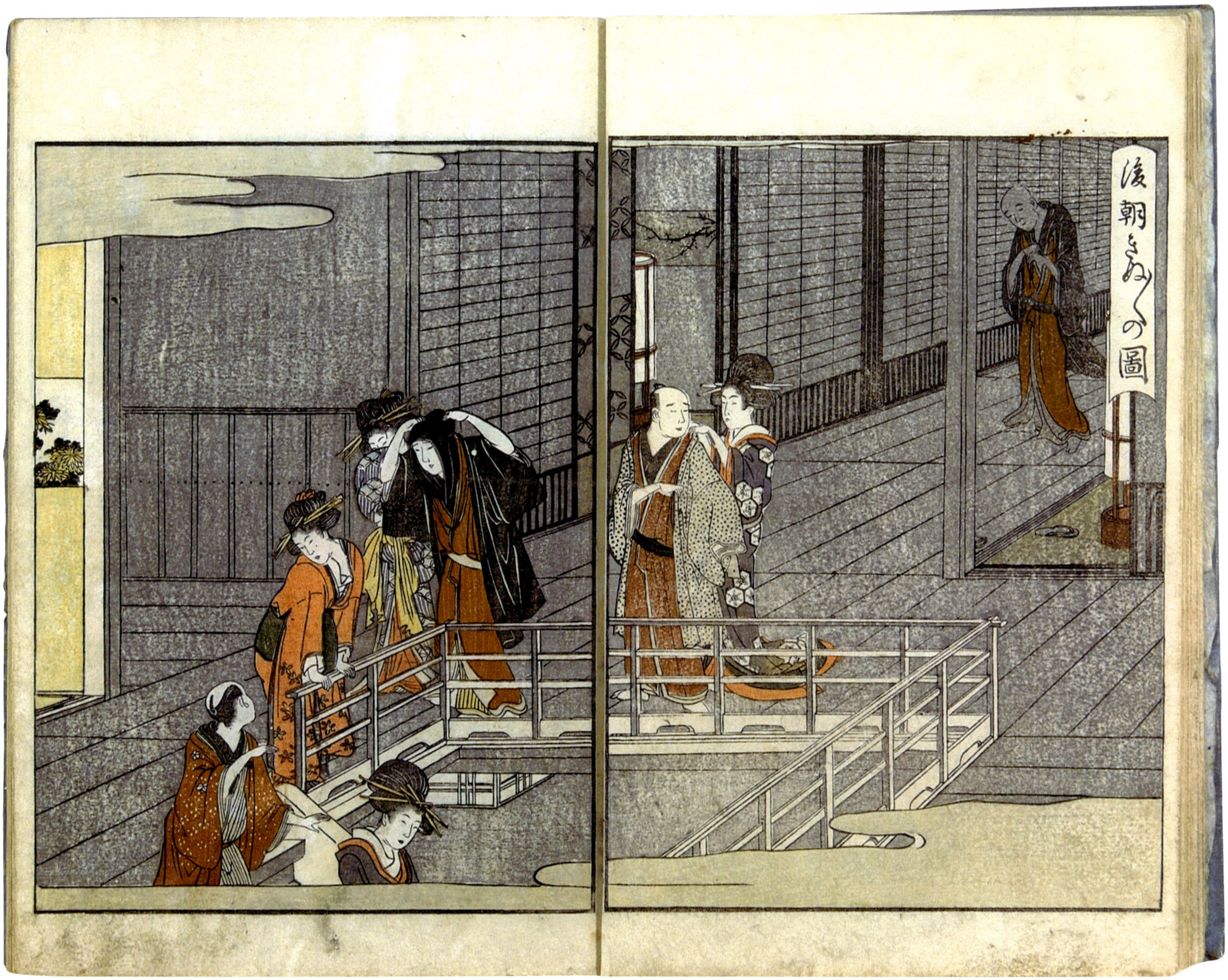

During the Tokugawa period, both puppet theatre (*bunraku*) and the *kabuki* theatre with all-male casts were wildly popular forms of entertainment. Whereas only men could enjoy the company of 'celebrity' courtesans, and even then only if they had the wealth to support themselves, the theatre was accessible to men and women, rich and poor.

The origins of *kabuki* lay in a rather licentious, cross-dressing performance of dances and skits by a troupe of women, led by a woman called Okuni, on the dry riverbed in Kyoto in the early 1600s. The verb *kabuku*, from which the name derives, suggested something deviant, alternative, irreverent. Concerned by the secondary, sexual services being offered by the performers, in 1629 the government had banned women from performing. Their replacement with attractive young men did not resolve this problem, however, and so the actors were required to shave off their forelocks, the marker of an adolescent male. *Kabuki* actors were born or adopted into a lineage, and were awarded a succession of hereditary names as they progressed through their career. Just like modern-day film stars, a particular actor would attract a loyal following of fans, eager for the latest news and images of him. Attending *kabuki* was a lively, multi-sensory experience, with plentiful food and drink, and vocal responses at set moments in the play. The repertoire of *kabuki* theatre often drew on popular pieces from puppet theatre, as well as thinly disguised contemporary or recent events, despite a ban on using such material. Multiple-sheet colour print designs of the popular plays were produced by the most famous *ukiyo-e* artists,sometimes before a play's run had even begun.

Social control and censorship

Erotic images were widely produced and consumed, and were not subject to the moral constraints customarily imposed on them in European cultures. Nevertheless, the Tokugawa shogunate recognized the power of the print medium as a form of mass communication, and it issued many regulations to control the publishing industry, including its erotic output.

According to Neo-Confucian philosophy, the harmony and order of the cosmos should be replicated in society, in the household and in the individual. It was held that under the rule of a virtuous regime the world was inherently free of conflict, and thus political debate and criticism of the government was neither needed nor permitted. For the sake of political stability, the shogunate forbade travel abroad and limited external trade to the Chinese and to Protestant nations (because those of the Catholic faith refused to renounce adherence to a foreign potentate, i.e. the Pope). The government outlawed Christianity, and was wary of intellectual currents other than the Neo-Confucian orthodoxy. It imposed a ban on the representation of current events or of recent history (in effect, after 1600), especially anything touching on the Tokugawa dynasty or the Toyotomi clan, which they had annihilated. However, artists often found inventive ways to circumvent the ban, transposing events to a different time period and subtly altering the characters' names.

For the individual, correct conduct meant observing one's proper station within the social hierarchy, and observing the frugal lifestyle of Neo-Confucian teaching. Impropriety was a greater offence than sexual explicitness, as it contained an implicit threat to the social order.

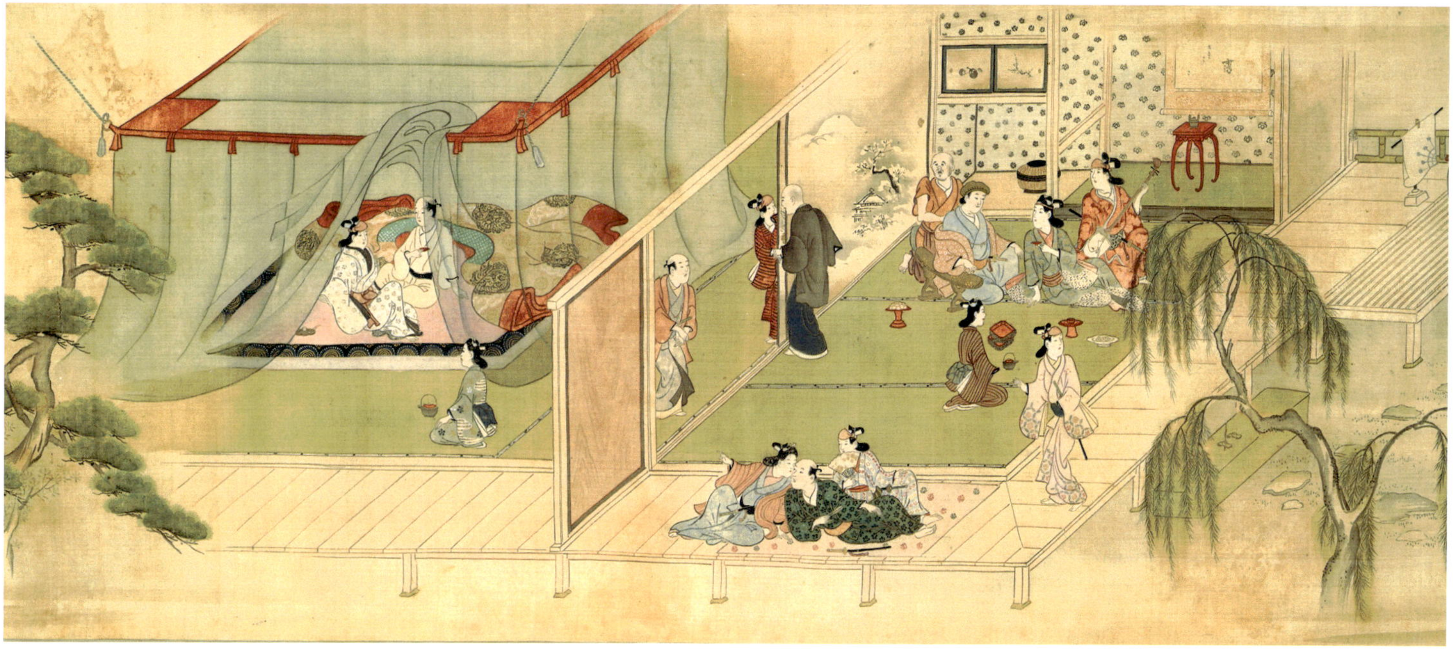

Hishikawa Moronobu
Scene in a theatre tea-house (detail)
1685
Handscroll painting, ink and colour on silk, 31.5 × 147 cm

The luxurious 'stage tea-houses' (*shibai-jaya*), situated near the theatres, were places where patrons could meet their favourite actors and also hire the young trainee *onnagata* (female role specialists) for their sexual services. In this deluxe painting we see patrons relaxing in the front room and being entertained with *sake* and music by attractive young actors. In the bedroom to the rear an *onnagata* relaxes with a client beneath the mosquito net.

Nishikawa Sukenobu
One Hundred Women Classified According to their Rank
(*Hyakunin jorō shina-sadame*)
1723
Woodblock-printed book,
28.5 × 19.5 cm (covers)

This book presents women of all classes and occupations. In the first volume there are imperial and court women, shrine maidens and nuns, women of samurai and townsman rank, professionals, women engaged in craftwork, and manual labourers. The second volume is devoted to courtesans in the three capitals, as well as tea-house and bath-house attendants (often available for other services), and finally street-walkers. Apparently, because the book presented upper-class women alongside prostitutes, it was put on the list of banned works. There was possibly greater sensitivity as the book was published in Kyoto, the imperial capital.[5] In this scene we have an intimate view of prostitutes getting dressed in the evening (indicated by the lantern). One fixes her hair with a hand-mirror, another relaxes with a tobacco set. Outside the door a palanquin is waiting to carry one of the women off to an appointment. The category of woman is written next to each figure.

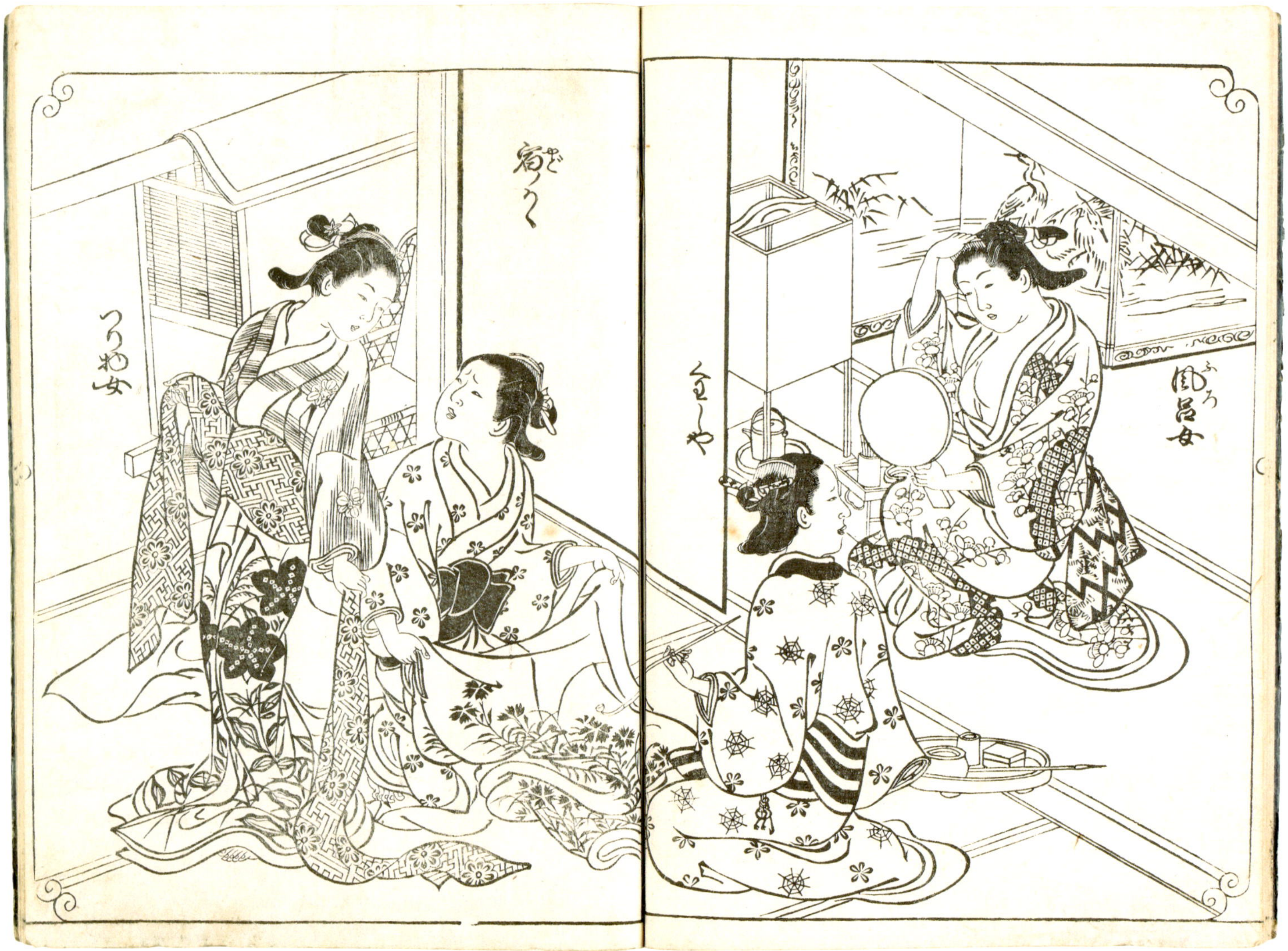

Though not realistically enforceable in a culture of rapidly expanding consumerism, the government nevertheless strove to control consumption, issuing regulations specifying the type of residence, clothing and other material goods permitted to each class, and forbidding luxurious items, such as prints employing an excessive number of colour blocks. When the lowest social stratum, the merchants, was in fact the wealthiest, it was clear that society was disordered. Townspeople were therefore the obvious target for official restrictions on pleasure-seeking.

Already in the Kanbun era (1661–73), when the publishing industry was still relatively small, an edict listed erotic books, military stories, songs, calendars and rumours as 'dubious materials' which required authorization before publication. As the audience for prints and books expanded over the decades, the need for control of content grew accordingly. Specific edicts of this type were issued repeatedly during Tokugawa rule, and it is often speculated that the repeated banning of certain practices or products in fact indicates how often the rules were being violated – requiring regular reinforcement. There were periods of greater liberality according to the shogun in power and the tenor of his government, and enforcement was always dependent on the individual censors. However, at three points during the 250-year rule of the Tokugawa dynasty there were more thoroughgoing attempts at comprehensive reform, provoked by conditions of economic and social unrest. Each of these had far-reaching effects on the print medium (see pp. 80, 113 and 149).

Although for much of the Tokugawa period, erotic prints and books were nominally banned commodities, *shunga* survive in large numbers from all eras, suggesting that the law was not strictly enforced. The primary motivation for the control of material and visual culture was political rather than moral, and this seems to have resulted in relative tolerance. In effect, *shunga* and *shunpon* did not constitute legitimate publications and it seems officials were therefore willing to turn a blind eye, as long as their sale was conducted discreetly. As *shunpon* were contraband, they had no need to conform to regulations and so lacked the colophon containing the author's and artist's names required in publications after 1720. Artists still managed to take credit for their erotic designs, using fairly transparent pseudonyms which were referred to in the preface or half-hidden on a painted screen or fan within the image.

Erotica might have broken the rules, but it was not regarded as politically dangerous. Sex was not used as a vehicle for political satire, as for instance in the prints of Thomas Rowlandson or the pamphlets against Marie Antoinette printed during the French Revolution. Nevertheless, erotica might still have the power to disrupt by its irreverence. The elegant 'reworkings' of high culture that were popular in mainstream *ukiyo-e* had erotic versions too. Some of the earliest examples of erotic books were parodies of the literary classics, such as *The Tale of Genji* and *The Tales of Ise*. Confucian conduct books for women and certain medical texts were also rewritten as erotic parodies. Thus, when artists and publishers were prosecuted, it was not for explicit designs, but for scenarios that challenged the approved Confucian social hierarchy.

The legal restrictions regarding erotica dealt exclusively with published material, and there was no attempt made to control painted works. These were available only to the elite, and therefore posed no threat to the fabric of society.

Erotica in the modern era

Throughout the rule of the Tokugawa shogunate erotic images were officially banned but in practice were tolerated to a large extent. In 1868 with the establishment of a new government, which initiated the Meiji era, there followed a thoroughgoing programme of modernization and industrialization of the country, looking to Western nations for administrative and social models. The shogun's capital, Edo, was renamed Tokyo. As part of this came new legislation in the 1870s to suppress erotic material based on the newly introduced concept of 'pornography'. To the present day the sale of photographic images showing genitalia and pubic hair is still illegal in Japan. Until recently, when *shunga* were reproduced in modern publications, chequered or black squares were placed over the area of the genitalia. These legal restrictions have seriously impeded research on this area of Japanese art, even though the artists who produced these works were the same as those who created the most celebrated examples of woodblock prints, works which have been enthusiastically promoted as icons of Japan's culture. There are clearly reasons why 'adult themes' will always need to be treated with sensitivity, but there is at last a growing opinion in Japan that the suppression of sexual material is unjustifiable. Within the past ten years there have been no legal actions taken against the reproduction of *shunga*, and unexpurgated catalogues and both scholarly and popular works have been published in some quantity.

In the West attitudes towards *shunga* specifically have followed those towards erotica generally. During the nineteenth century *shunga* were classified as pornography, and, though collected as examples of foreign customs and culture, they were stored in the 'secret museum' of restricted or simply unregistered collections. Historically the accession of objects into the collections of the British Museum has generally been painstakingly recorded, but for the majority of the Japanese erotic art there is no information on provenance or acquisition. The collection was finally registered only in the 1970s as part of a Museum-wide audit.

With the changes in attitude in Japan now allowing fuller exploration of this rich area of Japanese art and visual culture, together with the acknowledgement of the historical importance of these works, the way is open for fruitful study, research and exhibition of these fascinating images, allowing them to be freely appreciated and enjoyed, as their makers intended.

Torii Kiyohiro
Awabi diver
1722
Colour woodblock print, 30 × 13.8 cm

After a government crackdown on explicit pictures in 1772 there was an increase in the genre of *abuna-e*, 'risqué pictures'. These were eroticized depictions of women shown engaged in ordinary tasks, such as bathing, washing their hair, breastfeeding or walking outside, where the physical movement provided tantalizing glimpses of naked breasts or shapely calves and thighs. The women-divers (*ama*) who gathered abalone (*awabi*, a type of edible sea-snail) from the seabed were a popular subject matter for *abuna-e* (see pp. 134–5). They wore only a red underskirt when diving, so genre scenes showing them standing or sitting on the shore after a dive allowed the artist to depict the divers' breasts and their legs as they lifted their skirts to wring out the water.

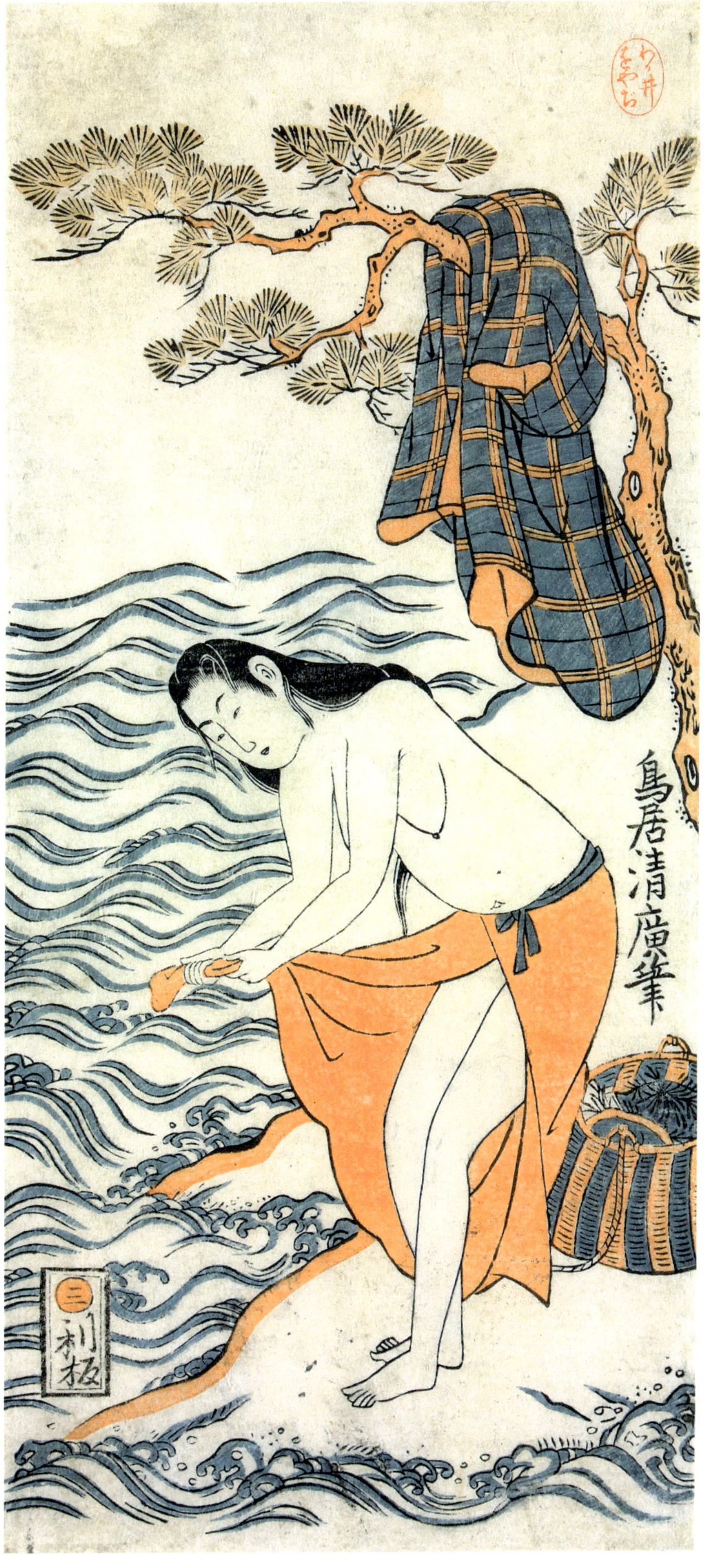
鳥居清廣筆

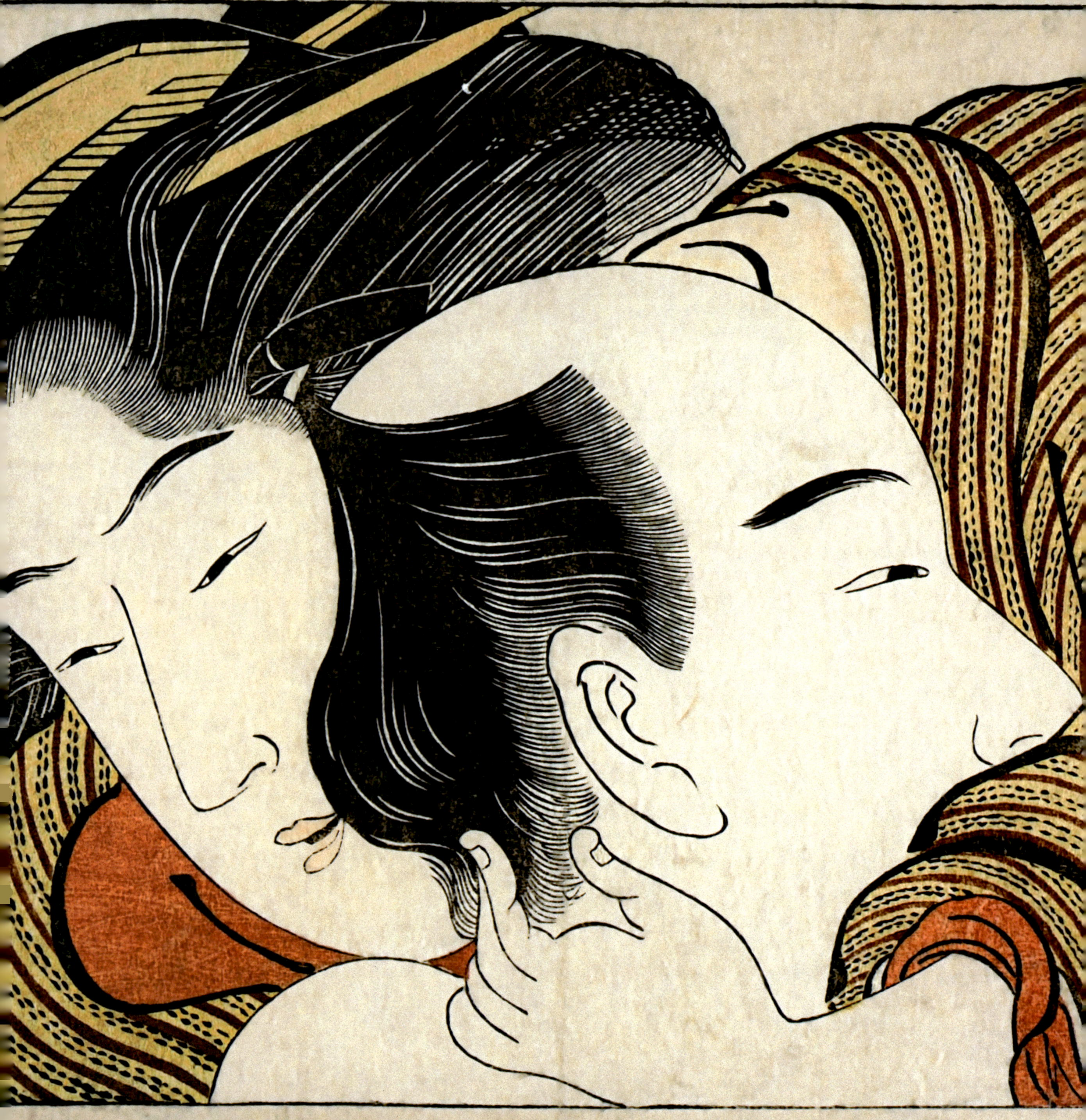

Features of *shunga*

Torii Kiyonaga
***Scroll for the Sleeve* (*Sode no maki*)**
1785
Colour woodblock print, 12.6 × 67.4 cm
Caption details p. 50

A full appreciation of *shunga* requires some understanding of its particular characteristics, including subject matter, visual conventions, and social and cultural context. Although *shunga* present us with imaginary scenes and cannot be taken as faithful representations of the society which produced them, they are nevertheless grounded in reality and may well indicate what was considered typical.

Characters

It is a commonly held misconception that the people depicted in *shunga* are sex-workers and their clients. In fact, as can be seen from the works illustrated in this book, the majority of explicit images depict ordinary men and women from all ranks of society and all manner of professions. Even those who have devoted themselves to a spiritual path are shown ineluctably drawn by the desire for both physical stimulation and emotional connection. The female partners include young women, wives, maids, mistresses, widows, wet nurses, *geisha* and tea-house girls; among the males are young townsmen, heads of house, samurai, servants, merchants, shop-owners, clerks, priests, doctors, craftsmen, itinerant salesmen and *kabuki* actors.

The glamorous courtesans were, however, certainly the object of men's erotic focus (and some women's admiration and emulation), and images of them were plentiful. The world of the pleasure quarters provides the subject matter for many *ukiyo-e* prints and paintings, and there were certain periods when *shunga* which presented such prostitutes were popular. During the second half of the seventeenth century, in the early stages of 'floating-world' culture, artists such as Hishikawa Moronobu created erotica showing gorgeous courtesans in sumptuous surroundings entertaining clients. Such images no doubt appealed to wealthy men who could afford the women's services. In later *shunga*, however, artists tended not to depict prostitutes, or when they did, the women were shown making love not with their clients but with their secret lovers (see pp. 14–15). From about 1700 to the 1820s, at the height of *shunga*'s popularity, many artists concentrated on depicting ordinary men and women. Only in the mid-nineteenth century did prostitutes from the licensed and unlicensed quarters again appear in large numbers as characters in *shunga*. Overall, however, it has been estimated that only ten per cent of the women in *shunga* are sex-workers.[1]

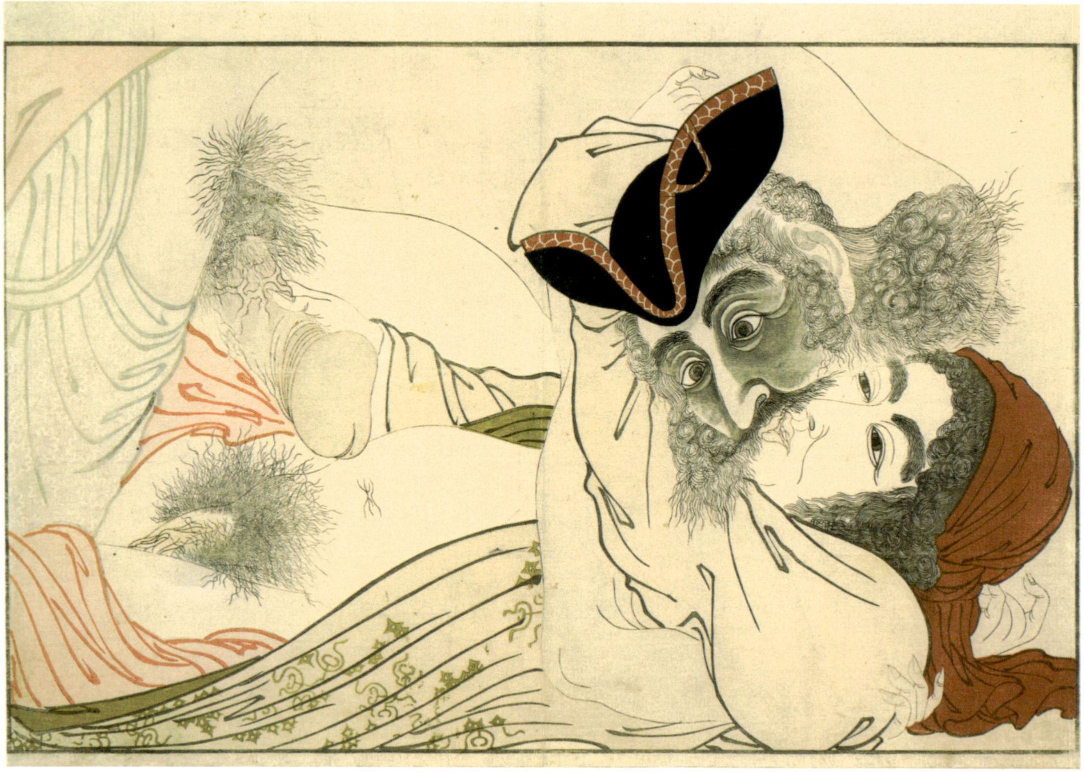

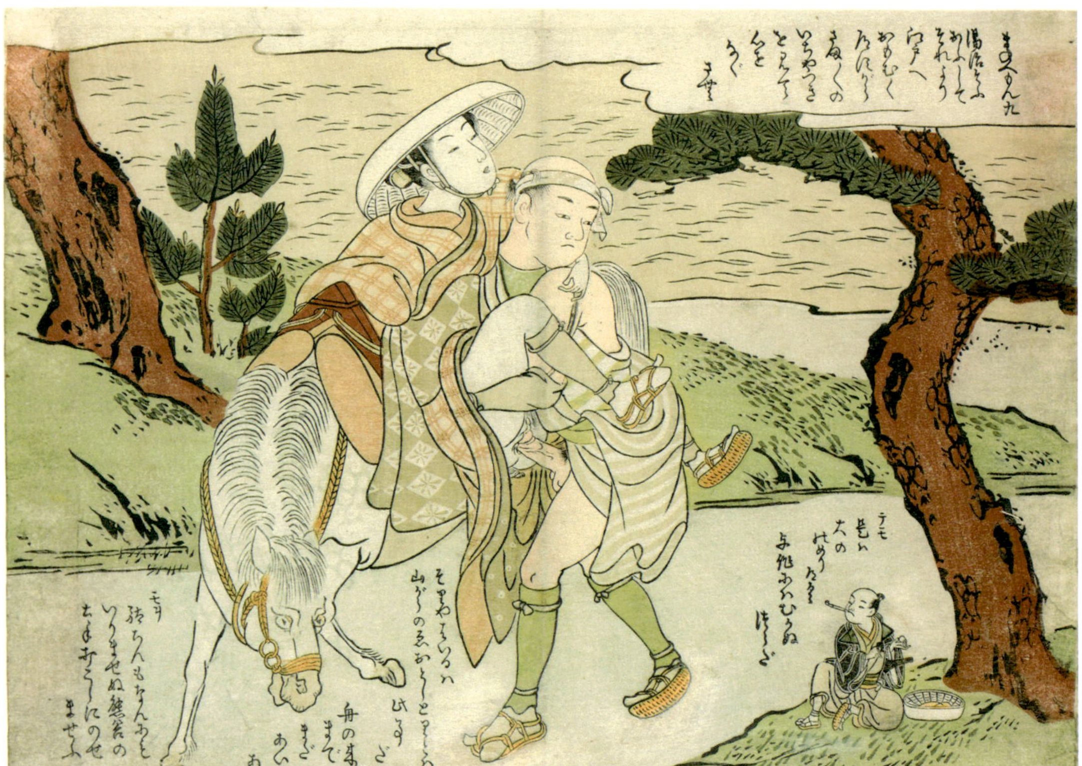

Kitagawa Utamaro
***Poem of the Pillow* (*Utamakura*)**
New Year 1788
Colour woodblock-printed album, each sheet approx. 25.5 × 37 cm

Dutch and Chinese traders were permitted to reside in Nagasaki, Japan's only international port. There was tremendous interest in the Europeans particularly, and they even appear in *shunga*. The Dutchman keeps his exotic headgear on while making love to his wife, and his abundant hair and sideburns are depicted in great detail.

Suzuki Harunobu
***Fashionable Lusty Mane'emon* (*Fūryū enshoku Mane'emon*), no. 9**
1770
Colour woodblock print, 20.6 × 28.5 cm

The settings for *shunga* can be mundane situations. On the way back from Ikaho hot-springs resort, Mane'emon (the 'Bean Man') watches a scene from the roadside at a ferry-crossing. The woman traveller says, 'I still have some time until the boat comes' and the road-horse boy replies enthusiastically, 'You don't need to pay the riding fee. I'll take you on my horse for free…'.

Types of sexual activity

The majority of sexual encounters in *shunga* are heterosexual, and most of the characters are between the ages of twenty and fifty, although there are sometimes adolescents and elderly people. Many scenes show married couples, but there are also young lovers, cheating spouses and amorous widows, as well as male and female prostitutes. All manner of sexual positions are explored, with both penetration and oral stimulation. One frequently encounters men and women masturbating, sometimes using sex aids, often while watching others engaged in love-making.

In Tokugawa-period Japan, the adult male had a choice of genders for his sexual partner. There existed a category of young men, known as *wakashū*, who were sexually available, to older men in particular but also sometimes to women. Sexual relations between men were socially acceptable provided the senior partner maintained the dominant role, though in reality there may have been more nuanced relationships. In depictions of such encounters, little attention is paid to the genitalia of the younger man and the penis is usually flaccid. However, such scenes become relatively rare in *shunga* after 1800, perhaps reflecting changing social custom. Scenes of female–female sex are not uncommon in *shunga*, and almost invariably feature the use of some kind of dildo.

Also depicted are combinations of a man with both female and younger male partners, or one man pleasuring multiple women simultaneously (up to ten!). Occasionally rape and even bestiality or necrophilia are shown, but such scenes are few and far between, certainly in works dating from before the nineteenth century.

Women

It is sometimes mistakenly believed, perhaps influenced by tendencies of Western pornography, that *shunga* depict male enjoyment and female submission. Examination of the examples in this book, however, shows that in *shunga* the women are generally equal partners in the sexual experience. It is assumed that they possess equal desire for sexual activity, and that they are due sexual satisfaction to the same degree as men. Within domestic situations, this is held to be the key to harmonious relations. Many *shunga* show women actively wanting sexual relations, urging their partners to commence intercourse, and then being overcome by the intensity of pleasurable sensations.

However, all known producers of *shunga* (with the possible exception of Katsushika Hokusai's daughter, Oi) were men, and thus the scenes presented are the result of male imagination or fantasies. Nevertheless, the predominance of representations of mutual sexual fulfilment suggests something significant about the expectations of those who produced and consumed these commodities.

Kitagawa Utamaro
Poem of the Pillow **(*Utamakura*)**
New Year 1788
Colour woodblock-printed album,
each sheet approx. 25.5 × 37 cm

From the woman's blackened teeth and plump figure we can surmise this is a more mature, married couple. The husband grasps his wife tightly round the chest, and she thoughtfully pulls over his kimono to stop him catching a chill.

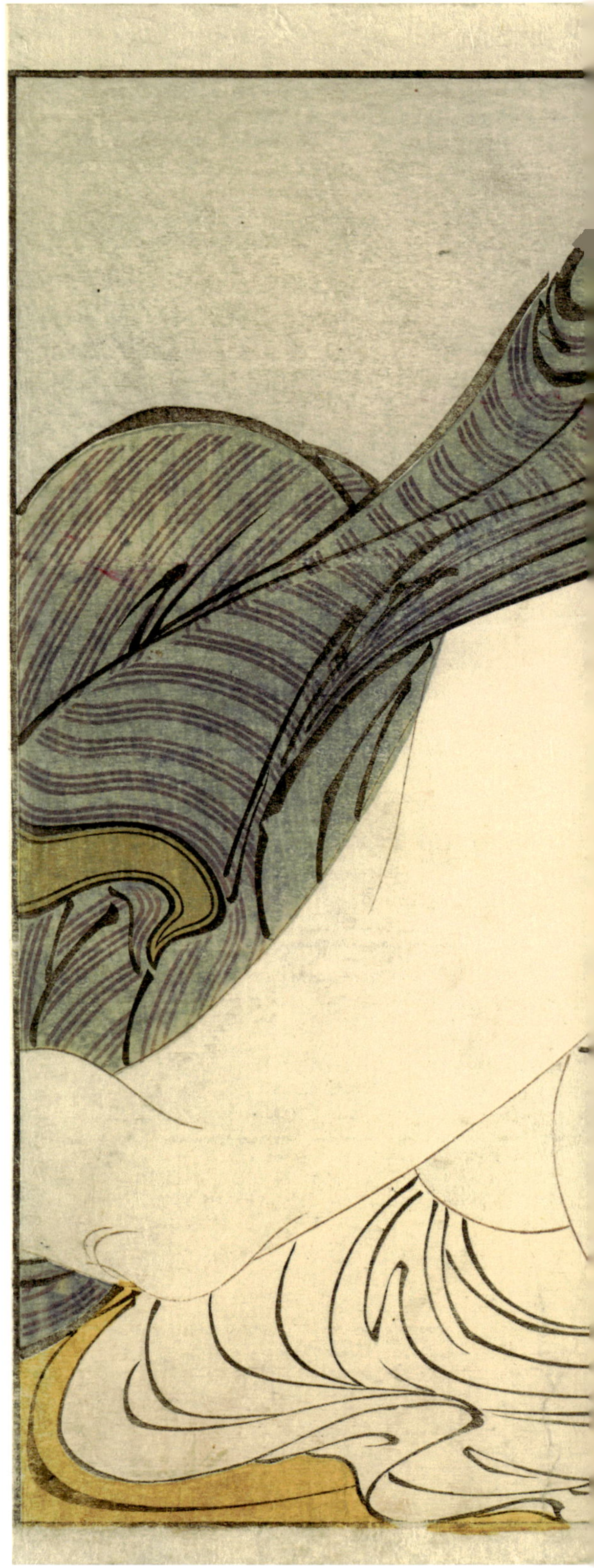

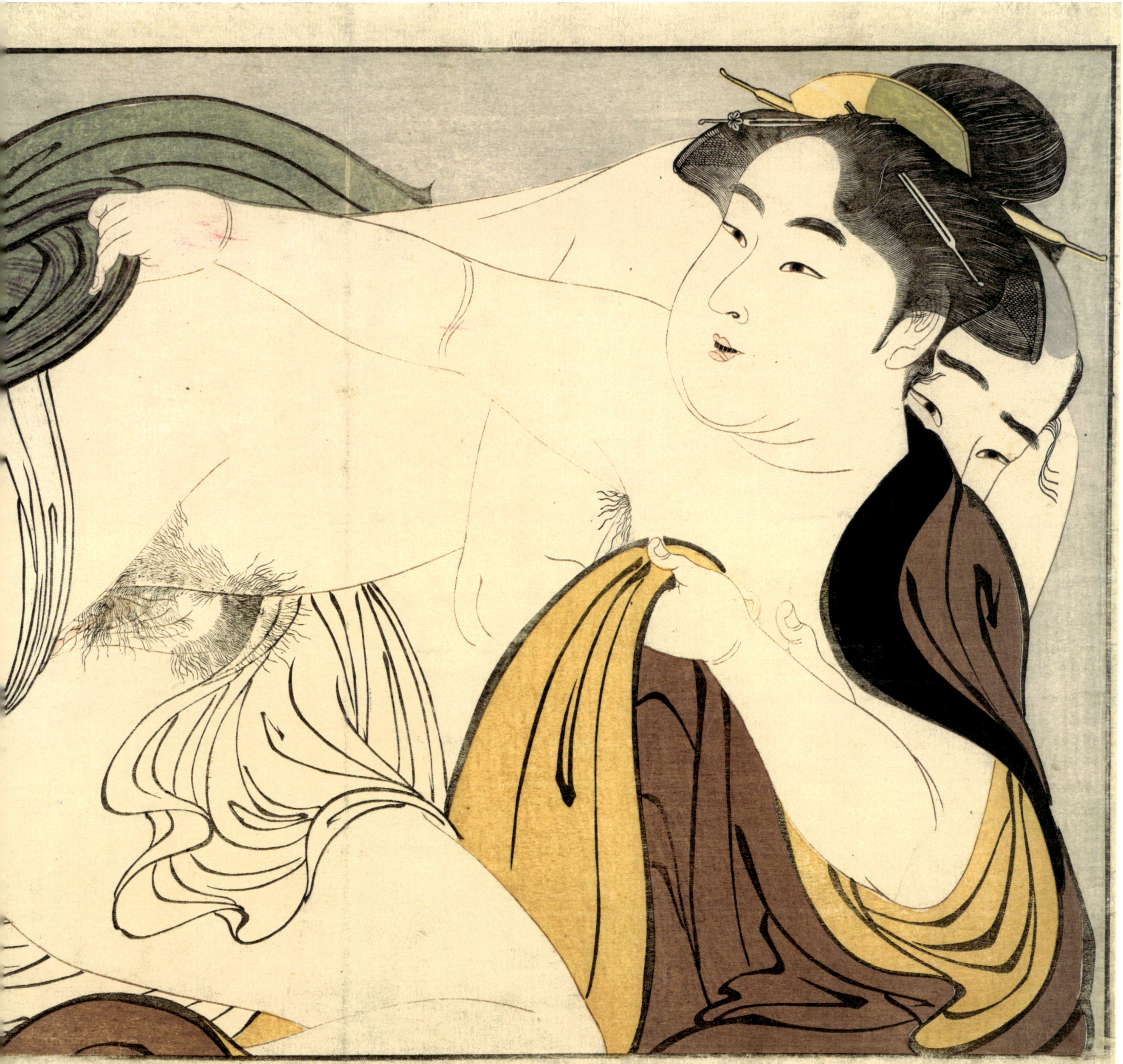

Locations

The venues for sex in *shunga* are as diverse as the characters. As mentioned, a large proportion of the scenes are domestic, whether in the bedroom or other areas of the house. Nevertheless, danger and the risk of being discovered form an essential element of many *shunga* designs, adding an atmosphere of tension and excitement to the scene depicted. Even married couples are often concerned that they will be discovered by other members of the household. In fact, the voyeur (or voyeuse) is a common occurrence in *shunga* – he or she functions as an empathetic stand-in for the viewer. In reality people would indeed have had little opportunity to be completely alone: the architecture of Japanese houses, of wooden construction with moveable partitions and translucent door panels, afforded many opportunities for glimpsing or overhearing people's sexual activities.

Artists competed in creating locations and positions that conveyed the idea of *kiwadoi*, the 'dangerous, risky or pressing', for example, staircases, the garden, the veranda or the drying platform on top of houses. There are often outdoor scenes, such as cherry-blossom viewing outings.[2]

Many couples are concerned about secrecy because theirs is a forbidden relationship. A common figure is the maid who has little opportunity to leave her employer's house and meet her lover, or the courtesan who must conceal the existence of her secret lover, a man who makes love with her but brings no profit to her employer. There are also many scenes of married men or women conducting affairs. Romance did not play a significant part in people's expectations of marriage in Japan, and considerations of economic and social status were more important (though the importance of such concerns varied according to class). As a result, there were fewer moral or ethical reservations about sexual relations outside marriage, at least for men. Nevertheless there was a need to be discreet about such liaisons. For couples who needed to meet in secret, there were establishments known as 'rendezvous tea-houses' (*deai-jaya*) where they could enjoy a few hours in private.

Representations of gender

Ascertaining the gender of the figures depicted in *shunga* is culturally determined. Whereas in European erotic pictures gender is indicated by the shape of the body – men usually portrayed as lean and muscled, and women as round and rather fleshy – in early Japanese erotic imagery there is often little distinction between the bodies and clothing of men and women. With the introduction of colour printing, different skin tones were used: women tend to have white skin whereas men are more flesh-coloured. The clearest indicator, however, is to be found in the hairstyles, though fashions changed over the decades. Generally, men who have reached maturity have the crown of their head shaved, and the remaining hair is long and tied back (and sometimes fixed on top); adolescents retain their long forelock, but the shaved crown can be seen underneath.

Likewise, there are aspects of female representation that require an understanding of contemporary customs. The type of kimono can indicate status, with townswomen in plainer

Suzuki Harunobu
Fashionable Lusty Mane'emon
(*Fūryū enshoku Mane'emon*), no. 5
1770
Colour woodblock print, 20.6 × 28.5 cm

In Edo-period Japan, a man could take a younger male lover if he chose. At tea-houses near the *kabuki* theatres, the young female role specialists (*onnagata*) worked as prostitutes. Here, an attractive youth stimulates himself as he mounts his client. The narcissi on his robe are a symbol of male love. The 'Bean Man' comments, 'Good heavens, the method of having male sex involves some elaborate armwork.'

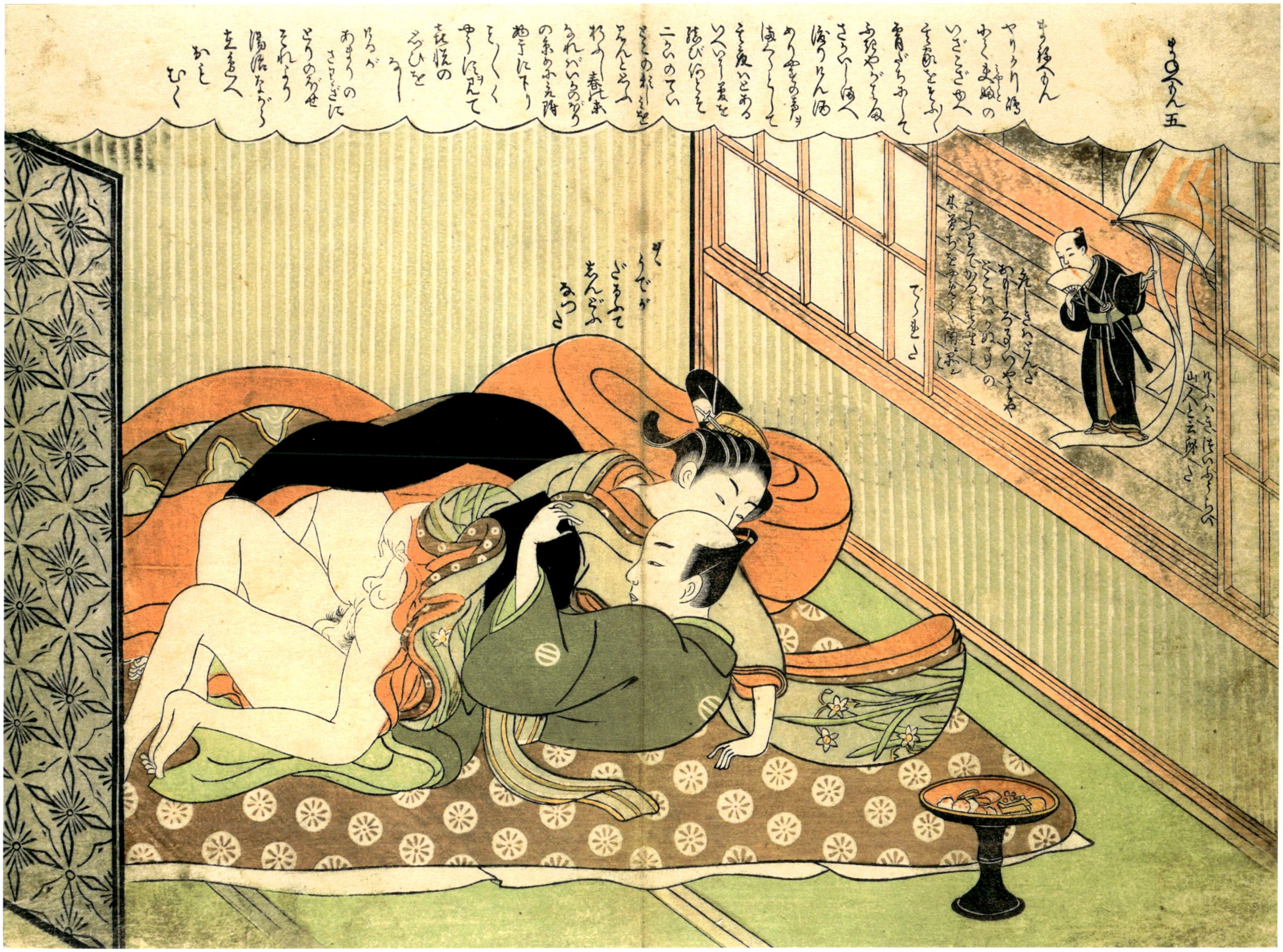

Katsukawa Shunshō
***Picture-book: Haikai Album of the Cuckoo* (*Ehon haikai yobuko-dori*)**
New Year 1788
Colour woodblock-printed album,
25.2 × 18.2 cm (covers)

Shunga emphasize the pleasure which women experience in sex. In this design of a married couple, the husband complains of the exhausting effects of the Chōmeimaru aphrodisiac. His wife, meanwhile, throws her head back in orgasmic ecstasy, clutching the pillow and curling her toes.

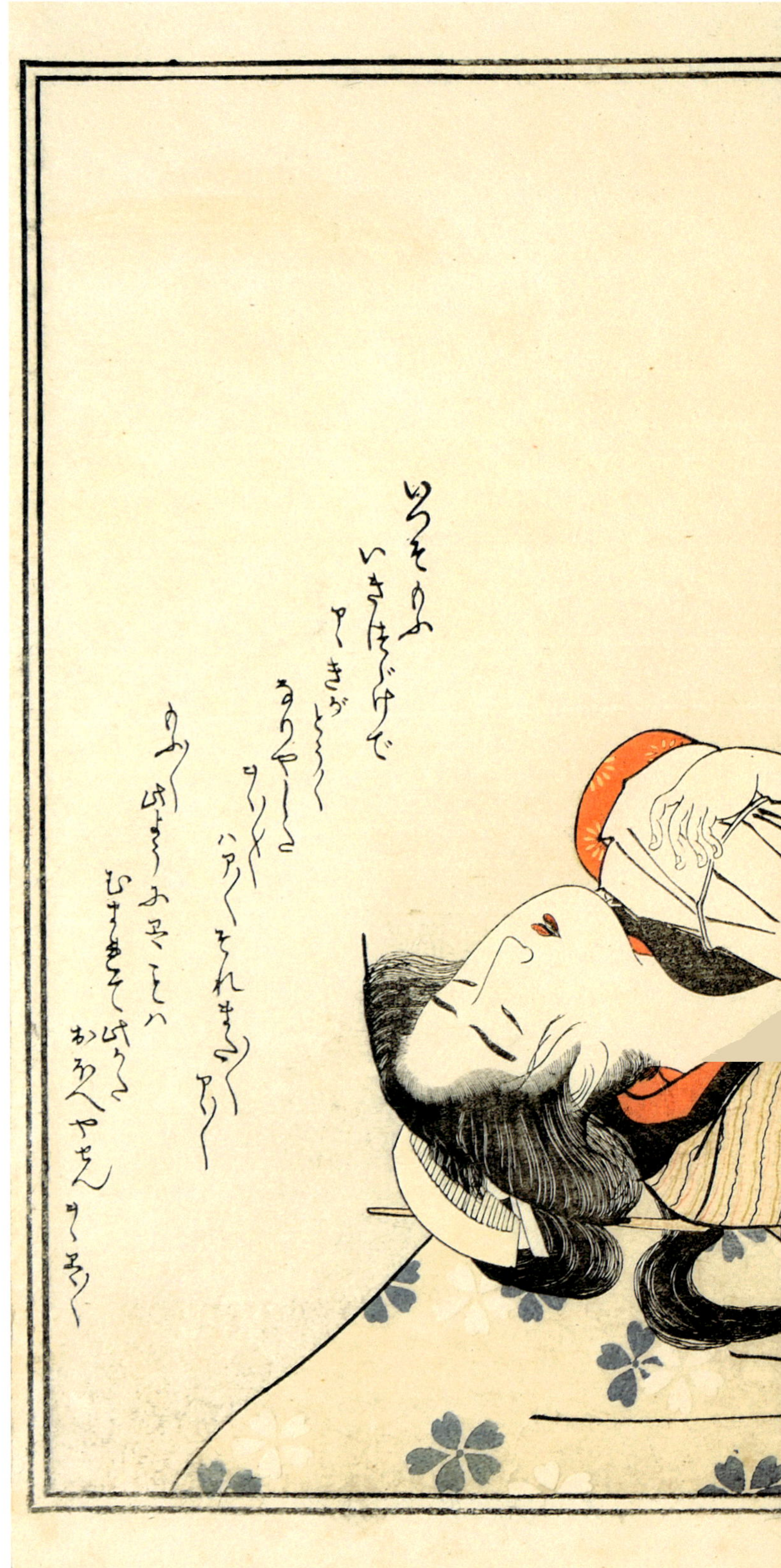

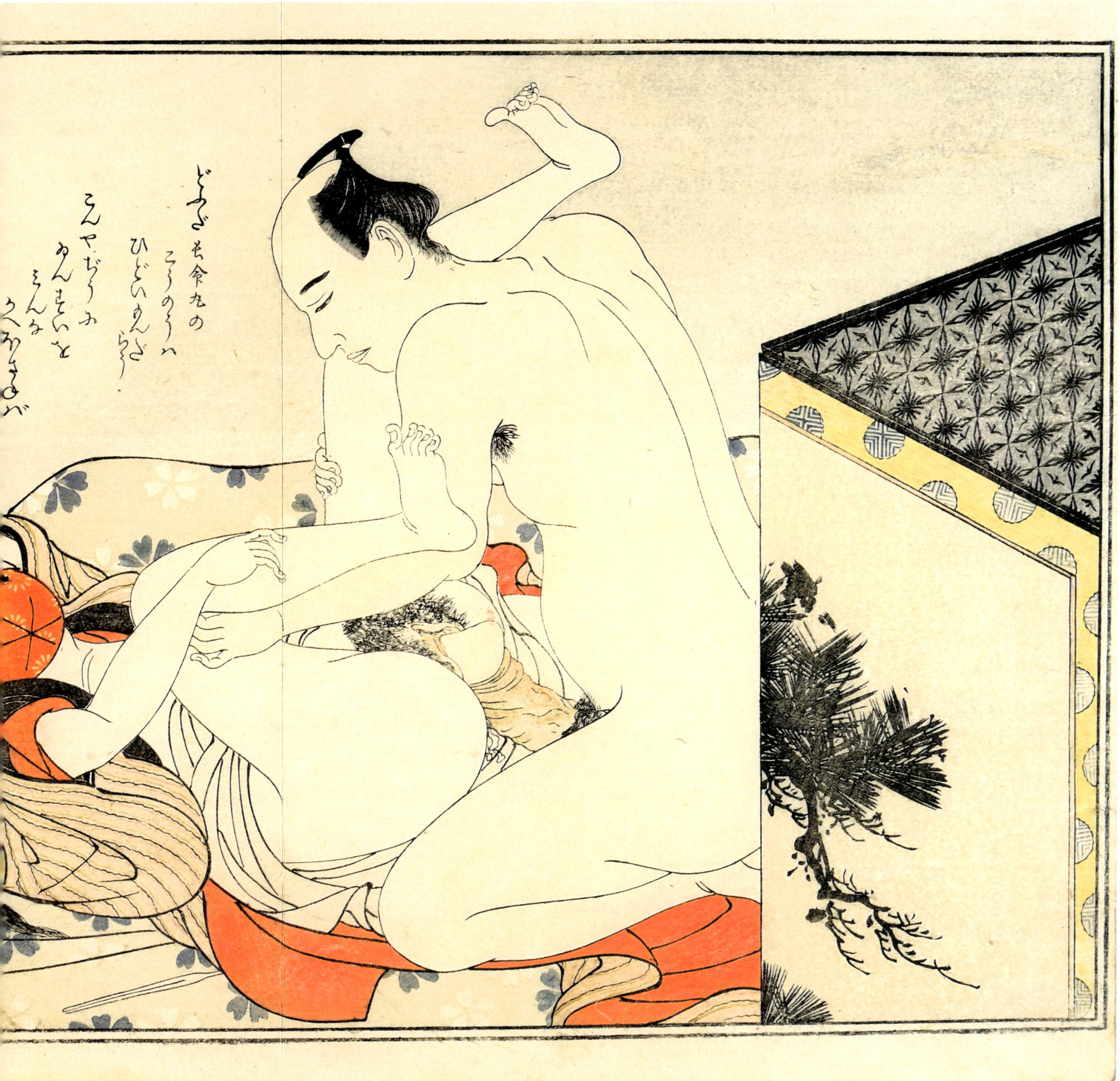

Below: Isoda Koryūsai
Making love on the veranda
c. 1774–5
Colour woodblock print,
24.4 × 37.9 cm

Couples in *shunga* often choose 'risky' places for their secret encounters, and are fearful of being caught. The veranda which wrapped around traditional architecture is one such locale. The energetic thrust of the young man's love-making here pushes the woman back into the room, and she braces herself on the door. The surging waves on the screen painting echo the powerful sensations.

Opposite: Okumura Toshinobu
Types from Osaka, Kyoto and Edo
1716–46
Woodblock print with hand-colouring,
31.2 × 15.7 cm

Despite the flowery robe, the attractive companion from Osaka whom the townsman from Edo is leading off is a male prostitute, indicated by the shaved crown. Both men turn to look at a female prostitute from Kyoto, seated within a room: perhaps the client is reconsidering with whom he should spend the night. The characters on the robes indicate the cities the figures represent, and the design suggests the rivalry of the three great cities of Edo-period Japan.

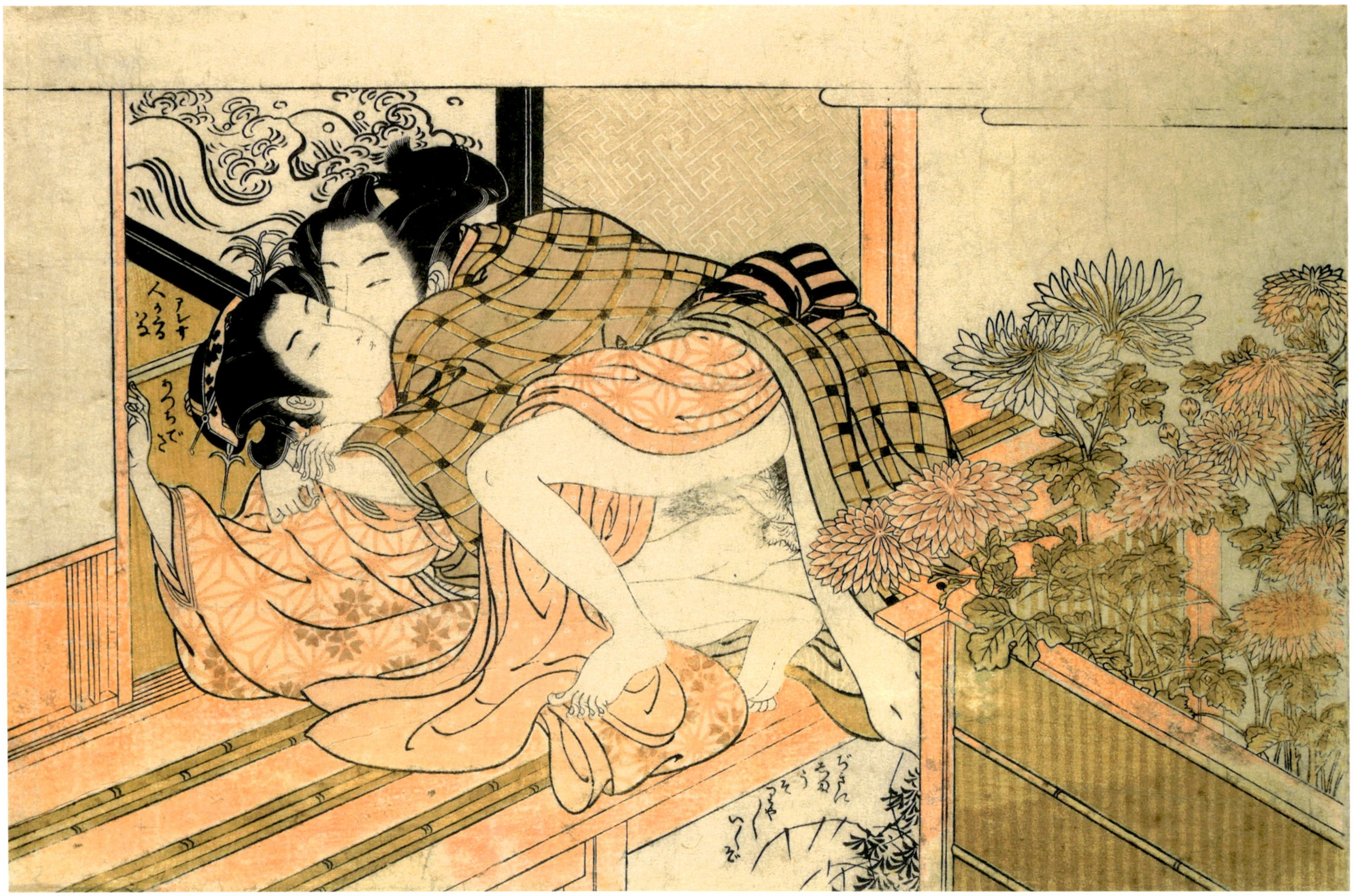

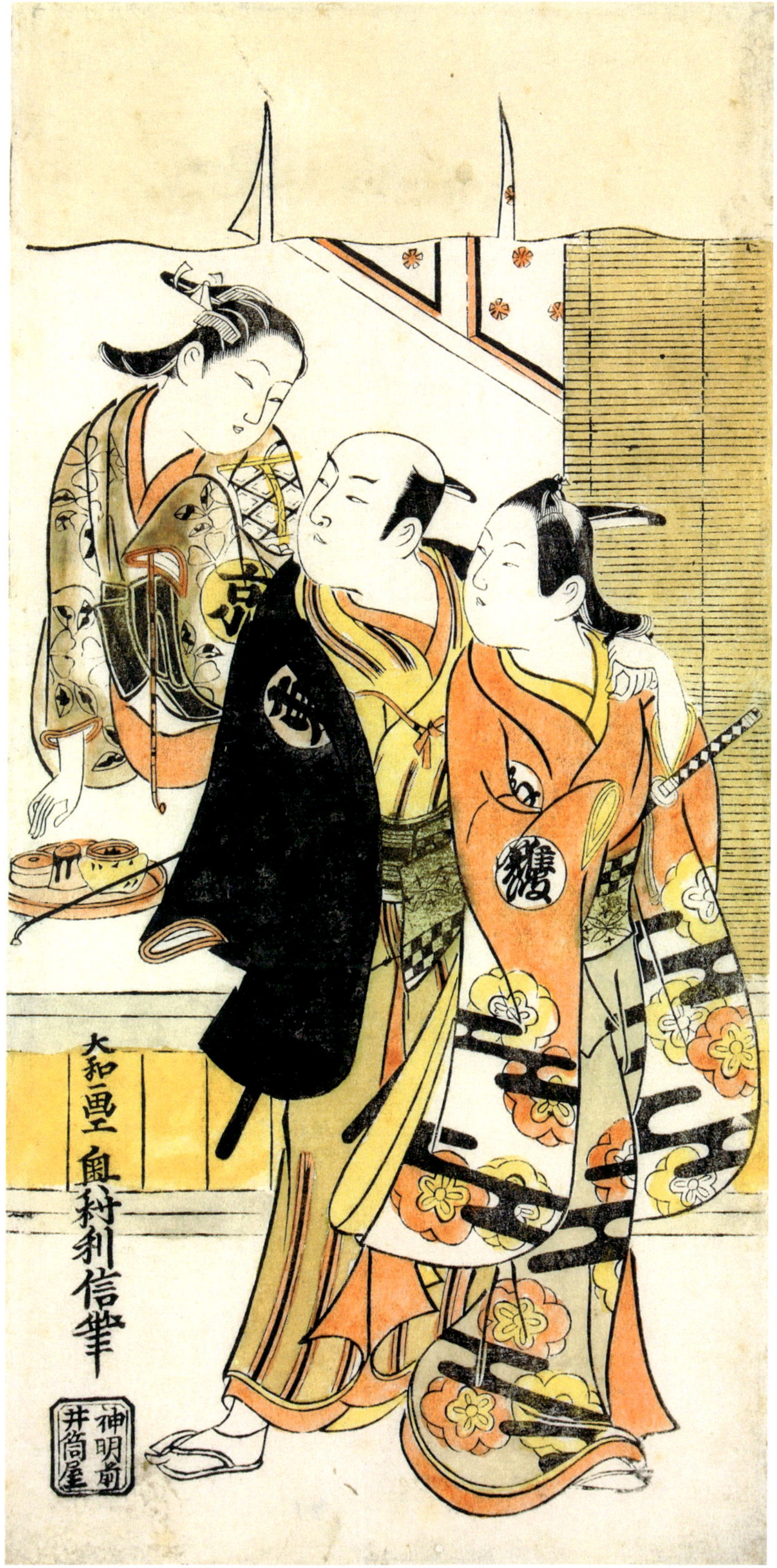
大和画工 奥村利信筆
神明前 井筒屋

Attr. Katsushika Hokusai
Picture-book: Patterns of Couples
(*Ehon tsuhi no hinagata*)
1817
Colour woodblock-printed album, each opening 25.3 × 18.5 cm

The fabric of the robes and bedcover envelop the bodies of this young couple, filling the composition. The wave pattern on the woman's robe with long sleeves (*furisode*) provides a particularly strong visual element. The man has crept into her room at night (the lantern he used to find his way in the dark stands at the side) and she hides her face in embarrassment. He asks her, 'Is it really your first time?'

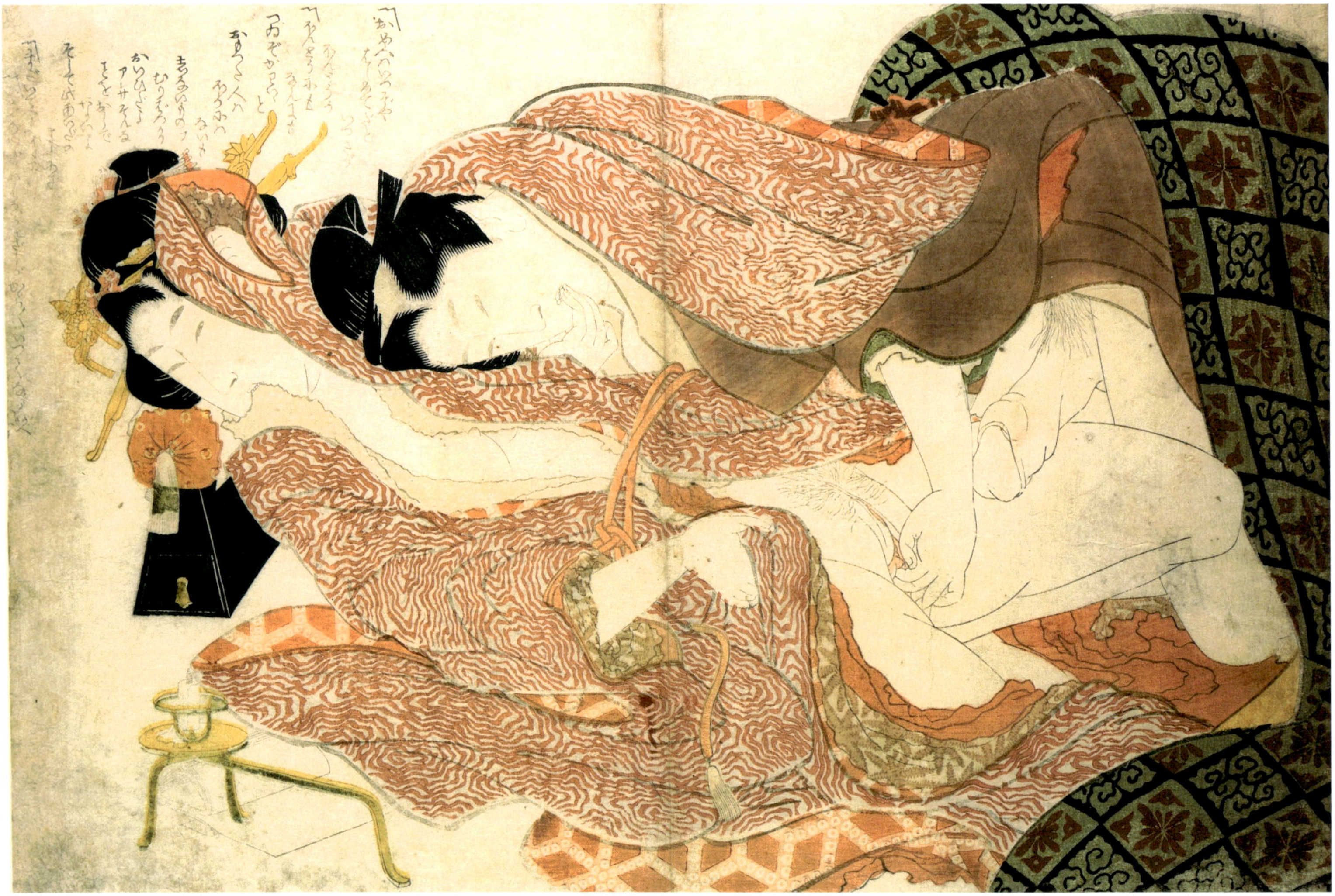

garments, and courtesans wearing the most elaborate. Young women wore long, hanging sleeves, which they would give up on marriage. Married women, usually after their first child, shaved their eyebrows and painted their teeth black. Rather than jewellery worn on the neck or hands, women of the Tokugawa period ornamented their hair, creating elaborate styles according to their income, and wearing combs and pins made of tortoiseshell, lacquer, gold, silver and inlays.

Fabrics

The sexual organs constitute the fulcrum of *shunga*, acting as the 'energy centre' of the composition.[3] The artist's aim is to convey the sensations and ecstasy associated with sexual intercourse, so it is natural that genitalia are the focus. Yet surrounding and framing these in almost every design are the undulating, rippling folds of luxurious robes (many of the lovers keep their clothes on) and bedding.

The inclusion of clothing relates to particular attitudes towards the human body. In Western cultures, the unclothed body has often been regarded as shameful because associated with sexual relations. Within the Japanese visual tradition, however, nakedness did not possess these connotations, but suggested merely the discarding of clothing in informal situations, such as the neighbourhood bath-house or the home. Therefore, rather than naked bodies, it is the material, patterns and forms of gorgeous robes that possess erotic appeal. A courtesan depicted naked, were it even imaginable, would have lost much of her appeal for a would-be client. Tremendous attention was paid by artists to the detailed depiction of fabrics, which also allowed publishers to showcase the supreme technical achievements of woodblock-printing technology. Clothing defined characters, literally by rendering the shape of their bodies, and by providing the viewer with narrative information.

When looking at *shunga*, clothing gives us information about the class, status and age of the players, helping us to interpret the picture, for example the hat and fine robes of a courtier, the swords identifying a samurai, or the long-sleeved robe of a young apprentice courtesan. Crucially, however, the women in *shunga* never wear undergarments, allowing an endless variation on scenarios of hasty and furtive sexual encounters, where only a skirt needs to be lifted for intercourse to commence.

Genital exaggeration

An immediately noticeable, and much commented on, feature of *shunga* is the exaggerated size of the male genitalia. As explained, the simple depiction of naked bodies had little intrinsic erotic force, and so in *shunga* the sex organs are imbued with extra power through their exaggerated size. Less often acknowledged is the enlargement of the female genitalia: the man in *shunga* wields an impossibly large penis, but he meets his match in his female partner. With the genitalia serving as the enlarged focus of many *shunga* designs, they are given a tremendous amount of visual detail. The shape, textures, folds and pubic hair of both penis and vulva, as well as the fluids emerging, are all carefully depicted. In the majority of designs

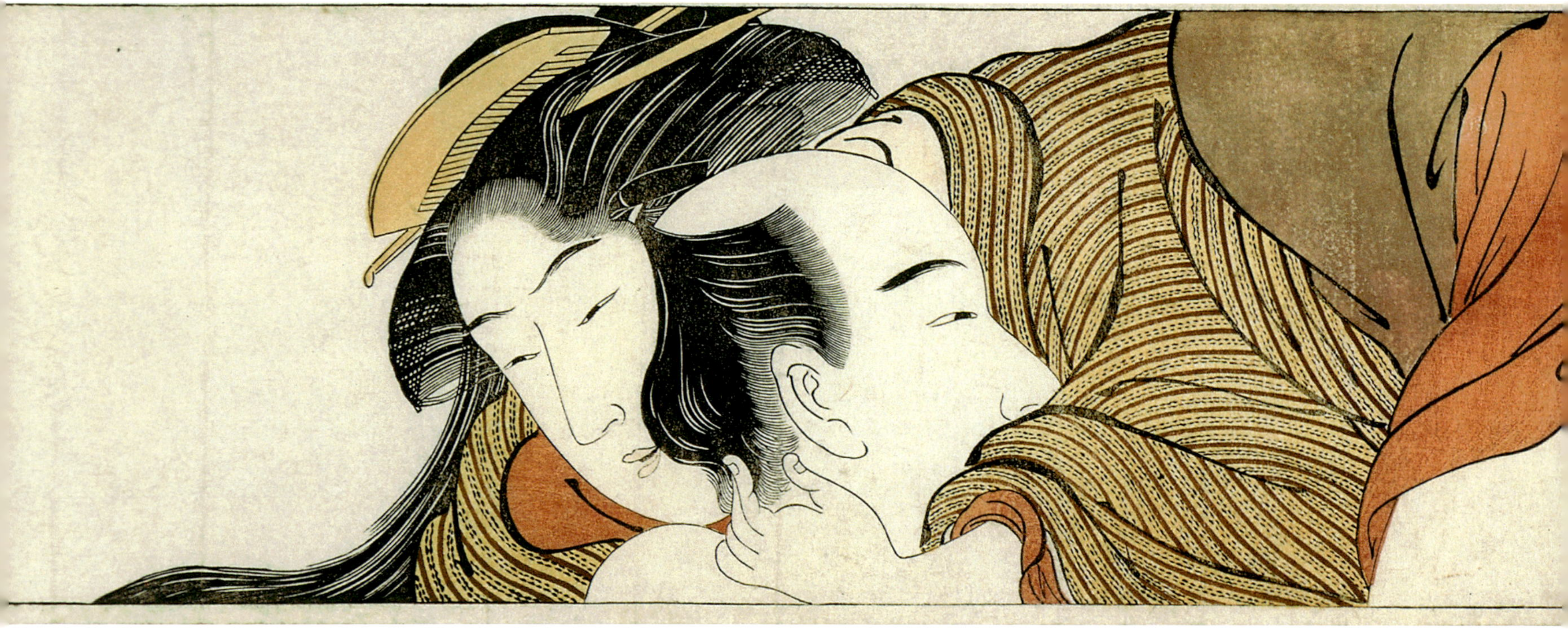

Torii Kiyonaga
***Scroll for the Sleeve* (*Sode no maki*)**
1785
Colour woodblock print, 12.6 × 67.4 cm

The focus of *shunga*, both visually and thematically, is the genitals, and so these are depicted larger than life. However, it is not only the penis that becomes a huge organ, the vagina is also comparably engorged. Here, an older married woman straddles her lover energetically, dislodging her coiffure.

the sex organs are of roughly equal size as the figures' heads, and serve as a balance in terms of their position within the picture. It has been argued that the equal visual weight given to heads and genitalia implies the inseparability within each individual of the public life as a member of society and the private sexual life.[4]

This compositional imperative to present the genitalia and faces equally results in artificial contortions of the body, which are another common feature of *shunga*. The woman's legs are often placed at impossible angles given the position of her hips, and sometimes abbreviations are made in the proportions of torso and limbs for the sake of visual simplicity. The exaggeration and fictionality of *shunga* was acknowledged at the time, however. A contemporary humorous verse can be translated, 'The foolish couple copy *shunga* and pull a muscle.'[5]

Humour

A humorous light-hearted tone plays a central role within many *shunga* designs. In Tokugawa-period Japan sex was regarded as something to be enjoyed, and something that could even provoke laughter, which may explain why erotic images were known as 'laughter pictures' (*warai-e*) and sexual aids were called 'laughter tools' (*warai-dōgu*).

The playfulness of *shunga* can be seen first and foremost in their settings. With sexual activity represented as an integral part of everyday life, there are all manner of situations where humour is possible: a wife catches her husband having it away with the maid, a couple are spied on by a curious servant, mice start copulating in imitation of the humans, painted figures on a folding screen point with glee at a couple having sex.

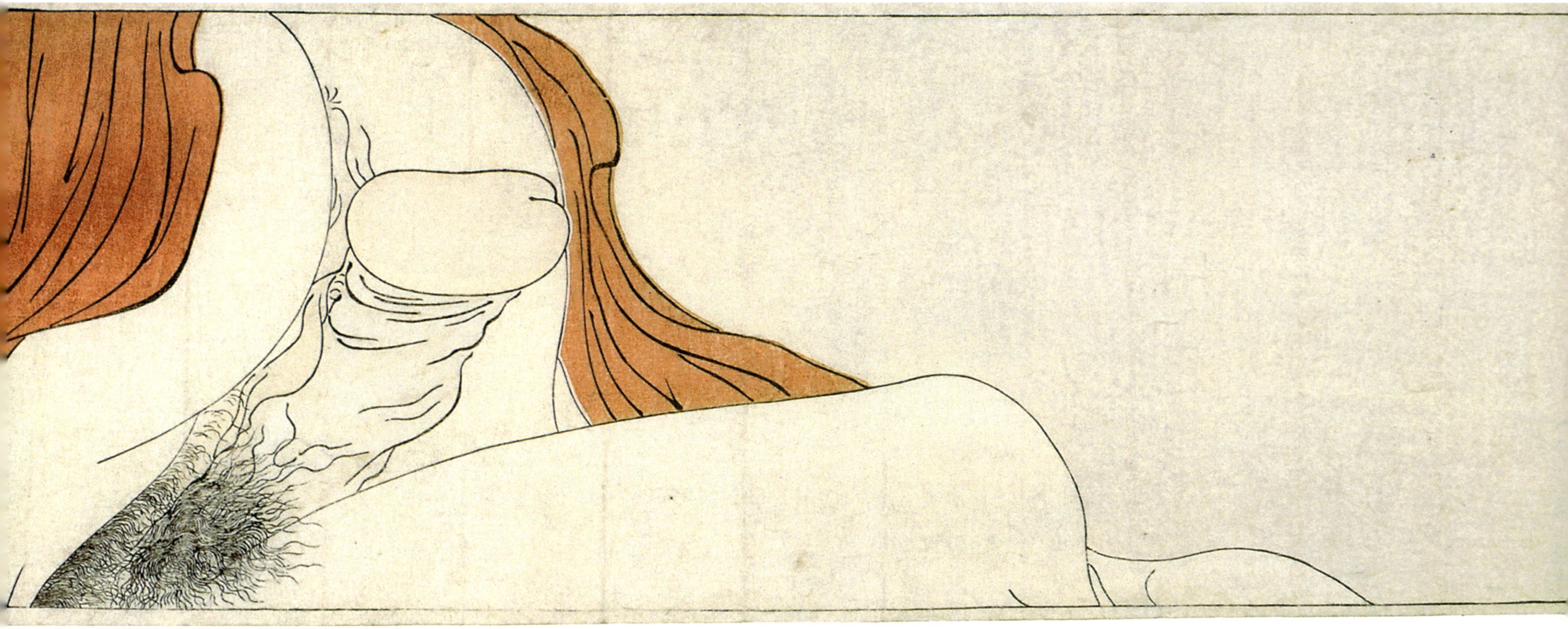

The medium for the humour is often the text rather than the pictures. It was a feature of some genres of light fiction of this period that text and image were integrated within one visual field. Erotic novels would present the amorous adventures of the hero, with accompanying text describing the excitements and mishaps encountered. The titles of books draw on the plentiful supply of homophones in the Japanese language to make double entendres. Prefaces are often written in *kyōbun*, a pseudo-classical style reliant on puns and humorous juxtapositions, with irreverent references to Chinese and Japanese history and mythology. These jokes would have appealed to the reader's sense of his (or her) own erudition, while simultaneously making sexual innuendo.

Dialogue

In many *shunga*, the dialogue between the participants is an essential element of the work, and it is impossible to understand the tenor and mood of each situation without taking this into account. The dialogue was often written by the artists themselves. The inscriptions are usually written in the phonetic syllabary, using a smaller number of Chinese characters than is customary in modern written Japanese. They are full of contemporary idioms and slang, and can be challenging to read even for Japanese people today.

The dialogue often gives information on the types of people portrayed, their relationship to one another, and their attitudes towards the sex taking place. It contains a temporal aspect: one character describes what he or she is feeling, and the other then responds. The speech may have taken place just before the moment depicted in the image, where, for example, a

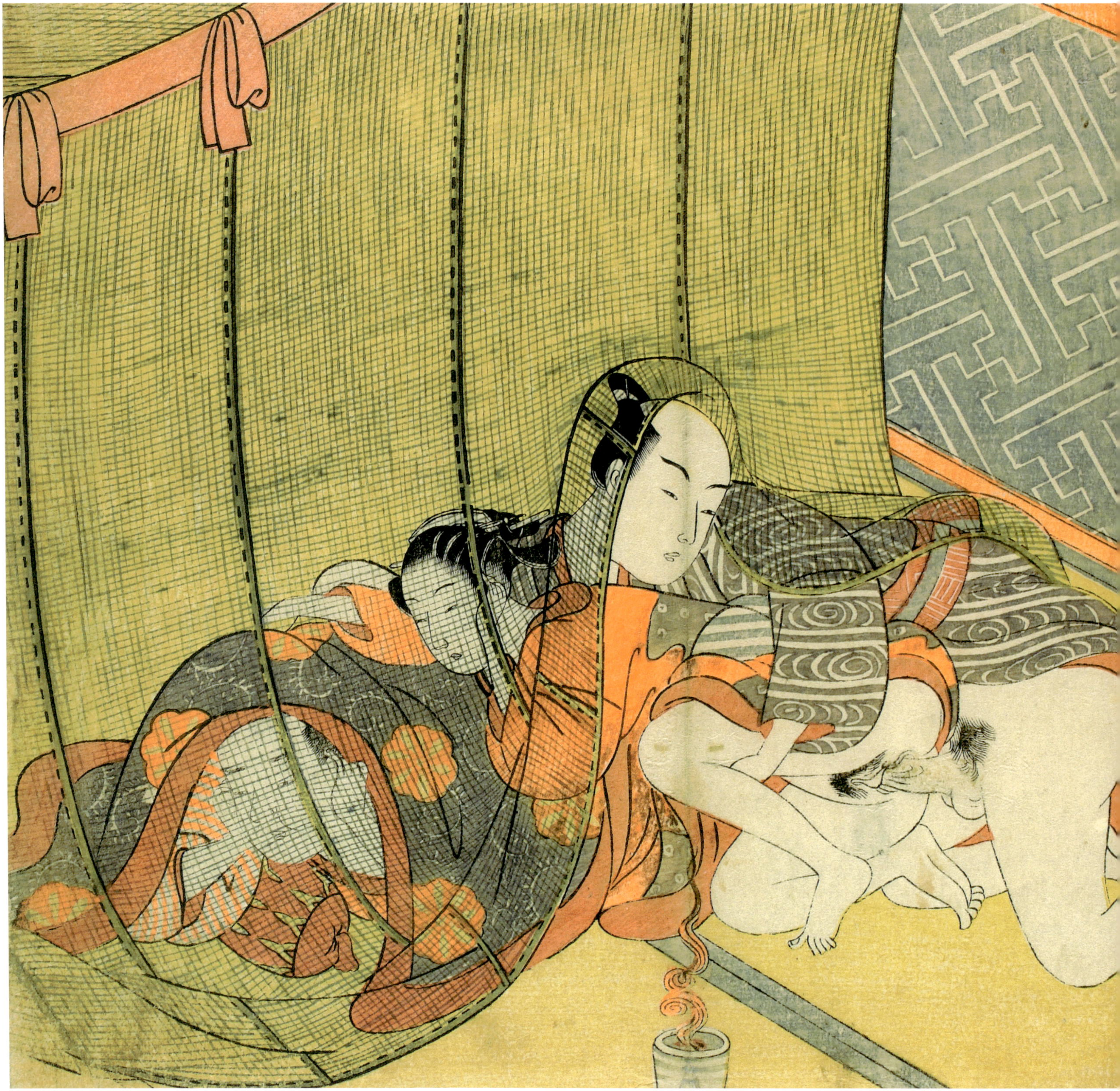

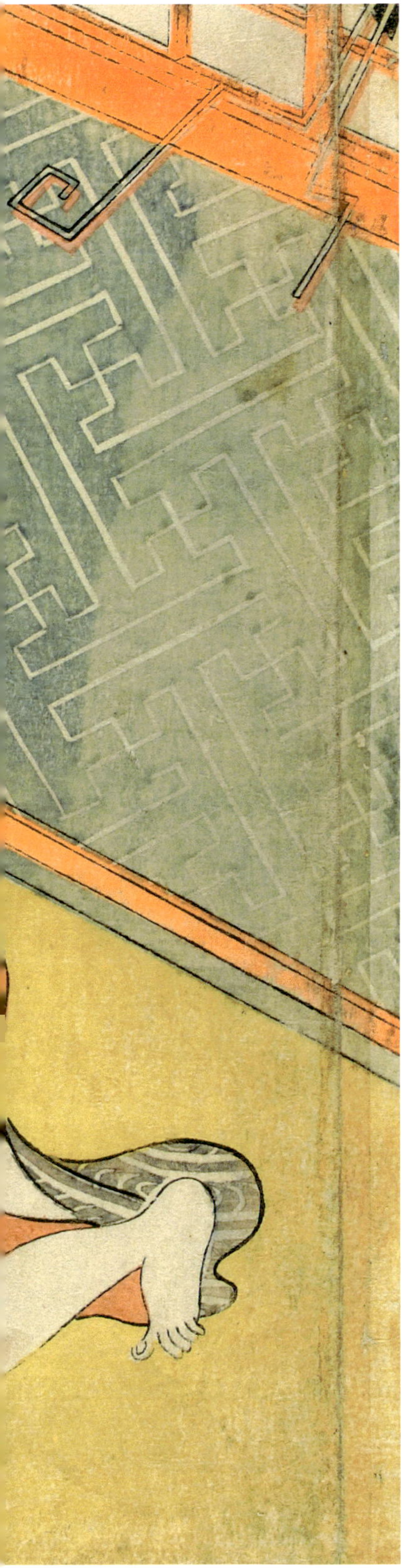

Style of Suzuki Harunobu
Husband cuckolded during a thunderstorm
1769–70
Colour woodblock print, 18.7 × 24.8 cm

Under the mosquito net in summer, a husband takes fright during a powerful thunderstorm (indicated by the stylized pattern entering through the window). His wife comforts him with one arm, but also takes the opportunity to entertain her lover.

woman says she must bite on her sleeve so she won't cry out, and the picture shows her doing so. The actors are much more articulate than one would expect of people engaged in energetic sex, but the viewer is asked to suspend disbelief!

Technology

The production of woodblock prints and books involved the collaboration of artist, block-cutter and printer, coordinated by the publisher, who was the financial backer of the project. The artist brushed the outline design in ink on thin paper, with indications of the colours and patterns to be used. This paper was then pasted face down on to a block of cherry-wood and 'sacrificed' in order to carve out the design through it. The cutter produced a block for each stage of the printing process, usually one for each of the colours. An elaborate design could require twenty printing blocks, or even more. Carvers served an apprenticeship of many years and specialized in the various types of print, with portrait subjects held to be the most demanding. The blocks were passed to the printing workshop, where each member would concentrate on one stage in the process, passing the printed sheets on to the next member of the team in the form of an assembly line. The sheets were placed face down on the inked blocks and rubbed on the verso using a *baren*, a pad made of coiled bamboo fibres covered with lacquered papier mâché and bamboo leaves. Registration marks (*kentō*) notched into one corner and one edge of each block ensured exact alignment of the printed colours at each stage. Modulation of the tone and intensity of the colours was possible through both careful application of pigment and variation in the pressure exerted during printing. Special finishes were possible by the use of metallic pigments, or by pressing the paper into the block without pigment, creating an embossed or textural effect.

Both images and text were produced by the same printing process, allowing for their easy integration on the page. This made for a dynamic viewing/reading experience, with the eye led to explore every corner of the page.

Kitagawa Utamaro
Picture-book: The Laughing Drinker
(*Ehon warai jōgo*)
c. 1803
Colour woodblock-printed book,
20.7 × 15 cm (covers)

Dialogue plays an important role in imparting information about scene and characters. Here, the young *geisha* says, 'I'd like another five or six men as cute as you, and I'd have them do me day and night without stop.'

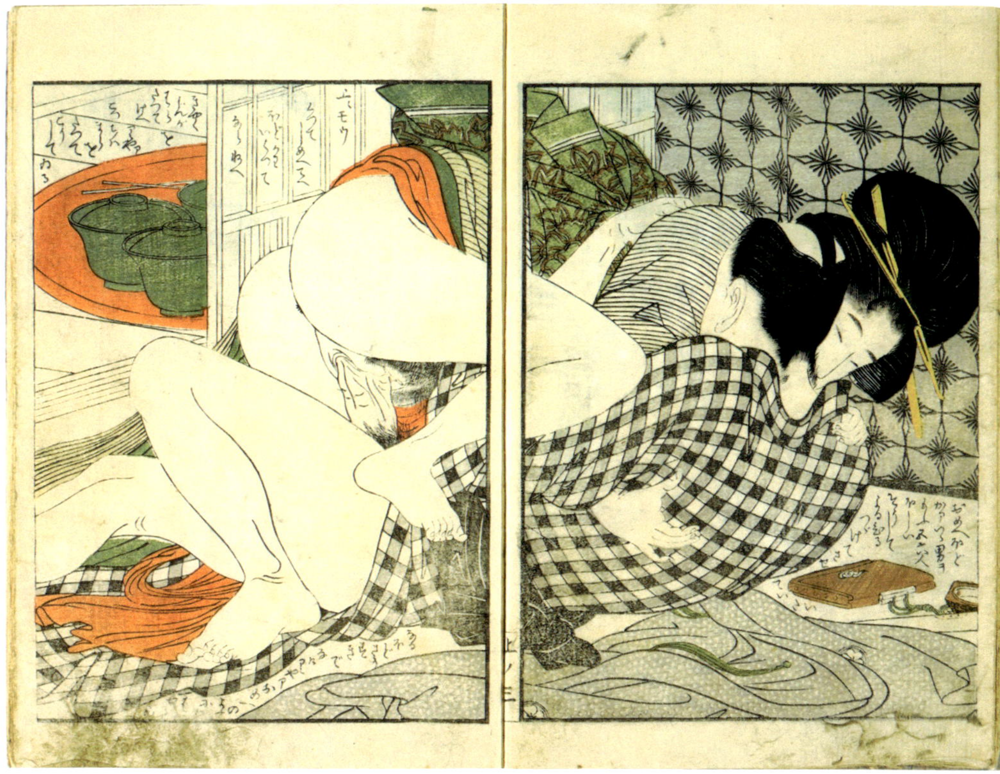

Kitagawa Utamaro
Making Brocade Pictures, a Famous Edo Product
(*Edo meibutsu nishiki-e kōsaku*)
1801–3
Colour woodblock prints,
left-hand sheet 36.5 × 24.7 cm,
right-hand sheet 36.4 × 24.2 cm

Though women may have assisted in some stages of woodblock-print production, Utamaro has here created a fanciful scene, placing his customary elegant beauties in a workaday scenario. On the right, one woman has paused before starting an initial design, another carves a woodblock and a third sharpens a knife. On the left, the women are applying coating to the paper and then hanging the sheets up to dry.

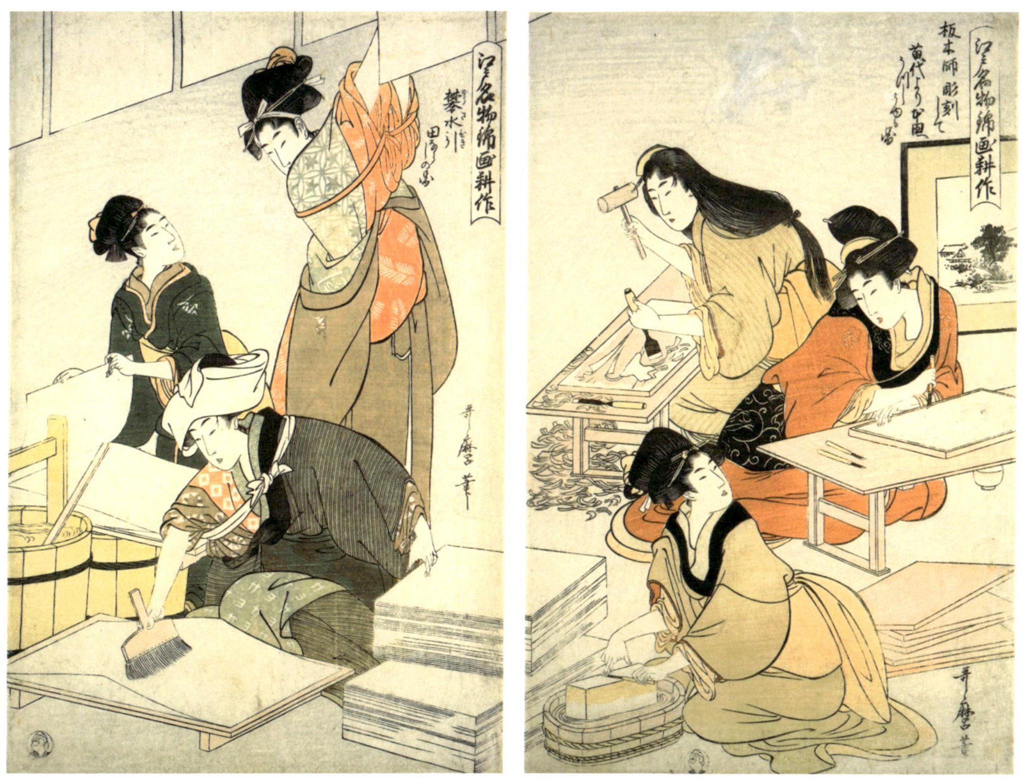

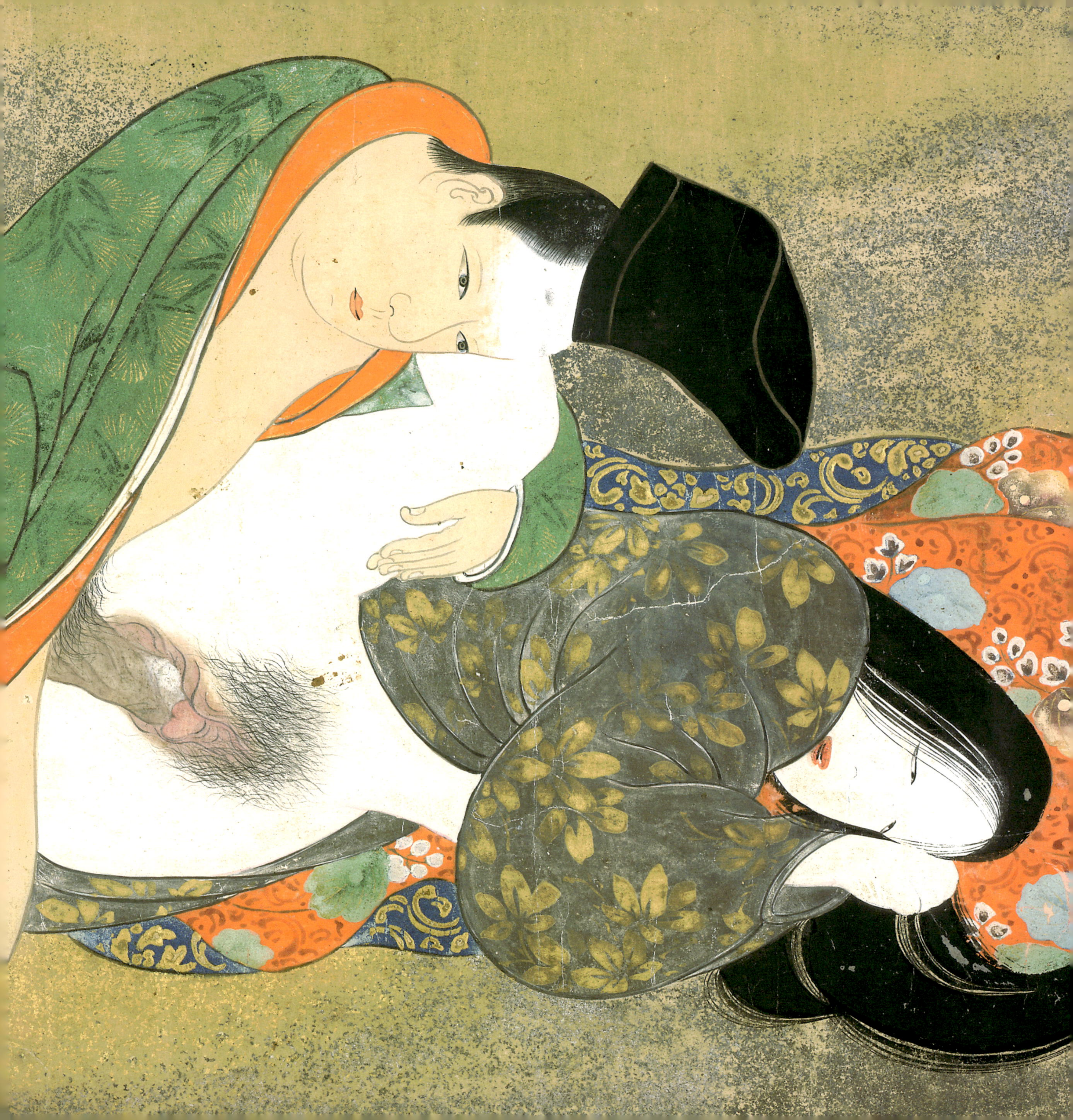

Patterns of sensual pleasure: from luxury paintings to popular prints, 1600–1750

Opposite: Erotic scene (detail)
c. 1600
Handscroll painting, ink, colour, gold and silver on paper, H: 27 cm
Caption details p. 65

Right: Scenes of phallic strength (detail)
1848–68
Three sections of a handscroll painting remounted together, ink, colour and gold on paper, 29.7 × 369 cm

In this handscroll painting, attributed to a pupil of the renowned print artist Utagawa Kuniyoshi (see pp. 153–7), a man demonstrates the strength of his member in a variety of situations. In the section illustrated here, he thrusts his phallus energetically through six roof-tiles, and in the text above cries, 'Ow! Let me show you how I can stick it through these.' Elsewhere in the scroll he shatters a metal cauldron and makes love five times in one night.

Erotic imagery was already being created during the Heian period (794–1185) in the form of painted handscrolls, a small format which was suitable for intimate viewing. A handscroll, usually about 20 to 30 centimetres high, would be unrolled for viewing in sections about 60 centimetres wide. They employed a narrative framework, sometimes alternating between pictures and passages of text. The earliest known erotic handscroll is the 'Tale of the Brushwood Fence' (*Koshibagaki-zōshi*; also known as the 'Initiation scroll', *Kanjō no maki*), though it survives only in much later copies. With text supposedly by the Retired Emperor Goshirakawa, it relates a real-life scandal of 986, when a princess undergoing ritual purification prior to taking up the position of shrine maiden at the Ise Grand Shrine had an affair with an imperial guard. The original was said to have been presented to the imperial consort Taira no Tokuko by her aunt as a present upon her marriage in 1172 to Emperor Takakura, although this was perhaps an odd kind of instruction.

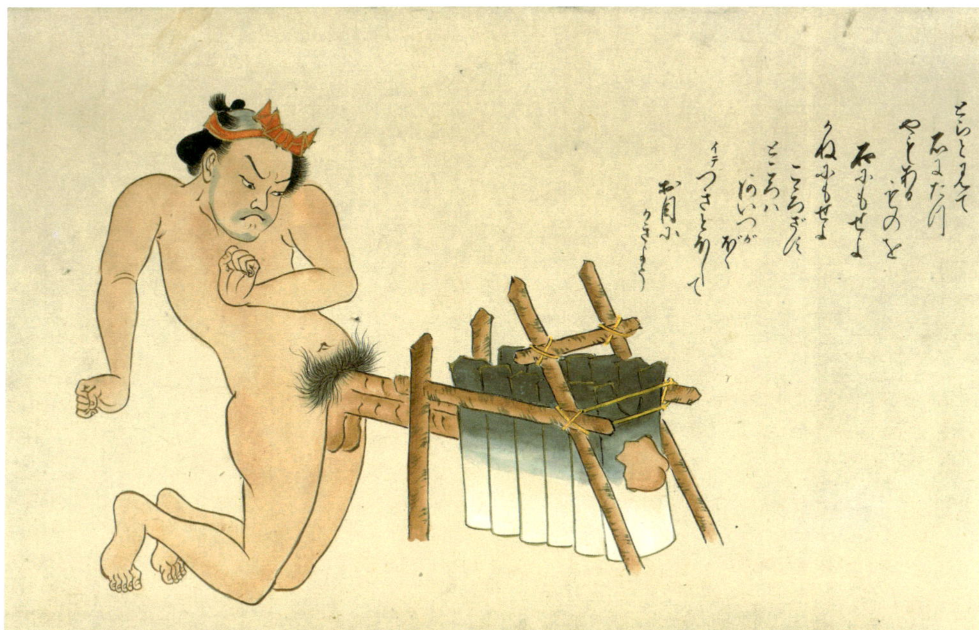

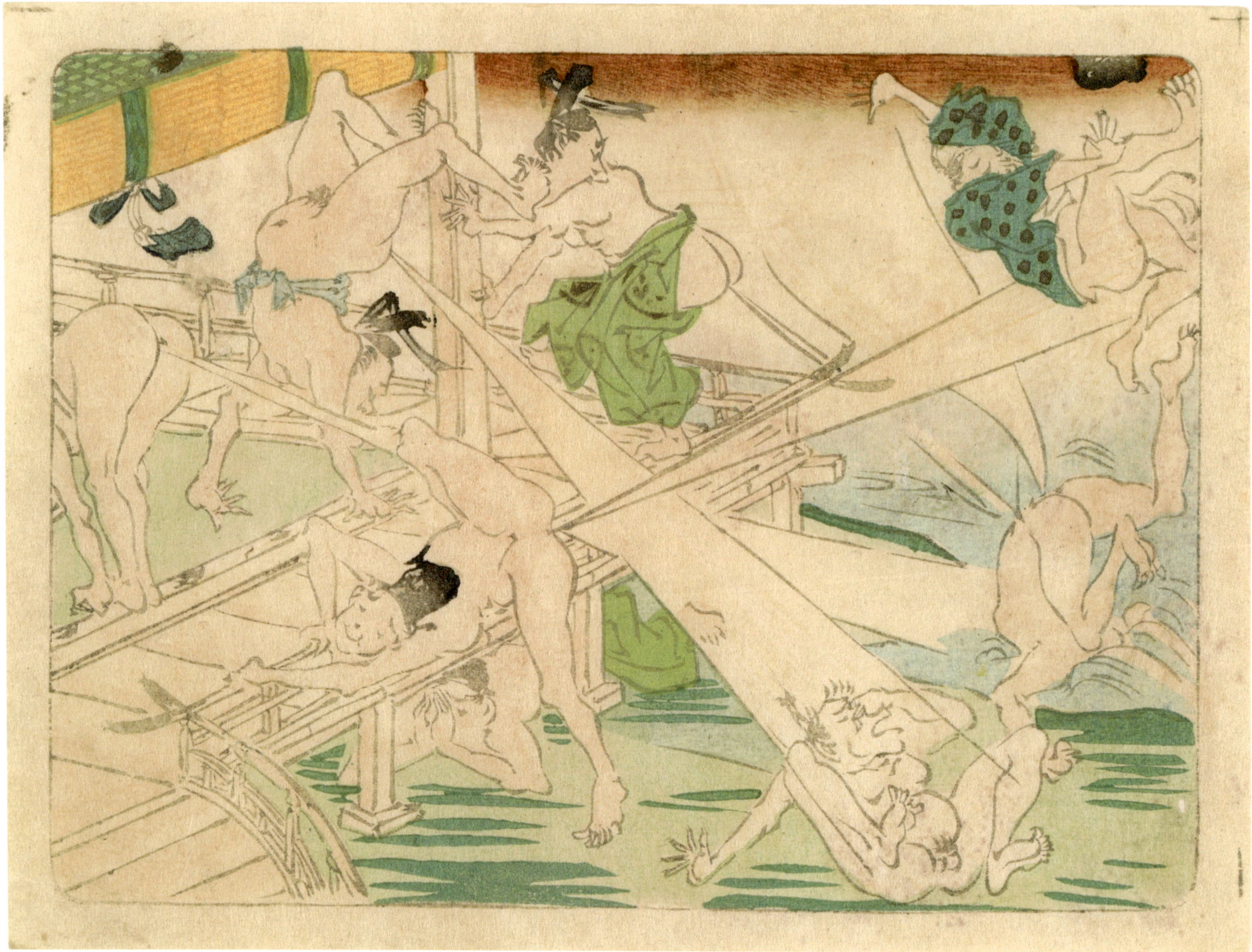

Kawanabe Kyōsai
***Farting Contest* (*Hōhi gassen*)**
1870s
From a set of twelve colour woodblock prints,
9.7 × 13.3 cm
Israel Goldman Collection, London

This image is from a set of twelve small woodblock prints depicting the medieval theme of a farting contest among courtiers. The set of prints is designed to emulate a handscroll. Here, a group of aristocrats perform acrobatics on the veranda of a mansion, all the while demonstrating their 'talents'.

There are two further notable medieval erotic scrolls: the 'Tale of the Acolyte' (*Chigo no sōshi*), dated 1321, the earliest *shunga* extant in its original version, which tells of the not uncommon practice of sexual relations between monks and young acolytes in a Buddhist temple, and the 'Illustrated Tale of the Bag-Priest' (*Fukuro hōshi ekotoba*), also of the fourteenth century, in which a priest who pesters three women who have lost their way gets his comeuppance and is taken hostage by them for their sexual pleasure.

Scrolls depicting contests of bodily attributes or functions were also produced during this period. These are often more humorous than erotic, but they feature plentiful naked men (and sometimes women) cavorting. The genre emulated and parodied elegant competitions of poetry or incense. The most famous is the 'Phallus Competition' (*Yōbutsu kurabe*), with text attributed to Jōken (1162–1231), the abbot of Sambōin sub-temple of Daigoji. Another is the 'Farting Contest' (*Hōhi gassen*), which was copied repeatedly. The persistence of such subjects over the centuries can be seen in two works from the nineteenth century illustrated here.

Handscrolls of the seventeenth century

With the growth of a wealthy, if still small, class of merchants during the late sixteenth to early seventeenth centuries, there was an expansion of the scope of erotic imagery. The typical format remained the handscroll, convenient for private viewing, but rather than a continuous narrative these works tended to present a series of unrelated compositions, depicted in abstract space with only a few accoutrements. There is no description of architectural settings, but within these paintings textiles play an important role: the lovers lie on colourful ornamented rugs and their sometimes naked bodies are concealed or framed by gorgeously decorated robes and bedding. The handscrolls usually contained twelve scenes, a structure probably derived from the paintings depicting the customs and activities of the twelve months (*tsukinami-e*) which had begun in the Heian period. This approach was subsequently continued with sets of twelve woodblock prints and print albums containing twelve designs. The scrolls generally depicted courtiers or samurai in full armour making love to court ladies with long, flowing tresses.

There exists a great energy and diversity in representations of sexual intercourse during this period: painted scrolls present a wide range of positions, practices and combinations of partners (of various ages, and including priests, nuns, and even Chinese couples). It was a convention derived from earlier paintings to depict men and women of the court, the men wearing stiff, lacquered hats and the women with long tresses. Such scrolls were copied repeatedly, and the same scenes and compositions can be found in works of different dates. Painters would either have taken existing works as their models, or have relied on studio copybooks.[1]

Scenes of love-making (details)
Late 17th century
Handscroll painting, ink on paper,
29 × 412 cm

This handscroll contains ten erotic scenes, several of which can be found repeated in other works of the period. The opening image (below) is of a naked nun (identifiable by her shaved head) masturbating with a dildo attached to her foot, the box lined with expensive gold leaf lying to one side.

Opposite: Another common motif in painted handscrolls of this period is the combination of a man kissing one woman as he penetrates another. This derived originally from a composition of a man together with a woman and a young male partner.

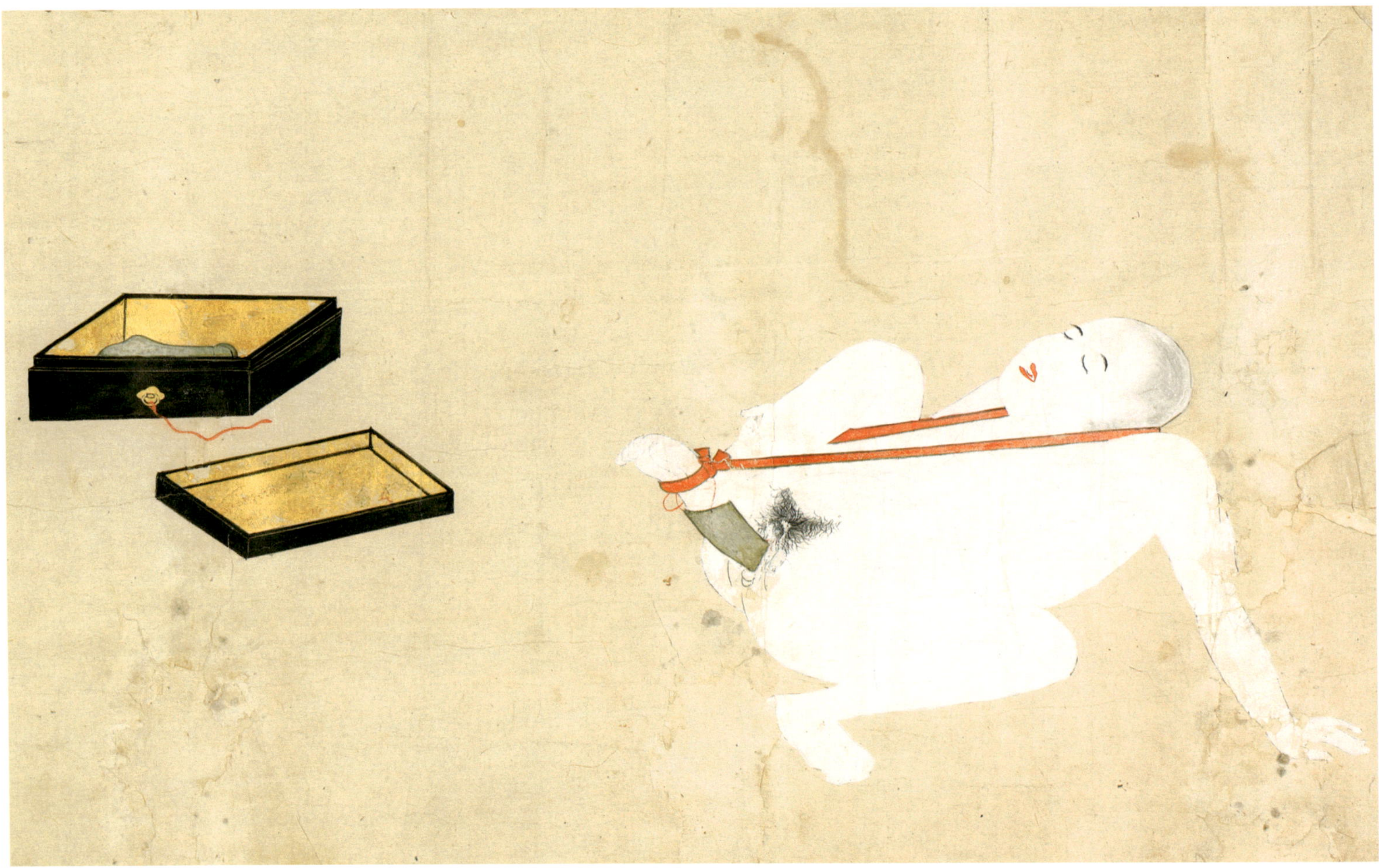

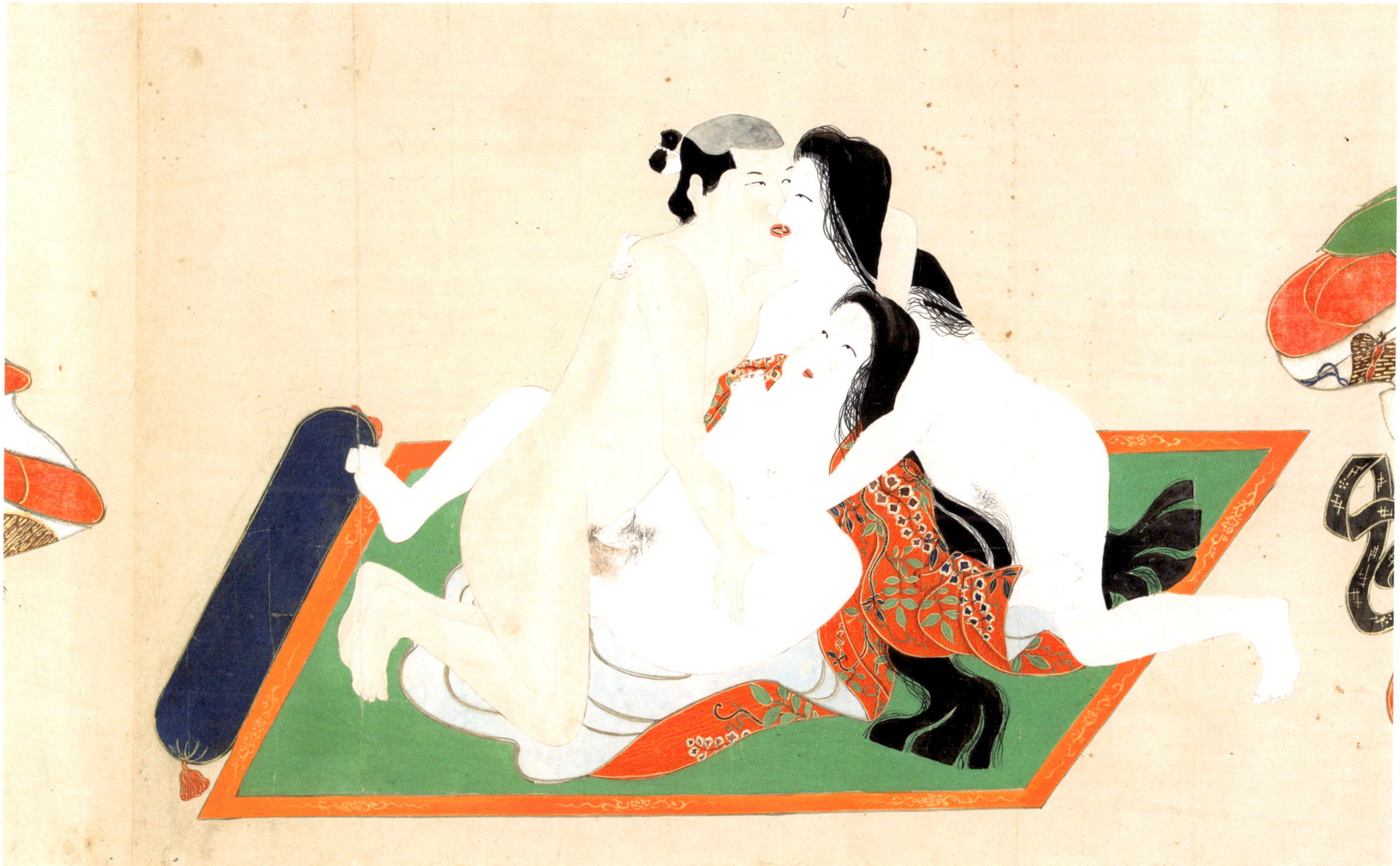

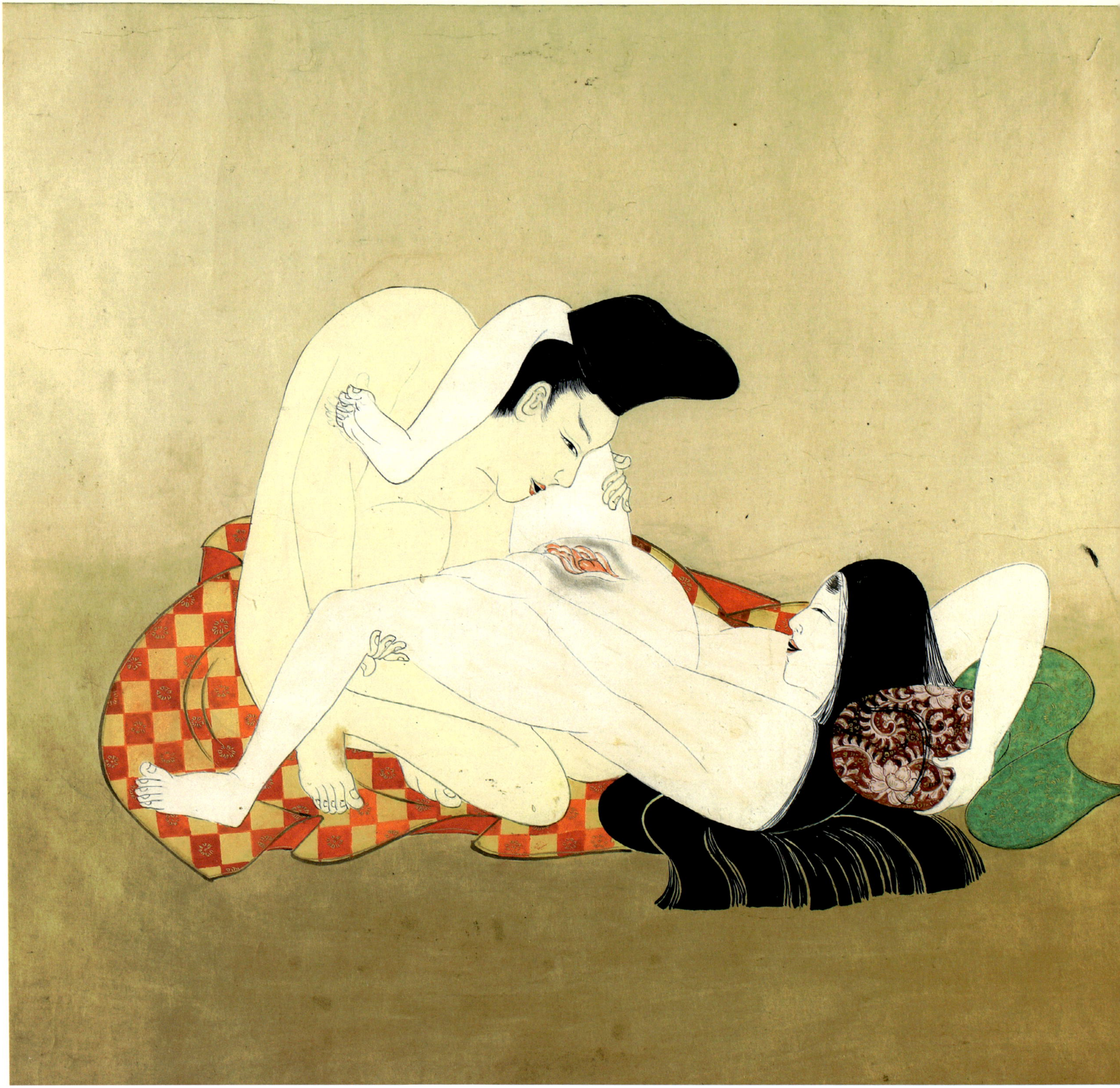

Courtier and court lady
Late 1600s
Section of a handscroll painting, ink, colour and gold on paper, 29.6 × 35.1 cm

This section from a handscroll shows a man about to perform cunnilingus on his partner. This composition is found frequently, but it seems that anatomical precision has been lost during the iterations of copying, and the transition from the woman's torso to her legs is awkward, with her hips poorly defined.[2] Moreover, at an early date it seems a more fundamental mistake has crept in: the woman reaches her right hand back to grasp the pillow, but the thumb is on the wrong side of the hand.

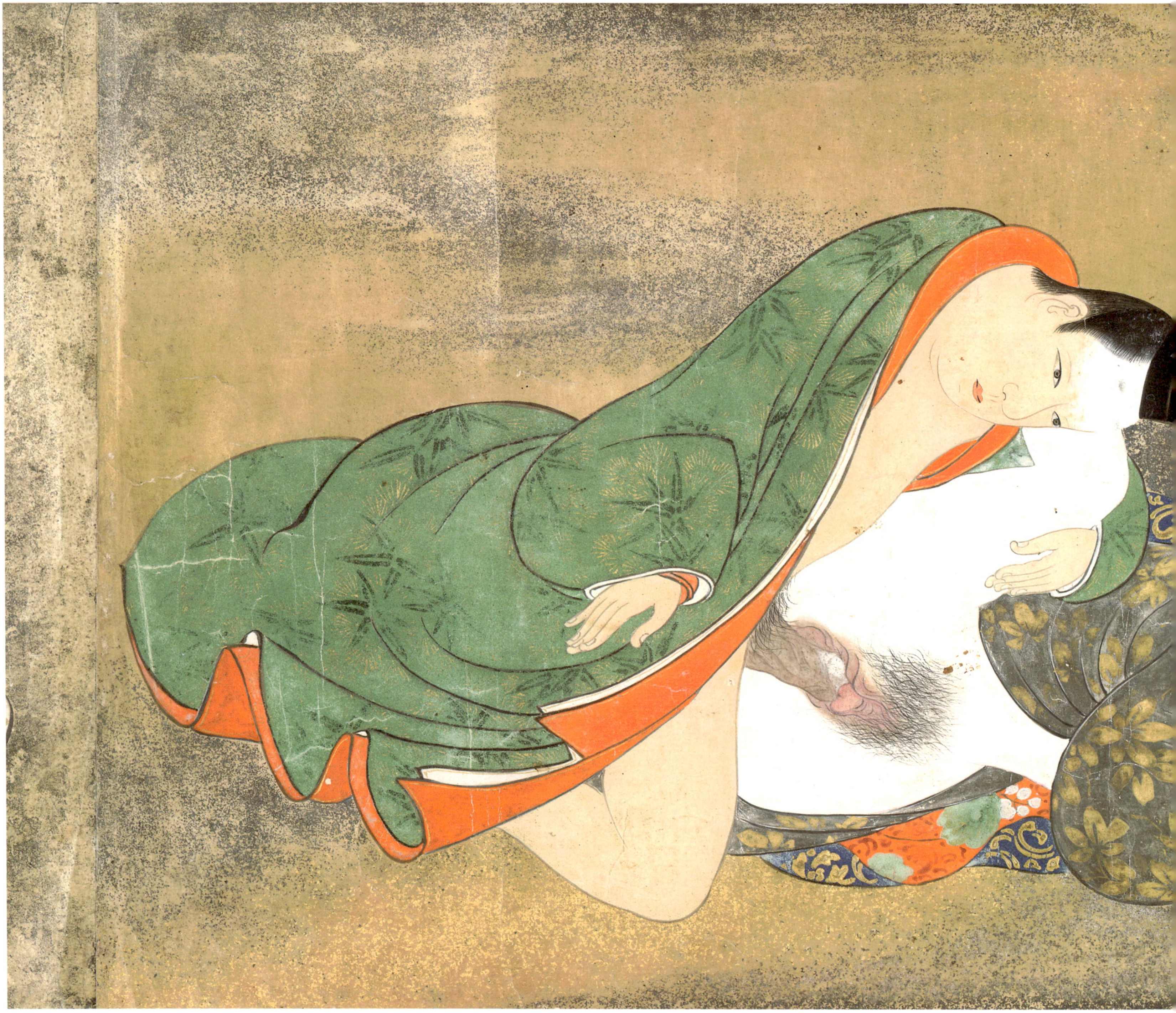

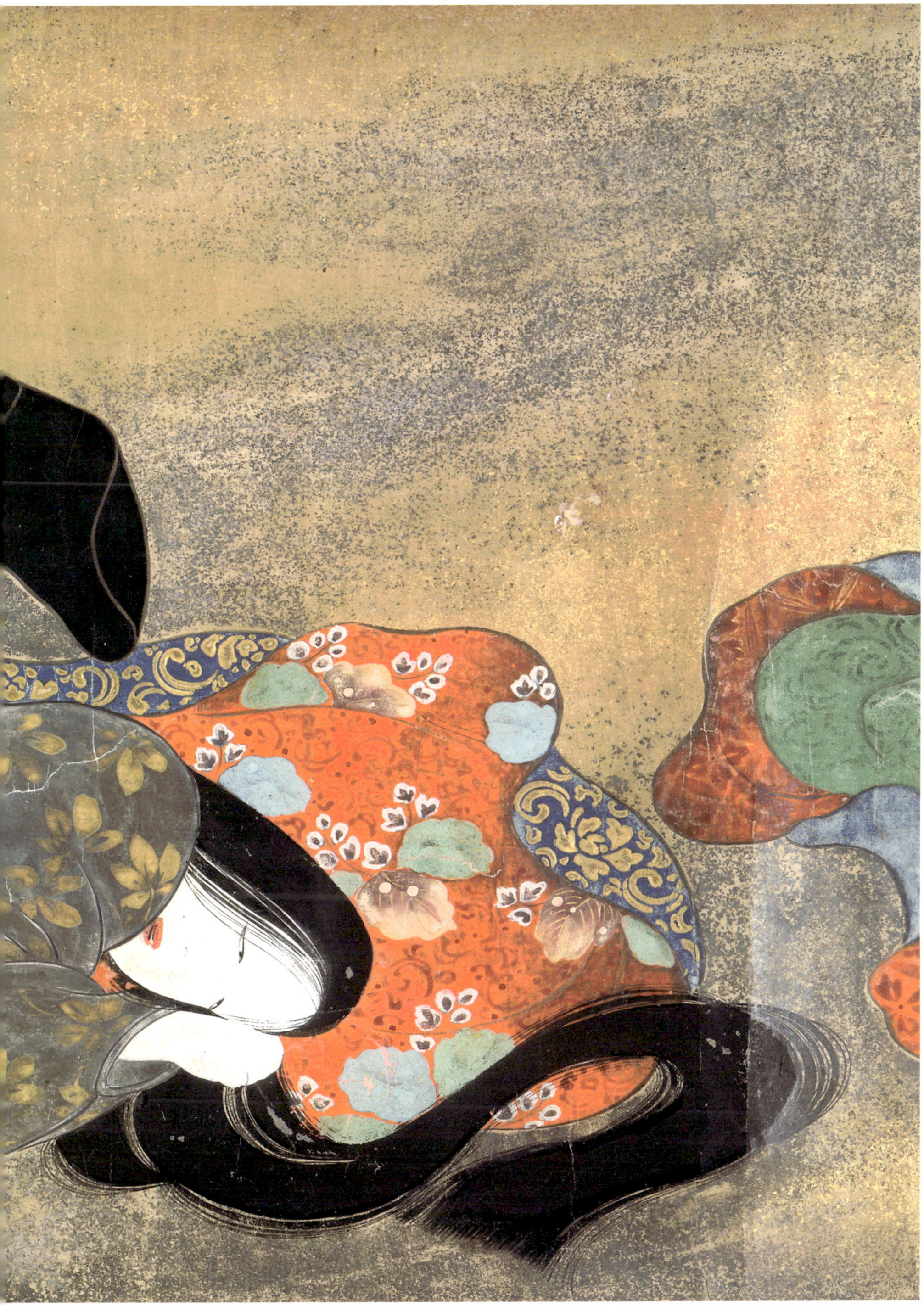

Erotic scene
c. 1600
Section of handscroll painting,
ink, colour, gold and silver on paper,
H: 27 cm

This section from an early surviving example of erotic handscroll painting presents a typical coupling of courtier and court lady, both clad in richly coloured robes. The artist has arranged the composition so that the woman's right leg is lifted, revealing her genitals. There is an air of gentleness, however, in the way the man rests his hand on her leg and inclines his head towards her. Her face, meanwhile, expresses the intensity of the sexual sensations she is experiencing. Intriguingly, the woman's robe bears a design of the paulownia plant. This was the crest of the Toyotomi clan, whose hold on power was at this very point being challenged by Tokugawa Ieyasu.

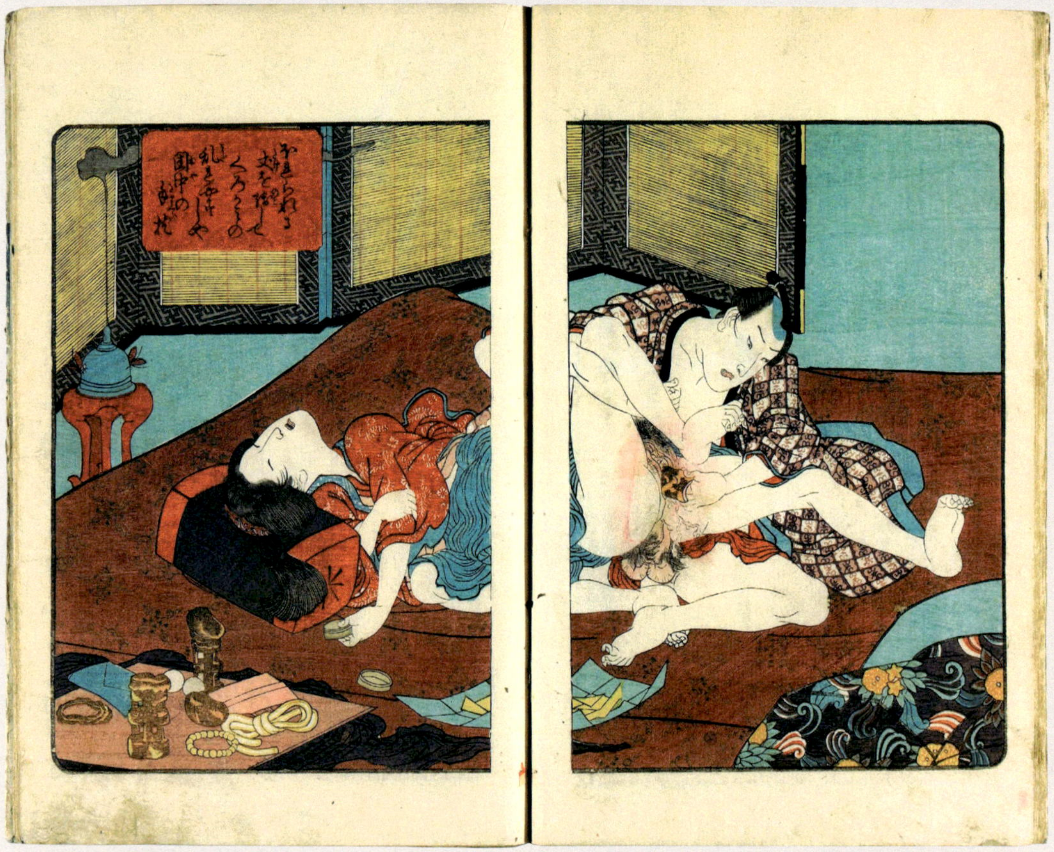

1

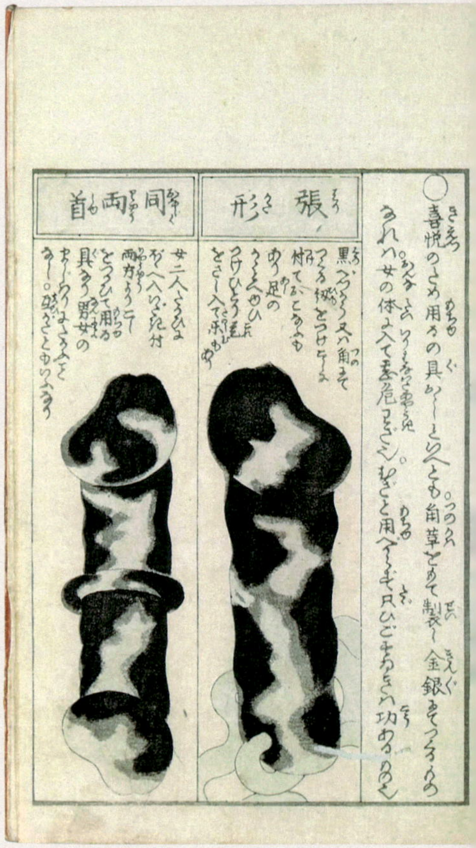

2

Sexual aids

As early as the 1660s books included practical information and advice on how to maximize pleasure during sex, as well as illustrations of available sexual aids. Many of these appear in *shunga* scenes, being used for both solitary masturbation and couples' play. The aids were often sold in boxed sets by itinerant pedlars. Most frequently encountered is the dildo (*harikata*), often shown being used by a maidservant aroused as she watches or listens to her mistress's love-making in an adjacent room (see pp. 78–9). Pictures also show a dildo being used as a 'strap-on', tied with strings around the waist of either a male or female lover, or tied to a woman's ankle.

A particularly explicit illustration from Utagawa Kunisada's *The Eight-Petal Wisteria of Love* (*Koi no yatsufuji*, 1837) (**1**) shows the passionate session of a couple on a hot summer's evening (to the left, smoke rises from an incense-burner to deter mosquitoes). An impressive array of sex toys is laid out on a tray beside them. The man lifts the woman's leg to insert a tortoiseshell dildo into her vagina while he penetrates her anally. She flings her head backwards and curls her toes in ecstasy, still grasping a small container of lubricant or aphrodisiac ointment, hastily removed from its paper wrapping.

Erotic publications sometimes included sections illustrating and explaining the uses of these devices, fulfilling a sex-educational purpose. A section entitled 'Tools for women in the bedroom' (*Keichū joetsu no gu*) in the book *Stories from the Bedroom: The Pillow Library* (*Keichū kibun makura bunko*, 1822) illustrates the various items available with notes on their use (**2** & **3**). The book, which has been described as 'a kind of illustrated encyclopædia on sex and sexual attributes',[3] has images by Keisai Eisen and text by Tamenaga Shunsui (1790–1843). It also contained a recipe for the aphrodisiac ointment Chōmeigan ('long-life medicine'), supposedly brought by traders to Japan via the port of Nagasaki, and redolent of exotic foreign sexual practices. The ointment was applied to the shaft of the penis and then washed off before sex, ensuring 'long life', in other words a prolonged performance.

The set of sex toys illustrated opposite is made from carved tortoiseshell. It comprises a full-size dildo; two smaller dildos placed on the forefinger for masturbation; a tube with openwork sides to support an erection; another similar item with a cap for enhanced sensation

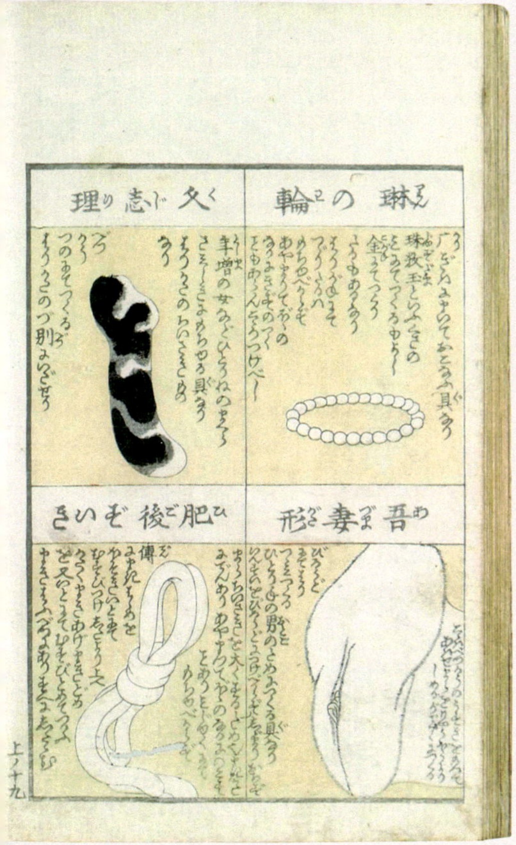

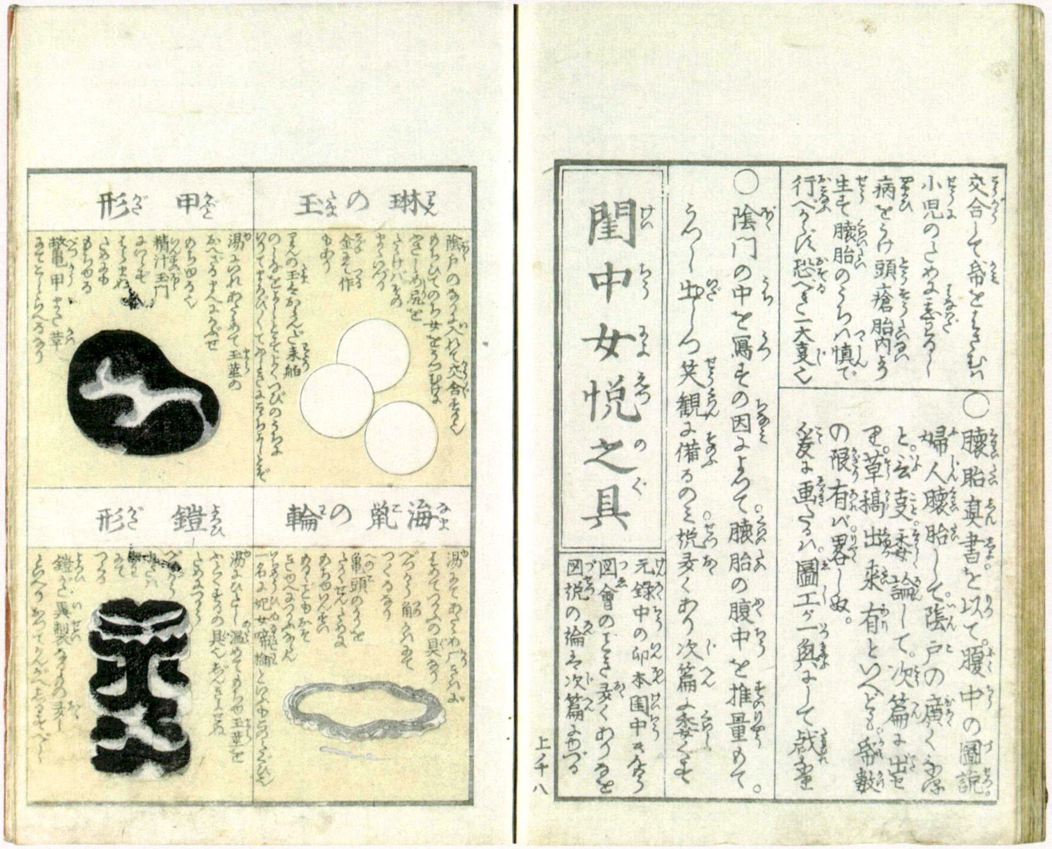

3

and also contraception; a simple 'helmet' for the penis head; and two cock rings designed to stimulate the vagina. There is also a small hollow sphere of silver containing a metal ball, which was placed in the opening of the vulva; as the woman moved about, the ball rattled, producing prolonged pleasurable sensations. As the page on sex toys in Settei's parody *Love Letters and a River of Erect Precepts for Women* of 1768 instructs, 'When finished, it can be removed by patting her bottom'.

Below: Set of sexual aids
Late 19th century
Horn and metal,
L: 13.4 cm (dildo)

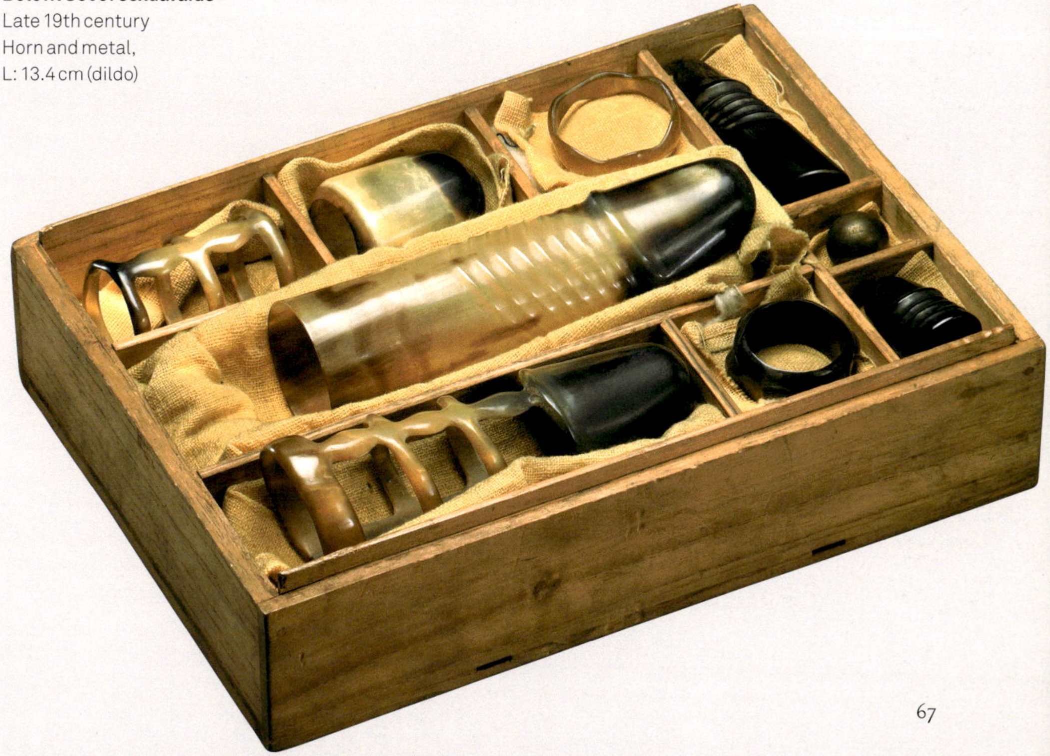

1. **Utagawa Kunisada**
***The Eight-Petal Wisteria of Love* (*Koi no yatsufuji*)**
1837
Colour woodblock-printed book, 25.4 × 17.5 cm (covers).
Private collection, Ritsumeikan ARC Database

2 and 3. **Keisai Eisen**
***Stories from the Bedroom: The Pillow Library* (*Keichū kibun makura bunko*)**
1822
Colour woodblock-printed book, 22 × 14.7 cm (covers).
Private collection, Ritsumeikan ARC Database

Hishikawa Moronobu

One of the most devastating of Edo's repeated conflagrations, nicknamed the 'flowers of Edo', occurred in 1657: for three days the fires raged, destroying two-thirds of the city. The shogunate's subsequent efforts to revive commerce proved advantageous to the publishing industry, which saw considerable expansion in the following decades. The new popular art movement, which came to be known as *ukiyo-e*, was no longer concerned with idealized views of courtiers, but instead depicted the burgeoning urban culture. Its most important artist was Hishikawa Moronobu (d. 1694), regarded as the originator of popular printed erotica. He was responsible for about 150 illustrated books and albums, one quarter of which was erotic.[4] All Moronobu's works were printed in monochrome.

As with many of the publications of this period, and especially the erotic ones, very few impressions of any given title survive. The British Museum has one of only three known surviving copies of *The Sources of Love* (*Koi no minakami*), illustrated by Moronobu and published in 1683. The book presents twenty-one unrelated episodes in the love affairs of young men and women of the samurai class in fashionable urban society. Above each double-page picture the (unknown) author provides a brief anecdote followed by two poems drawn from the classic imperial anthologies. Each scene depicts attractive figures engaged in pleasurable, amorous pastimes, with plentiful dancing, music-making and drinking, both in the open air and at indoor parties. There are also more intimate scenes, with men and women reclining in bedrooms, but no explicit depictions. Women play an unusually active part in this work, and the several scenes of women absorbed in reading novels are notable.[5]

No undisputed erotic paintings by Moronobu survive. However, a rare handscroll in the British Museum by Hishikawa Morohira (active 1688–1711), assumed to have been a direct pupil, may suggest something of the sophistication and artistic skill of Moronobu's lost works. The scroll is notable for its delicacy of pigments on both flesh tones and fabrics, and for the charming compositions, by turns passionate, humorous and tender. The scroll opens, as was customary, with a non-explicit scene of two lovers in bed, the heavy covering kimono beautifully ornamented with a phoenix in flight.

Yoshida Hanbei

The author Ihara Saikaku (1642–93) is renowned for his novels recounting the amorous adventures of men and women of fashion. *The Great Mirror of Male Love* (*Nanshoku ōkagami*), published in 1687, was the longest of Saikaku's novels, running to eight volumes.[6] It contained forty tales describing both the passionate pursuit of the 'way of youths', the attractive young dandies of the theatre districts who were available to merchants and monks, and the devoted relationships of elder and younger samurai men. The depictions of elegant entertainments and dramatic fight scenes were provided by Yoshida Hanbei (d. c. 1693), who had illustrated earlier novels by Saikaku, and had produced the first encyclopedia of erotica the previous year. Hanbei filled his images with activity and movement, defining each scene at the top with drifting mist-banks derived from medieval handscrolls.

Hishikawa Moronobu
***The Sources of Love* (*Koi no minakami*)**
1683
Woodblock-printed book with later hand-colouring, 27 × 17.5 cm

A man and woman share a passionate embrace beneath the cherry blossoms on a spring day. A folding screen and curtain have been set up to create a private area, and a servant sits at a discreet distance with refreshments. Their privacy has been disturbed, however, as two women lift the curtain to peep in on the scene.

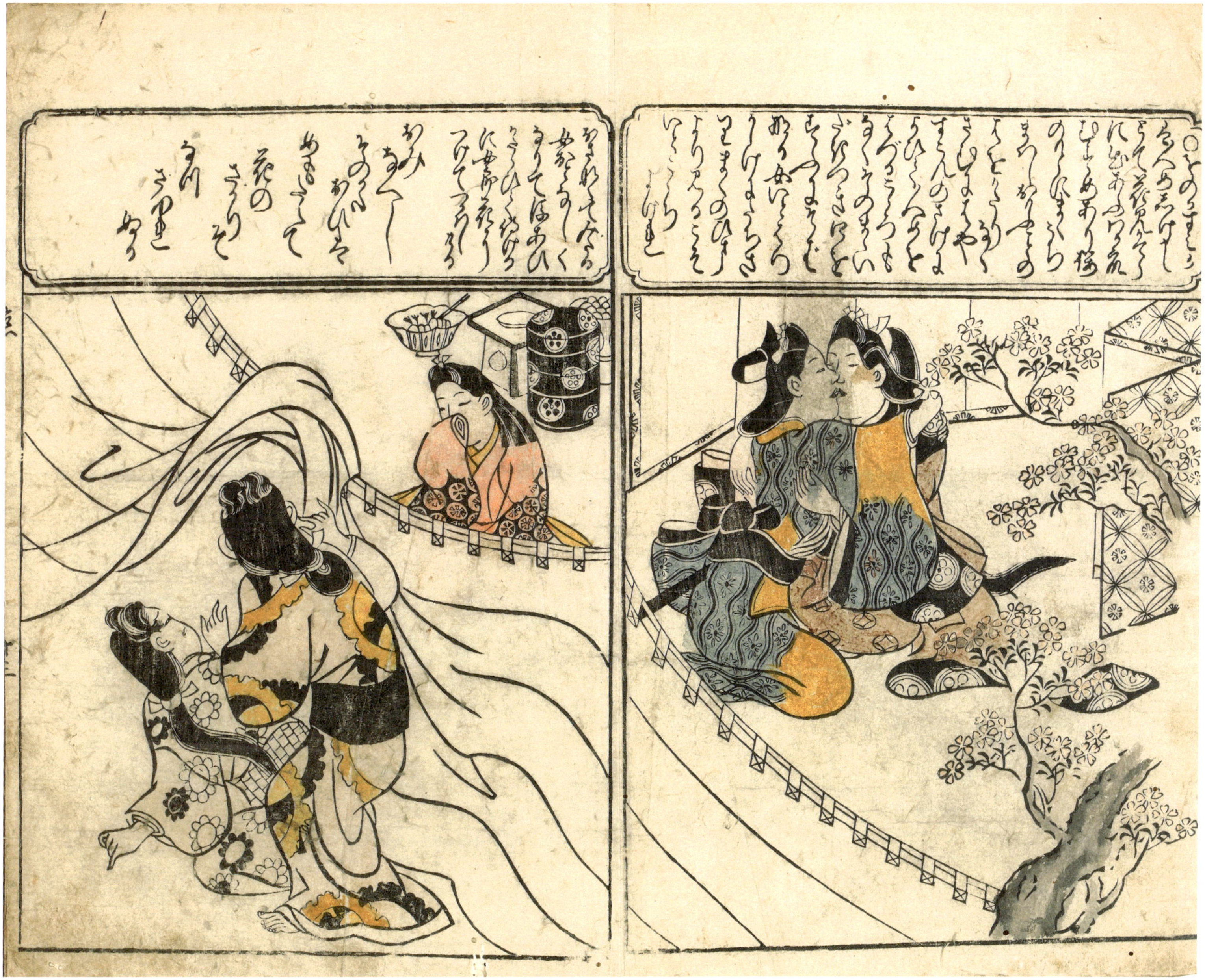

Hishikawa Moronobu
Fragment of a page from *The Amorous Thread of Willow* (*Kōshoku ito yanagi*)
1684
Woodblock-printed book with hand-colouring, 12.9 × 16.3 cm

This fragment is from a guidebook for young dandies on how to seduce various kinds of women. This is the image for 'the deposit type' (*azuke-mono*), describing a situation when a man cannot afford to maintain his lover in her own residence, so installs her in a friend's house and provides her living costs.[7] The couple are lying on a white rug and the woman straddles her partner, her arms wrapped tightly around his shoulders. Her face is hidden behind his head, but her closed eyes are just visible. He seems to lean forward with the effort of the love-making, and his feet are crossed in a rather uncomfortable way. The book was woodblock-printed, but this print has subsequently been coloured by hand. Metallic pigment was added to give a sheen to the orange quilts piled up to the left; this has subsequently oxidized and discoloured.

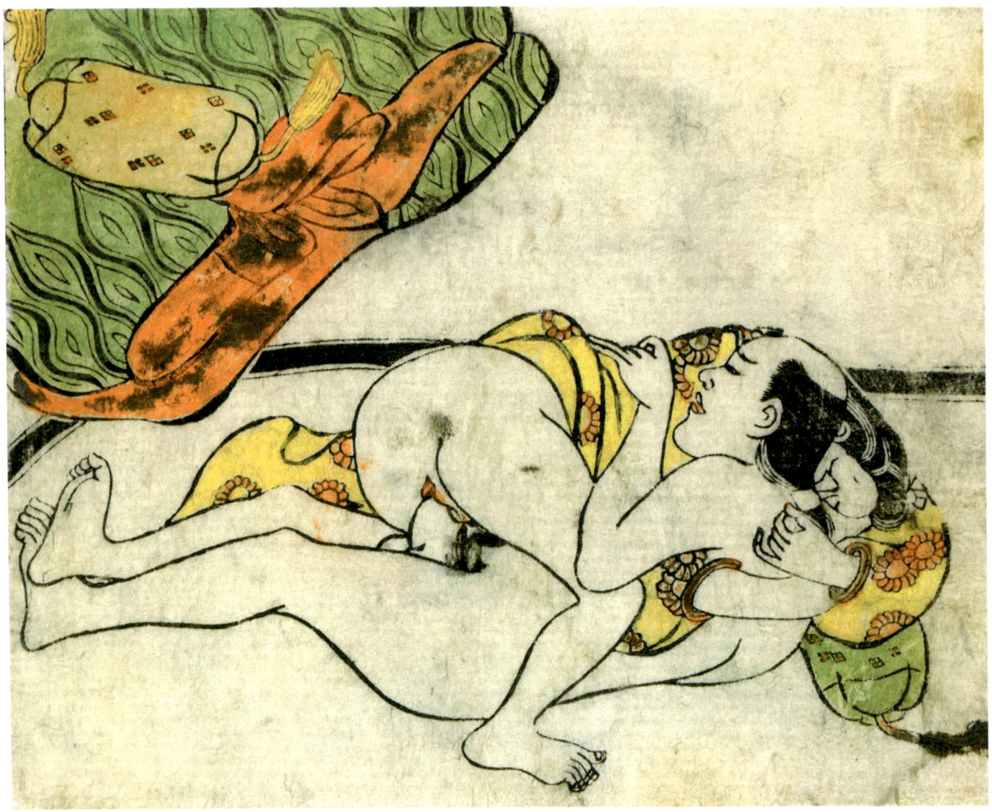

Hishikawa Morohira
Scenes of love-making
1688–1711
Section of handscroll painting, ink, colour and gold on silk, H: 32.6 cm

This is a scene of anticipation rather than actual intercourse. The woman is naked, and the man's robe has slipped off his shoulders, but the composition does not present us with a clear view of the sex organs, as in other parts of the scroll (see pp. 72–3). Instead we see the moment when she reaches down to guide her partner's penis inside her. The two lovers hold each other gently around the shoulders as they both concentrate their gaze downwards.

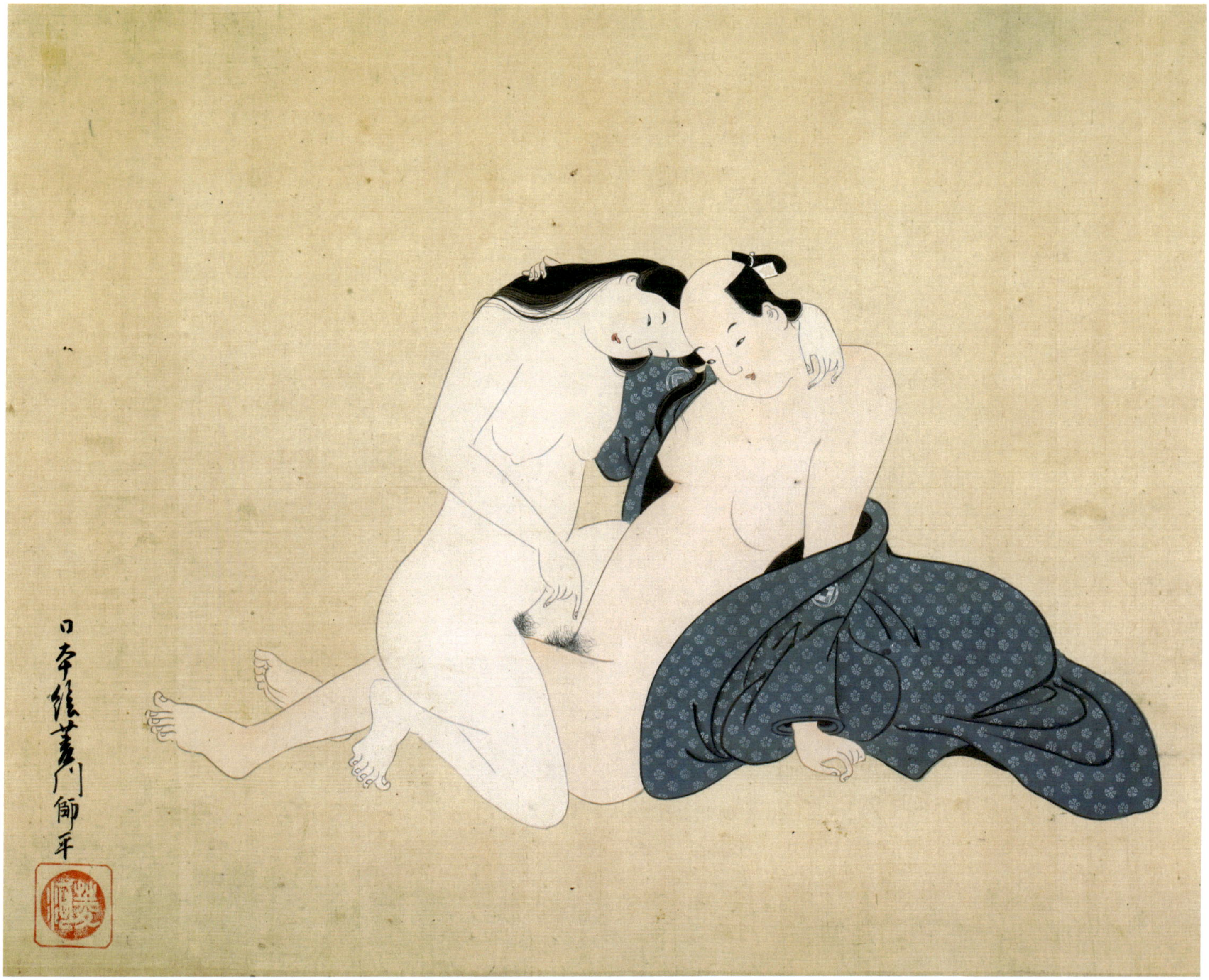

Hishikawa Morohira
Scenes of love-making
1688–1711
Section of handscroll painting, ink, colour and gold on silk, H: 32.6 cm

Taking refreshment during love-making is a common theme in *shunga*. Here the man has not even paused to withdraw his penis from his partner (who looks a little put out by the sudden movement), but reaches around to hold out his cup to the maid, requesting a refill of *sake* from the ewer close at hand. The maid seems rather embarrassed to be in such close proximity, and averts her eyes.

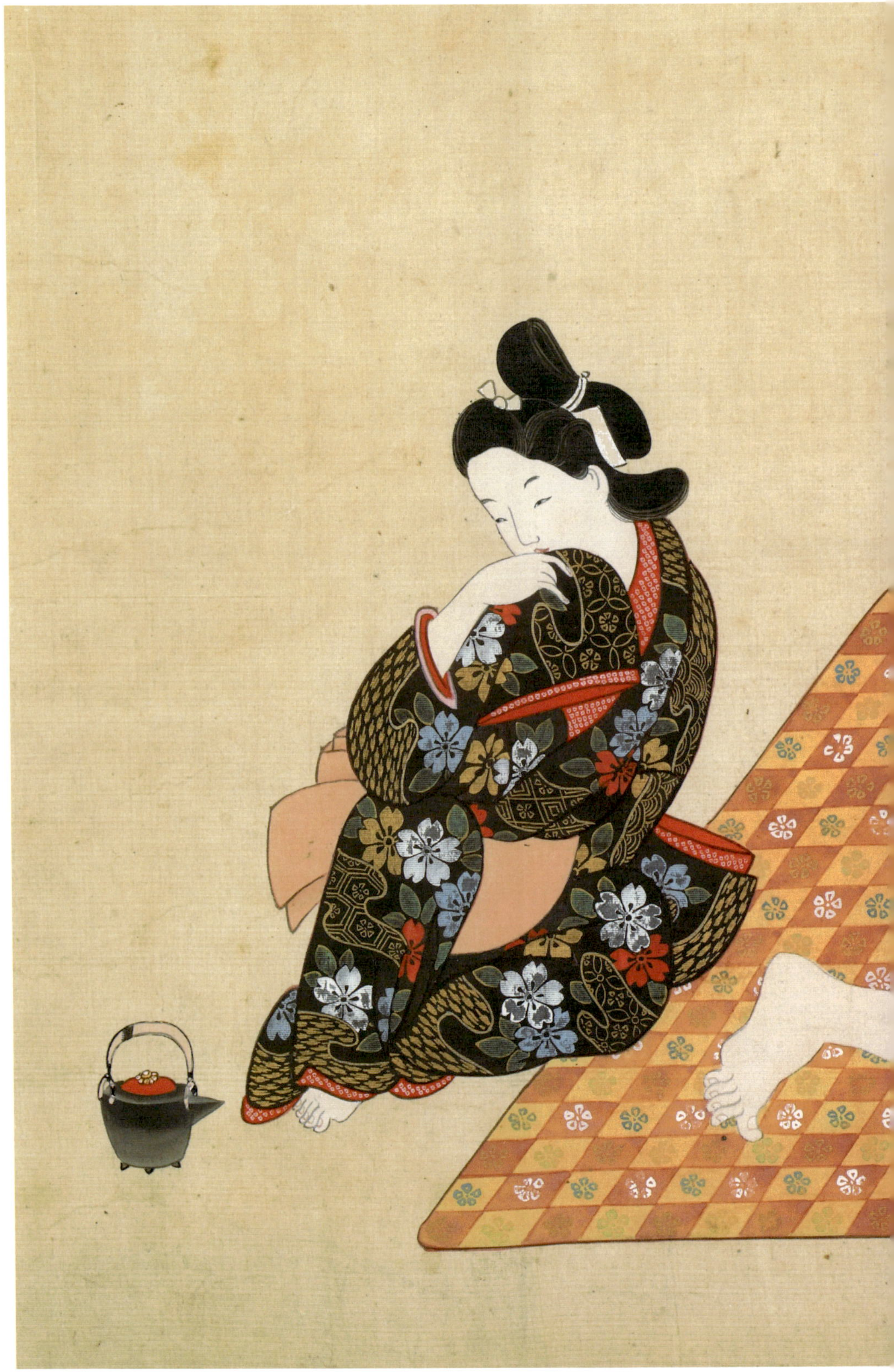

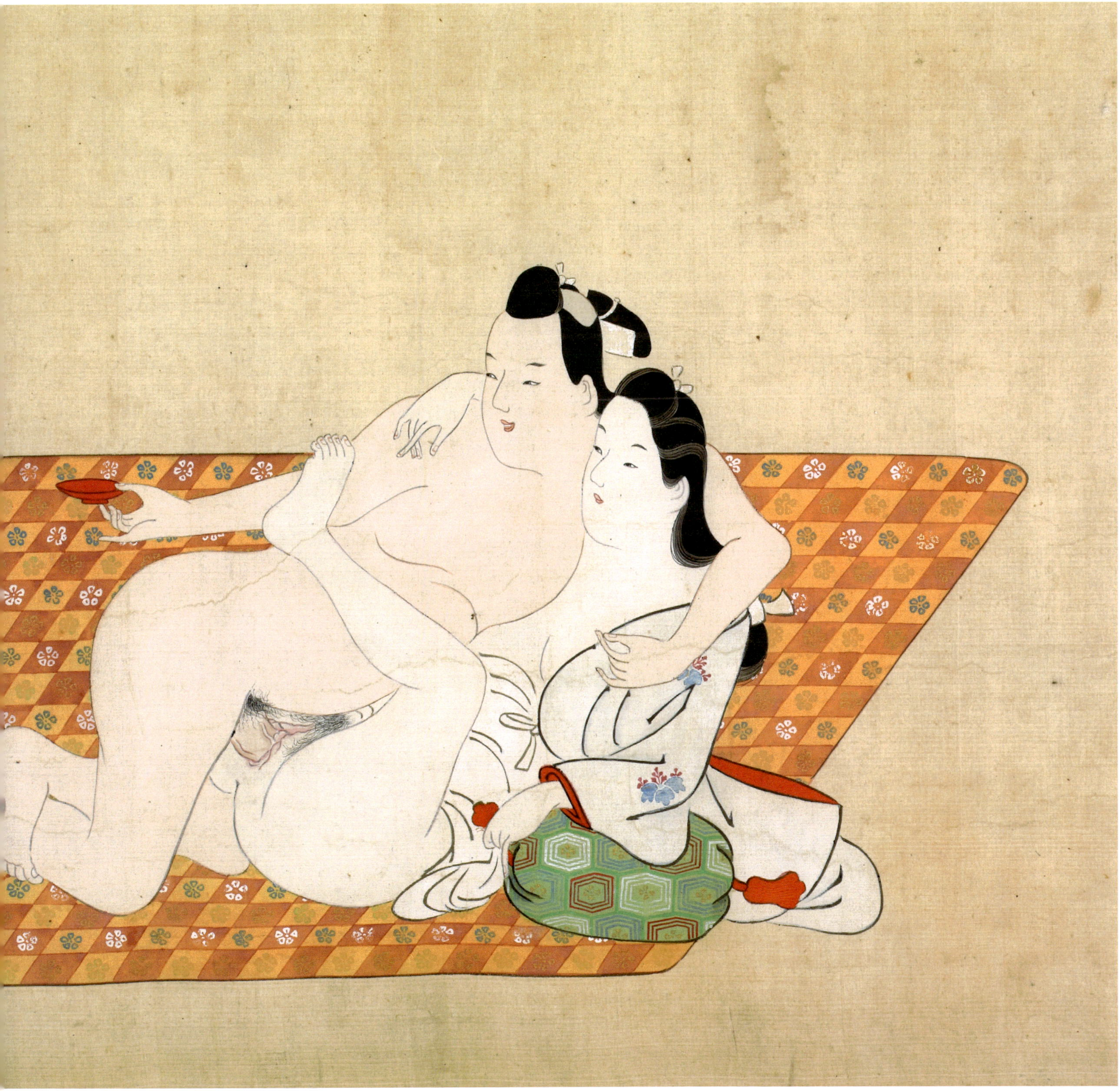

Yoshida Hanbei
The Great Mirror of Male Love
(*Nanshoku ōkagami*), vol. 8
1687
Woodblock-printed book,
25 × 18.5 cm (covers).
British Library

In summer, a party of young actors has travelled up from Osaka to Kyoto to enjoy the cool evening breezes. After an evening of carousing, they relax on platforms set up over the River Kamo, drinking, eating, smoking and playing the *shamisen* under the light of the moon until after midnight. Suddenly, they see the figure of a woman on the roof of a nearby tea-house and they start reciting a sutra in terror. They realize the woman must be in love with one of their party, and when she tosses them a letter, they surmise it is Minanojō, whom the story describes as 'like an unopened plum blossom… immature yet wonderfully fragrant'. We are told that, 'The fact that both men and women fell in love with him in this way was one of Minanojō's most attractive traits'.[8]

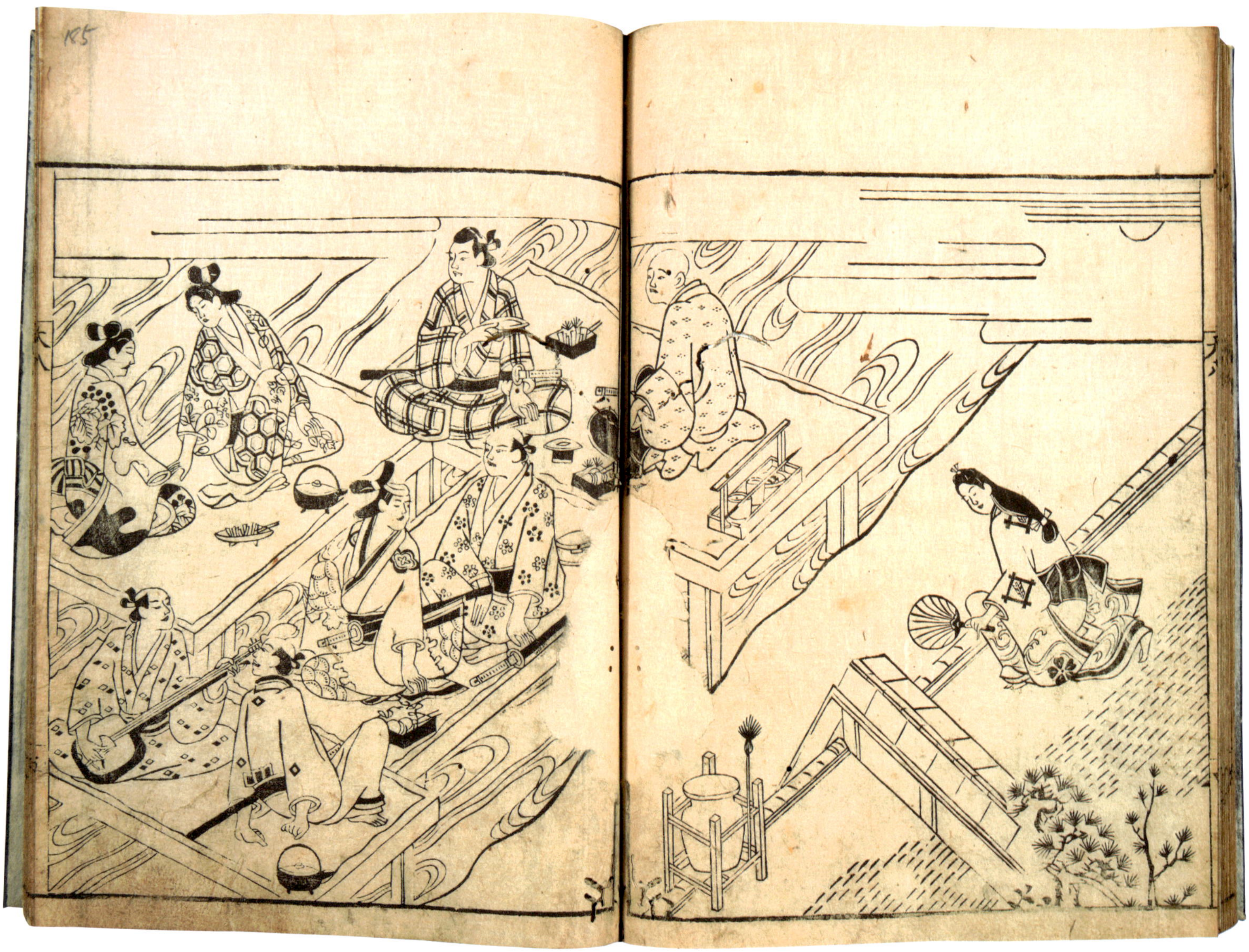

Torii Kiyonobu I

Kiyomoto Shōshichi (n.d.) was an actor from Osaka who moved to Edo in 1687 and dominated the production of painted signboards for the four main theatres. The signboards served to entice customers in to see a performance, and their visual style required thick graphic lines, bold colours and exaggerated postures. His studio operated under the name Torii, and his son Kiyonobu I (1664–1729) expanded the repertory to single-sheet prints of actors as well as erotica. Rendered in monochrome lines (sometimes with hand-colouring), Kiyonobu's coupling figures possess rounded, fleshy limbs and full faces. As before, the naked or semi-naked bodies are set in empty space with only a screen, a food tray or a lantern to suggest the physical setting.[9]

Nishikawa Sukenobu

As the political centre, Edo dominated *ukiyo-e* production throughout the Tokugawa period, but the cities of Osaka, Kyoto and Nagoya also had active publishing industries. Woodblock printing at this time was monochrome, but a fair number of surviving copies of printed books were hand-coloured by professionals. The most influential artist in the first half of the eighteenth century was Nishikawa Sukenobu (1671–1750), an accomplished painter and prolific book illustrator working in Kyoto, whose productivity was aided by an unusually long lifetime. Like many *ukiyo-e* artists, Sukenobu worked in a variety of genres, producing illustrations for light fiction and actor critiques, as well as pattern-books, images of beauties, and erotica. Unlike paintings, which were expensive privately commissioned items, books were readily available to the common man or woman, especially through book lenders (see p. 144). Books containing Sukenobu's illustrations were widely available in Edo as well as in the region around Kyoto and Osaka, and his style of depicting beauties, refined and with ample figures, had a lasting influence on artists of the following generation.

Over sixty books with erotic pictures have been attributed to Sukenobu, and his name was so closely associated with this material that 'Nishikawa books' (*Nishikawa-bon*) came to be used as a generic term for them. The title of *Iro hiinagata, Patterns of Sensual Pleasure,* plays on the name for kimono design books, which Sukenobu also illustrated. Published in 1711 in five volumes, it depicts the love-making of all the social classes. The first volume portrays the aristocracy in their mansions, in an ox-cart and within elegant gardens; in the second are samurai liaisons; the third contains one hundred women of the farmer class; and the fourth and fifth present the artisan and merchant classes, with hasty liaisons in all manner of situations. It has been suggested that a sequel publication presented the significant category lacking here, the courtesans.[10] Sukenobu's elegant and alluring pictures were obviously a selling-point of the book, and the preface boasts his signature in large characters. The book is in a horizontal format, allowing for wide compositions that stretch across both pages of each opening, similar to the spatial possibilities in medieval handscroll paintings. Sukenobu also borrowed from handscrolls the pictorial technique of removing roofs, affording us aerial views into rooms and gardens. Usually on one page a couple is shown making love, while opposite people can be seen close by, sometimes oblivious to the activity, but often listening or watching and themselves also becoming aroused.

Torii Kiyonobu I
Erotic scene
1703
Woodblock print, approx. 22.7 × 33.2 cm

A courtesan in a sumptuous robe reclines against her client, seductively locking his gaze. Behind them are a *sake* ewer and two wine-cups, and they are perhaps just proceeding to physical intimacy. The folding screen set up behind them bears Kiyonobu's signature.

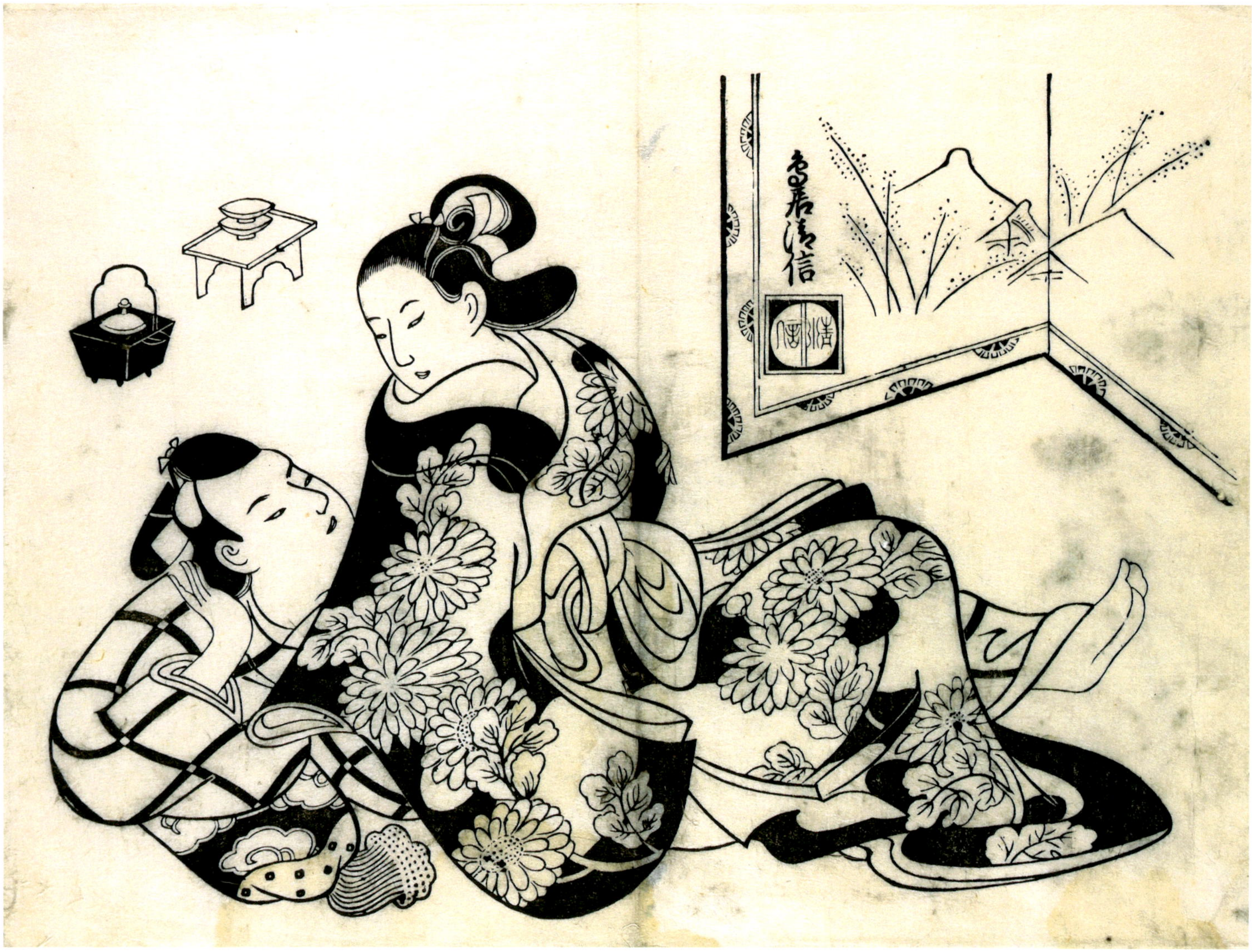

Torii Kiyonobu I
Erotic scene
1703
Woodblock print, approx. 22.7 × 33.2 cm

The client leans forward as he starts making love to the courtesan. He holds her sash firmly, and his open mouth and intense eyes suggest the strength of his desire. She reaches her arms around him, but turns her head aside, obviously overwhelmed by the sensations.

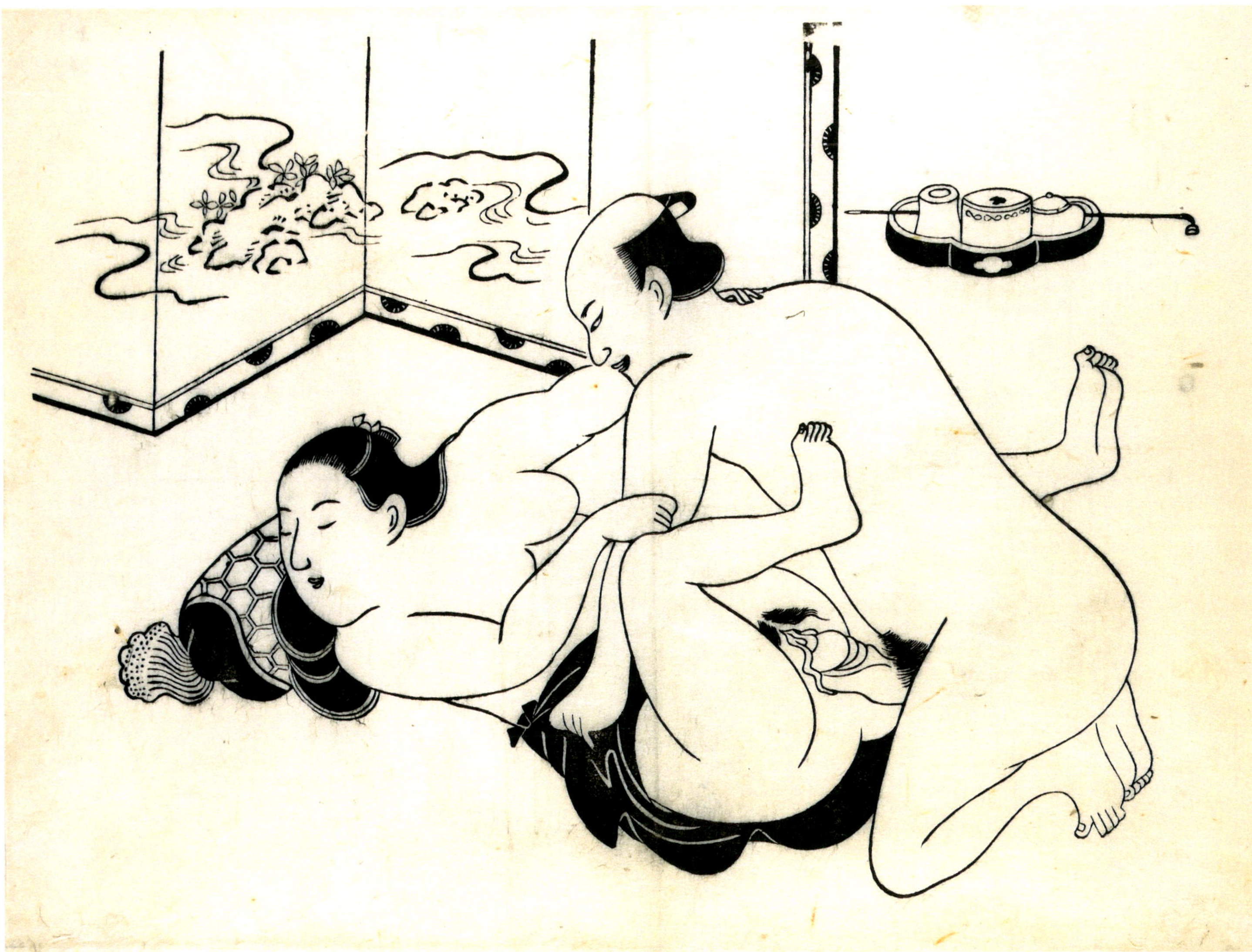

Nishikawa Sukenobu
Patterns of Sensual Pleasure
(*Iro hiinagata*)
1711
Woodblock-printed book,
13.1 × 18.7 cm (covers).
Private collection,
Ritsumeikan ARC Database

'Night-time in the Mansion' (*Yoru no otodo*) shows a bedchamber in an aristocratic residence, furnished with wall-paintings, a recessed cupboard and standing screens. The man supports his wife's leg as she lowers herself on to him, gasping. Meanwhile, a maid spies on them through the gap in the sliding doors, stimulating herself with a dildo and sighing, 'Oh, I'm jealous. I want that to happen to me.' Hanging from the ceiling above the couple is a bundle of 'suspended bedding' (*tsuri-yagu*), a method used to reduce the weight of heavy bedcovers for the sick or elderly.

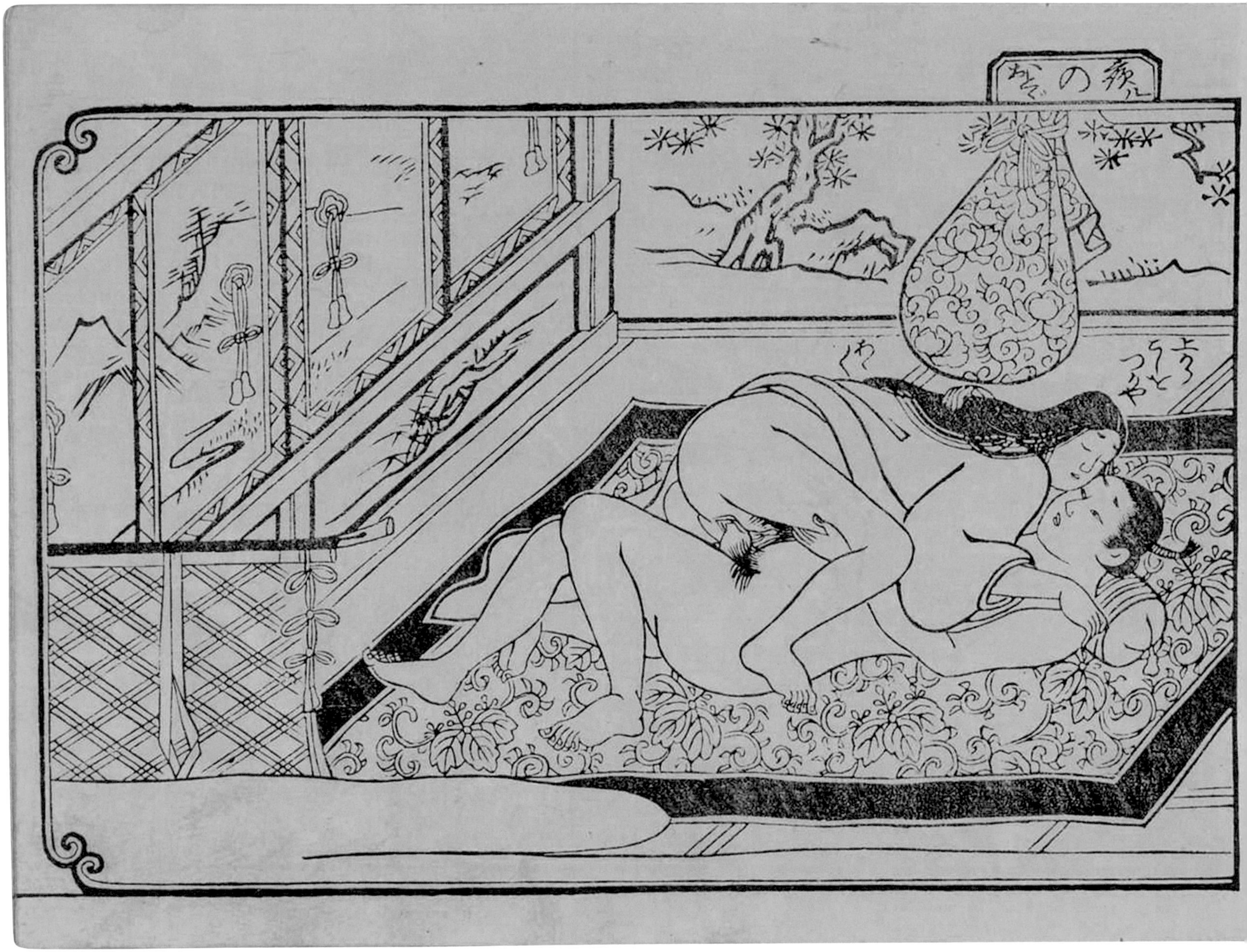

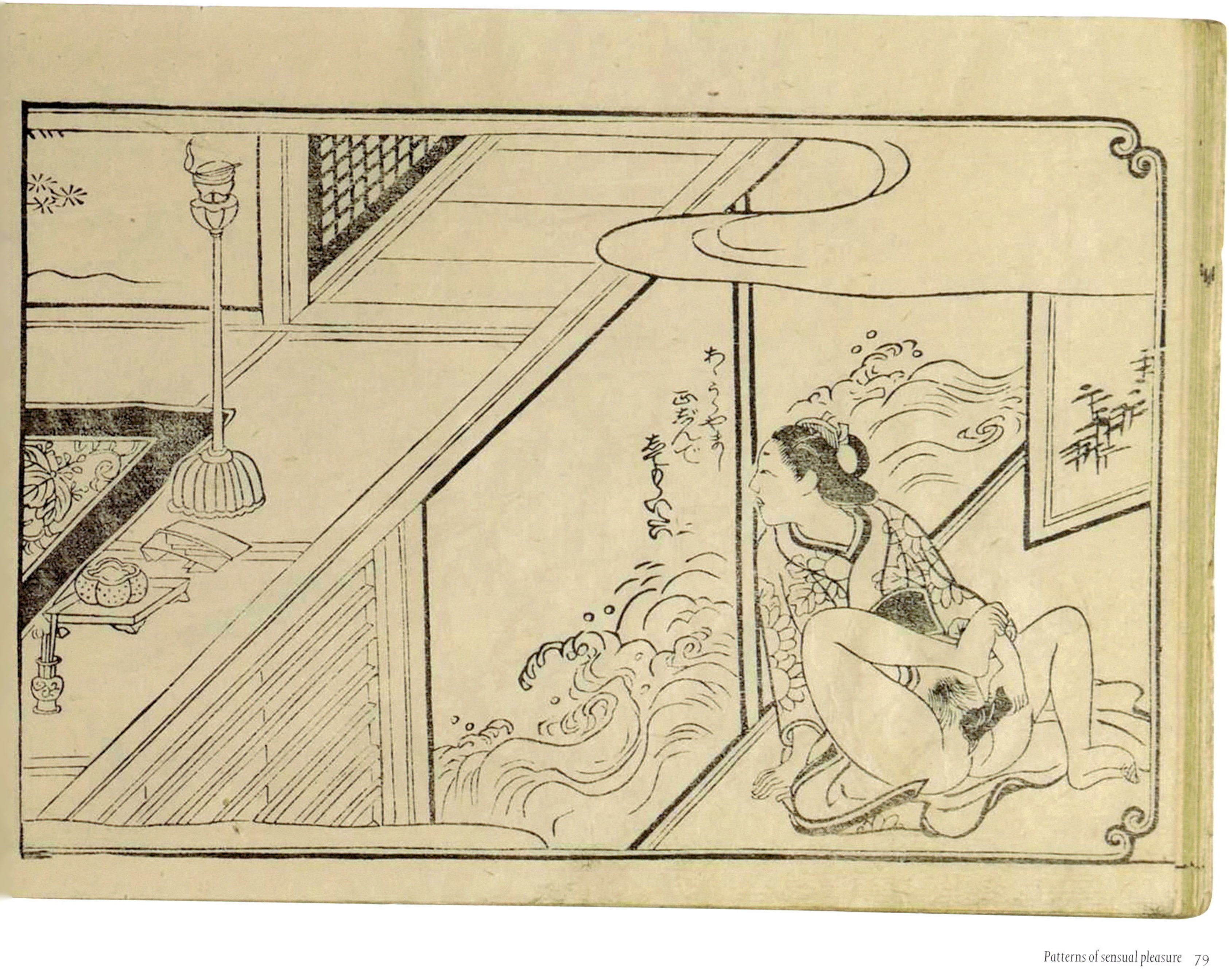

Kyōhō Reforms

From 1721 (Kyōhō 6), the government introduced a programme of reforms aimed at stabilizing the social structure and the economy. Both samurai and townsmen were exhorted to pursue a modest, if not frugal, lifestyle. The crackdown included restraints on the publishing industry.
The representation of current events was forbidden, as well as any reference to the ruling Tokugawa family, and new works were not to discuss any unconventional theories or baseless rumours. It now became mandatory for a book to contain a printed colophon listing the publisher's name and address, and the professional (rather than common) names of all authors and artists involved, together with the date when the printing-blocks had been cut. The new laws also banned 'amorous books' (*kōshokubon*) as being injurious to social order and customs (*fūzoku*). The regulation of people's private lives extended also to adultery, lovers' suicide pacts and the spreading of scandal and rumours. The inspection of publications was to be carried out by the publishers themselves, creating a system of self-regulation which was to characterize censorship throughout the Tokugawa period. Though the number of erotic books dropped off sharply as a result of the new law, publishers did continue to produce them – but now they had to do so cautiously, and avoid including the names of all those involved in their production.[11]

Okumura Masanobu

The technology of colour-printing was brought from China to Japan in the early seventeenth century, but costs remained prohibitively high until there came a time when market demand justified the outlay. Thus for several decades colour was added to prints by hand by specially employed artisans. One of the most influential figures in *ukiyo-e* of the early 1700s was Okumura Masanobu (1686–1764). He claimed credit, whether rightly or wrongly, for the introduction of block-printing with colours (in 1741), as well as for other innovations, such as lacquer printing to impart gloss, the use of metallic powder, and the introduction of the triptych and pillar-print formats. It is thought that Masanobu took inspiration from the work of Torii Kiyonobu I, and by about 1720 he had established his own publishing business, giving him an unusual degree of control over the print-making process, and allowing him to pursue such technical experiments.[12]

In the early 1740s, Masanobu designed a series of twelve *ōban* (large-format) prints entitled *Mountains of Dyed Colours, Models for the Bedroom* (*Someiro no yama neya no hinagata*), distinctive for their charming, fresh hand-colouring. The subtitle alludes to the theme of kimono patterns, and the characters of the series title are presented as if dyed into the back of a kimono. The title also called to mind a popular novel on male–male relations of 1687, *The Dyed Robe of Love* (*Iro no someginu*), which had been illustrated by Masanobu's predecessor, Kiyonobu. The main title, however, better conveys the actual content of this work, suggesting 'the peak of love-making'. It seems the series was published not in the customary format of a folding album, but as a continuous handscroll (the example opposite was subsequently mounted as an album, and the resultant centrefold is visible).

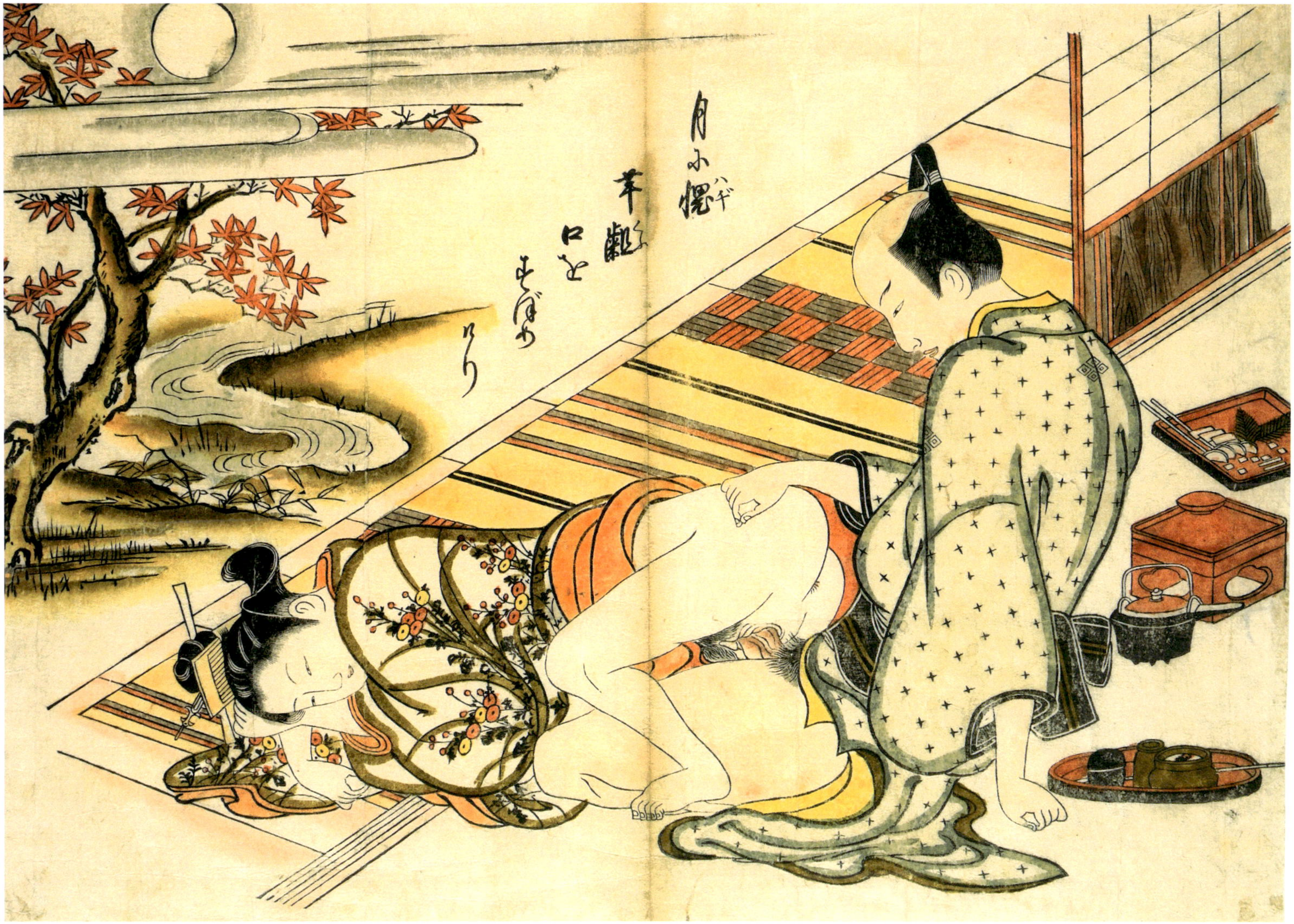

Okumura Masanobu
***Mountains of Dyed Colours, Models for the Bedroom* (*Someiro no yama neya no hinagata*)**
c. 1740
Woodblock print with hand-colouring, 27.1 × 33 cm

Perhaps the finest design in this series is that for the tenth month, depicting a couple making love on a veranda. She uses her right arm as a pillow, and he looks down with concentration, resting his hand gently on her buttock. Behind them are various lacquer utensils from the meal they have interrupted, including a plate of sushi and a *sake* ewer, together with a smoking set, suggesting an assignation in a tea-house. Outside, the harvest moon illuminates a garden scene, with a maple tree by a stream. The print employs a dynamic composition, with the lovers forming a right angle in the centre and the veranda providing diagonal lines in two directions. The calligraphy of the poem inscribed above follows the diagonal of the veranda. With obvious sexual allusion, it translates, 'Shy of the moon, the potato-eating mouth, puckered.' The 'rear-entry' position was a relatively popular one in *shunga*, and is also employed in another design in this same set.

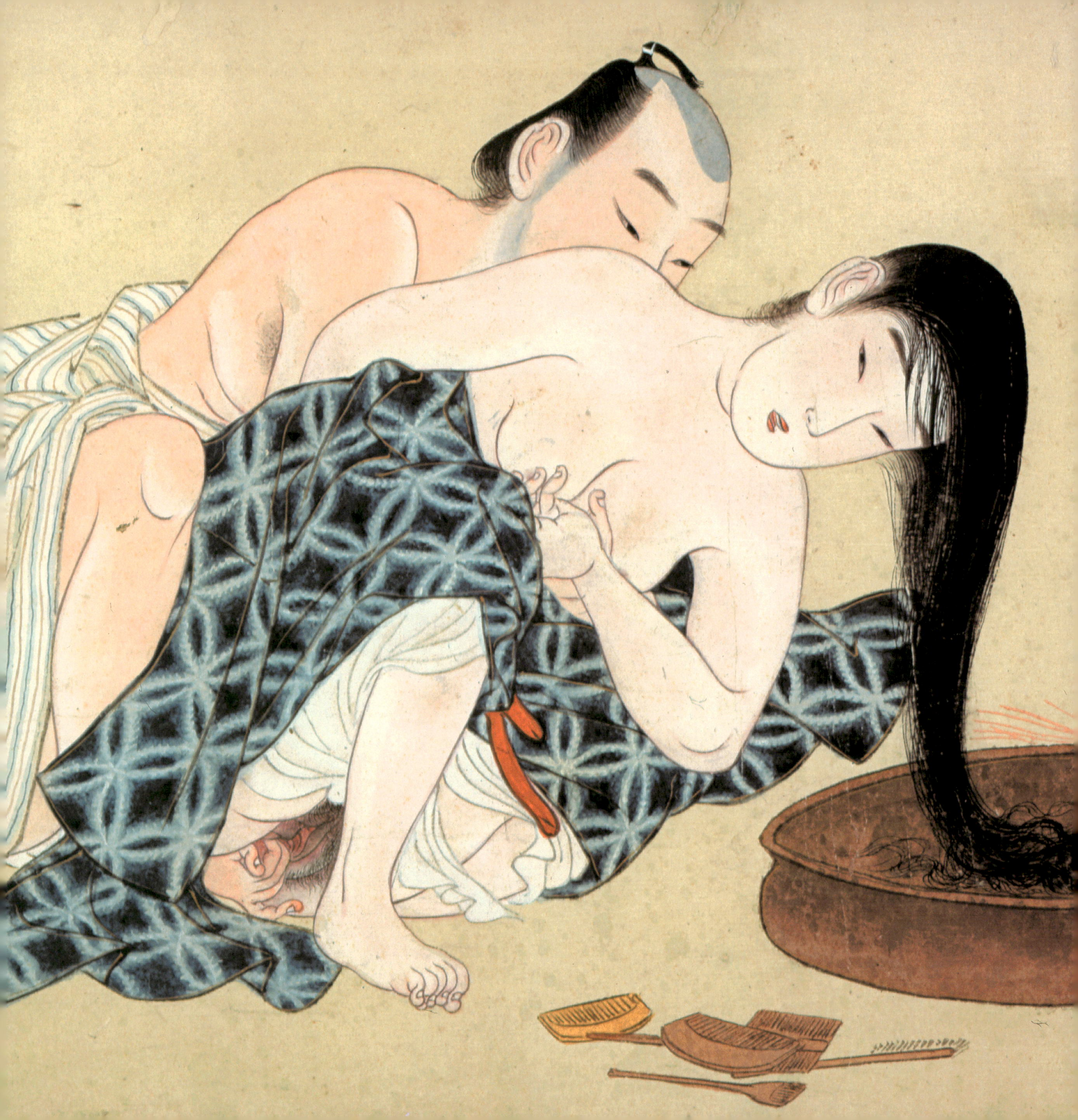

Poem of the Pillow: masterpieces of the late eighteenth century

Katsukawa Shun'ei
Ten erotic scenes (detail)
1792–5
Handscroll painting, ink and colour on paper, H: 28 cm
Caption details p. 116

By the mid-eighteenth century, the shogun's city of Edo was possessed of a rich artistic environment, drawing to it talented young men and women, along with patrons eager to experience its delights. Edo was by now the unquestionable centre of fashion, confident in its rapidly changing modern culture, distinct from that of the ancient capital Kyoto. The successes of the fashionable arts – theatre, dance and poetry – were celebrated by the publishing industry, with proprietors sponsoring large-scale, often lavish books to appeal to the upper end of the market. As well as luxury poetry books and painting commissions, some of the finest examples of erotic art in Japan, and perhaps the world, were produced as books and albums during these years. These masterpieces were characterized by the superior quality of their draughtsmanship and the technical achievements of the block-cutters and printers.

Tsukioka Settei

The artist Tsukioka Settei (1710–86) worked in Osaka from the 1750s to the 1770s, producing an unusually wide range of work. He had studied with Takada Keiho (1674–1755), who practised the classical Kano style of Chinese-inspired ink painting, and this training undoubtedly contributed to the strength and vitality of Settei's draughtsmanship. He was a prolific book illustrator, producing genre scenes and pictures of beauties, and also contributing to painting manuals, encyclopedias, topographical guidebooks and erotic works.

Among his erotic productions, Settei was notable for three parodies of Confucian instruction manuals for women. These manuals were widely read and were established as the basic sources of correct behaviour and attitudes for women, in relation to their parents and more particularly to their husband and parents-in-law when they married and entered the husband's household. Settei himself had on occasion illustrated the very conduct books (*ōraimono*) that he was here mocking. Parodies depend for their success on the reader's familiarity with the original: these works preserve the size and format of the serious manuals, while their texts (possibly written by Settei, at least in part) cleverly twist the original meaning. The pictures likewise maintain the ostensibly serious subject matter, but add a salacious element. *Womanly Virtue and a Library on the Private Parts* (*Onna teikin gesho bunko*), published around 1768, is a parody of the conduct manual *Womanly Virtue and a Palace Library* (*Onna teikin gosho bunko*) of the previous year. Should an unsuspecting reader open its cover, the first illustration is an innocuous image of a yellow

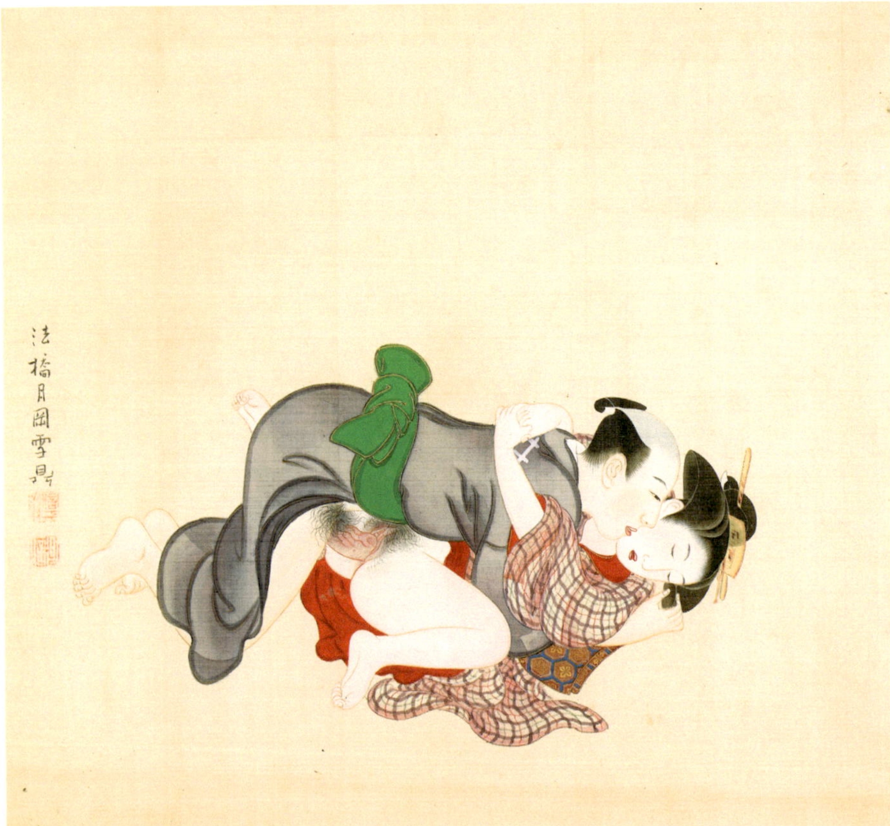

Tsukioka Settei
Scene of love-making
c. 1770
Unmounted painting, ink and colour on silk, 30.3 × 33.3 cm

Settei, renowned for his erotic book illustrations, also made many paintings. This couple is locked in a passionate embrace. The woman holds her partner tightly around his shoulders, but turns her head away as he makes to kiss her, closing her eyes to concentrate on the sensation as he penetrates her. As with the earlier painted scrolls, the lovers are depicted against an undefined blank space. The painting demonstrates Settei's characteristic style, quite literally 'fleshed out', with particular care taken in rendering the skin tones of both partners, especially on the genitalia. The figures' clothing is very finely painted; the man's robe of translucent black gauze reveals his body underneath, and his rich green sash is edged with gold lines. Her robes fall around her gracefully, the red underskirt providing a vivid backdrop for the genitalia, which are the focus of the picture. The work is individually signed, suggesting it came originally from an album.

peony, but there follows a bawdy comparison of the three capitals (see pp. 18–19). The book continues with the events of the twelve months, sections on 'Famous Women of China and Japan' and on male–male relations in the two countries. It closes with two compositions of couples making love spread over several pages. The particular copy of the book reproduced here bears the seal of a book lender (*kashihonya*), indicating its circulation and suggesting the reach in society it must have had.

It has been argued that the popularity of these parodies, and the evidence of their widespread circulation, points to an alternative discourse regarding women's sexuality in eighteenth-century Japan. Beneath the public presence of the respected, authoritative didactic manuals, there was the subversive world of the erotic take-offs. Thanks to the itinerant book lenders, who made house-calls (see p. 144), women were first in line as customers for such works. The parodies promoted the importance of sex within conjugal relations, and went even further, arguing that women too should enjoy sex and should be brought to orgasm. A passage from another of Settei's parodies, *Great Pleasures for Women and Their Treasure Boxes* (*Onna dairaku takara-beki*), published mid-1750s, a spoof on the Confucian text *A Treasure-chest of Greater Learning for Women* (*Onna daigaku takara-bako*), translates as follows: 'For a wife whose husband is poor, to escape the cares of the household she will have no greater pleasure than sex. Therefore she should be coquettish and talk about erotic things with him, and make him feel good. Your husband will forget his troubles and, feeling happy, he will no longer feel poor.'[1]

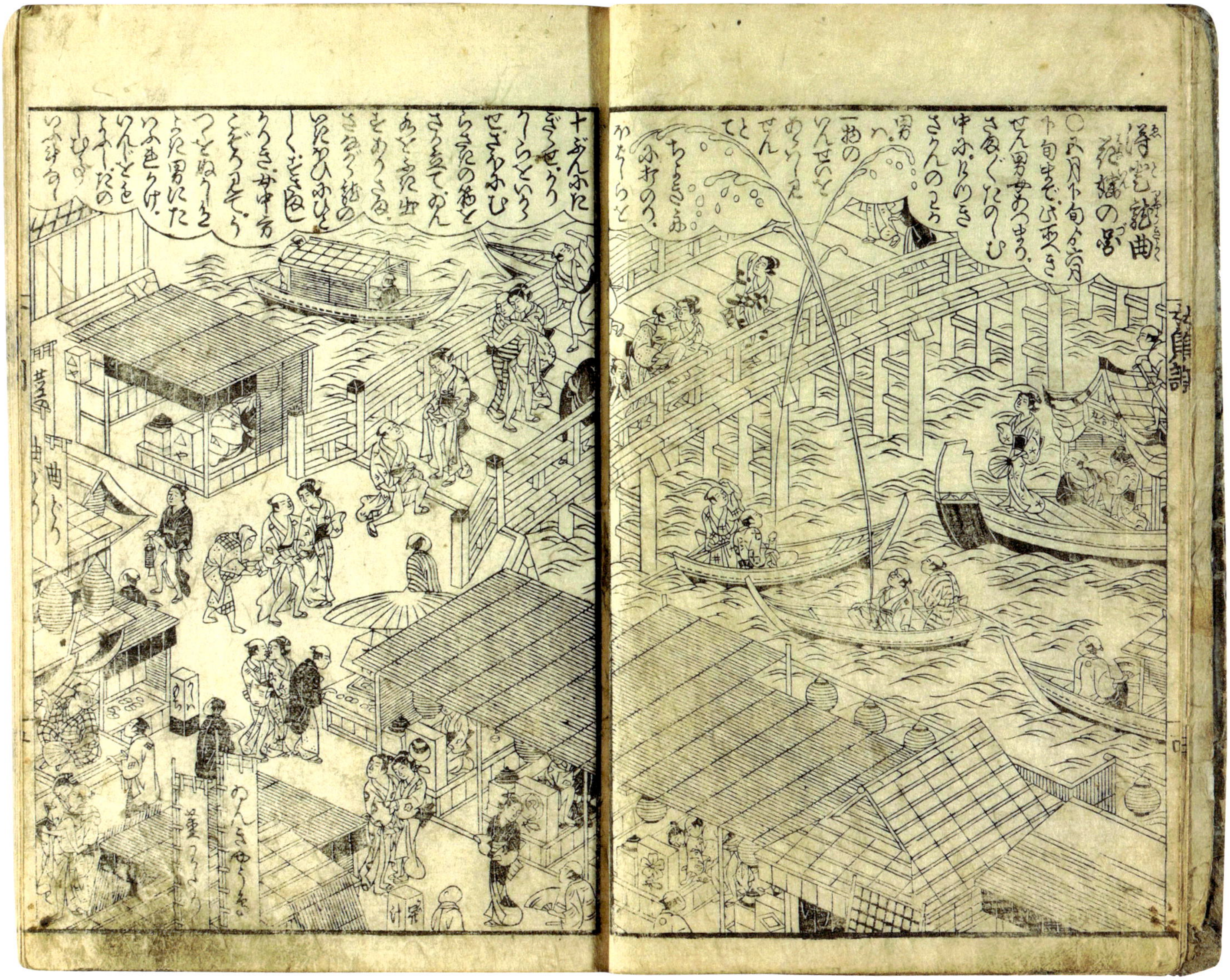

Tsukioka Settei
***Womanly Virtue and a Library on the Private Parts (Onna teikin gesho bunko)*, vol. 1**
c. 1768
Woodblock-printed book, 26 × 18.5 cm (covers).
Private collection, Ritsumeikan ARC Database

The book opens with three views of licentious behaviour in Japan's main cities. In summer, Ryōgoku bridge in Edo is busy with strollers enjoying the cool air by the Sumida river, and they do not restrain their urges. Many are already in flagrante or preparing themselves, and the customary river firework displays have been replaced by powerful jets of another kind.

Suzuki Harunobu

Suzuki Harunobu (d. 1770) is the artist most closely associated with the development of full-colour prints, around 1765. He is thought perhaps to have been born in Kyoto, and it is possible he studied with Nishikawa Sukenobu, the leading book illustrator of the time. After moving to Edo, it seems that Harunobu turned to designing prints relatively late in life, perhaps in his mid-thirties, around 1760. Though he lived only ten years longer he produced many hundreds of print designs. Harunobu benefited from the enthusiasm for poetry of wealthy patrons, who commissioned 'calendar prints' (*egoyomi*) for the New Year in which, as a leading professional artist, he was asked to work up their amateur ideas for compositions. The new patronage of these deluxe prints made possible the development of woodblock-printing technology from just two or three colours to full colour using multiple printing blocks. The new multicolour prints were likened to richly ornamented fabric, gaining for themselves the name 'brocade pictures' (*nishiki-e*). *Ukiyo-e* prints were in essence a popular form of art, but the eager consumers of Harunobu's new full-colour designs included affluent merchants, shogunal retainers and scholars.

Woodblock prints of this period often had several layers of meaning to be decoded and enjoyed. The classics of Chinese and Japanese literature, as well as mythological and religious themes, provided a rich source of subjects for modern-day 'reworkings', where the ancient themes were seen through the prism of contemporary dress and settings. In Japanese, this process of reworking was known as *mitate* or *yatsushi*. Such designs are often incorrectly described as 'satires' or 'parodies', whereas in fact they usually possessed little of the critical intent implied by such terms. Artists would use their creative imagination to hide witty allusions in the design, and viewers enjoyed working out the puzzles. The popularity of this convention was based in a well-established practice of superimposing the 'elegant' (*ga*) on to the 'mundane' (*zoku*), or finding the sacred within the profane.[2]

Erotic print designs also adopted this playful approach to subject matter. In his series *Eight Fashionable Parlour Views* (*Fūryū zashiki hakkei*) of 1768, Harunobu played on the classical Chinese theme of the 'Eight Views of the Xiao and Xiang Rivers' (in Japanese, *Shōshō hakkei*).[3] This was a region, in present-day Hunan province, at the confluence of the Xiao and Xiang rivers. Renowned for its natural beauty, the area was popular with Chinese literati, who had long celebrated it in painting and poetry. Such works were taken back to Japan by Zen monks who visited China in the Muromachi period (1333–1573), and the theme became established as an elegant expression of idealized landscapes. The set of eight views was also soon adapted for beauty spots in Japan. In his version, Harunobu layered the eight landscapes on to scenes of everyday life in Edo, with the motifs from the original painting subjects likened to domestic furnishings. The series was inspired by the 'humorous verses' (*kyōka*) of the young poet Fukuo Kichijirō (n.d.), and versions of these poems appear above each design.

Two years later, just before his death in the summer of 1770, Harunobu designed two related sets of prints entitled *Fashionable Lusty Mane'emon* (*Fūryū enshoku Mane'emon*). The work is unusual in that it presents a continuous narrative from picture to picture among its twenty-four designs. The text on the first print explains that a man of Edo named Ukiyonosuke

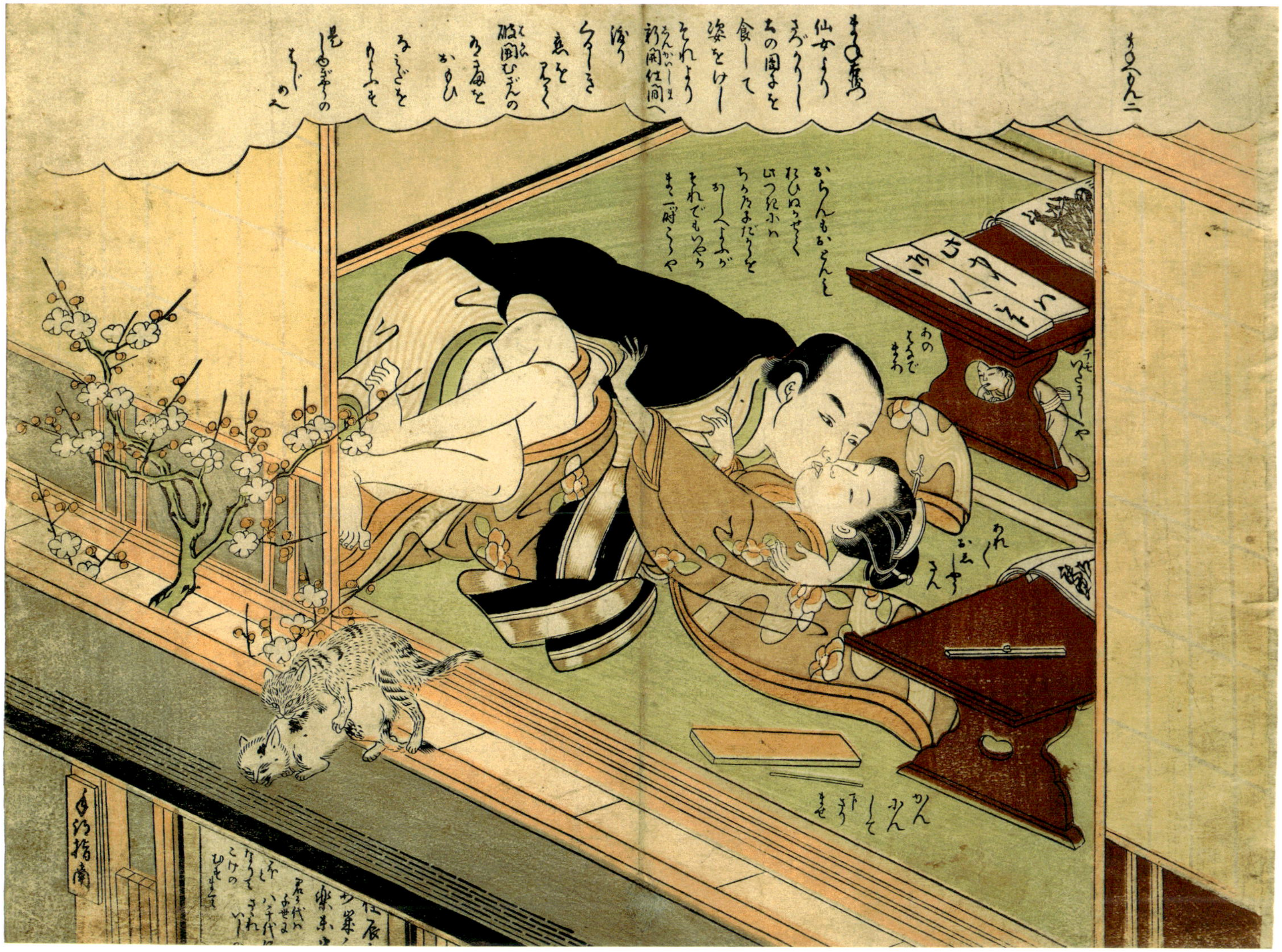

Suzuki Harunobu
Fashionable Lusty Mane'emon
(*Fūryū enshoku Mane'emon*), no. 2
1770
Colour woodblock print, 20.6 × 28.5 cm

On his travels to understand the mysteries of love, Mane'emon first goes to the 'Island of Virgins'. We know from the sign hanging outside the ground-floor entrance and from the materials on the table that a girl has come for a calligraphy lesson. The teacher is trying to force himself on his young pupil – she wears the robe with long, hanging sleeves of an unmarried woman – telling her, 'I'll pass you ahead of your fellow students Oran and Oton, and will teach you the methods of the next level. In that case, is it still disagreeable? Be patient for just a little while longer.' She tries to push him away, saying 'Oh dear! Teacher, please let go of me!'. Mane'emon watches from beneath the table, and comments, 'What a pitiful, wretched thing. And look at his nose!'. Outside a male cat appears to be equally determined to mate. The text above is critical of the teacher who is abusing his position, and says that to force a woman is an atrocious thing.

Suzuki Harunobu
***Returning Sail at the Towel Rack*, from the series *Eight Fashionable Parlour Views* (*Fūryū zashiki hakkei*)**
1768
Colour woodblock print, 20.2 × 27.6 cm

Here Harunobu replaces the billowing sail of a ship with a hand-towel blown by the breeze. A middle-aged man is having his beard plucked by a young woman, who wears a robe with long, hanging sleeves. He reaches one hand inside her skirts and gently holds her shoulders; the closeness of their embrace is emphasized by the reflection of their faces in the hand-mirror. From the age difference we can surmise that the man is visiting his young mistress, and he has possibly slipped in by the rear-gate of the garden, across the stepping stones. The poem above translates, 'The boat over there / With sails swelling to the front / Is it coming into the harbour? / Ah yes, it's coming in.' With a clear double entendre, the man represents the 'returning sail' of the title, and his mistress provides the 'harbour'. The painting of waves on the standing screen behind the couple reinforces the nautical theme.

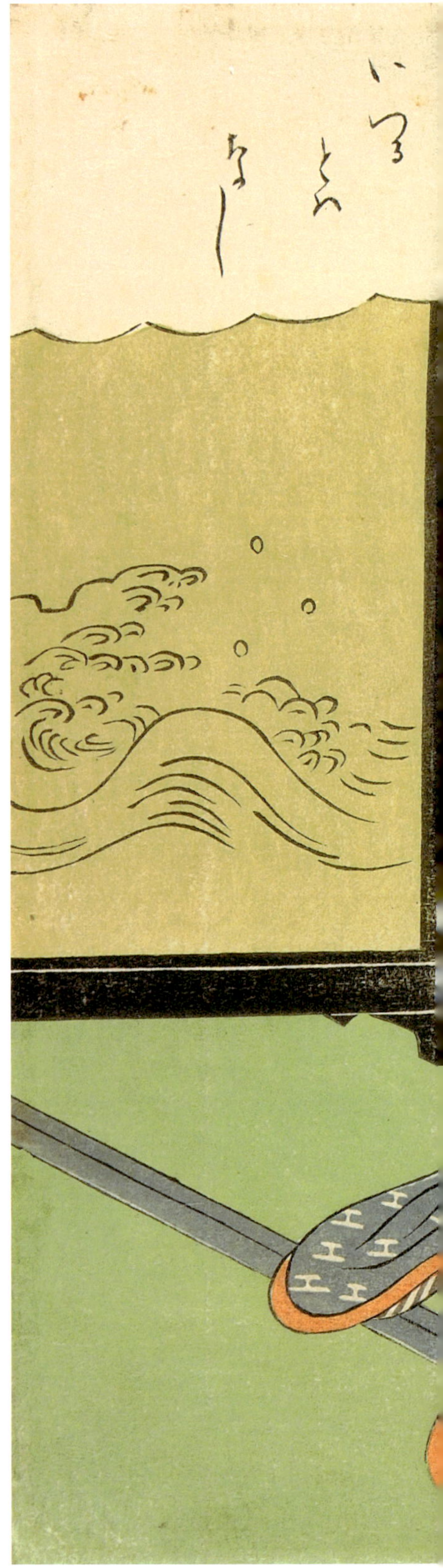

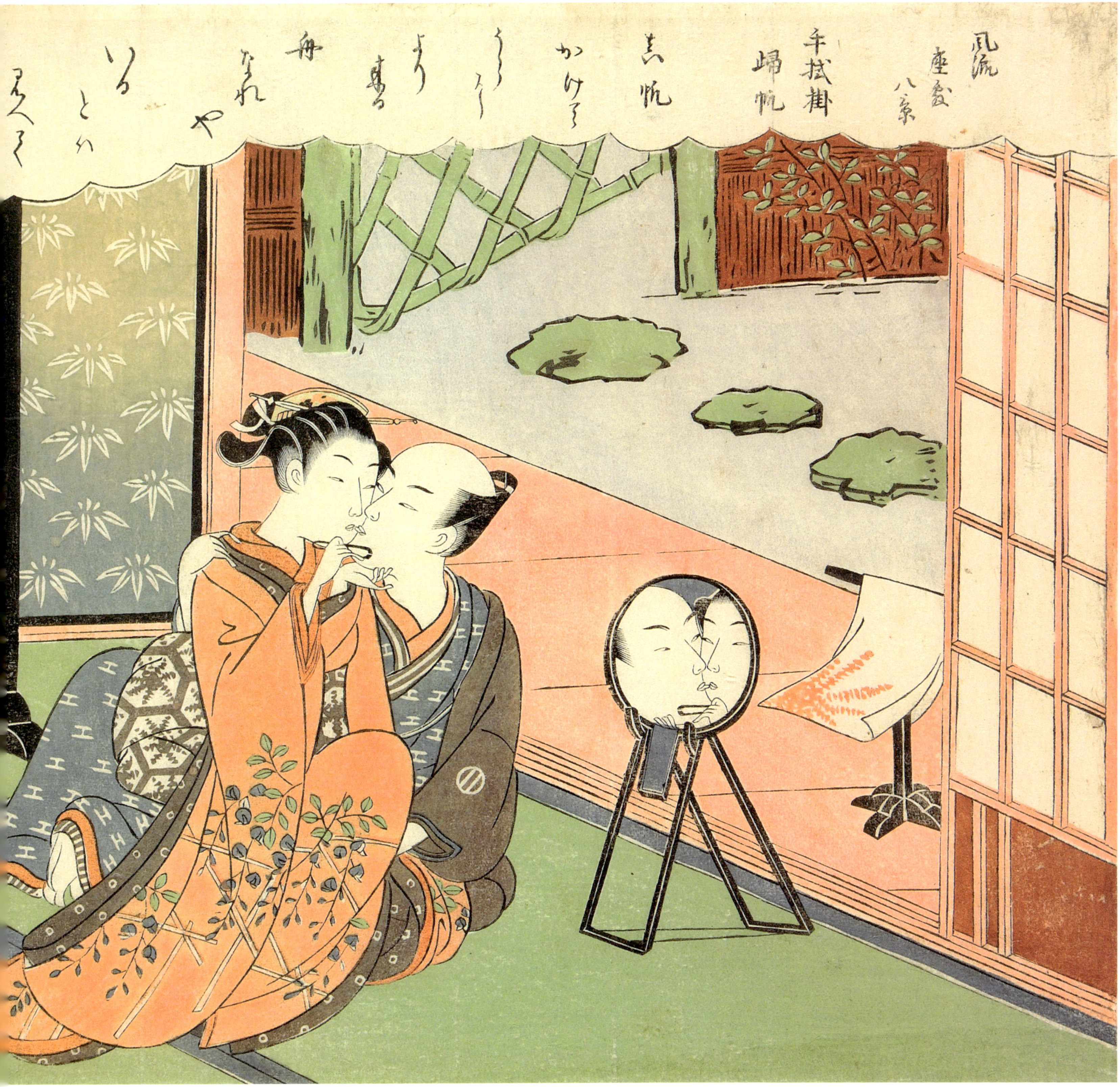
風流
座敷八景
手拭掛
帰帆

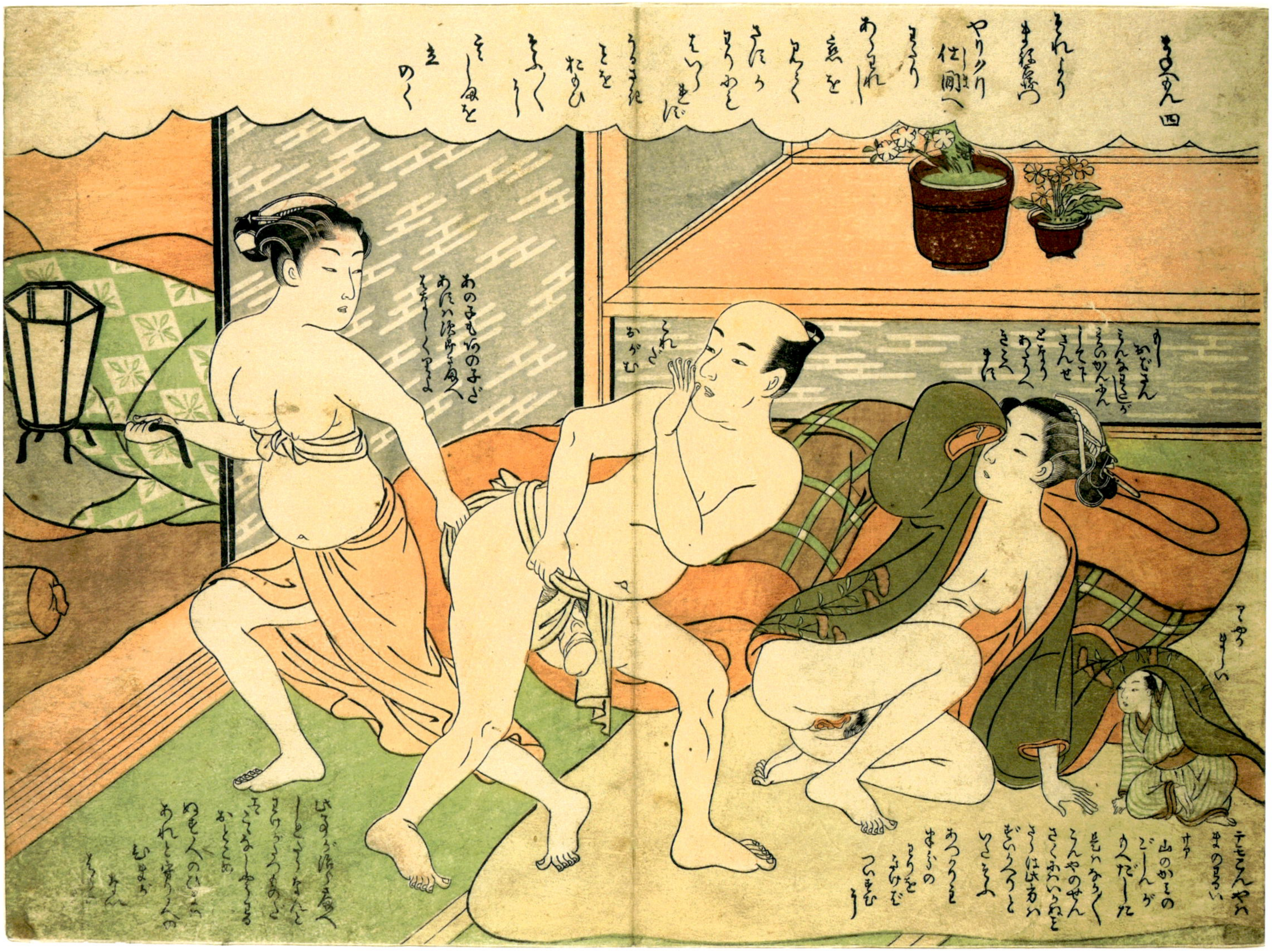

Suzuki Harunobu
Fashionable Lusty Mane'emon
(*Fūryū enshoku Mane'emon*), no. 4
1770
Colour woodblock print, 20.6 × 28.5 cm

Mane'emon visits 'Excuse Island' and finds a cheating husband caught by his wife. The bedding visible through the sliding doors suggests that the man has got up in the night to visit the young woman in the adjacent room. His wife, carrying a lantern, has woken and caught him, and now drags him away by the loincloth. With his drooping penis, he holds up his hand in apology. From her swollen belly and the protective white sash (*iwata-obi*) we know that the wife is pregnant. The dialogue informs us that the young woman is staying with the couple to help the wife during her pregnancy. Covering her face in shame, she pleads, 'Pardon me, ma'am, I'm the one at fault.' Hiding beneath her robes, Mane'emon comments sagely, 'This situation probably won't calm down until morning.'

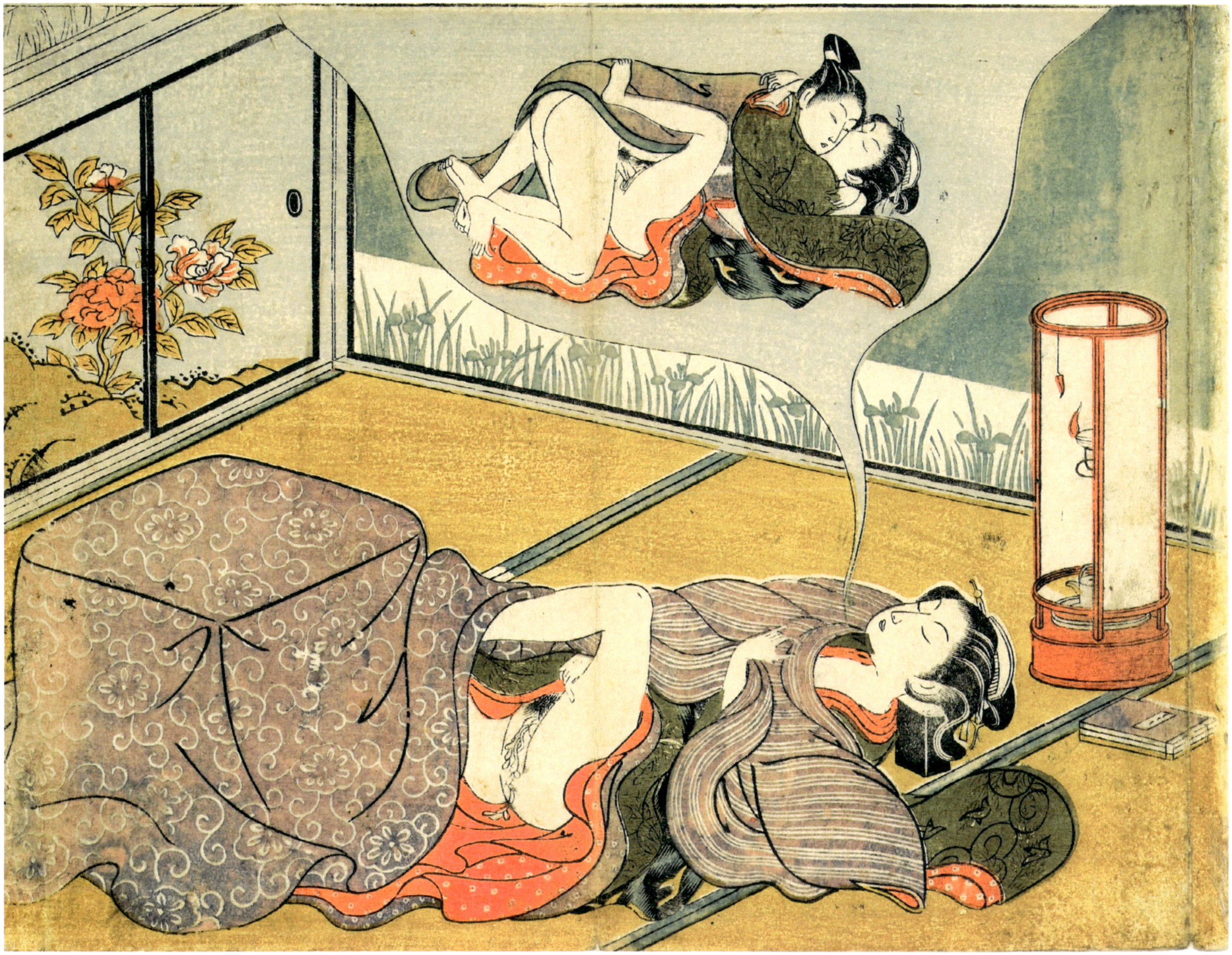

Style of Suzuki Harunobu
Woman dreaming of an erotic scene
c. 1770
Colour woodblock print, 18 × 25 cm

Seated at the *kotatsu* (covered brazier) on a winter's evening, a woman's thoughts have drifted, perhaps inspired by the book lying beside the lantern. The covers have fallen back to reveal the pleasurable effects of her reverie.

Suzuki Harunobu
Lovers in winter
1768–70
Colour woodblock print, 18 × 25 cm

The print captures a moment of dramatic tension as a jealous woman spying on two lovers prepares to extinguish their passion by hurling a snowball through the window. We can surmise that she is a courtesan and the man is a regular client who is betraying their relationship by having an affair with her young apprentice. Snow lies heavily on the bamboo outside the building, given a textured effect by a special printing technique.

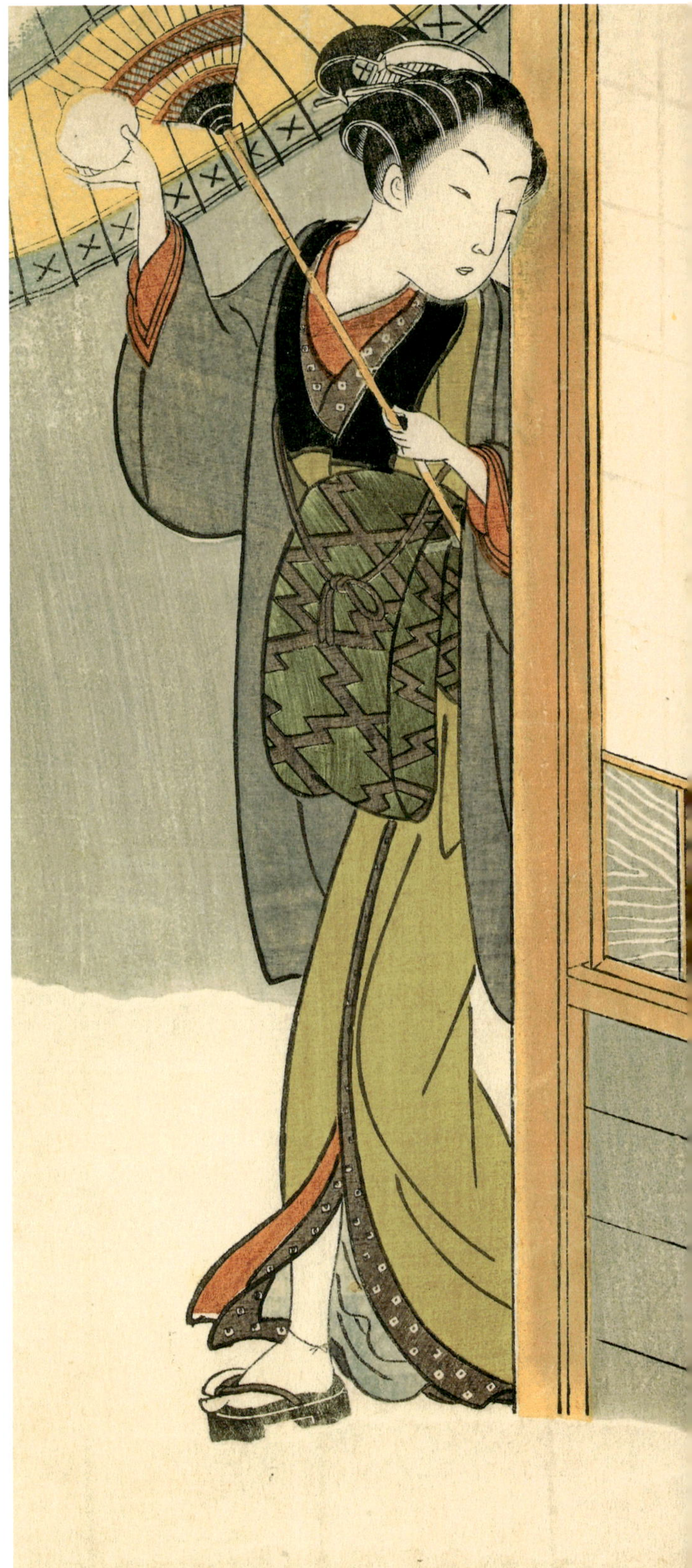

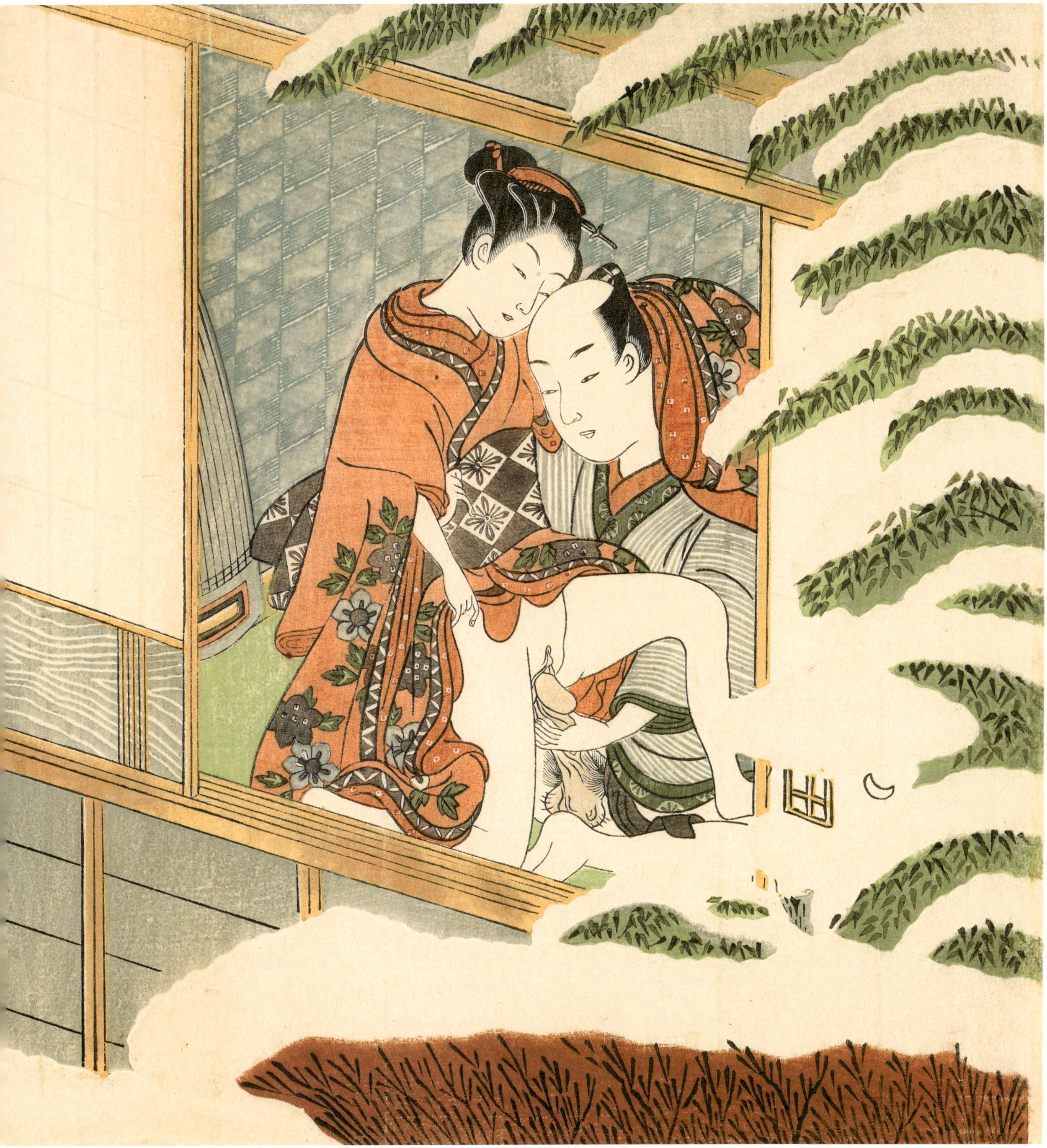

('floating world chap'), being of an amorous nature, visited a shrine and petitioned for mastery of 'the secrets of the art of love-making'. Two shrine deities (depicted as two celebrated Edo beauties) presented him with magical dumplings to shrink him to the size of a bean and a potion for eternal youth. Mane'emon ('Bean Man') then set off on his travels to observe the ways of sex of 'men and women, young and old, business and pleasure, city and country'.[4] In the first twelve prints Harunobu presented the ordinary citizens of Edo, and the second series focused on encounters in the pleasure district, Yoshiwara. The introduction and text above each picture were written by Komatsuya San'emon Hyakki (1720–93), proprietor of a large pharmacy and keen poet; Harunobu himself probably provided the dialogue. The device of an invisible man who could observe sexual practices undetected was a useful one, allowing Harunobu to link together a series of disparate sexual situations. Such a character had appeared as early as 1712 in a work illustrated by Sukenobu; likewise, in 1763 Harunobu's friend Hiraga Gennai (1729–79) had published a story of a man granted invisibility and the means to speed across land and sea, who visits strange peoples all around the world, taking in Korea, China, India and Holland.

Isoda Koryūsai

In the late 1760s the *ukiyo-e* artist Isoda Koryūsai (1735–90) began to produce many designs of elegant, fashionable beauties. His early style shared close similarities with Harunobu's, and he first used the name Haruhiro, suggesting that he may have trained in that master's studio. Later he moved away from his fascination with the 'floating world', and concentrated on producing paintings. Like Harunobu, Koryūsai produced a large number of *shunga*. The erotic album *Prosperous Flowers of the Elegant Twelve Months* (*Fūryū jūniki no eiga*) was published around 1773, demonstrating Koryūsai's style as it developed after Harunobu's death. The album is structured according to the calendar; each design includes the name of the month, an appropriate poem (containing innuendo and sexual puns) and associated motifs and observances. The album presents ordinary men and women engaged in love-making, usually in a domestic setting, and the dialogue incorporated into each design helps convey their feelings. In all the scenes sexual intercourse is already underway, with the bodies twisted to afford a view. The elegant designs, explicit sexual content and textual play produce a work that rewards viewing on many levels.

In *shunga* albums, the first design was usually not explicit, but rather depicted a more innocent scene of a couple (or group) relaxing together. The first design in this book is of a young couple dozing as they play a boardgame on the last night of the year, and they share an auspicious dream for the New Year. Because their themes were more innocuous, these opening designs were often removed and sold separately. This was apparently the case with the British Museum's album, which is missing the design for the first month and has only eleven remaining illustrations. It came from a small collection of Japanese erotica with an admirable pedigree of previous artist owners. The group was assembled by the American painter John Singer Sargent (1856–1925), who shared in the contemporary fascination with Japanese art. He gave it to a fellow painter, Philip Wilson Steer (1860–1942), who in turn passed it to the print-maker John Wheatley (1892–1955). The final owner was the portrait painter and President of the Royal Academy, Sir Gerald Festus Kelly (1879–1972), whose widow donated the items to the British Museum.

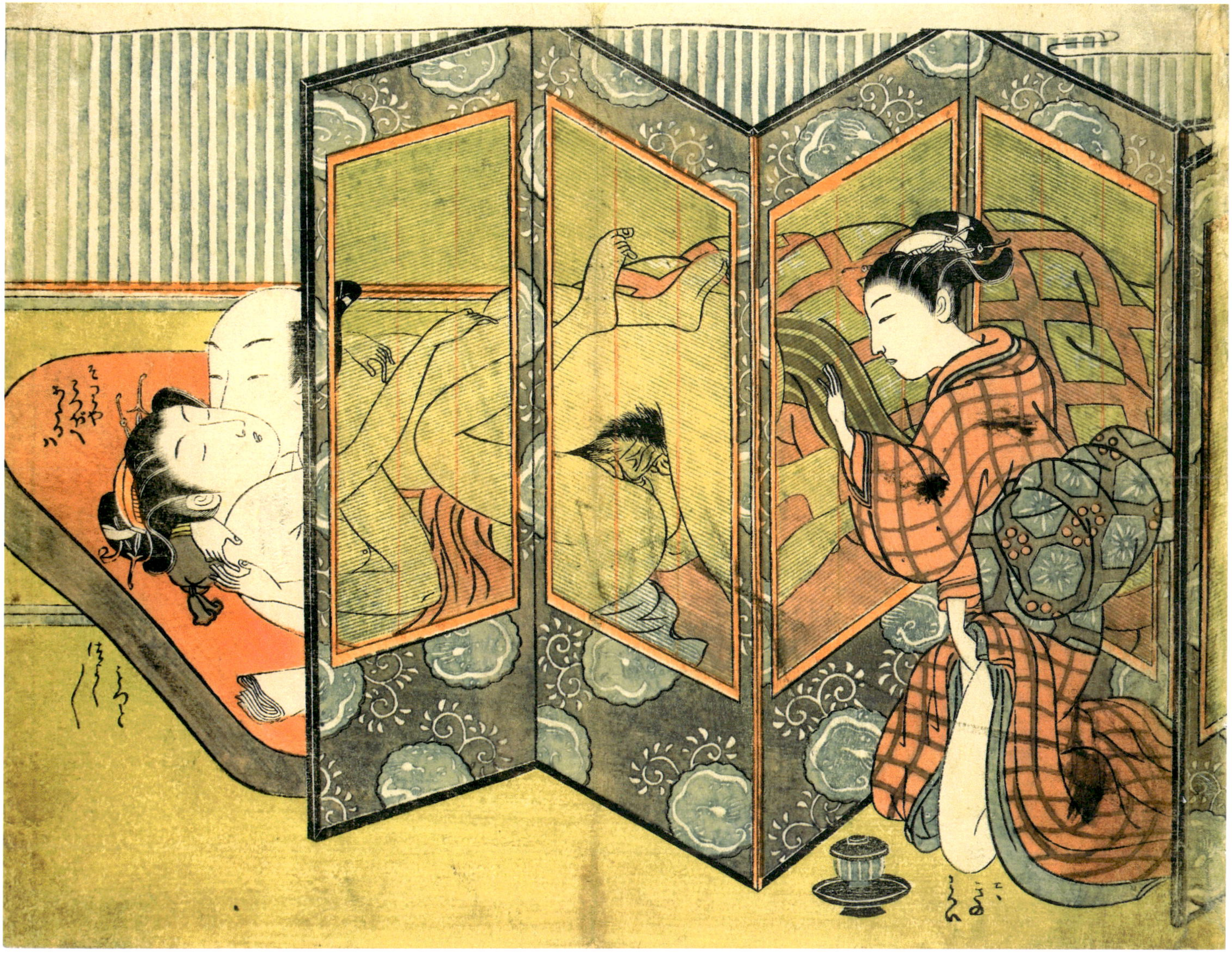

Attr. Isoda Koryūsai
Lovers behind a screen
1772–3
Colour woodblock print, 18.8 × 24.8 cm

A maidservant bringing a cup of tea has placed it on the ground and stopped to watch the couple's love-making through the transparent folding screen. Aroused by what she sees, she has slipped her right hand between her legs.

Isoda Koryūsai
***Prosperous Flowers of the Elegant Twelve Months* (*Fūryū jūniki no eiga*)**
c. 1773
Colour woodblock-printed album, 21.2 × 14 cm (covers)

The image for the fifth month, *Satsuki*, or the 'month of rice seedlings', is a scene of a husband becoming aroused at the sight of his wife undressing for a bath, a theme common in *shunga*. She has cast her robes over a clothes rail, and is just stepping into the high tub. The poem translates, 'Iris bath / with edges so wet! / Entering the rainy season.' Irises blossomed in the fifth month, and on the fifth day people scattered the leaves into bathwater to dispel the malignant vapours of summer. This was just when the rainy season began, bringing with it the strenuous work of rice-planting. The poem contains double entendres, with its 'wet edges' and 'entering', and 'getting wet' was also a slang term for sexual relations. In the dialogue below, the woman scolds her husband, saying, 'What do you think you are doing? Stop acting silly!'. He tries to cajole her: 'Silly? Don't be so heartless. Come on.' His half-hidden face suggests his stealthy approach, but he holds his wife gently and their gazes meet in apparent mutual understanding.

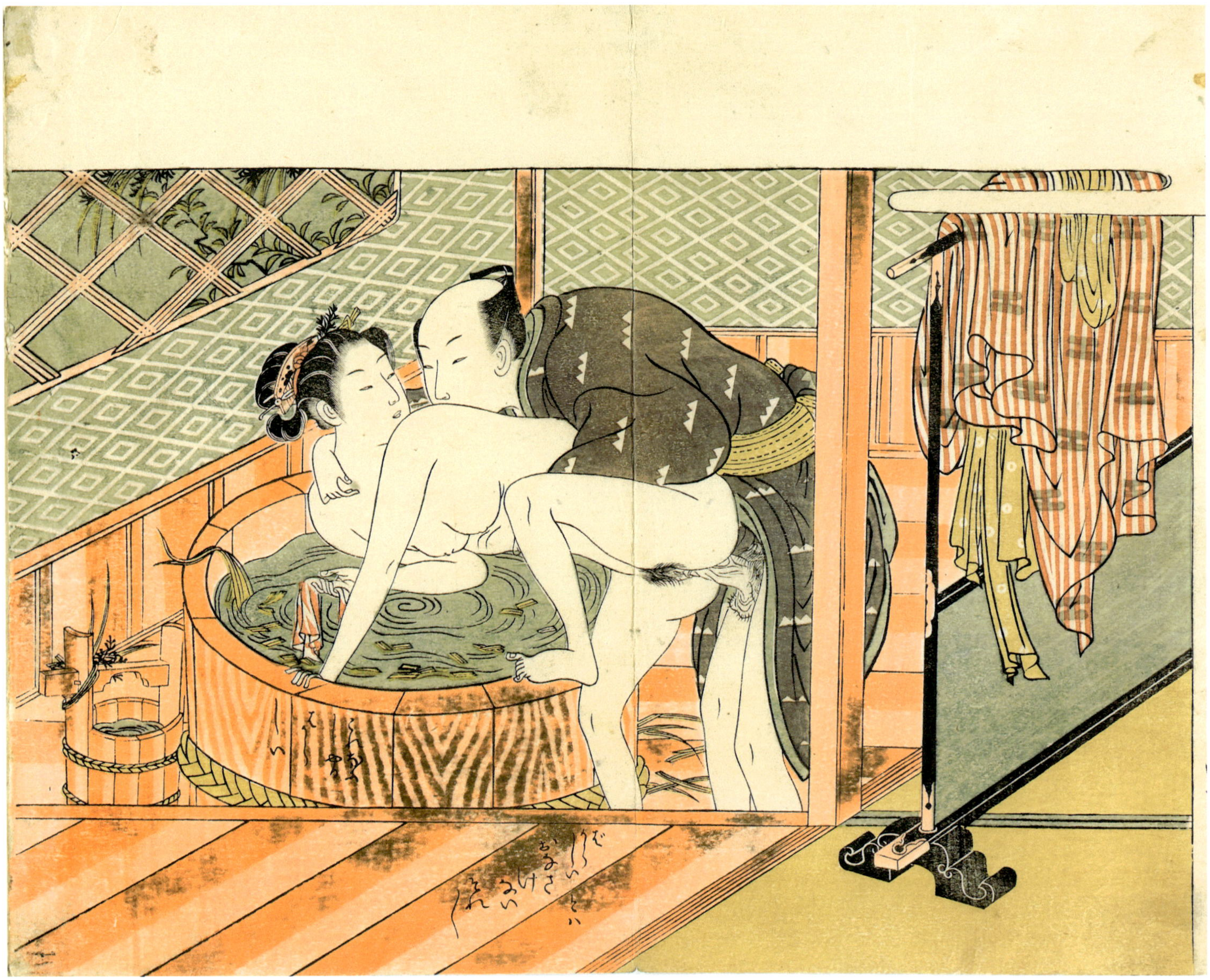

Isoda Koryūsai
***Prosperous Flowers of the Elegant Twelve Months* (*Fūryū jūniki no eiga*)**
c. 1773
Colour woodblock-printed album, 21.2 × 14 cm (covers)

In the ninth month, chrysanthemums bloom outside the window. A townsman has just smoked a pipe, and is taking a nap with his wife. In yet another common *shunga* scenario, he is unaware that her lover has slipped in, a male servant who has worked in the house since he was a child. The poem alludes to how quickly the young man has matured: 'In an instant it has grown / over a foot long: / the crimson carp of autumn.' She whispers to him, 'Careful! Your panting… your panting…', while the husband snores on peacefully.

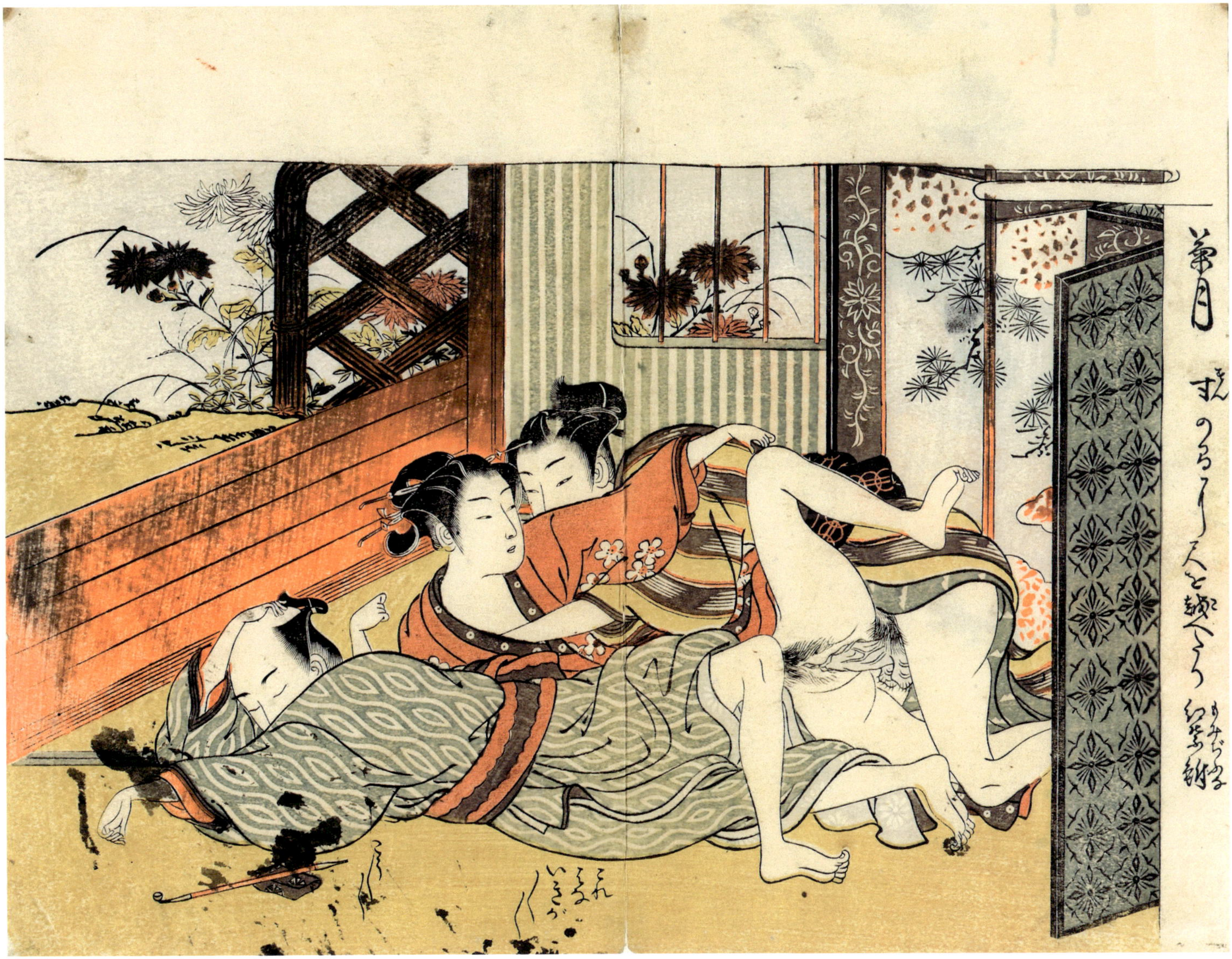

Katsukawa Shunchō
From the series *Twelve Tastes in the Classification of Passion* (*Shiki burui jūni-kō*)
c. 1785
Colour woodblock print, 39.2 × 52.7 cm

Much of the erotic imagery in Tokugawa-period Japan offered the viewer escapism and scenes of sexual fantasies, often with no strings attached. In this extra-large print, twice the size of a normal 'large-sheet' (*ōban*) design, one man dexterously pleasures six women at once, possibly in a comical inversion of the Seven Gods of Good Fortune, one of whom is a woman. The multiple creases in this unusually large print indicate that it was folded, probably sold in a wrapper which may have borne a non-explicit design.

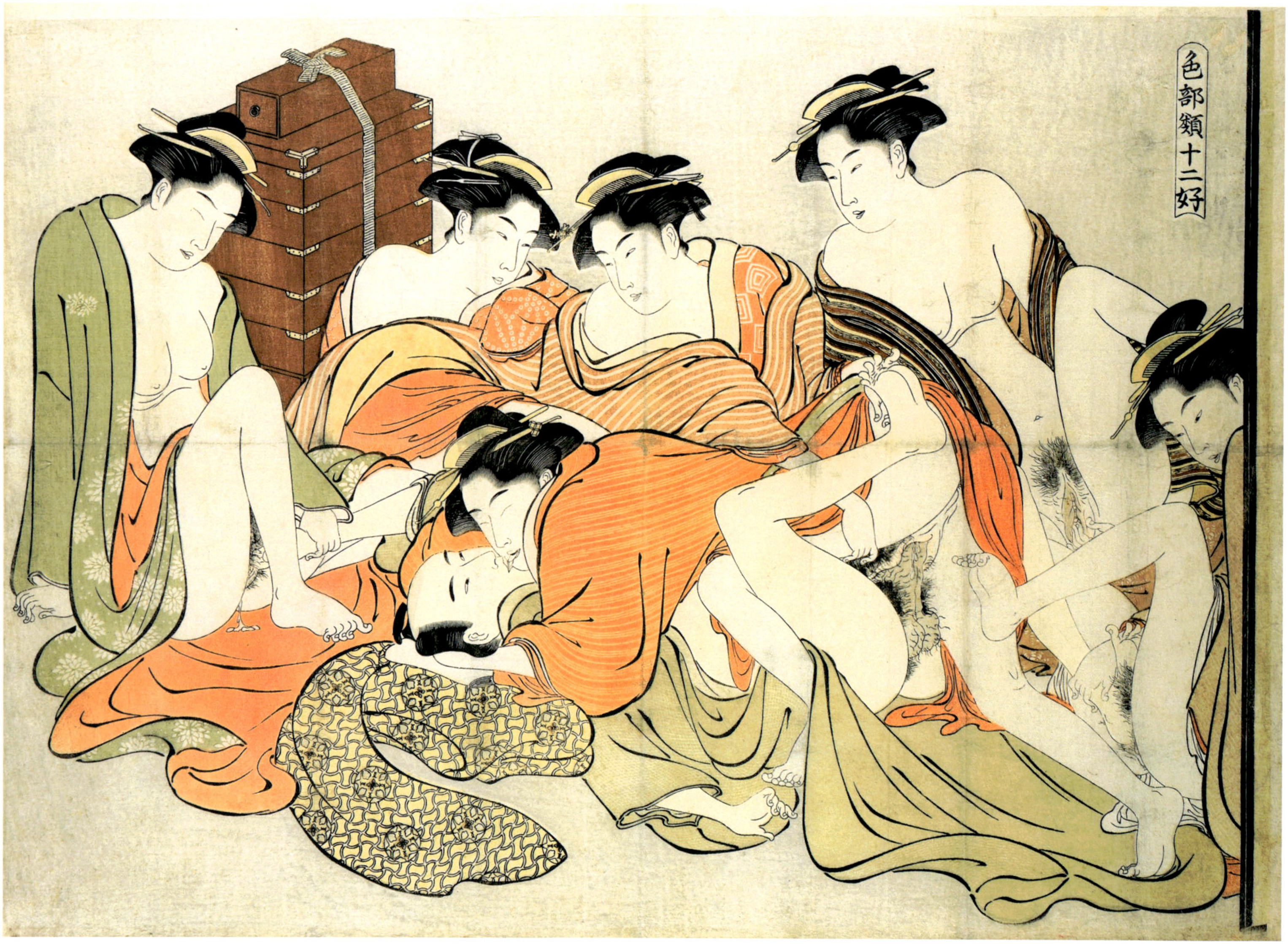

Tenmei masterpieces

Tanuma Okitsugu (1719–88), one of the Senior Counsellors to the shogun Tokugawa Ieharu, is credited with encouraging a more liberal regime, introducing proposals – which were ultimately vetoed – for currency reform and relaxation of the restrictions on intercourse with foreign nations. Though censorship laws remained in effect, their enforcement was generally lax. In a society usually preoccupied with distinctions of class and rank, the more liberal atmosphere of the Tanuma years, broadly coinciding with the An'ei (1772–81) and Tenmei (1781–9) eras, made it possible for intellectually and artistically inclined samurai (and even *daimyō*) to associate with like-minded, often wealthy, townsmen. The climate of social and cultural exchanges fostered a remarkable flourishing of the arts.

The leading artist of the Tenmei era was Torii Kiyonaga (1752–1815). In his teens he had studied with Torii Kiyomitsu, and was adopted into this lineage, which specialized in portraying the actors of the *kabuki* stage. Early in his career Kiyonaga produced many illustrations for comic novellas, but he later came to concentrate on single-sheet print designs. He was renowned for his designs of tall, statuesque beauties in attractive surroundings, either landscapes with carefully rendered perspective or elegant interiors. His erotic masterpiece was published around 1785, probably at the New Year. Known (from a phrase in the preface) as the *Scroll for the Sleeve* (*Sode no maki*), the prints were pasted together to form a continuous handscroll. This made a relatively affordable substitute for a deluxe handscroll painting. The conceit of the title is that the scroll could be hidden inside the hanging sleeve of a *kosode* robe.

The work opens with a text mimicking the calligraphic preface of a handscroll, sealed 'Onobore' ('the self-infatuated'), perhaps referring to the artist himself. In the twelve erotic designs that follow, Kiyonaga turned the vertical 'pillar-print' (*hashira-e*) format on its side, confining each pair of lovers within the elongated frame, dramatically cropping their bodies and thereby bringing the viewer right up close to them. To conform to the tight compositions the couples are all shown lying down, holding each other closely with their faces pressed together. This long, narrow, horizontal format had been used for painted handscrolls as early as the 1750s by Tsukioka Settei, and in printed form by Shimokōbe Shūsui, but Kiyonaga exploited its compositional possibilities to the greatest effect. He provides very little physical setting for the love-making, and there is no room for text or dialogue. With such tight compositions, the focus is fully on the characters' facial expressions and the forms of the genitals. The naked bodies are rendered with long, delicate lines, which achieve a convincing sense of volume without the use of shading, and the narrowed eyes and partly open mouths give rich expression to the faces with a remarkable economy of line. Kiyonaga lavished much attention on the fine patterns of fabrics and the delicacy of hairstyles. He used a thicker, calligraphic line for the robes, which cascade in rhythmic folds, parting to reveal the sex organs beneath.

The New Year 1788 was a milestone in the history of Japanese erotica, seeing the publication of not one, but two masterpieces. The first, *Picture-book: Haikai Album of the Cuckoo* (*Ehon haikai yobuko-dori*), was designed by Katsukawa Shunshō (d. 1792) and issued by an unknown publisher in the medium *aiban* size. Although about twenty erotic publications by Shunshō are known, this is his superlative expression of erotic art. An alternative translation of the title, as written in

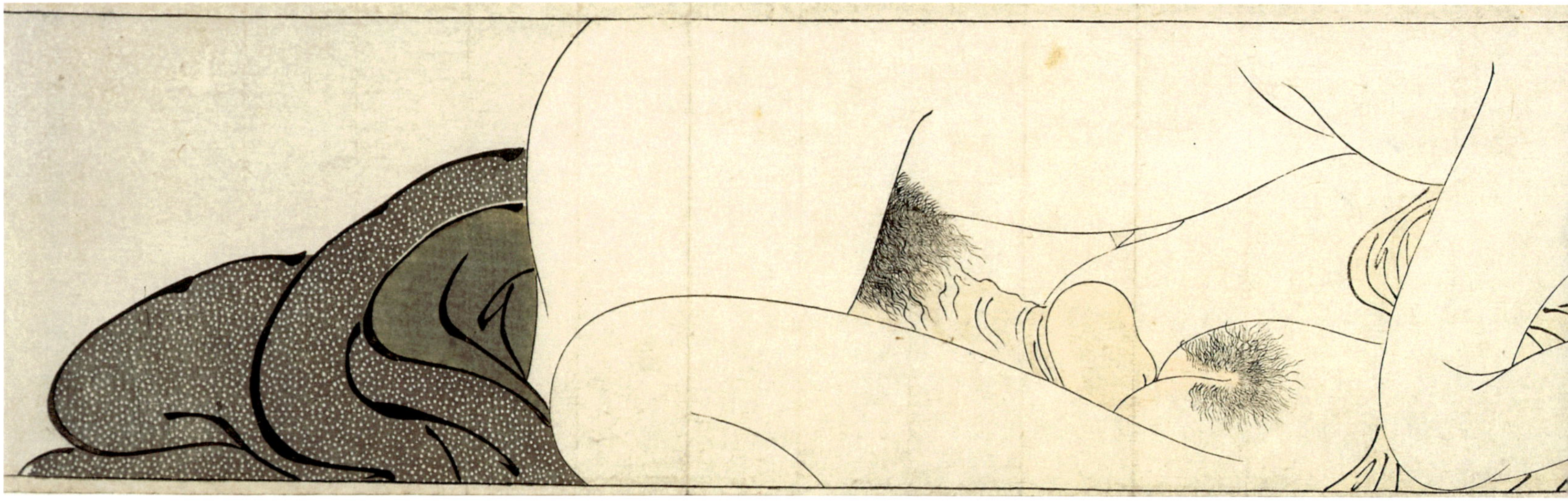

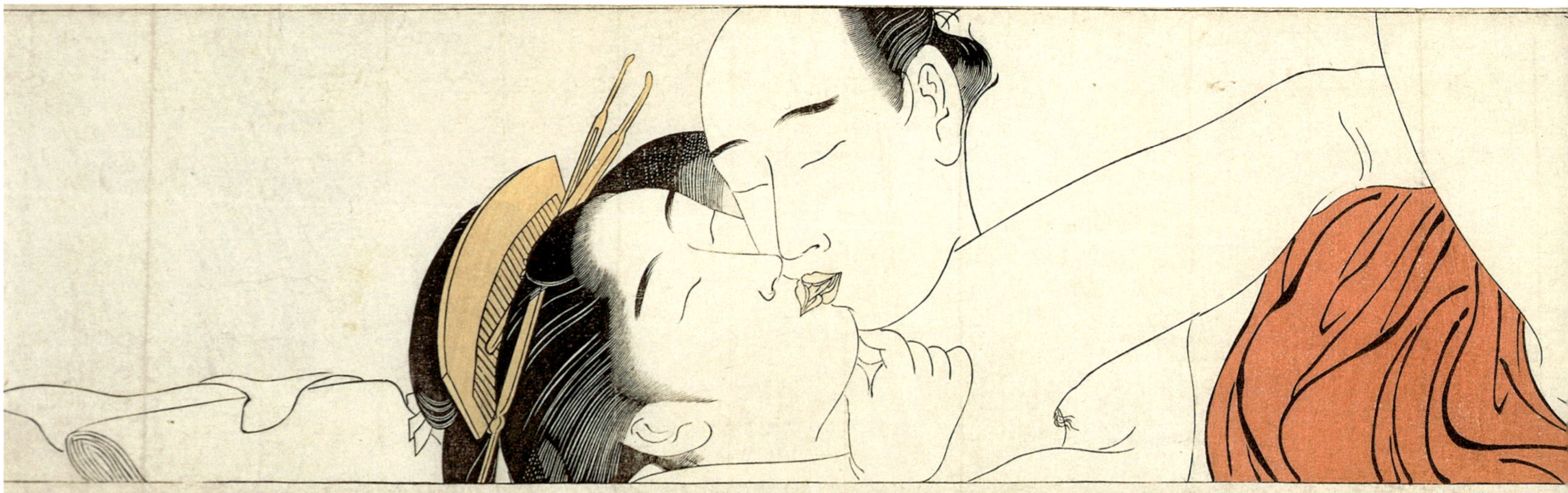

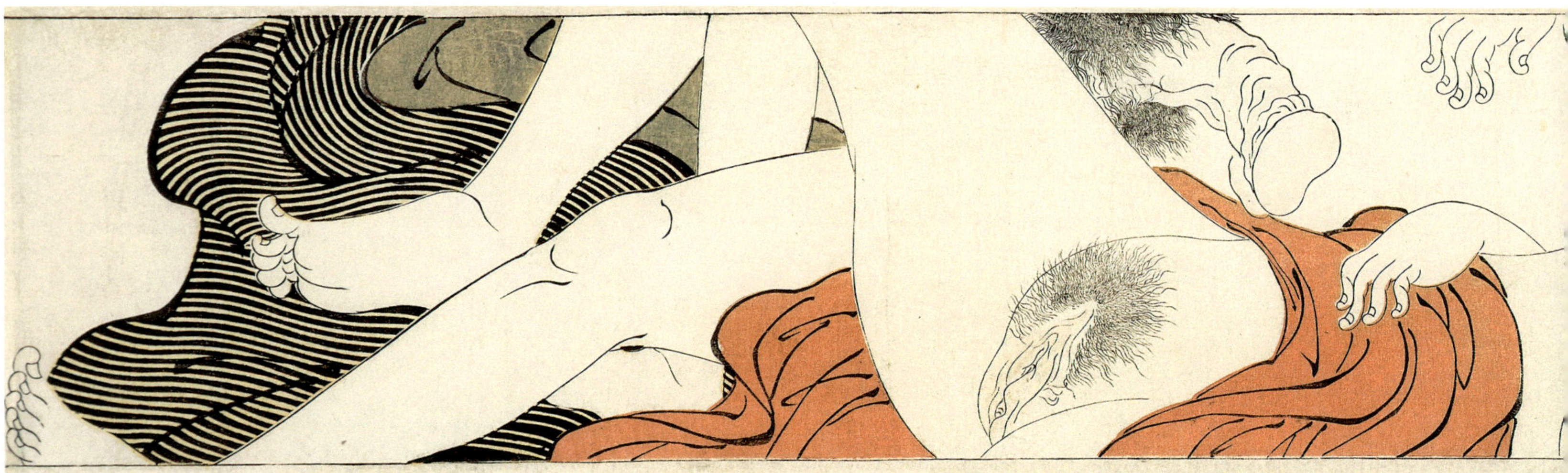

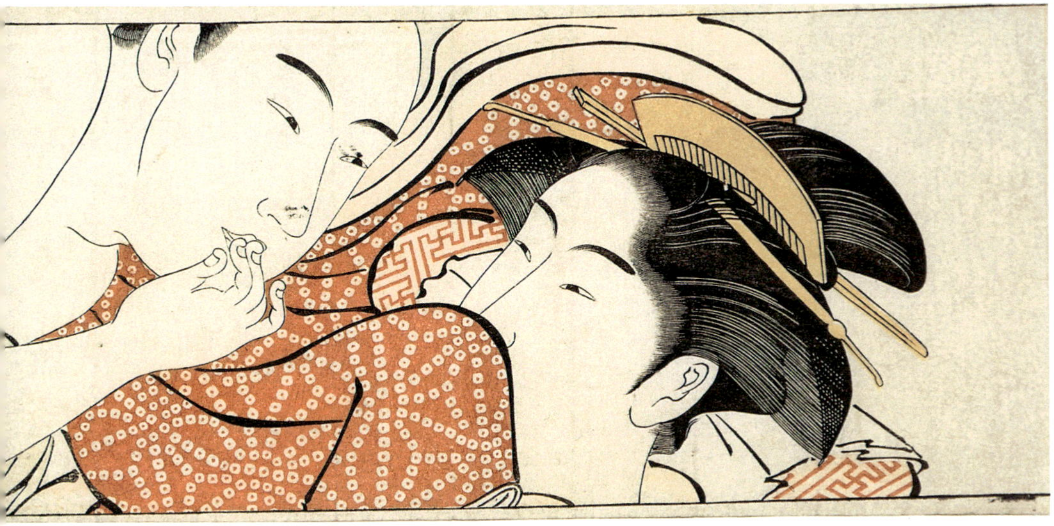

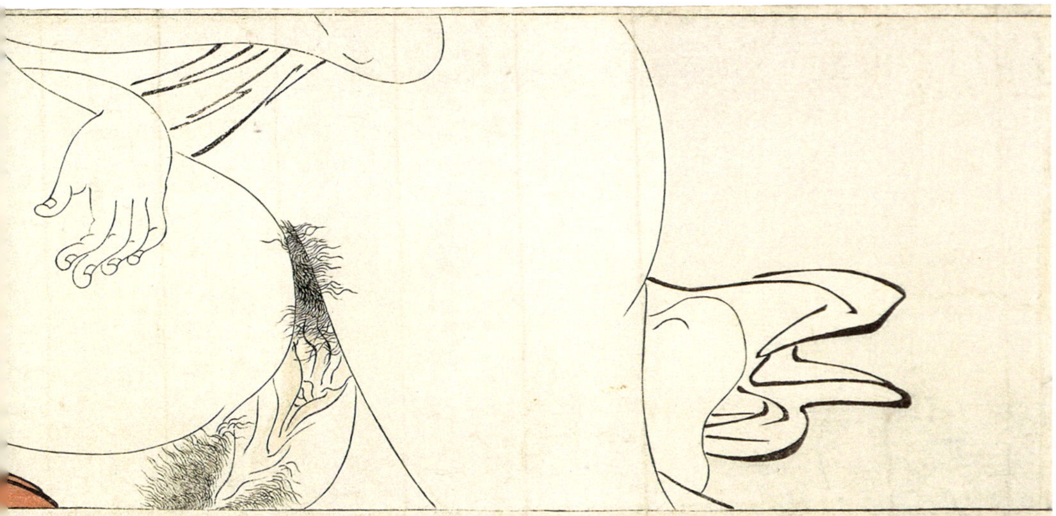

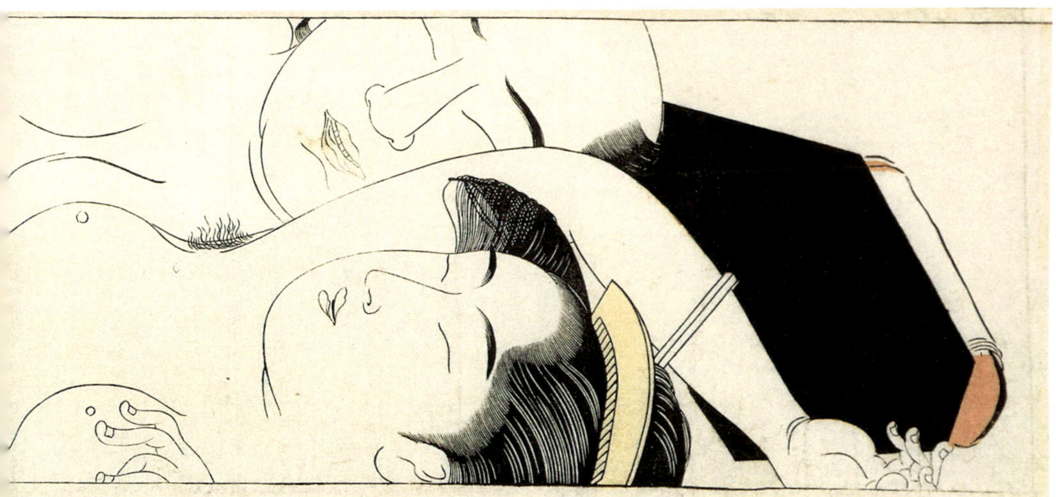

Torii Kiyonaga
***Scroll for the Sleeve* (*Sode no maki*)**
1785
Colour woodblock prints,
each print 12.6 × 67.4 cm

Top: *Scroll for the Sleeve* describes the full gamut of sexual intercourse, from the moment of anticipation, through the height of passion, to the sleep following its completion. Here a client at a brothel is just about to penetrate his partner, a courtesan's teenage apprentice. He has slipped off his stylish grey robe and wets his fingers to moisten her. She holds his gaze firmly, but demurely tries to hide her face with her hand, covered in the long, hanging sleeve of a young woman's *furisode* robe.

Centre: A young woman lifts up her leg to receive her lover, who wraps his arms tightly around her. As their lips meet, they close their eyes in mutual rapture. The woman's red underskirt provides an area of solid colour in a composition otherwise filled with their naked bodies. To either side the picture is balanced by the folds of his loincloth and some tissues placed in readiness.

Below: A middle-aged couple lie in post-coital bliss. Sated with their exertions, their bodies relax, with eyes closed and mouths partly opened. She stretches her lower leg over his thigh and he gently rests his hand on her navel. As his penis begins to droop, its form is echoed by her right arm thrown back, and even by the pillow lying on its side.

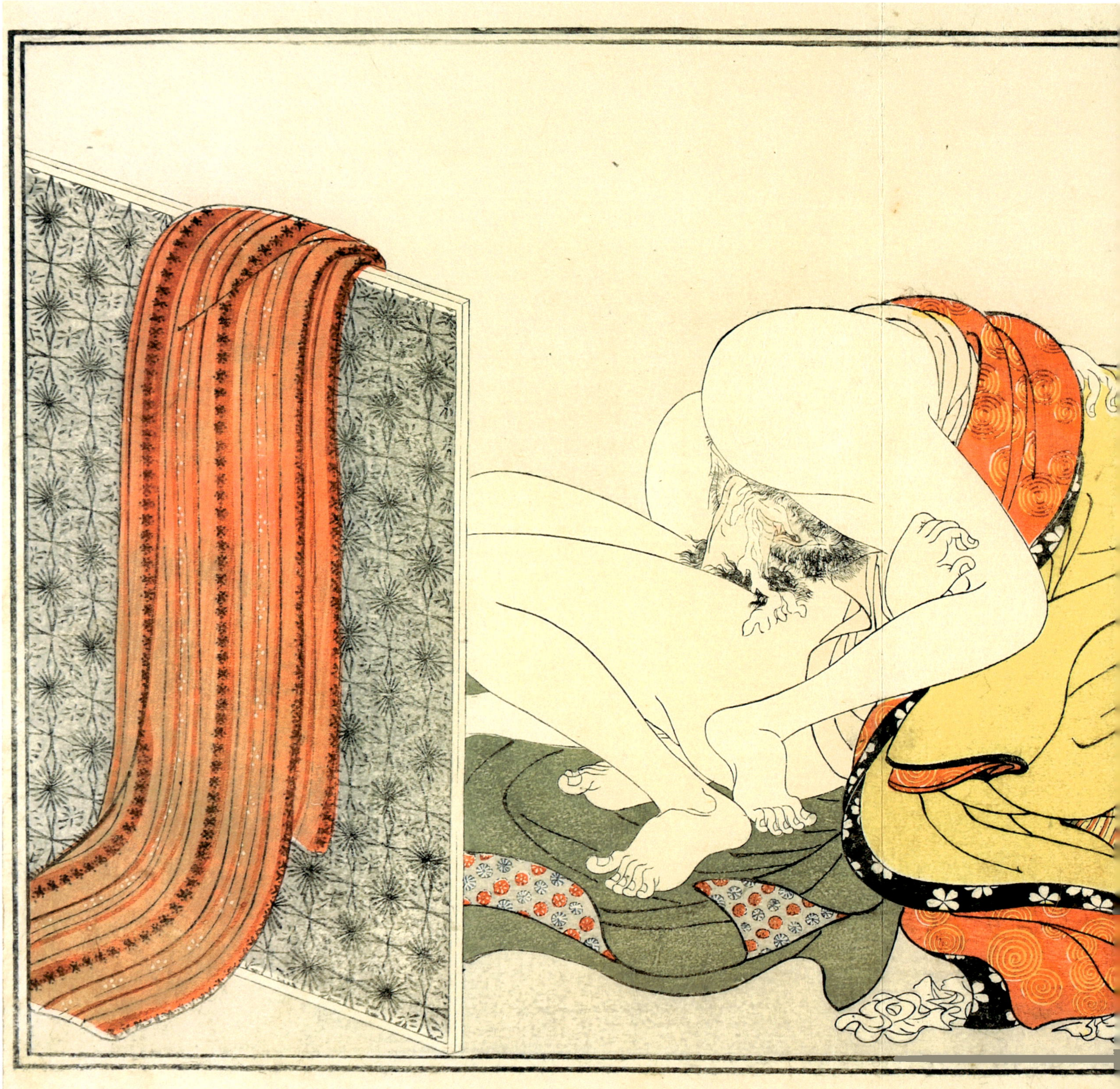

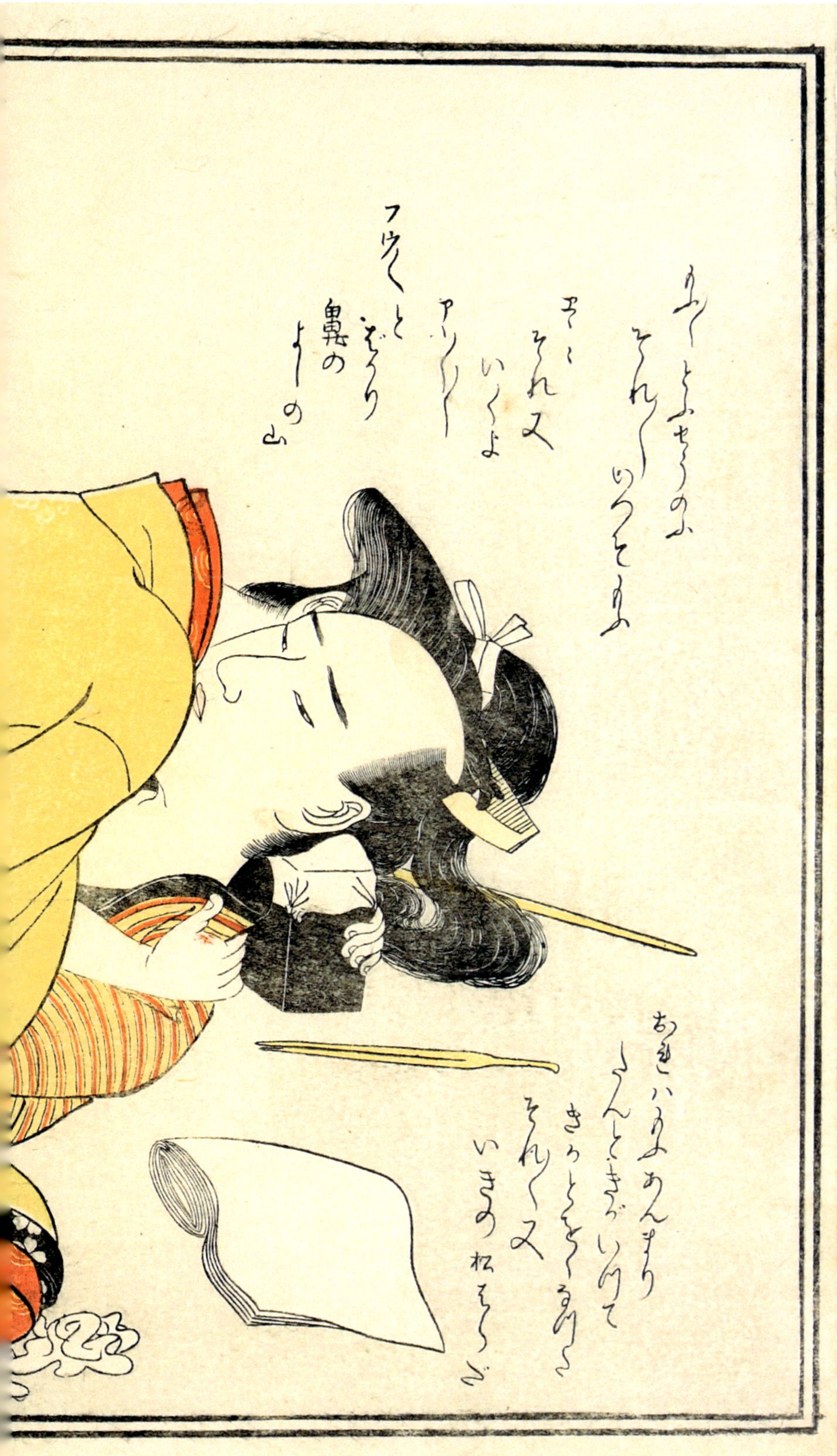

Katsukawa Shunshō
***Picture-book: Haikai Album of the Cuckoo* (*Ehon haikai yobuko-dori*)**
New Year 1788
Colour woodblock-printed album,
25.2 × 18.2 cm (covers)

In over half of the scenes in this album, the face of one of the partners is partly veiled, increasing the sense of emotional as well as physical intimacy. Here, in perhaps the album's most intense scene, a couple make love behind a 'pillow screen', over which the woman has draped her sash made of fashionable striped fabric. A roll of tissues lies ready, but the discarded ones beneath her sleeve indicate that this is a prolonged session. Their bodies pressed close together, she grips tightly around his shoulder and the pillow, and he strains to push up with his thighs. Though we cannot read her facial expression, Shunshō suggests her enthusiastic movements by means of her hair, which is falling out of its arrangement and scattering hairpins on the ground. She moans, 'I can't help it... I'm coming again! Aah, aah, aah, fuu, fuu...'.

Katsukawa Shunshō
Picture-book: Haikai Album of the Cuckoo (Ehon haikai yobuko-dori)
New Year 1788
Colour woodblock-printed album,
25.2 × 18.2 cm (covers)

In a theme beloved of *shunga* artists, a husband steals up on his wife while she is bent over a tub, in this case trying to do the laundry. We know the scene is taking place outside (perhaps in a yard area) as they are both wearing sandals. The woman's fallen clog indicates the swiftness of her husband's move, and she steadies herself on the tub and his arm. He tells her that he couldn't resist the view of her from behind, but she scolds him for being foolish, as someone is bound to come along. Their puppy, meanwhile, yaps enthusiastically. The intertwining of the couple's legs, their eyes closed in bliss, and the fluids released indicate the intensity and pleasure of their sensations.

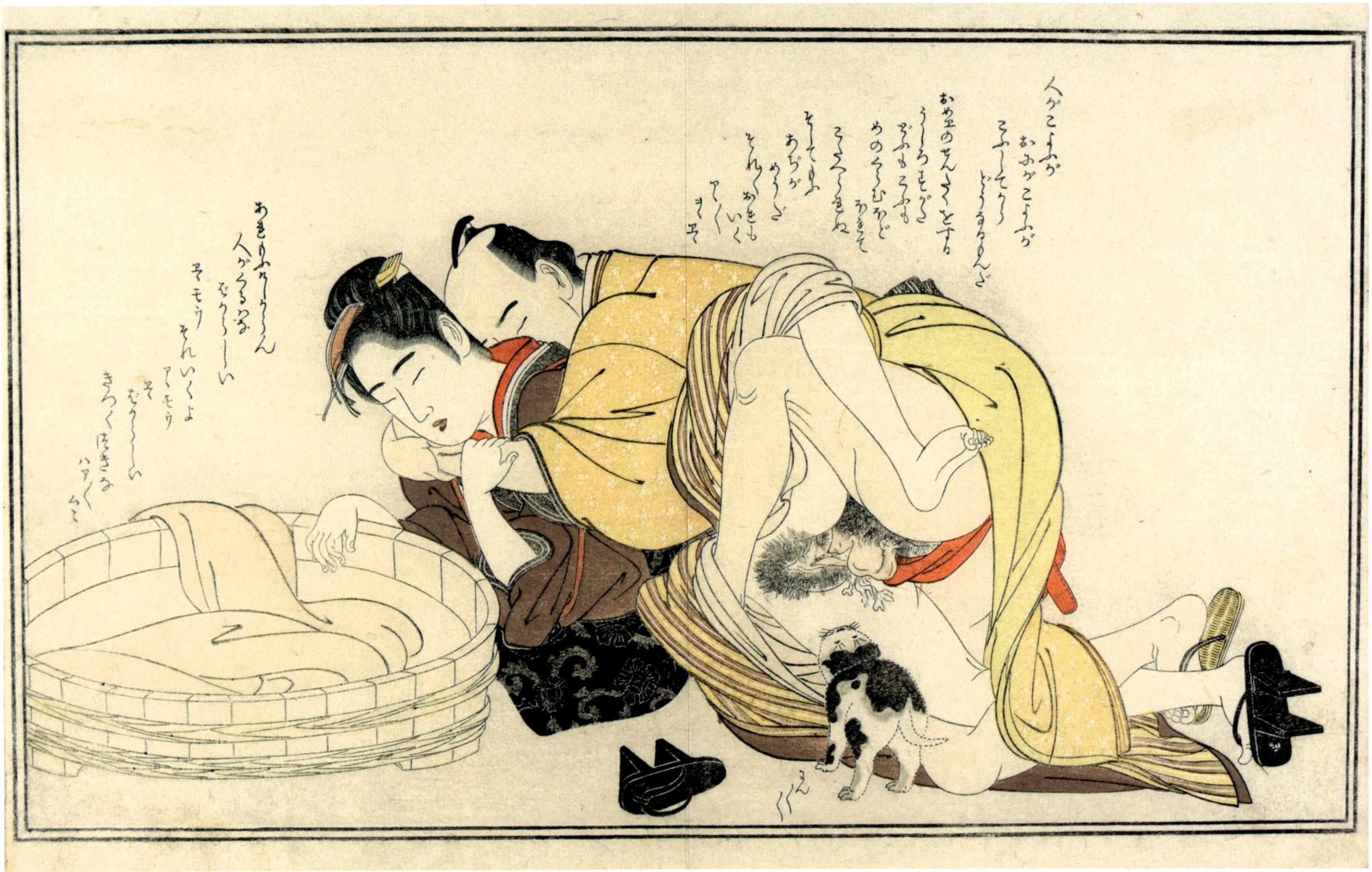

Katsukawa Shunshō
***Picture-book: Haikai Album of the Cuckoo* (*Ehon haikai yobuko-dori*)**
New Year 1788
Colour woodblock-printed album,
25.2 × 18.2 cm (covers)

This image shows how *shunga* can suggest a sense of eroticism and anticipation with only a minimal depiction of flesh. In winter, a man and a woman have been snuggling in the warmth of the brazier (*kotatsu*). As the man becomes amorous, with one hand he tries to pull his companion to the floor, and with the other he lifts up her skirts. Worried about someone coming into the room, the woman tries to pull herself up again, her face half emerging, but her raised knee serves only to reveal what the man is aiming for. As they move, the covering blanket is pulled off, dislodging the cat from its favourite hotspot. Aggravated, it stretches and yawns, complaining, 'Just when I was sleeping so nicely… They're such a noisy pair.' Shunshō conveys the sudden movement of the man's passionate impulse by the mass of the blanket and the folds of the woman's clothing. Underneath the cloth we can surmise the outline of the man's back, but he is concealed all but for his crown, one hand and one knee.

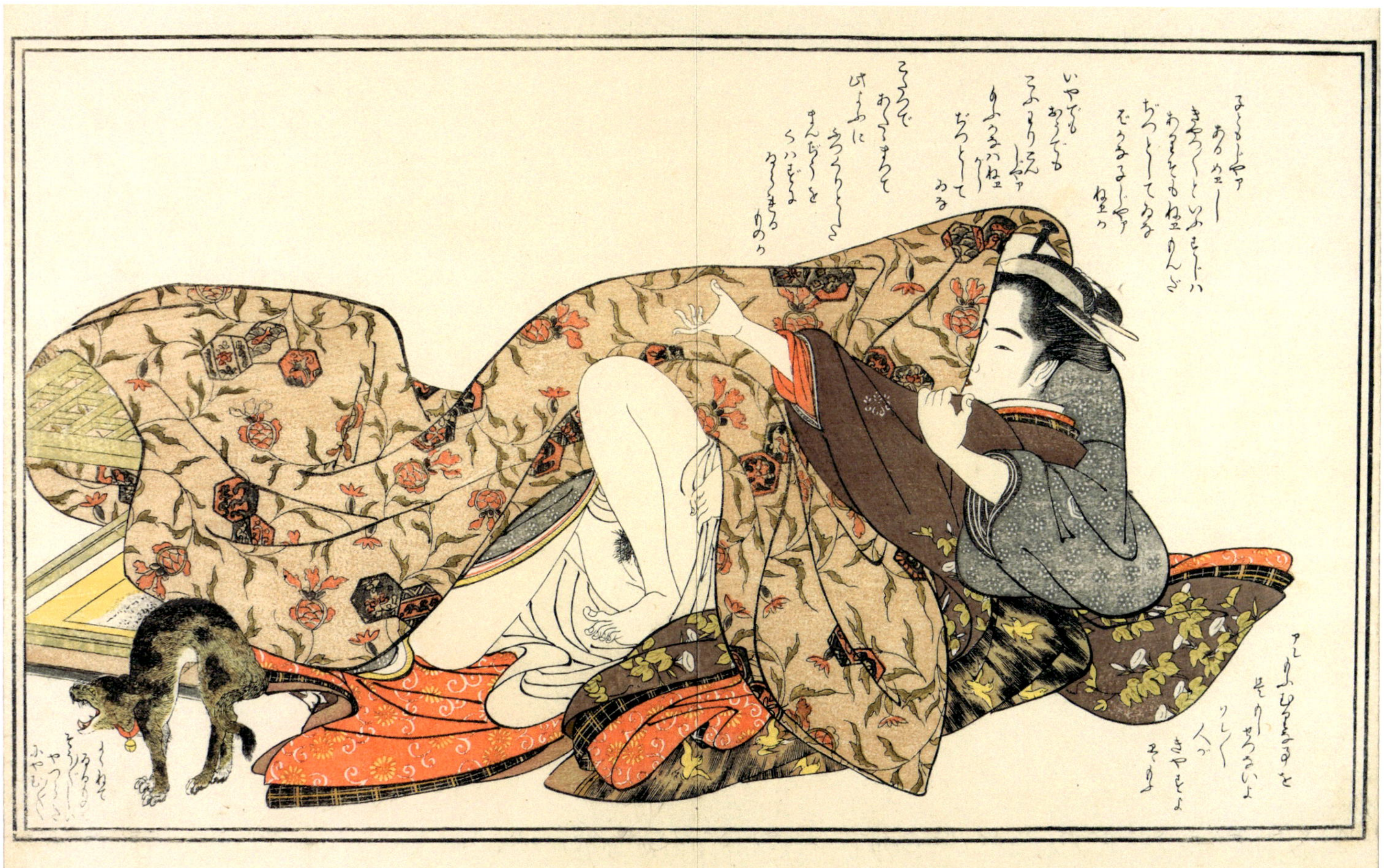

the preface (using different characters), is *Worshipping Pussy: Playing 'Gotcha!' with Women at Night.* The same playful punning continues through the one-page preface, signed 'Jintaku Sanjin', thought to be the erotic pen-name of Shunshō himself. Presented in folding-album format, the work contains the expected twelve designs, followed by three playful texts, entitled 'Finger Movements Chapter', 'Rear Entry Chapter' and 'Reverse Position Chapter'.[5] Shunshō reworked several designs already used in earlier publications (for example, the monochrome *Ehon eiga taigai* of the previous year). Few impressions of the album survive, but these suggest that it went through several printings, using slightly different colours and designs on background elements and robes.[6] As an indication of its success, the album was recut and reissued under a different title in the 1790s. Shunshō was renowned for his print designs of actors both on- and off-stage, but more particularly for his paintings of elegant, seductive beauties. The women appearing in this album exemplify the late Tenmei ideal of beauty, with soft yet expressive features, and a ratio of eight to one for the proportions of body and head. Here, however, the various poses of love-making do not allow the women to show off the elegance of their figures to quite the same effect as in Shunshō's paintings. In each design the lovers' bodies are surrounded by copious fabrics, described in fluid lines and rich colours.

The second major work to appear at New Year 1788 was the *Poem of the Pillow* (*Utamakura*). One of the undisputed masterpieces of Japanese erotic imagery, *Utamakura* presents a 'world of love-making' in its twelve scenes: young lovers as well as a mature couple, samurai, townsmen, servants, even a Dutch couple in exotic headgear; consensual relations as well as forced sex; and even a hallucinatory scene involving supernatural creatures. Though the album is unsigned, the preface describes the title as 'coming close to the name of the artist', and the style is unmistakably that of Kitagawa Utamaro. The preface (missing from the British Museum's set) is by Honjo no Shitsubuka (the 'Profligate of Soggy Honjo'), a pseudonym of

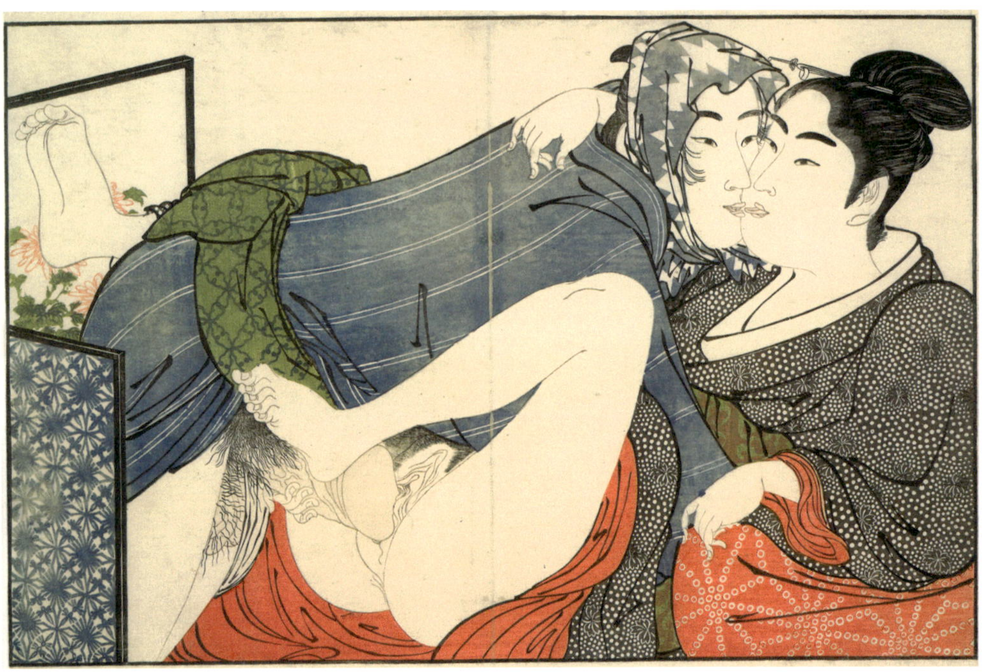

Below: Kitagawa Utamaro
***Poem of the Pillow* (*Utamakura*)**
New Year 1788
Colour woodblock-printed album, each sheet approx. 25.5 × 37 cm

This scene presents a mature woman with her young lover beside a low tea-screen painted with chrysanthemums. He has not stopped to remove his headscarf, but enthusiastically starts making love to her, and she responds eagerly by guiding his penis gently with her foot.

Opposite: Kitagawa Utamaro
***Poem of the Pillow* (*Utamakura*)**
New Year 1788
Colour woodblock-printed album, each sheet approx. 25.5 × 37 cm

A woman leans forward, and with a glance we see she is lowering herself on to her partner's penis, supporting herself with one arm. However, the man is not immediately visible, and it is only on closer examination that we can just glimpse his face through the transparent fabric of her summer robe. From her shaved eyebrows we know she is a widow, and the setting, of a room opening on to a bamboo veranda, with *sake* ewer, lacquer cups and porcelain bowl, suggests a secret rendezvous in the private room of a restaurant. She, too, modestly covers her face with her sleeve, as if not wishing to be seen by us, the viewers. The delicacy of the transparent fabric and the detail of the pubic hair is proof of the skill of not just the artist, Utamaro, but also the unrecorded block-cutter and printer.

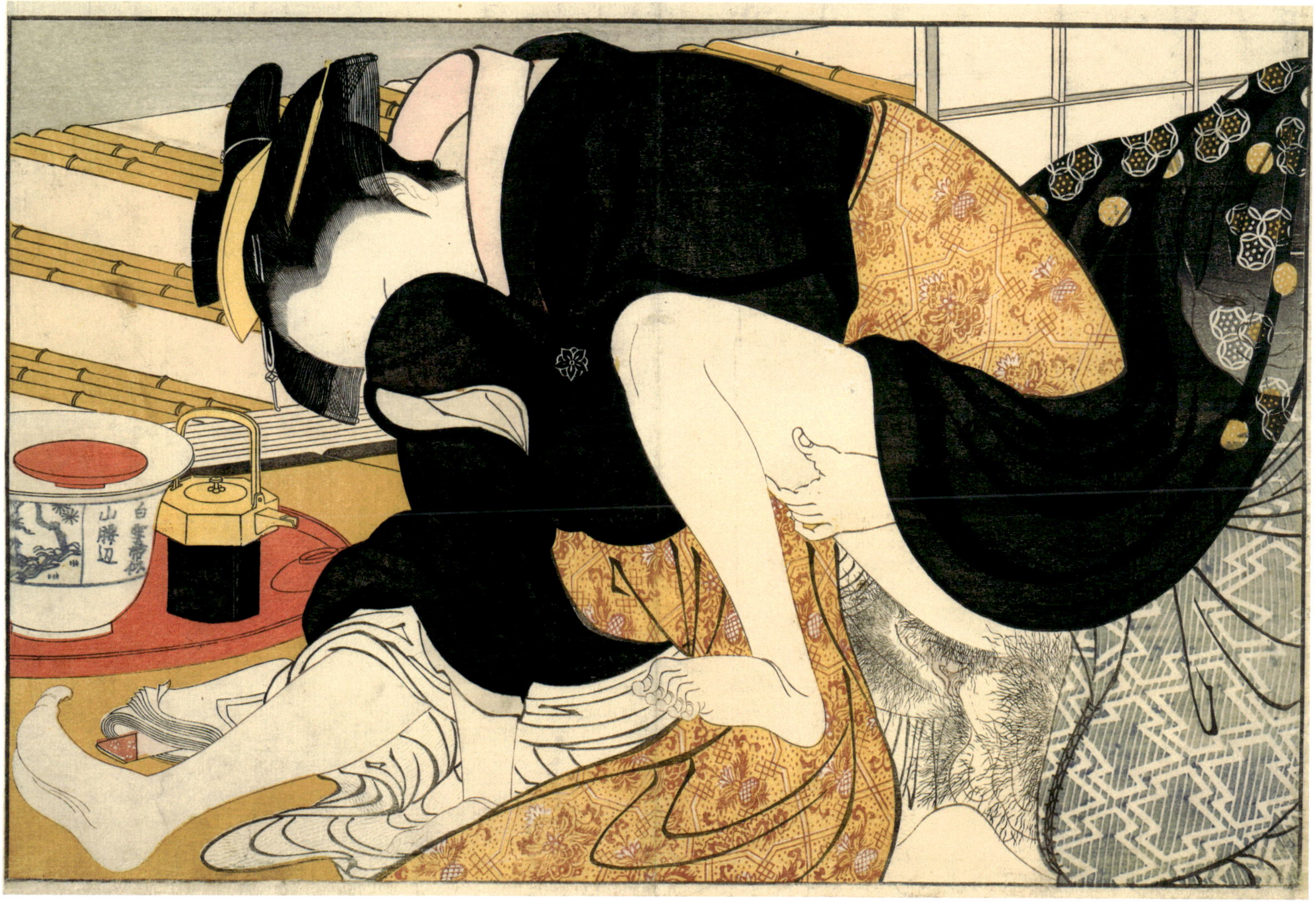

Kitagawa Utamaro
***Poem of the Pillow* (*Utamakura*)**
New Year 1788
Colour woodblock-printed album,
each sheet approx. 25.5 × 37 cm

Perhaps the most famous image from the *Utamakura* album, this design is a wonderful evocation of summer heat and mounting passion. A man and his lover are relaxing on a summer's evening in the upper-floor private room of a tea-house. In the background we see the upper branches of a tree beyond the bamboo blind and veranda railing. Rather than an explicit view, Utamaro presents the shock of white buttocks and thigh against the red fabric of the woman's underskirt. She slips her leg beneath the gauze fabric of the man's jacket, pulling his body closer. With just two fingers she lightly brings his face towards hers for a kiss, and though their faces are concealed, the man's right eye can just be seen. This is one of only two designs in the album to have text: the calligraphy on the man's fan is a suggestive poem by the comic author Yadoya no Meshimori (Ishikawa Masamochi; 1754–1830): 'Its beak caught firmly / in the clam / The snipe cannot fly away / this autumn evening'. This is a parody of a poem by the revered priest–poet Saigyō (1118–90). To the right a discarded clam-shell echoes the poem's imagery.

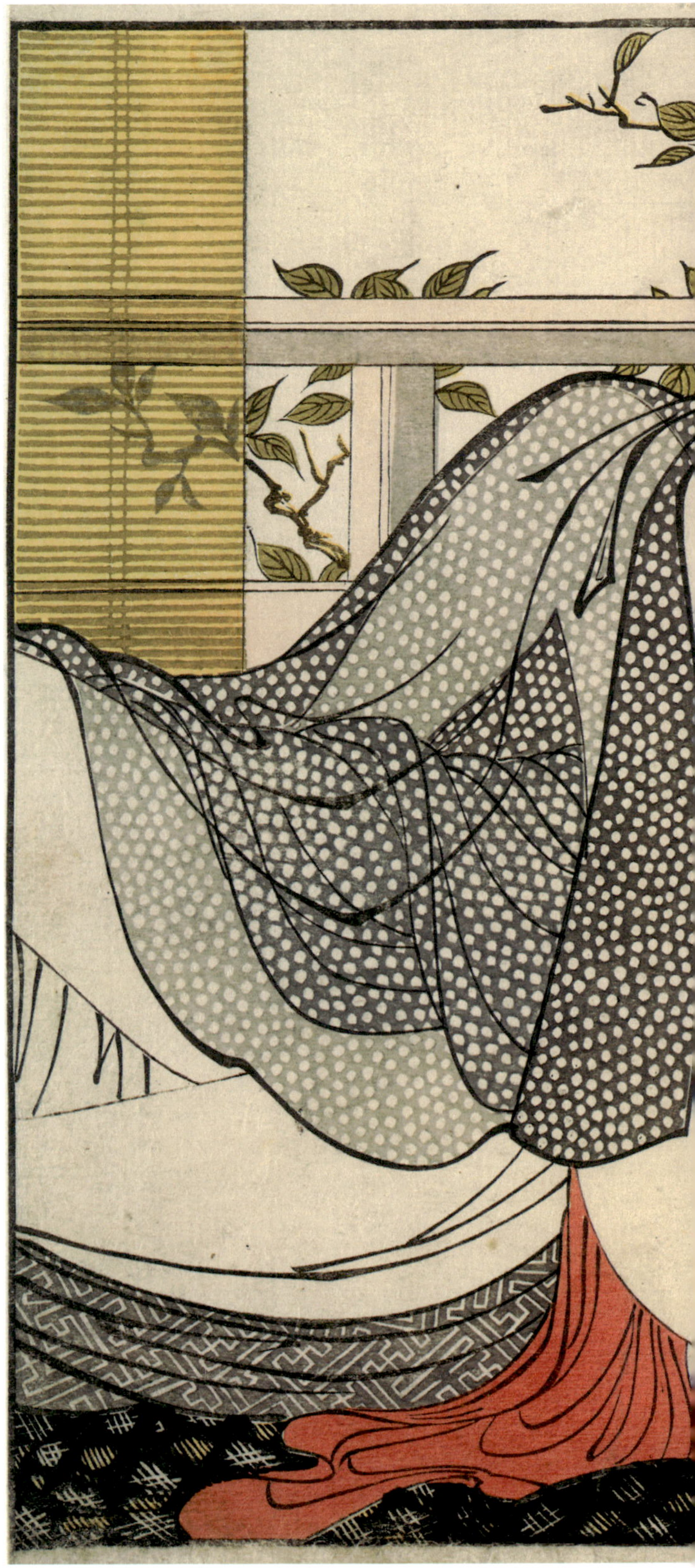

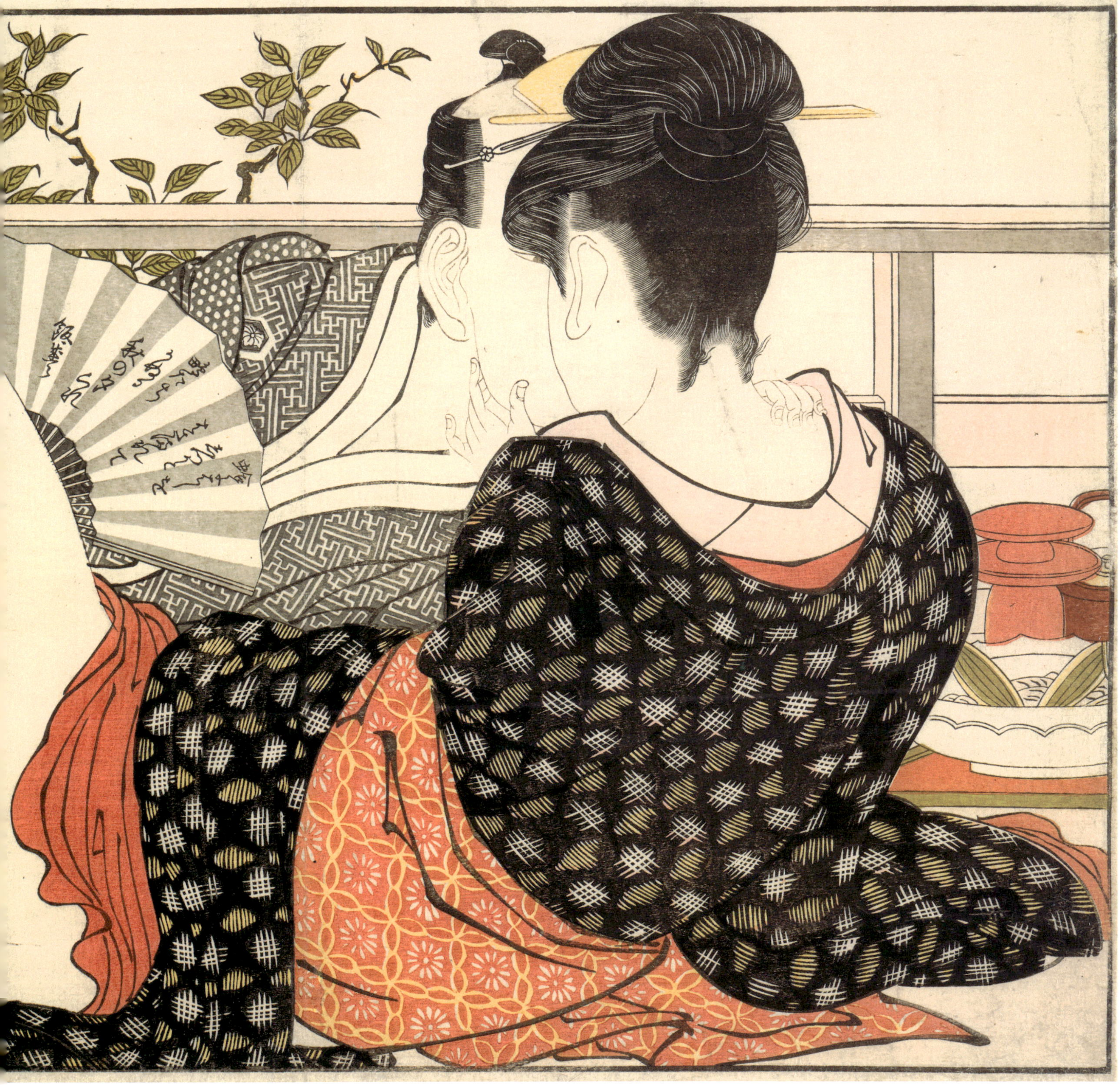

Chōkōsai Eishō
Clean Draft of a Letter
(*Fumi no kiyogaki*)
1793–1801
Colour woodblock-printed album, 25 × 35.9 cm

The success of *Utamakura* was such that it spawned an imitation, in flattery of its achievements. Half of the twelve designs (thirteen in the first edition) of this new work are direct adaptations of compositions in Utamaro's album. Some maintain the original composition almost unchanged, as here, though with a loss of subtlety in both the man's face concealed by the gauze fabric and the woman's shielded by her hand. The standing screen in the bottom right corner is also clearly a device to help fill the picture-plane, and the architectural setting has been largely omitted.

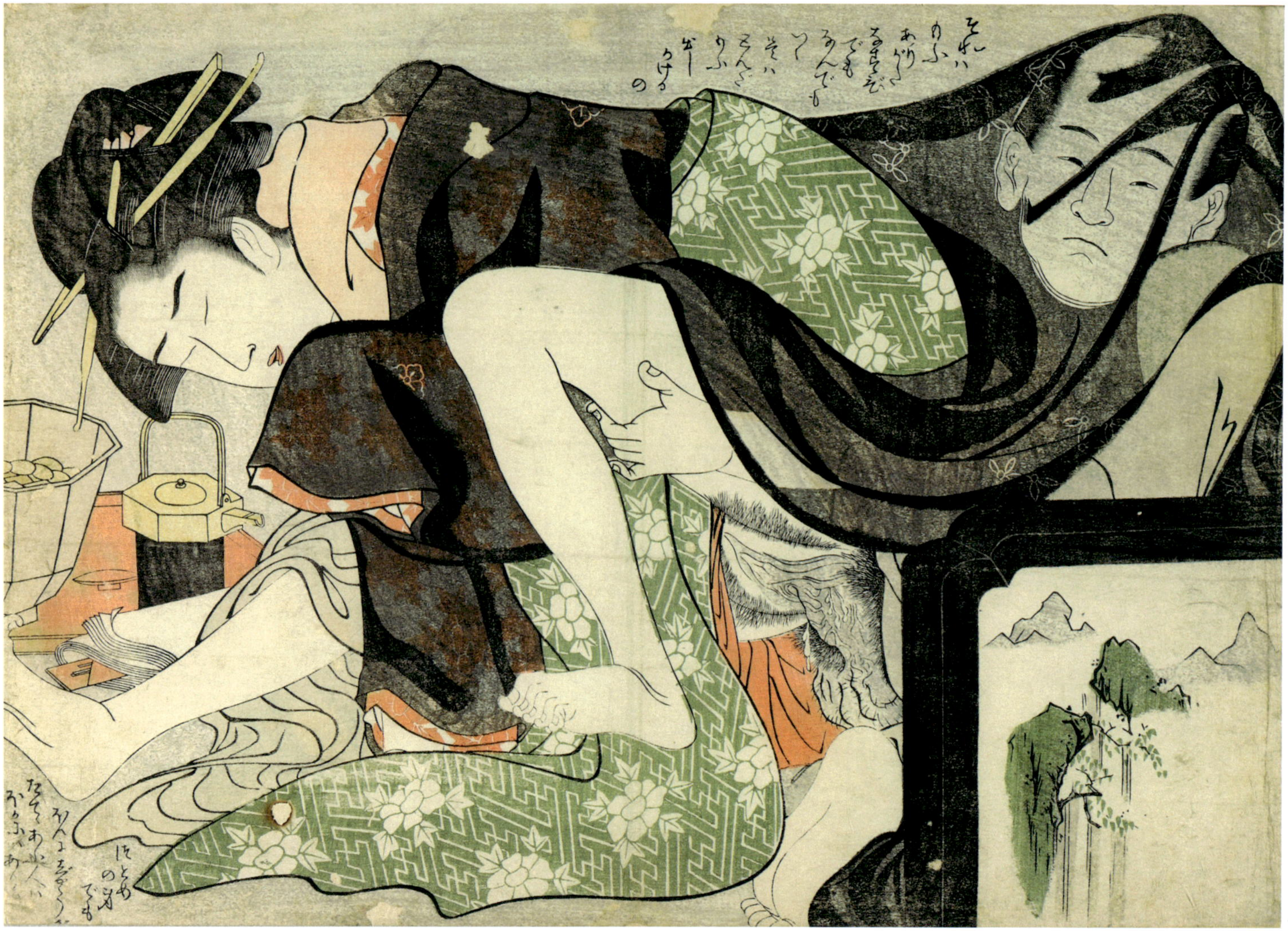

Chōkōsai Eishō
Clean Draft of a Letter
(*Fumi no kiyogaki*)
1793–1801
Colour woodblock-printed album, 25 × 35.9 cm

In other openings of the album, Eishō used the same characters but rearranged the scene, as here, where the Dutchman from the final image in *Utamakura* reappears (with disturbingly long fingernails; see p. 38), but is paired with a courtesan from the Maruyama quarter in Nagasaki. They are squeezed into the space of a Western-style window-frame, the curtain drawn aside. To the right incense burns on a stand, and on the packet beneath can be read part of the name of an aphrodisiac fragrance sold by the firm Yotsumeya, which specialized in aids for sexual enjoyment. It is even possible that the shop helped finance production of this album.[7] It is in the relatively coarser description of the foreigner's facial hair that Eishō's lesser skills of draughtsmanship are most apparent, in contrast to Utamaro. The careful shading of the skin tones seen in the original has also been simplified to a uniform pale brown.

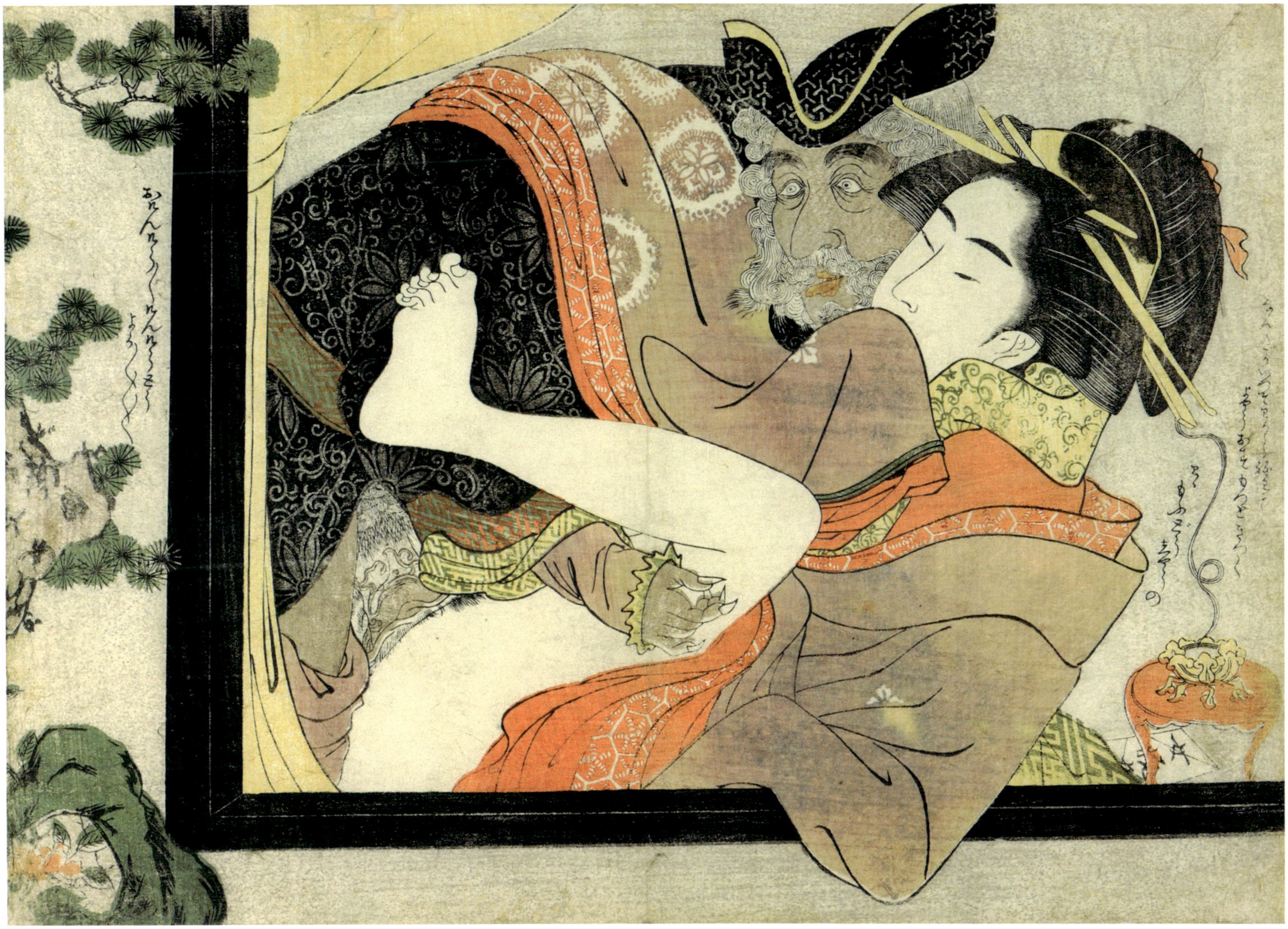

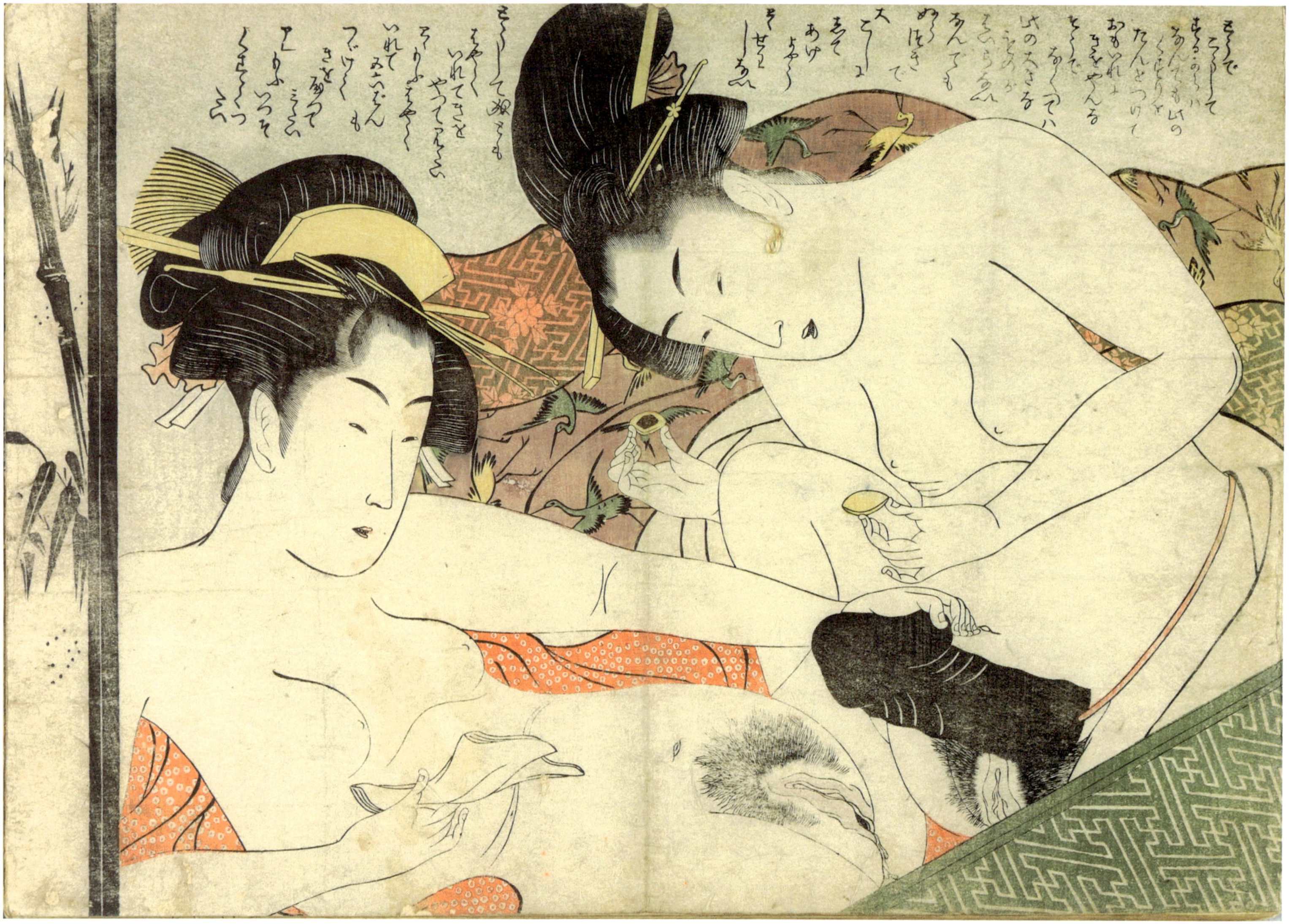

Chōkōsai Eishō
***Clean Draft of a Letter* (*Fumi no kiyogaki*)**
1793–1801
Colour woodblock-printed album,
25 × 35.9 cm

Two of the new compositions by Eishō in the album lack male figures altogether. Here, two women are naked beneath bedcovers: one has a large dildo made of horn tied around her waist and holds a small phial of lubricant to prepare her partner, who guides the dildo and holds tissues ready.

the author and poet Tōrai Sanna (1744–1810), and the calligraphy was possibly brushed by Akera Kankō (1736–98). After twelve erotic scenes, the album closes with two playful texts. It is thought that it was published by Tsutaya Jūzaburō (1750–97), a figure who was crucial in Utamaro's commercial success, and this identity is hinted at by the ivy-leaf crest on the man's robe in the design on pp. 108–9. This was one of several deluxe albums issued by Tsutaya containing Utamaro's designs, the others being anthologies of 'crazy verses' (*kyōka*) with illustrations of mainly natural motifs.

The *Poem of the Pillow* appeared at exactly the same time as *Picture-book: Haikai Album of the Cuckoo* by Shunshō, who was a generation older than Utamaro, but the contrast in compositional approaches is striking. Whereas Shunshō draws back from the lovers, setting them within a broad space, Utamaro zooms in, framing them from low angles. On *ōban*-sized sheets, the lovers seem larger than life, in one design even bursting beyond the confines of the frame. As with the other Tenmei-era erotic masterpieces, soft fabrics flow and drape, revealing elegant naked limbs beneath. These textiles are described with thick calligraphic lines which swirl and hook back on themselves, contrasting with the delicate outlines of the figures. Rather than the customary black, the lines of the figures are printed in a reddish-brown, providing a warm tone suitable to the description of soft flesh.

Kansei Reforms

After the cultural blossoming seen in the Tenmei era, a change of regime brought a new wave of reforms from 1787 to 1793, named after the Kansei era (1789–1801) during which they were introduced. A series of natural disasters – among them floods, poor harvests and famines (leading to rice riots), several volcanic eruptions and an earthquake, as well as a recession – prompted the new government to attempt to stabilize the economy and bring consumption under control. The reforms were instigated by Matsudaira Sadanobu (1758–1829), from 1787 Senior Councillor and from the following year regent for the fifteen-year-old shogun (until 1793, when the shogun reached majority). A highly cultivated individual, Sadanobu also wished to reverse the liberal excesses of the previous administration, and to bring the *daimyō* and samurai back to a proper understanding and expression of their position within society. For him, the mingling of the classes and the samurai's enthusiastic pursuit of floating-world pleasures posed a threat to the stability of the realm, so he exhorted them to return to the pursuit of literary and martial arts (*bunbu*). The reforms were extended to publishing in the fifth month of 1790, with instructions basically reiterating those of seventy years earlier: publishers were to limit their output to serious, edifying works, contemporary events must not be portrayed, erotica were not allowed, and all books and prints must bear the names of all producers involved. Once again, the publishers' own representatives were to be responsible for enforcement. When Tsutaya Jūzaburō flaunted these regulations in 1791 by continuing to publish satirical writings, he was penalized financially, with half his assets confiscated. The author, Santō Kyōden, literally had his hands tied when he was placed in manacles under house arrest for a period of fifty days.

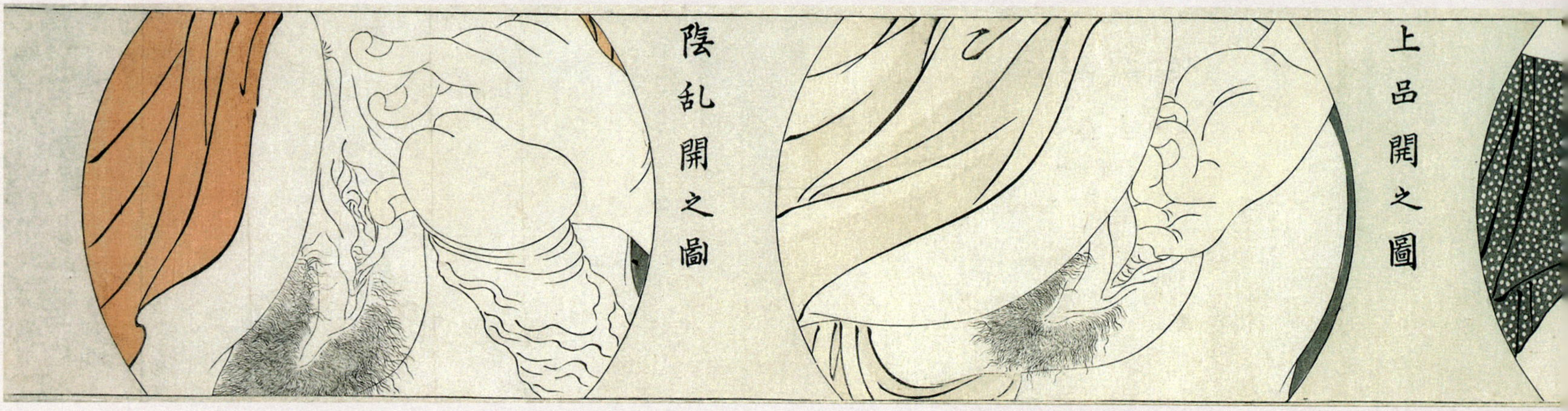
上品開之圖
陰乱開之圖

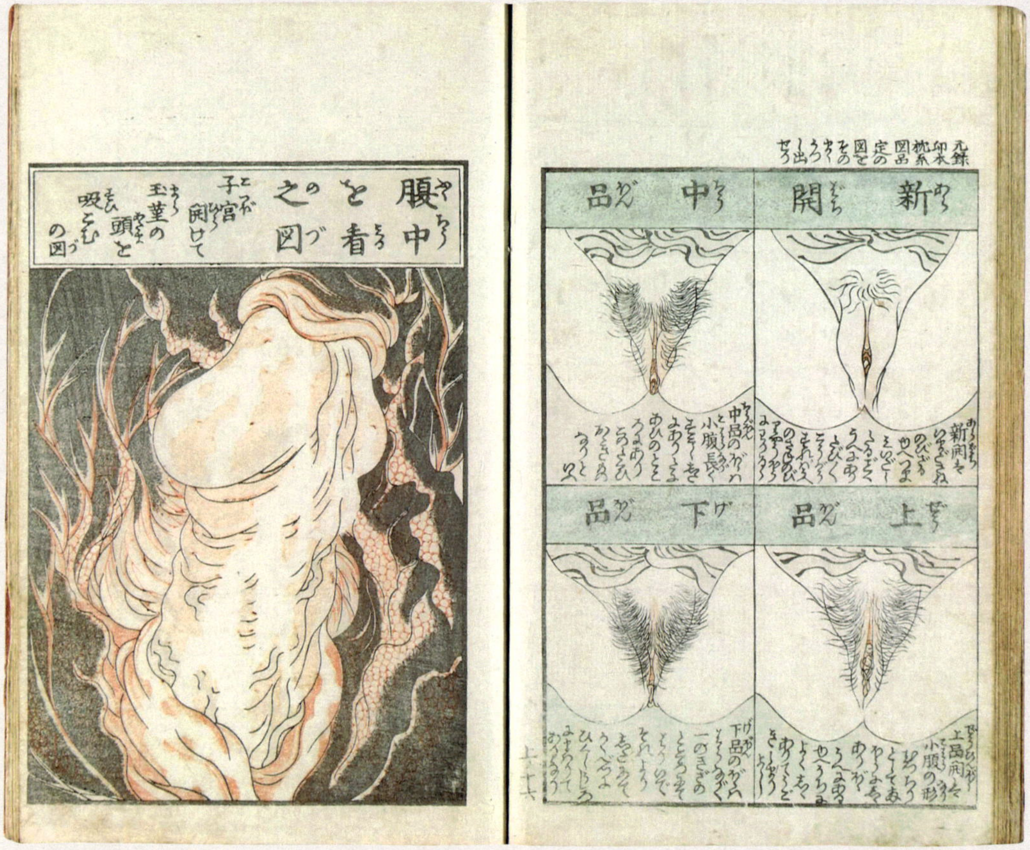
新開
中品
上品
下品

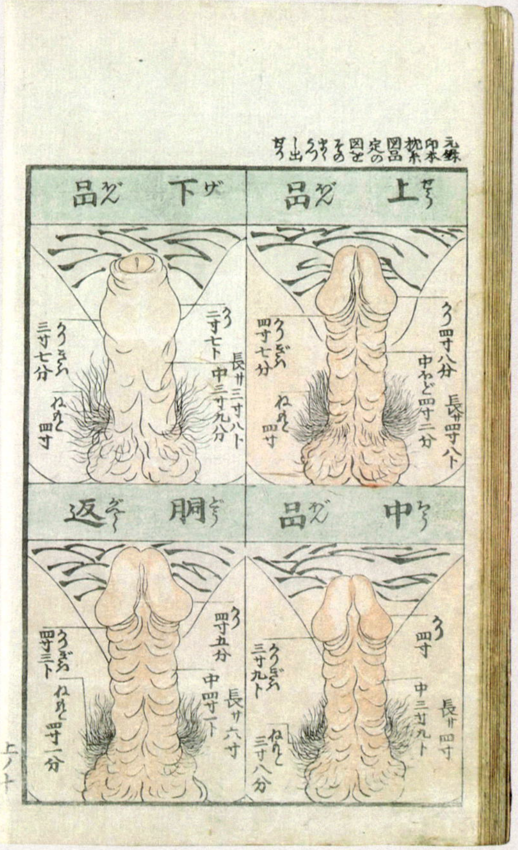
上品
下品
中品

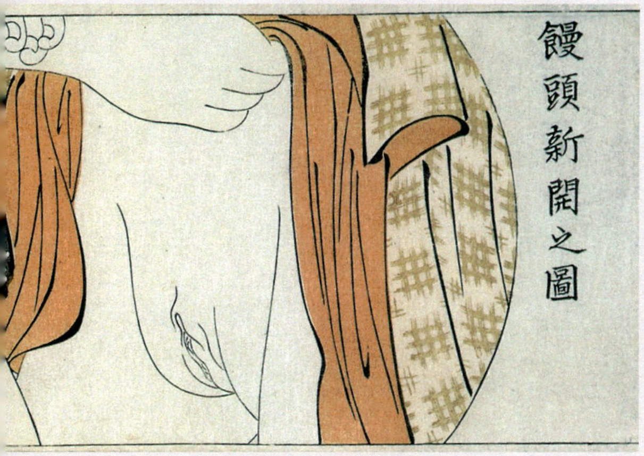

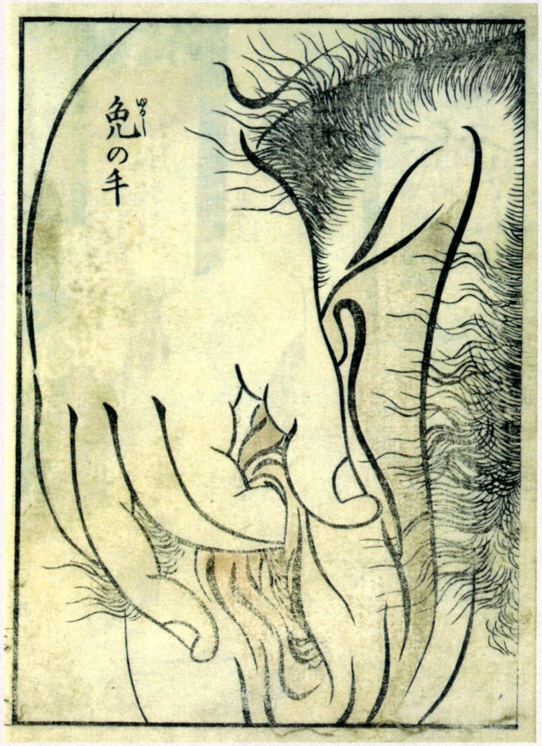

Anatomical comparisons

Genital close-ups (*ōtsubi-e*) were a humorous adaptation of the popular genre of bust-portraits of beautiful women (*ōkubi-e*). As a corollary to the opening portraits in the erotic book *Picture-book: The Laughing Drinker*, Utamaro closed each volume with a 'pussy portrait', presenting an intimate view of a woman's vagina, depicted with as much care and visual fidelity as the facial portraits. Here we see the woman's fingers beginning stimulation, with the title 'The hand of permission'.

Comparisons of the various types of genitalia of both men and women were a frequent feature in erotic books and albums, following the tendency to categorize many aspects of the natural world. Perhaps the most artistic example is the final image of Torii Kiyonaga's *Scroll for the Sleeve* of 1785, presenting a comparison of three types of vulva. Each is depicted within a circular frame, perhaps as if seen in a hand-mirror, and the labels translate roughly as 'Initiated Pussy', 'Quality Pussy' and 'Wanton Pussy'. As in the series as a whole, here too there is a temporal progression: in the first picture (top right) the woman is standing and a hand lifts her underskirt, in the second and third images the woman is bending over, and the hand explores inside her and then prepares for the penis to enter.

In *Stories from the Bedroom: The Pillow Library* (*Keichū kibun makura bunko*) by Keisai Eisen, published in 1822, there is a page comparing four grades of penis: the Top-, Medium-, and Low-grade, and the 'Stomach-Thwacker' (*Dōgaeshi*), with precise measurements of each section. A few pages later comes the corresponding comparison of vulvas, with Newly Opened, Top-, Middle- and Low-grades, with descriptive text beneath.

The next page indicates how contemporary scientific studies were being taken up and parodied in *shunga*. It illustrates what happens as the penis enters the vagina and hits the cervix. The accompanying text quotes the *New Book of Anatomy* (*Kaitai shinsho*), a Japanese version of European scientific studies imported into Nagasaki, translated by Sugita Genpaku (1733–1817) and others, and published in 1774. The following two pages then show several views of first the fingers and then the penis penetrating as far as the uterus, and even tickling the foetus growing there.

Top: Torii Kiyonaga
***Scroll for the Sleeve* (*Sode no maki*)**
1785
Colour woodblock print, approx. 12.6 × 67.4 cm

Below left and centre: Keisai Eisen
***Stories from the Bedroom: The Pillow Library* (*Keichū kibun makura bunko*)**
1822
Colour woodblock-printed book, 22 × 14.7 cm (covers). Private collection, Ritsumeikan ARC Database

Below right: Kitagawa Utamaro
***Picture-book: The Laughing Drinker* (*Ehon warai jōgo*)**
c. 1803
Colour woodblock-printed book, 20.7 × 15 cm (covers)

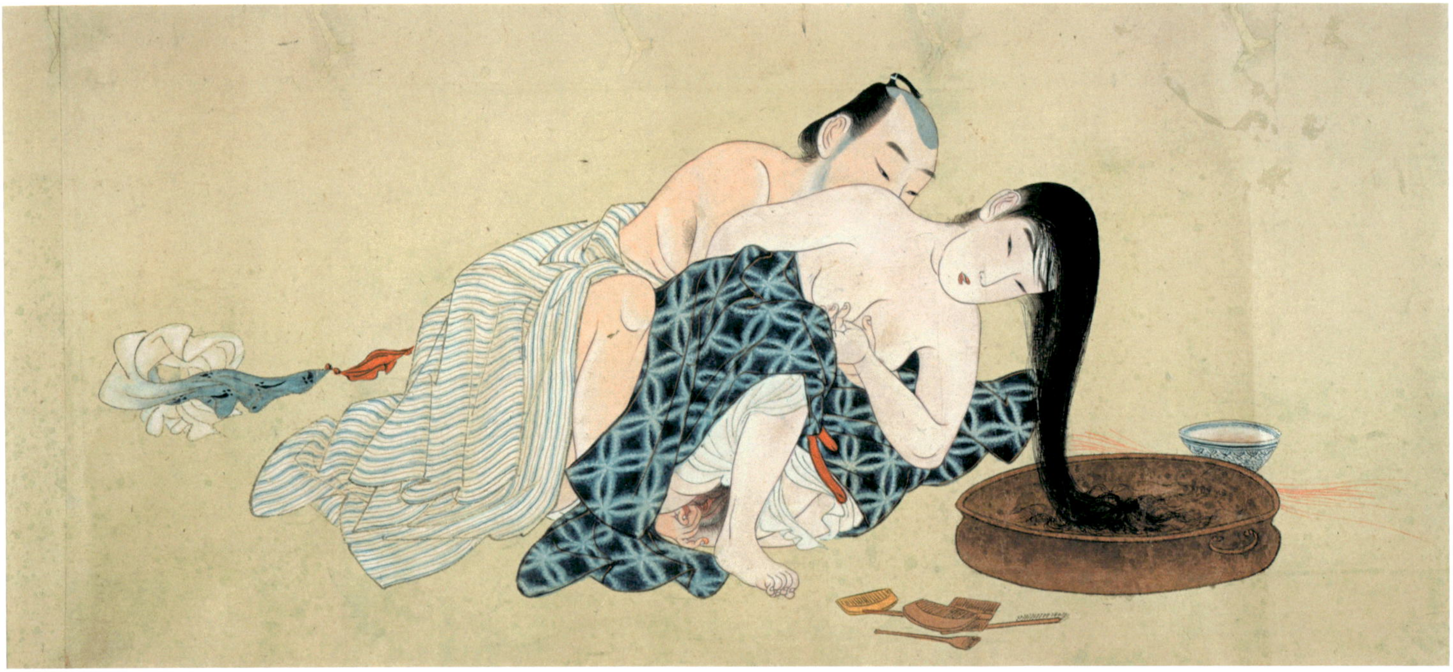

Shunga paintings

Though printed erotica was available at an affordable price to purchase or borrow, the tradition of expensive, deluxe handscroll paintings continued, and these generally contained a mixture of explicit and more contextual scenes. A fine handscroll in the British Museum's collection is unsigned but has been attributed to Katsukawa Shun'ei (1762–1819) on the basis of the sharp, dry brushwork, and of certain facial characteristics of the women (especially their eyelashes and plump chins).[8] Judging from the similarity to his teacher Shunshō's style, it probably dates from the years immediately after the latter's death in 1792. Like other artists of the Katsukawa lineage, Shun'ei was known primarily for actor prints and theatrical scenes, but in his pictures of beauties he strove to convey their emotional and psychological states to an unusual degree. The scroll contains ten images, apparently remounted in a different order at some point (it probably originally had the customary twelve). The scenes alternate between elegant and grotesque, among them a wealthy patron reclining on luxurious bedding with a sleepy courtesan leaning on his knee; an old couple engaging in oral sex; a *geisha* dozing after reading a love letter, followed by the violent content of her dream in which a couple make love one last time before they commit suicide together; and a man making love to his wife as she suckles their baby.

Katsukawa Shun'ei
Ten erotic scenes (detail)
1792–5
Handscroll painting, ink and colour on paper, H: 28 cm

In this scene from the handscroll, aroused by the sight of his young wife disrobing, a husband steals up as she washes her hair in a tub, and we catch them just as he begins to fondle her. Though his face is almost hidden behind her body, his intently narrowed eyes convey the force of his passion.

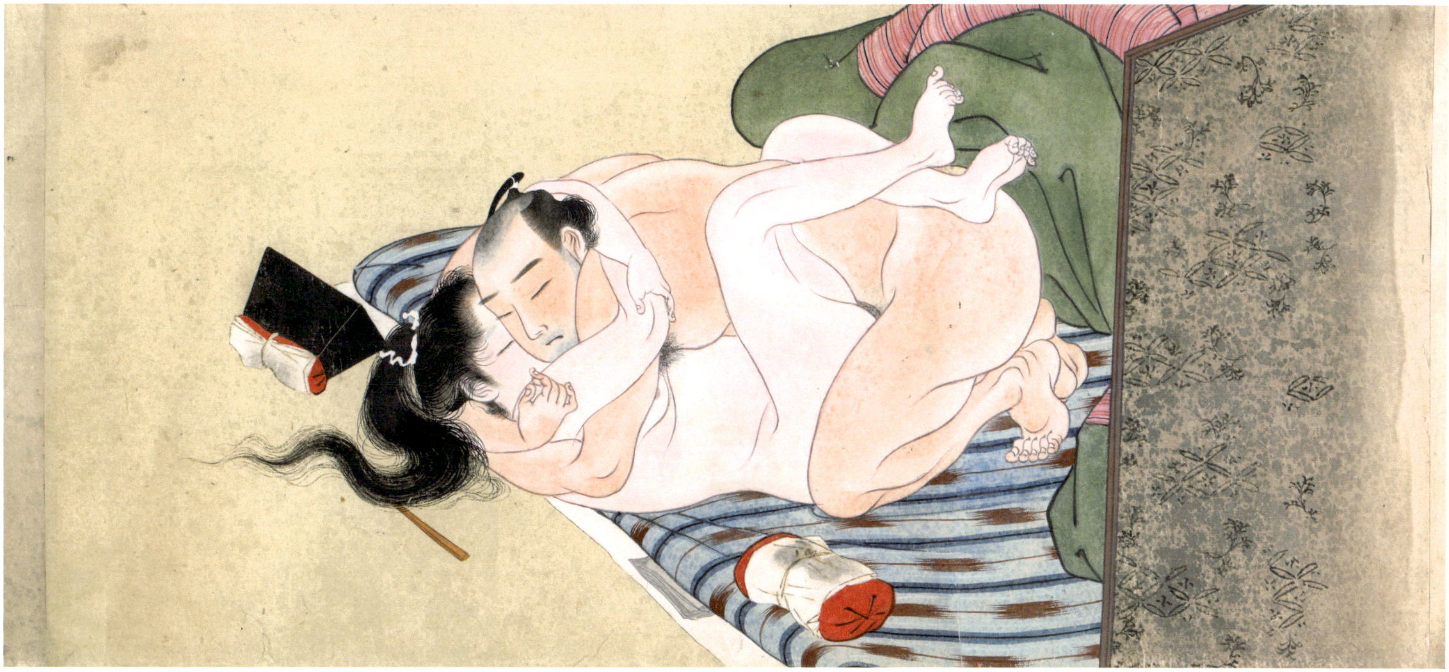

Katsukawa Shun'ei
Ten erotic scenes (detail)
1792–5
Handscroll painting, ink and colour on paper, H: 28 cm

In another scene from the scroll, the viewer peers past a folding screen into the bedroom of a married couple. As the man enters his wife, she locks him in a tight embrace with all four limbs. Their faces are pressed so close together that her face is hidden but for one eye. Shun'ei suggests the force of their exertions by the bodies gradually edging leftwards off the bedding, the toppled headrest, and the man's feet straining as he pushes.

Kitagawa Utamaro

Kitagawa Utamaro (d. 1806) was the foremost *ukiyo-e* artist of his generation, and was one of the Japanese artists most highly appreciated in Europe in the late nineteenth century. Born in Edo, he started his apprenticeship at a young age with Toriyama Sekien (1712–88), a Kano-trained painter known also for his book illustrations. Utamaro began his career illustrating popular novels, progressing to masterful designs based on the natural world made for the publisher Tsutaya Jūzaburō. However, he established his towering reputation principally in the genre of 'pictures of beauties' (*bijinga*), taking as his subjects renowned courtesans of Yoshiwara pleasure quarter. So closely did Utamaro become associated with this subject matter that he later came to be known as the 'painter of the Green Houses', a Ming-dynasty Chinese slang term for brothels. However, Utamaro also portrayed ordinary townswomen, and even when showing his subjects engaged in everyday tasks, he achieved powerful and seductive designs. His full-length figures were tall and elegant, with delicate features, but it was in bust-portraits (*ōkubi-e*) that he excelled, creating remarkable works imbued with psychological insight. Utamaro was prolific in the realm of erotica, producing several albums and no fewer than thirty-four books.[9] He produced three masterpieces of colour woodblock-printed erotic albums, all of which are represented in the British Museum's collection.

The *Poem of the Pillow* is remarkable for its voluptuous figures, bold experimentation with composition, and diverse range of sexual experience. In Utamaro's subsequent albums, appearing more than a decade later, however, we find quite a different approach: the viewpoint is drawn back, the figures are on a more naturalistic scale, the scenes feature a more conventional range of characters and situations, and the designs include dialogue helping to set the scene.

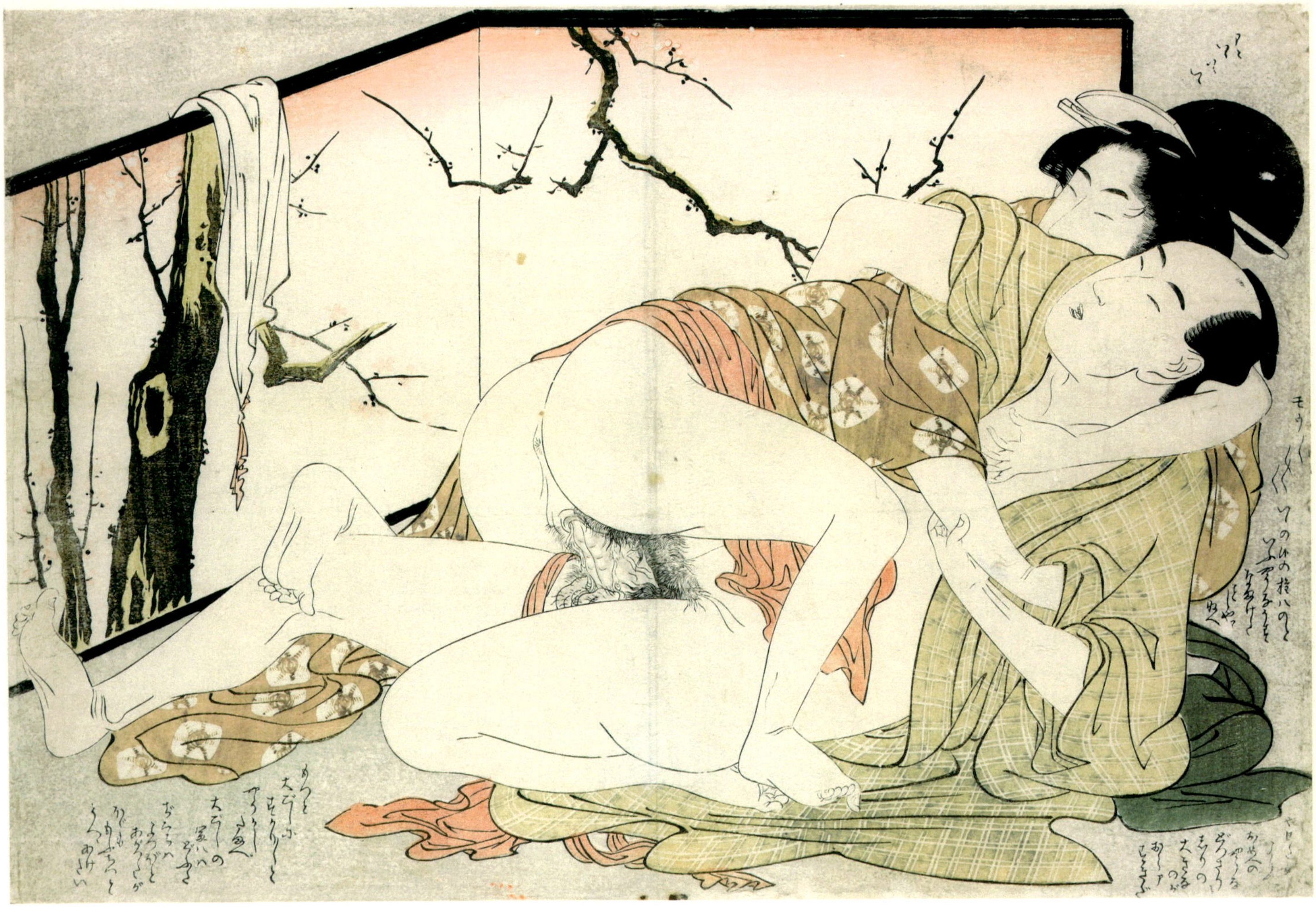

After about 1790, Kiyonaga and Shunshō apparently stopped producing print designs, erotic or otherwise. The second of Utamaro's great folding albums of erotic prints in the large *ōban* size, *Unravelling the Threads of Desire* (*Negai no itoguchi*), did not appear until 1799, when the censorship of the Kansei Reforms was on the wane. The preface was written by one 'Master of the Hostelry of Debauchery' (Intōtei no aruji), whose identity is otherwise unknown. The preface date indicates that, as was the case with most books, the deluxe album was published at New Year 1799.[10] The first edition contained an innocent frontispiece followed by the customary twelve erotic images and the volume closed with three erotic anecdotes. Less boldly experimental in its compositions than *Poem of the Pillow* of eleven years earlier, the lovers are drawn with more delicate features, and with a fine, fluid line. In the dialogue women openly express their sexual desires and take an active role in love-making. In the late nineteenth and early twentieth centuries, deluxe albums of this sort were often broken up by dealers to be sold individually, and the British Museum has only two sheets from the original sequence.

Utamaro's third erotic masterpiece was *Picture-book: Embracing Komachi* (*Ehon Komachi-biki*). References to recent events within the dialogues (an actor's name-change and a display of

Kitagawa Utamaro
Unravelling the Threads of Desire
(*Negai no itoguchi*)
1799
Colour woodblock-printed album,
25.5 × 38 cm

A couple make love in front of a low tea-screen, decorated with a plum tree in blossom, a motif that alludes to sexual pleasure. The towel thrown over the screen suggests that they have just returned from the bath. Their position seems rather uncomfortable, and he reaches around to hold her up as she lowers herself on to him. In the dialogue, he says that he prefers her full figure to skinny women, and she moans contentedly in response.

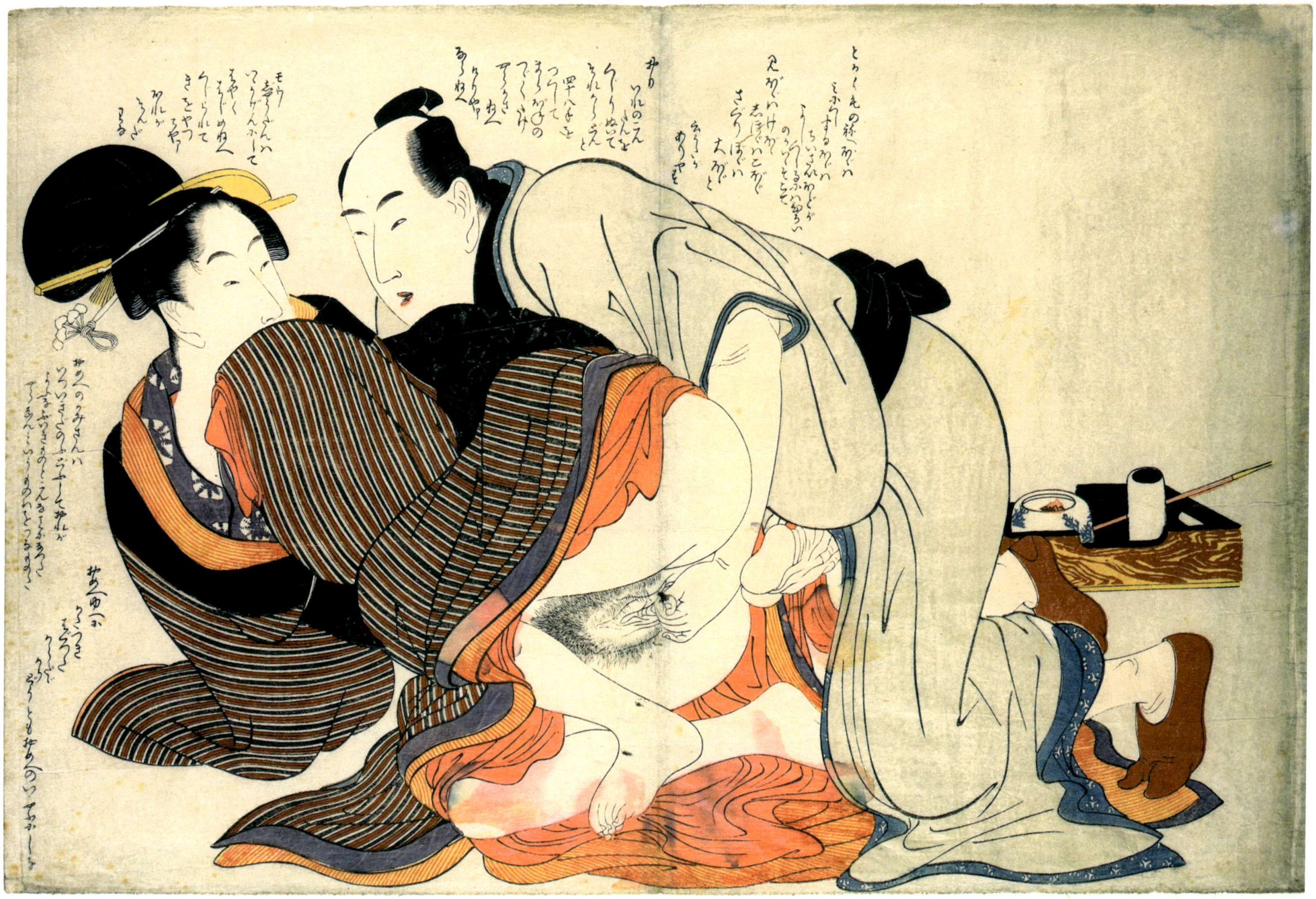

Kitagawa Utamaro
Unravelling the Threads of Desire
(*Negai no itoguchi*)
1799
Colour woodblock-printed album,
25.5 × 38 cm

Here a widow secretly meets her married lover. The importance of the eyes in Utamaro's art is clearly shown: the woman twists round to catch the man's gaze as he uses his fingers to stimulate her. She lifts her hand to her mouth in surprise at his bold move and raises her eyebrows in anticipation. He tries to engage in some humorous banter about her 'pussy', but she tells him to stop joking and to 'get started quickly'. She wonders aloud what he sees in her when he already has a 'chic wife', although she herself is dressed in a fashionable striped robe.

temple treasures from Kyoto) indicate that Utamaro designed the work in the autumn of 1801, ready for publication at the following New Year. After a frontispiece image of a young woman eagerly embracing her young male companion, there are twelve designs of couples making love in a wide variety of positions. Utamaro produced a relatively large number of depictions of sexual intercourse with the woman positioned on top; in this album these make up over half the designs. As with other albums, the order of plates varies according to the edition; and an early printing includes one variant design. The British Museum has nine plates of the full thirteen.

Alongside these three acknowledged masterpieces in the album format, Utamaro continued his designs for erotic illustrated books. Though the book is unsigned, reference to 'Utamaru' (*sic*) in the dialogue and the bold cropping of the figures indicate Utamaro's hand behind *Glossy Book: Dew on the Chrysanthemum* (*Ehon kiku no tsuyu*). As with *Poem of the Pillow*, the viewer has a sense of being up close to each couple portrayed. The first volume begins with a picture of a robe slung over a standing screen (bearing a painting of a pair of mandarin ducks, a symbol of marital fidelity); there follow eight illustrations, the last of which stretches over three pages, emulating

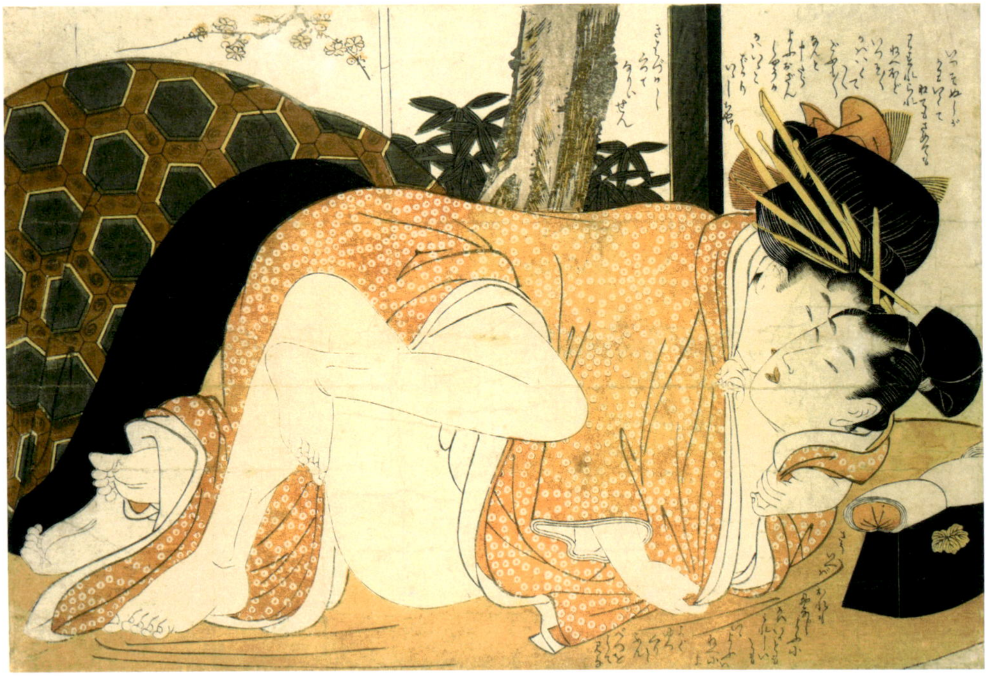

Kitagawa Utamaro
***Picture-book: Embracing Komachi* (*Ehon Komachi-biki*)**
1801
Colour woodblock-printed album,
25.2 × 37.8 cm

It is winter and the couple have come out from inside the quilted brazier. The courtesan climbs on top of her naked lover, pressing her face close against his and enfolding him in her robe. The man seems a little startled by her advances, and clings to the edge of her robe with one hand. Decorated with the popular tie-dyed 'hemp-flower' (*asa-no-hana*) pattern, the mass of the richly coloured robe emphasizes the passionate union of the bodies that it conceals.

a handscroll painting and making the figures appear monumental. Although it was published in three volumes, no complete set is known. The preface mentions the date Tenmei 6 (1786), but it has been argued convincingly that the style suggests a date of 1794 or 1795. The spurious date was probably included in order to circumvent the renewed ban on erotica which had been issued in 1790 as part of the Kansei Reforms.[11]

Based on a reference by one of the characters to a display of shrine treasures, we can surmise that *Glossy Book: Plum of the Bedchamber* (*Ehon toko no ume*) was published at New Year 1800. The artist is named in the preface cryptically as 'Mudamara' (Waste Prick), who also appears in the erotic story concluding the book. The preface is signed Sukitei, a pseudonym of the comic writer Shikitei Sanba (1776–1822), and other acquaintances of Utamaro are mentioned in the dialogue. The book is of medium size and contains the customary twelve scenes, using a so-called 'red-avoiding' (*beni-girai*) colour scheme featuring purple, green and blue.[12]

Picture-book: The Laughing Drinker (*Ehon warai jōgo*) was probably Utamaro's last erotic book, published at New Year 1803. The title refers to someone who invariably becomes jovial when inebriated. The preface purports to be a letter from the artist's wife, addressed in his absence to the publisher. Written in a suitably feminine calligraphic style, she explains that her husband 'Uta' has gone off on a pilgrimage, and so she has been so bold as to carry out the colouring of his designs. 'There is no better conjunction of the male and female principles', she writes, than such a connubial artistic collaboration. Each of the three volumes opens with a single-page bust-portrait (*ōkubi-e*) of a courtesan, which, after seven double-page pictures, is mirrored by a close-up 'portrait' of a woman's genitalia (*ōtsubi-e*; see p. 115). The volumes close with an erotic short story, unrelated to the preceding pictures. The main images are enlivened with raunchy, explicit dialogue, revealing the relationships between the characters, who for the most

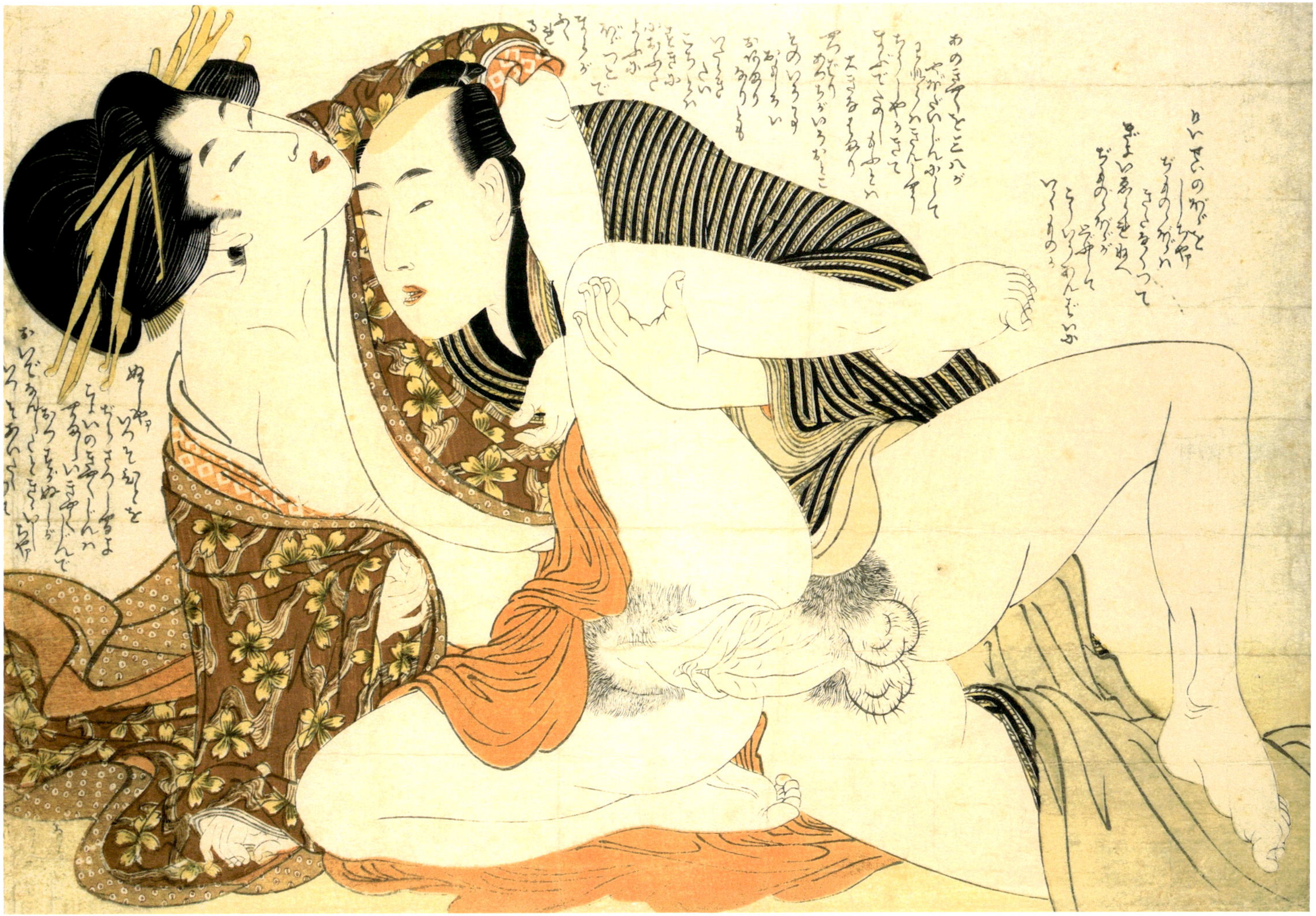

Kitagawa Utamaro
Picture-book: Embracing Komachi
(*Ehon Komachi-biki*)
1801
Colour woodblock-printed album,
25.2 × 37.8 cm

A high-ranking courtesan enjoys a rendezvous with her secret lover, who lifts up her leg to enter her from behind. In the conversation she warns him that she must soon return to the wealthy patron awaiting her in the salon.

Kitagawa Utamaro
Picture-book: Embracing Komachi
(*Ehon Komachi-biki*)
1801
Colour woodblock-printed album,
25.2 × 37.8 cm

This acrobatic position is known as 'clinging to the tower'. The woman is perched precariously on top of her lover, but, one would assume, is unable to achieve much movement. It is summer: a round fan lies on the ground and a bamboo blind is hanging at the left. The man comments on how good sex feels in summer, when a breeze cools their bodies.

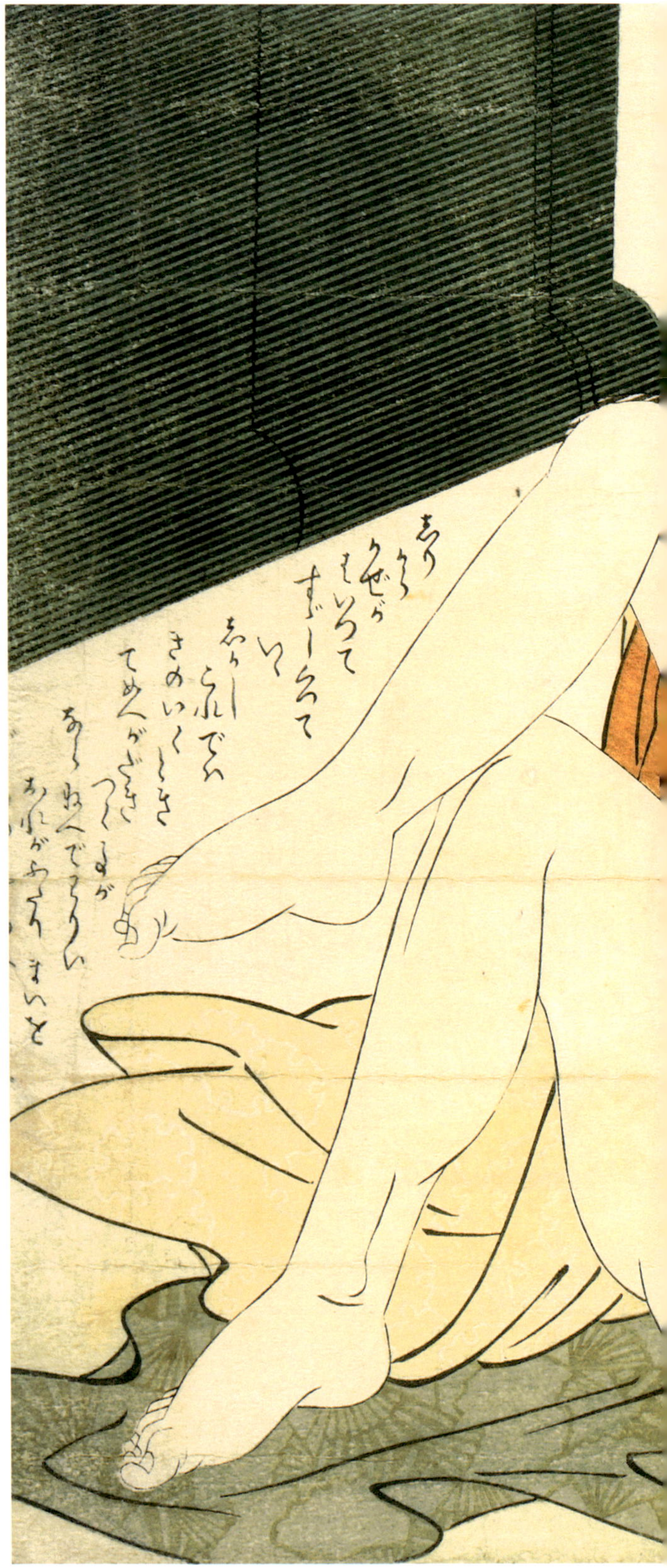

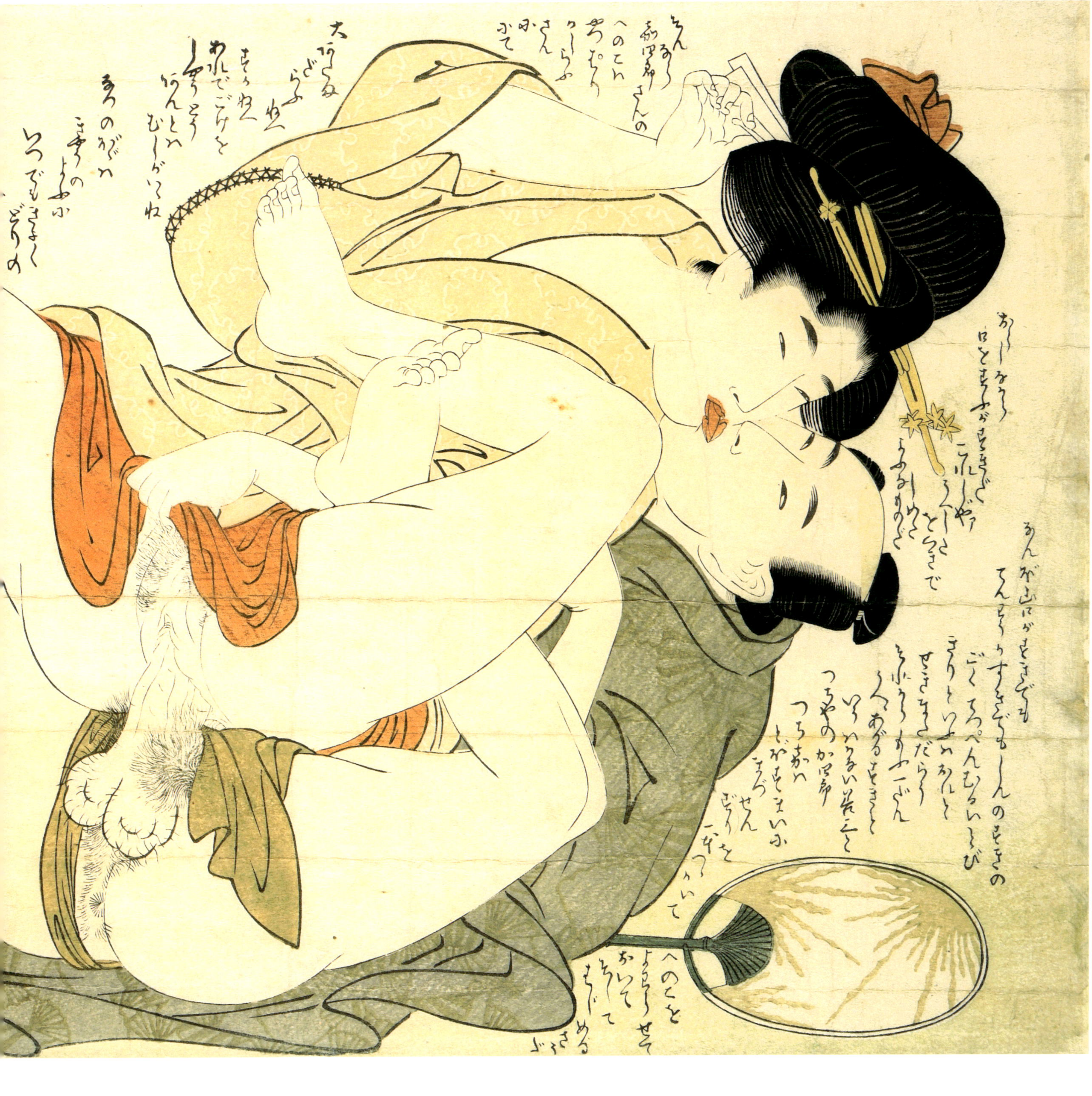

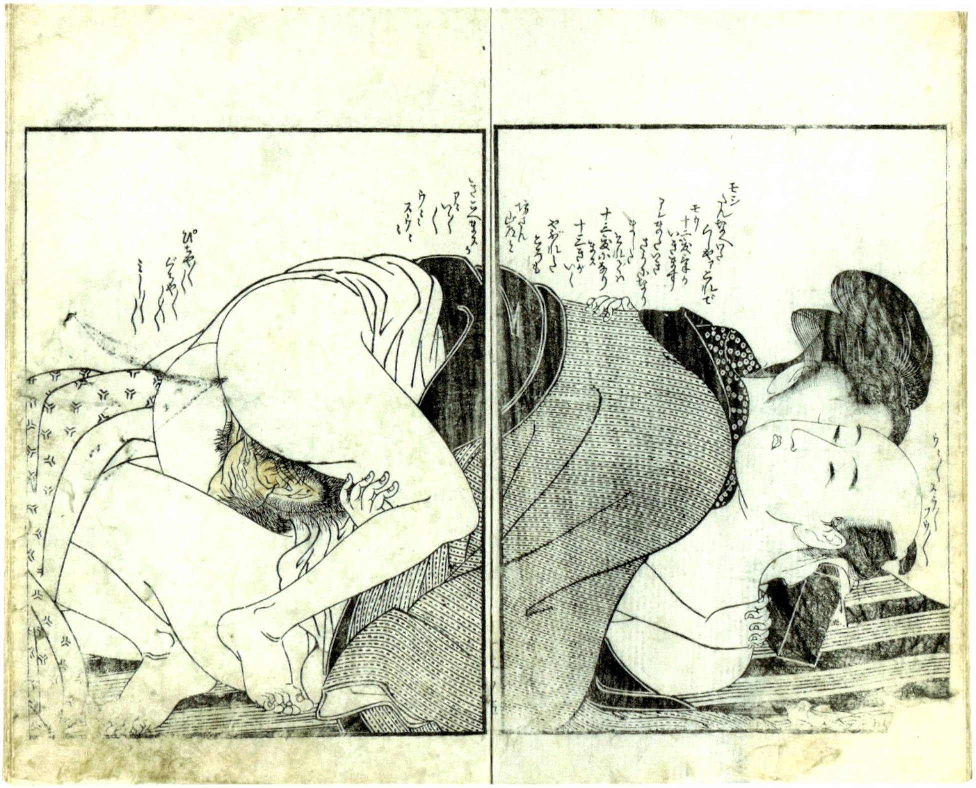

Kitagawa Utamaro
***Glossy Book: Dew on the Chrysanthemum* (*Ehon kiku no tsuyu*)**
1790s
Woodblock-printed book,
21.8 × 15.1 cm (covers)

Scenes of women on top during sex are relatively frequent in Utamaro's erotic imagery, as in the fourth image of this work, the only illustration in which both figures are lying down. The woman has straddled her lover, causing the headrest to tip back, and she clasps her hands tightly around his shoulder. Though her face is hidden behind his, one closed eye is just visible, and this, together with the man's expression of absorption, gives the image an emotional intensity. The woman comments that this is the thirteenth time they have made love and she will soon become tired. Intimate sound effects on the left augment the picture: 'Pichiya… pichiya… pichiya, guchiya… guchiya… guchiya… guchiya, mishi… mishi… mishi.' In this copy, a previous owner has enhanced the fleshier parts of the composition with hand-colouring.

part are ordinary townspeople. There were two further editions of the book around 1806, printed from recut blocks and of inferior quality, indicating the work's commercial success.[13] The book in the British Museum formerly belonged to the artist John Singer Sargent.

In 1804 Utamaro fell foul of the censorship laws for a number of designs that presented – and named – historical figures in what were considered frivolous situations. One triptych print was based on the popular historical novel *Picture-book: Record of the Regent* (*Ehon Taikō ki*), which had been banned because of its admiring portrayal of the great warlord Toyotomi Hideyoshi (1536–98). The Tokugawa were ever vigilant for expressions of support for the long-vanquished Toyotomi clan, whom they had destroyed in military campaigns of 1615. Utamaro's print showed Hideyoshi on a flower-viewing excursion with his concubines and contained cartouches explicitly identifying the characters. For this transgression the artist was arrested and sentenced to three days in jail and fifty days of house arrest in handcuffs.[14] It has been suggested that the traumatic experience caused a deterioration in his work after his release and he produced no more erotic works before his death in 1806.

Kitagawa Utamaro
Glossy Book: Plum of the Bedchamber
(*Ehon toko no ume*)
1800
Colour woodblock-printed book,
18.8 × 12.6 cm (covers)

Above: In a night-time scene beneath heavy bedcovers (with a lantern beside the bed), a young man holds his partner's leg and buttock as he enters her. She whispers to him that they are being too noisy; he looks around anxiously and replies, 'I think Mum has woken up – I can hear her coughing. We must be quiet.' Each design in the book contains lattices or screen-paintings as background props; here we see a screen pasted with paintings of the god of good luck, Hotei, and a lotus pond.

Below: In the last image of the album a couple in a well-appointed bedroom have abandoned their bedding. She uses her foot to brace against his leg as she 'clings to the tower'. The composition is centred on their sex organs, depicted with careful realism, and fluids indicate their climax; both partners have their eyes closed in bliss. Dialogue is scattered around the picture: the woman makes sounds imitating the chants of a festival procession as a float is bounced along; in the bottom left corner are numerous repetition marks for the onomatopoeic sounds of their love-making.

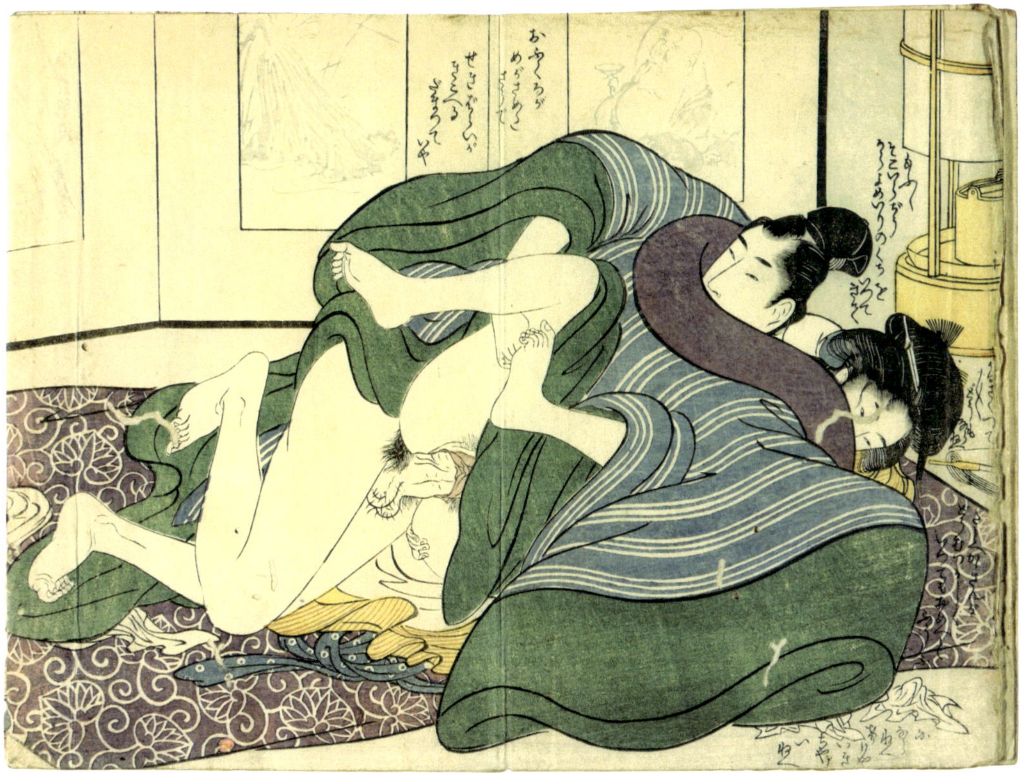

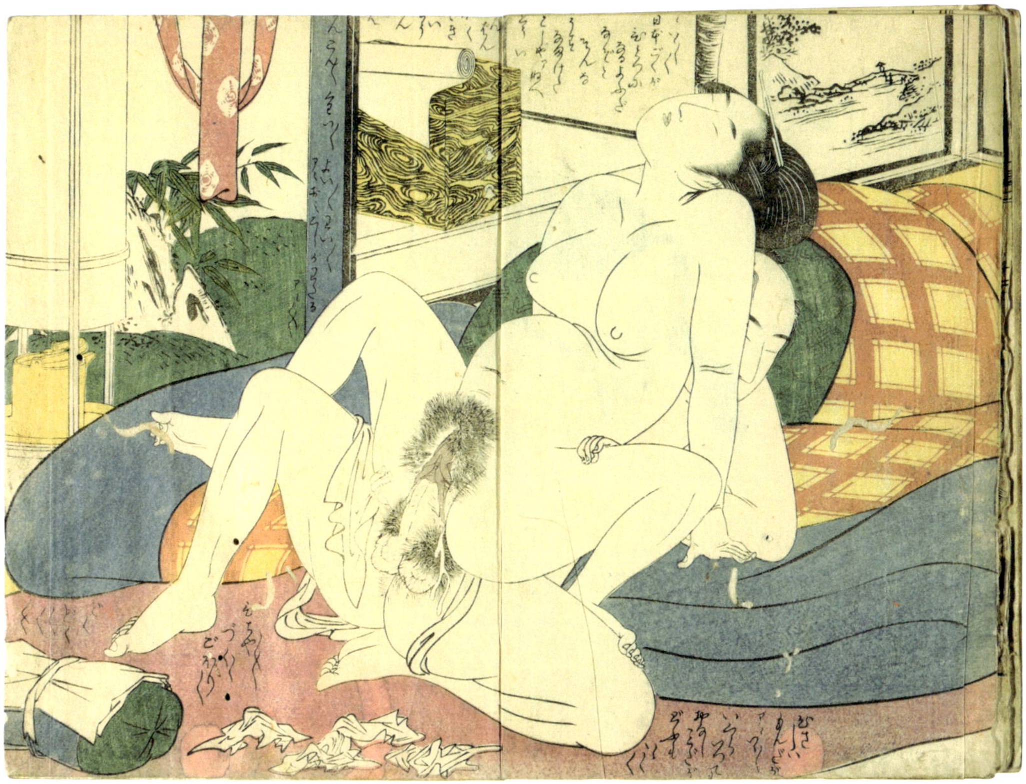

Kitagawa Utamaro
***Picture-book: The Laughing Drinker* (*Ehon warai jōgo*)**
c. 1803
Colour woodblock-printed book, 20.7 × 15 cm (covers)

Left: An image from the first volume shows a passionate couple making love beside the mosquito net. As he pulls her to him, she lifts herself on to one hand, her eyes closed in pleasure. She declares, 'I'm a born nymphomaniac. I'm an attractive woman and have taken on all kinds of cock, but I've never yet been on the receiving end of a whanger like yours.' He replies confidently, 'I suppose your husband's cock is really different from mine. I never forget a woman who's taken my cock in. It's a first-rate piece of equipment, of the very best quality!'[15]

Centre: In volume two we find an energetic – and acrobatic – married couple. The woman explains, 'That's the thing about being married – you have the freedom to do as you please. This way you don't tire so quickly of embracing.'

Right: A picture in the same volume presents a couple making love on a hot summer evening beside a mosquito net and lantern. The overwhelming sensual power of their love-making is conveyed by the woman's head thrown back in ecstasy, her ample breasts and curled toes, the intense absorption of their expressions, and, most crucially, the vivid depiction of the sexual organs and fluids. She cries, 'Ah... ah... wonderful... It's so good there is nothing I can compare it to. All the good things of this world seem to have concentrated in one place.' This opening seems to have elicited an enthusiastic response from a former owner, as evidenced by the stain!

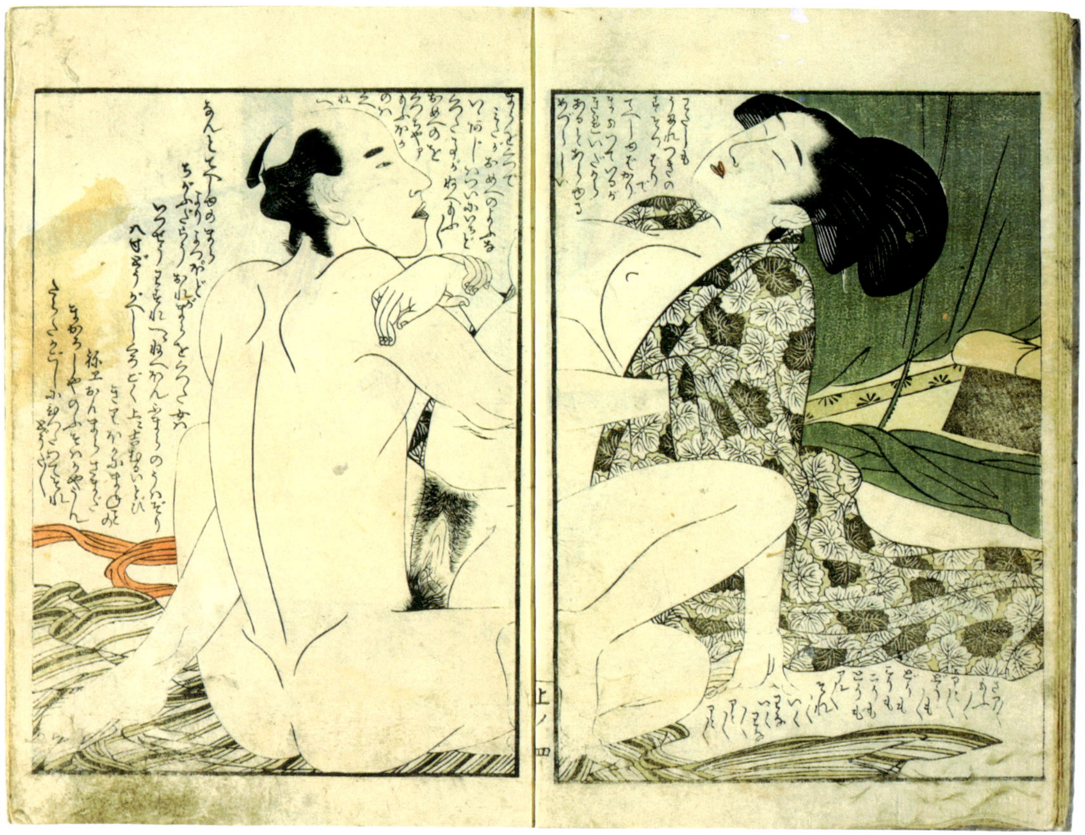

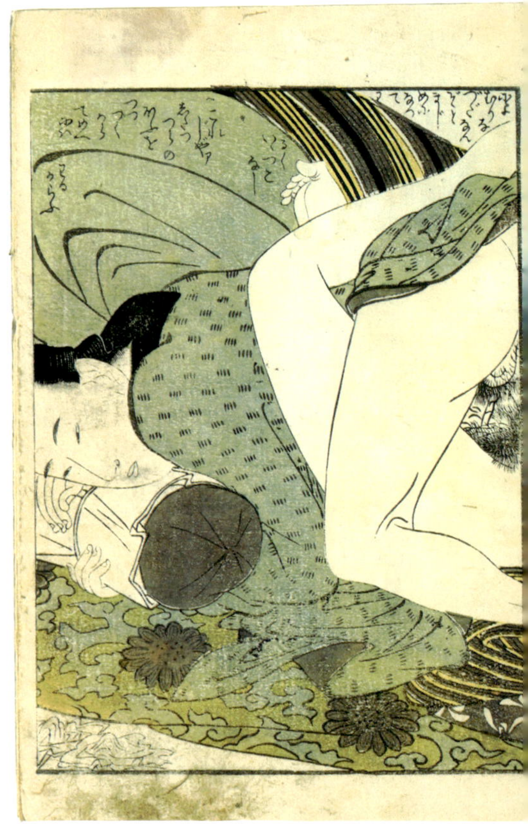

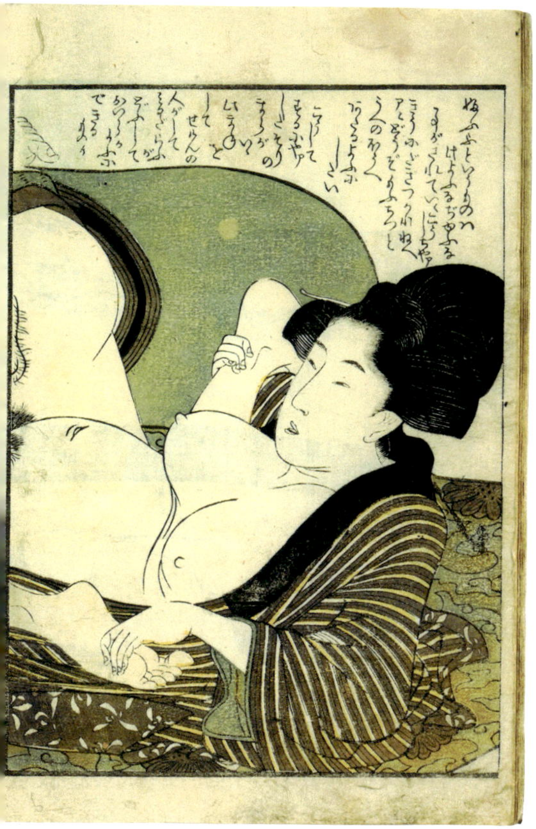

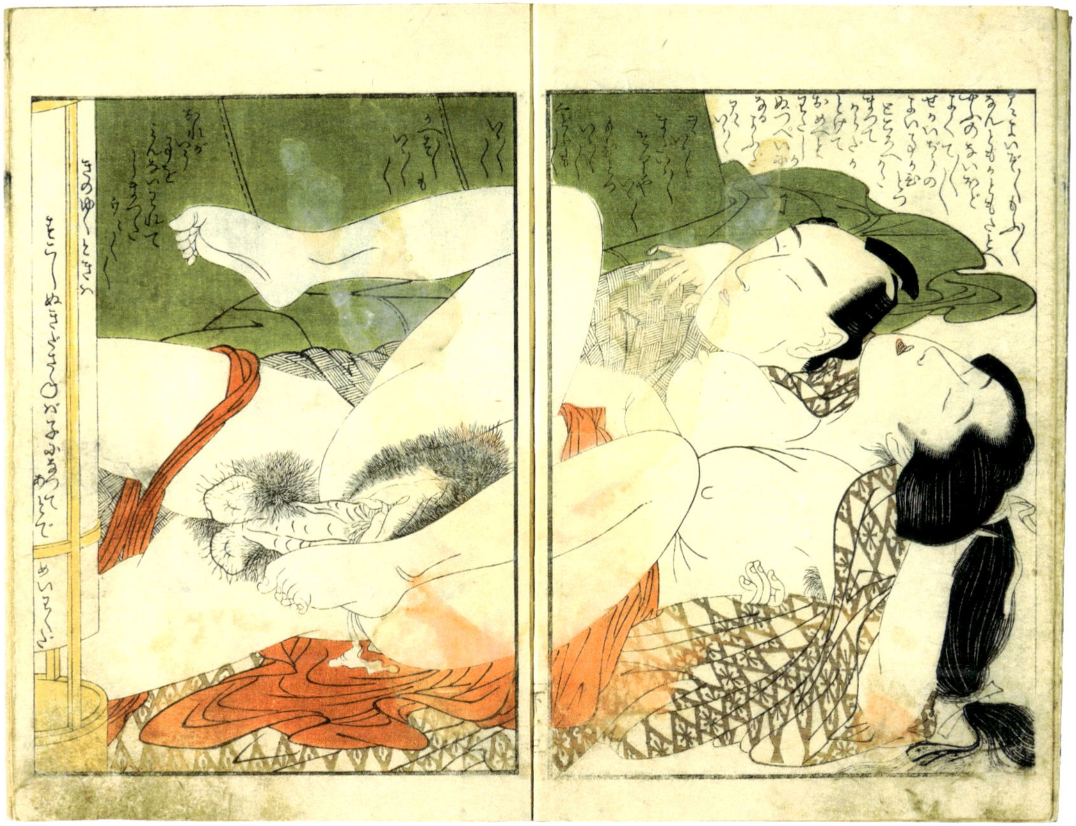

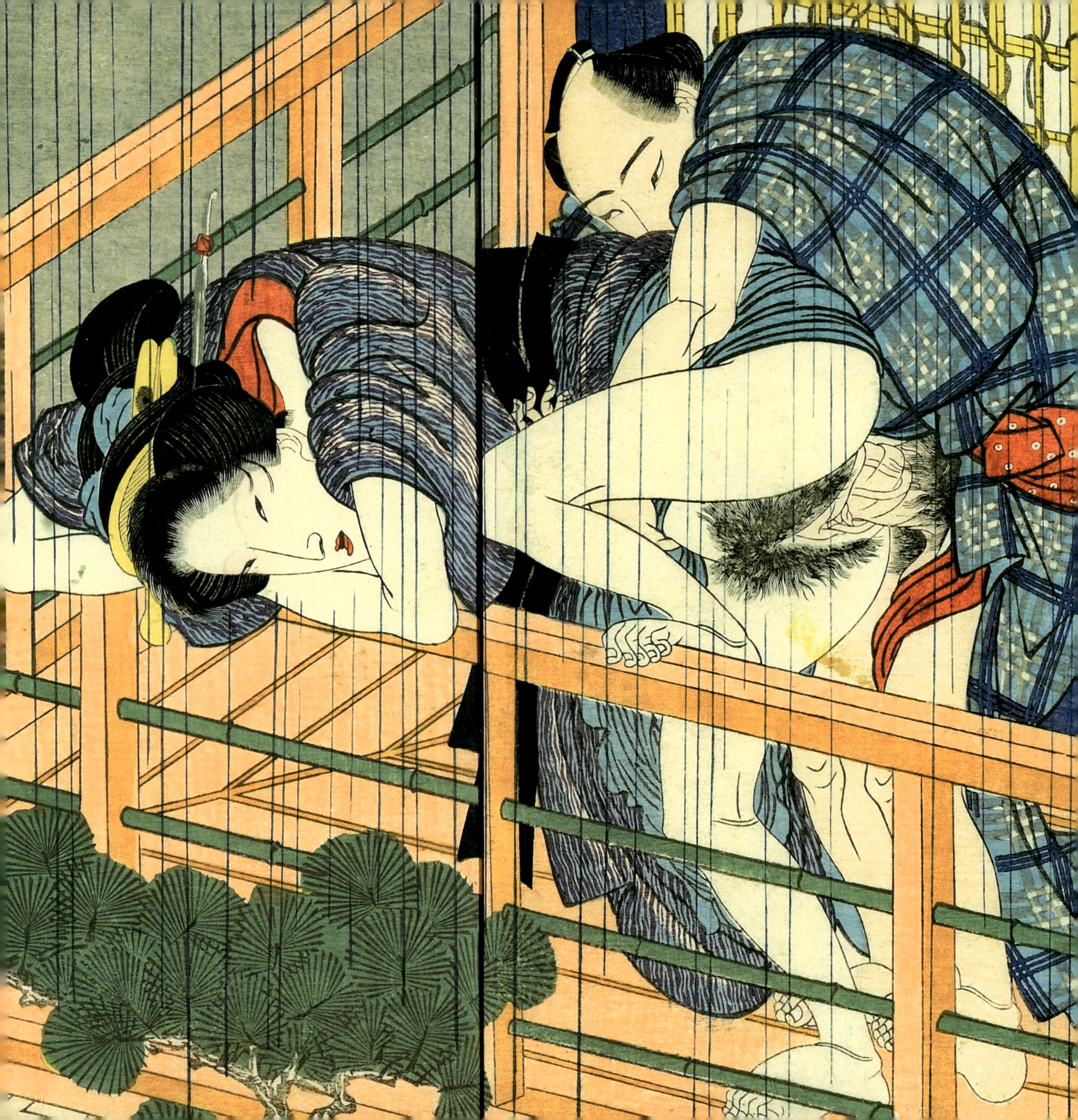

Erotic adventures: heightened drama in the nineteenth century

Utagawa Kunisada
***Spring, Summer, Autumn and Winter: Prospects for the Four Seasons* (*Shunka shūtō: Shiki no nagame*), vol. 1 (detail)**
1827
Colour woodblock-printed book,
25.5 × 18.5 cm (covers).
Caption details p. 148

The arts in Edo flourished during the Bunka and Bunsei eras (1804–30), having recovered once again from the strictures of the governmental reforms of the 1790s. Literature, poetry circles, painting and scholarly activities saw an unprecedented level of activity as the economy prospered. Both high and low tastes were catered for in this ebullient period. Some very fine erotic print albums appeared, especially from the brush of Katsushika Hokusai. Nevertheless, following the *Ehon Taikōki* incident (see p. 124) and renewed controls on erotica, artists of the Utagawa school held off from designing the more popular erotic books for about twenty years. After 1822, production increased once more and was dominated by this group, consisting of Utagawa Toyokuni I (1769–1825) and his pupils. In the 1840s print production was once again affected by tightened censorship regulations, part of a government response to a contemporary economic crisis. This led to a complete hiatus in the publication of erotic books for several years, though the genre recovered from 1848 onwards. Though Kyoto and Osaka had been important centres for erotica, after 1800 production seems to have been limited almost entirely to Edo.

The erotic art produced during the final decades of the Tokugawa shogunate, from the 1820s to the 1860s, possesses a greater intensity than that of the preceding period of the 1780s through to the 1820s, in terms of both visual qualities and the scenes depicted. In particular during the 1850s and 1860s, just before the ultimate fall of the military government in 1867, these developments can perhaps be seen against the political instability and social unease of the times. In visual terms, there is a tendency towards saturated colours, and the compositions extend to the very edges of the picture field, filling the entire space with furnishings and accoutrements. In terms of content, the sexual encounters tend to be more dramatic, with lovers lost in ecstatic abandonment, and with an increased number of scenes of sexual violence. This intensification is in keeping with the contemporary trend in popular culture – in prints, novels and *kabuki* theatre – towards grotesque and supernatural stories and motifs. The shared experience of sex which was characteristic of earlier decades, with couples engaging emotionally, is seen less often. In works by the two major artists, Kuniyoshi and Kunisada, there is a tendency to present 'the interiority of erotic rapture', with women particularly depicted lost in ecstatic climax.[1]

Katsushika Hokusai

Katsushika Hokusai (1760–1849) is one of a handful of Japanese artists whose name is known internationally. Over a career spanning seven decades he produced a huge output of paintings, prints, book illustrations and designs for decorative items. Though his fame derives quite rightly from his innovative and masterful landscape compositions, dating principally from later in his career, he was also productive in the realm of erotic imagery until 1821, a fact often overlooked.[2] From 1782 to 1794 Hokusai illustrated a number of erotic books, but it was long thought that for twenty years after this he did not produce any erotica owing to the restrictions on artistic expression brought about by the Kansei Reforms of the 1790s (see p. 113). It is possible that he produced one publication, however, during this period, titled *Erotic Book: Many Beautiful Women and Blessings* (*Ehon futamigata*), in 1802 to 1804.[3]

Young Pine Saplings (*Kinoe no komatsu*) was published in three volumes, with a preface date of 1814. Within the sixty-year calendrical cycle, based on the five natural elements and twelve animal signs, this was a 'senior wood' (*kinoe*) year. The style exemplifies the heavy, voluptuous figures of Hokusai's later erotica. It has been suggested that another artist's hand can be identified in some designs in the second and third volumes, which are possibly by Hokusai's third daughter, Oi. The texts above the illustrations do not relate to the longer passages in the rest of the book, but instead contain commentary and dialogue between the characters.

The great erotic album *Picture-book: Patterns of Couples* (*Ehon tsuhi no hinagata*) is unsigned, but it has been attributed to Hokusai on stylistic grounds, and is dateable to 1817. One design bears a hidden signature, 'Shishoku Gankō', thought to be a pseudonym used by Hokusai. Again, it has been argued that it was in fact a collaboration between Katsushika Oi, and the painter Keisai Eisen (1790–1848), the latter providing the text. Whatever the truth of the matter, the album's compositions possess marked similarities to previous designs by Hokusai. The large-sheet (*ōban*) album format allowed for ampler figures than are found in Hokusai's book illustrations, and the album marks the first appearance in the artist's work of massive figures with exaggerated sexual organs. Each couple is draped in gorgeous, elaborately patterned robes and bedcovers, and the undergarments feature the crinkly line which was to become a distinctive aspect of Hokusai's late style. The scenes of love-making are often dynamic and passionate, with lovers biting and kissing. The women comprise courtesans, *geisha* and ordinary women, including several older married women enjoying affairs with young lovers. As is often the case with erotic books, the title has both overt and covert meanings: while *tsuhi* indicates 'couple', it also alludes to *tsubi*, 'vulva'.

Katsushika Hokusai
***Young Pine Saplings* (*Kinoe no komatsu*)**
1814
Colour woodblock-printed book,
22 × 15.5 cm (covers).
Private collection,
Ritsumeikan ARC Database

An apparently possessive *geisha* uses a brush to inscribe her partner's penis with the words 'This belongs to…'. If the ink remains when she next sees him, she will know he has been faithful to her. He waits patiently, obligingly holding the inkstone. Behind them is a red fabric cord, a popular sex aid used to hold the partners together during strenuous love-making, often seen in *shunga*.

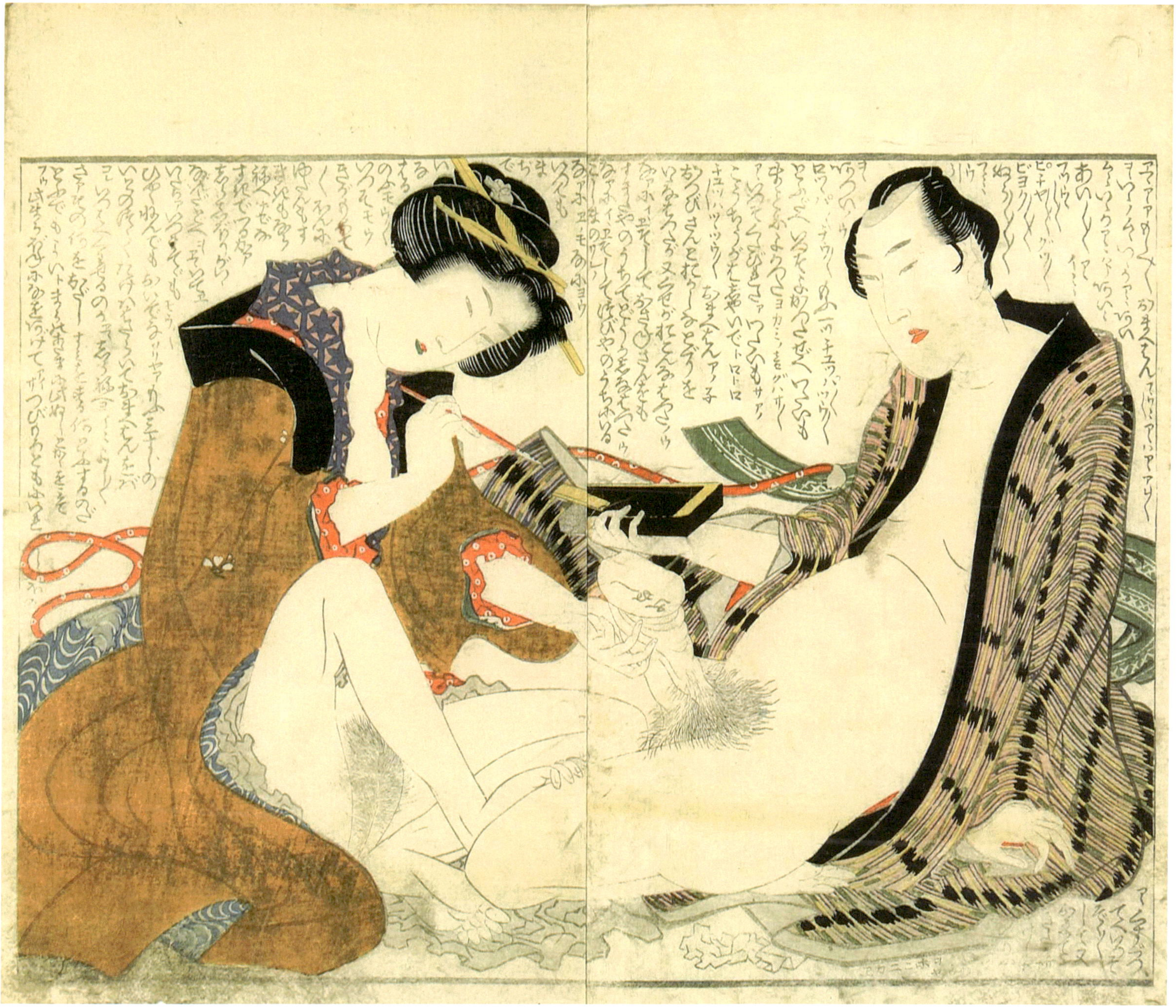

Katsushika Hokusai
***Young Pine Saplings* (*Kinoe no komatsu*)**
1814
Colour woodblock-printed book, 22 × 15.5 cm (covers).
Private collection, Ritsumeikan ARC Database

In another opening we see an imagined scene of a Chinese couple, a common inclusion in erotic books. The man, who is wearing a cock-ring (*namako no rin*), lifts his partner's leg in order to collect her vaginal juices, a practice that was thought to be popular in China, where both male and female vital fluids held a powerful role in Daoist belief. The explanation above mixes up syllables to create a pseudo-foreign language. The woman seems not to experience any discomfort, clasping her hands tightly together and curling her toes. Hokusai's distinctive style is visible in the agitated, crinkled line of the woman's undergarments.

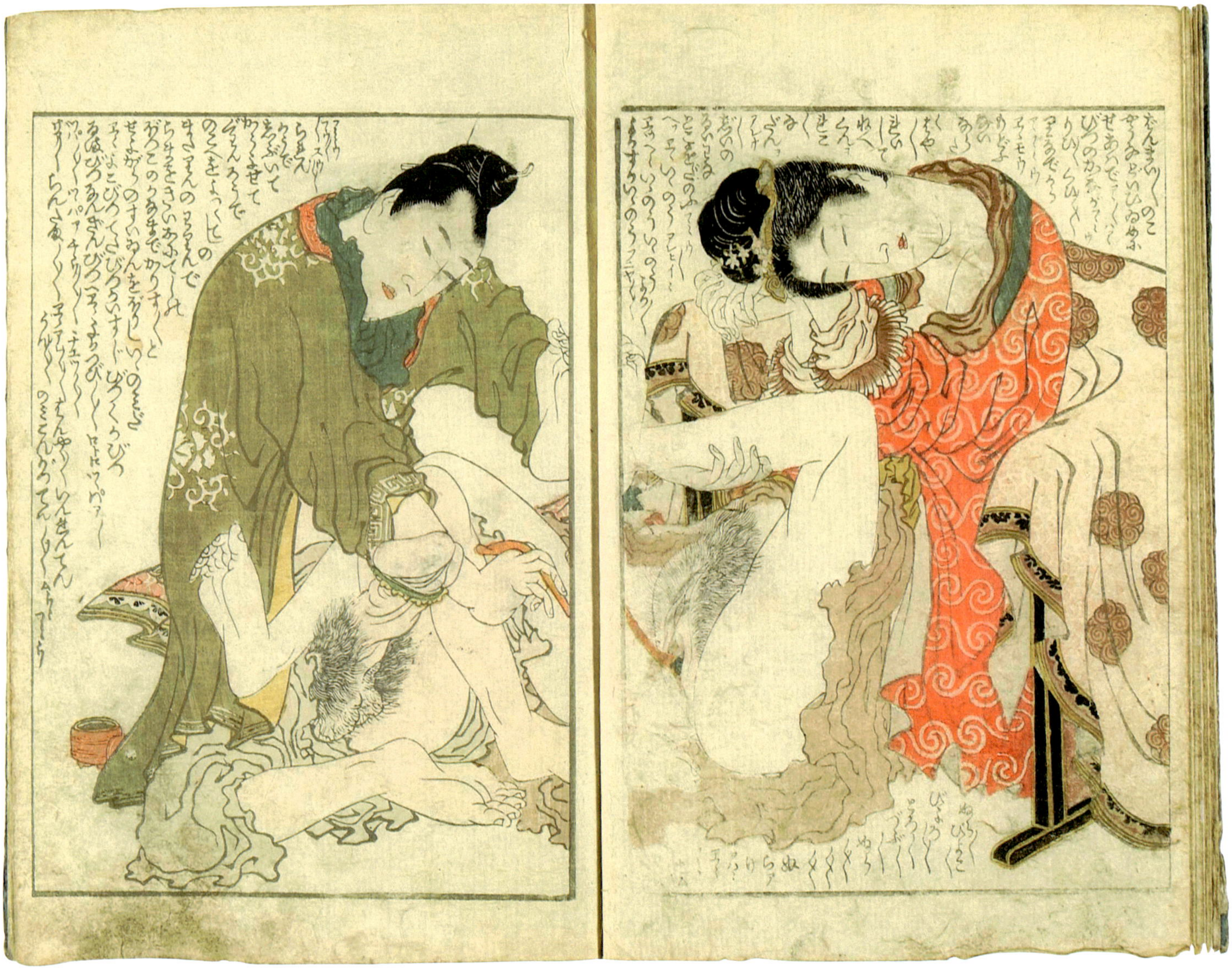

Katsushika Hokusai
***Young Pine Saplings* (*Kinoe no komatsu*)**
1814
Colour woodblock-printed book,
22 × 15.5 cm (covers).
Private collection,
Ritsumeikan ARC Database

The book includes two scenes of violence, in one of which a labourer is forcing himself on a young woman. She resists him energetically, pushing away his leering face, and jabbing her fingers into his eyes. In the dialogue below she cries repeatedly, 'Don't, don't!', and the text tells us that her screams alert the neighbours, who come to her rescue. A dramatic sense of movement is created by the man's lunging body and by the large pestle as it falls. Hokusai expends care on depicting not only the man's ugly face, but also the cracked skin on the soles of his feet. The differentiation in the depiction of the penis here is of note. It is given none of the customary strength and modelling, appearing instead rather lumpy and deformed, appropriate for a sexual encounter lacking the usual harmony and mutual enjoyment.

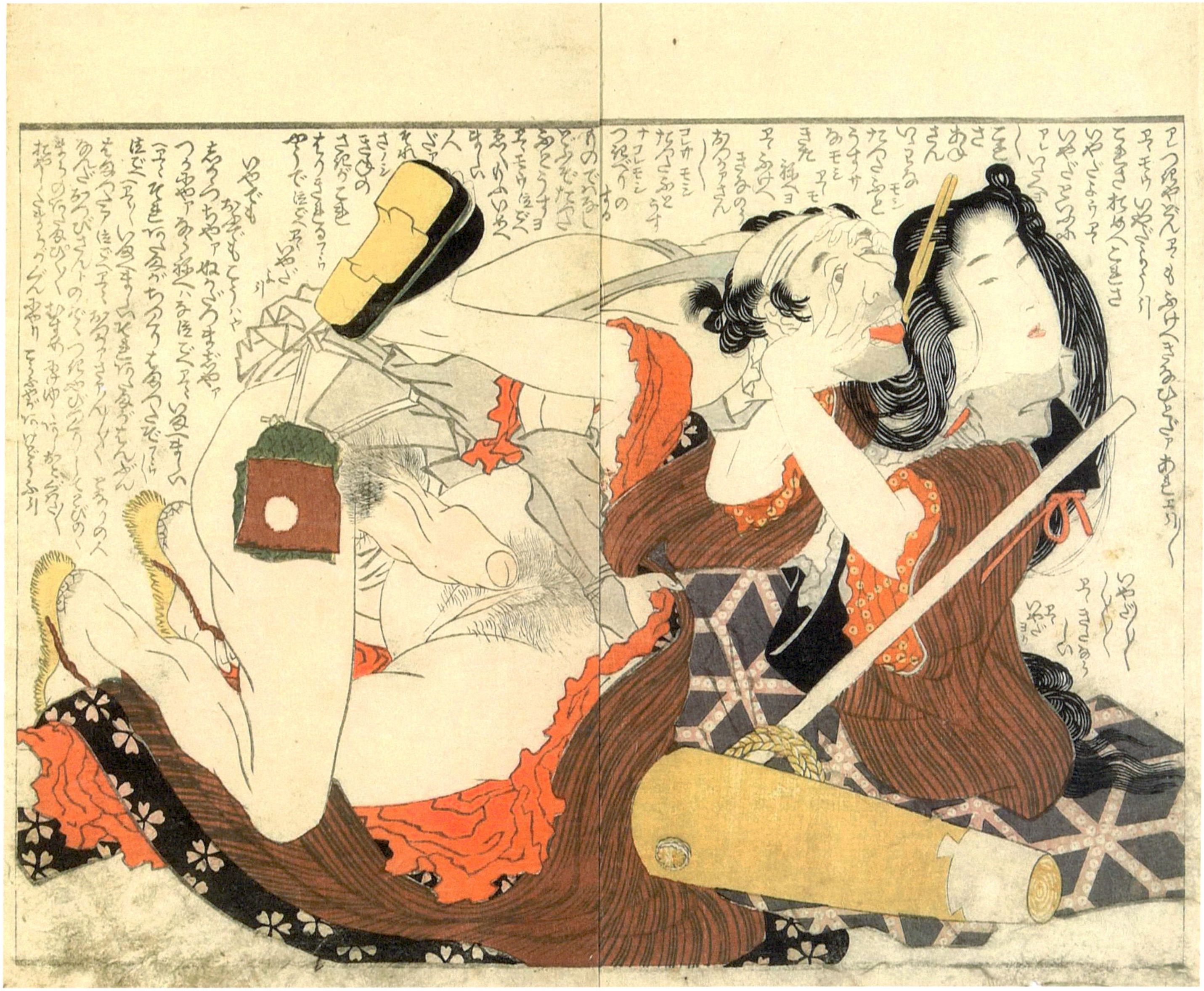

Katsushika Hokusai
***Young Pine Saplings* (*Kinoe no komatsu*)**
1814
Colour woodblock-printed book,
22 × 15.5 cm (covers)

One illustration from this publication has been reproduced repeatedly. Despite the passage of nearly two hundred years, it has lost none of its arresting graphic power. A naked woman lies between two seaweed-covered rocks, her legs spread to accommodate a huge octopus which penetrates her with its mantle. One of its tentacles curls around to stimulate her clitoris. At her head, a smaller octopus cradles her neck as it battens on to her mouth and tweaks her left nipple.

Although frequently reproduced, this image has often been misunderstood, providing an example of how close attention to the text embedded in the design can enhance our understanding. In the late nineteenth century two French enthusiasts of Japonisme, the writer Joris-Karl Huysmans (1848–1907) and the art writer Edmond de Goncourt (1822–96), wrote about the work, likening the woman to a cadaver. Later authors described the woman as being 'violated' by the sea creature. Yet she is very much alive and conscious of the experience, with her eyes open and cast upwards. Her hair falls down as she arches her neck in pleasure. In a rather human-like embrace, the octopus wraps its tentacles around her, two of which she grips firmly.

The dialogue here relies to a large extent on onomatopoeia, with the multiple vertical lines indicating repetition. As a sample, the woman moans, 'Ee, moo, I'm becoming ticklish. One after another until I lose track fu, fu, fu, fuu, fuu, limits and boundaries are gone. Oo, oo, oo, I've come, anna, aaaaaa, there, there, here, here, uu, mu, mu, mu, fun, mufu, umu, uuuuu. Good... good!'.[4] The woman is one of the female divers (*ama*) who gathered abalone shellfish. Women possess more subcutaneous fat so have an advantage over men in being able to endure the cold temperatures of the water, and these divers were renowned for their ability to hold their breath for long periods of time. *Ama* had appeared in various medieval stories, particularly *Taishokan*, the tale of a Buddhist jewel captured en route from China to Japan and taken to the Palace of the Dragon-King. An *ama* finally succeeds in rescuing the jewel, but only by cutting her breast open to conceal it, thereby sacrificing her own life. This story was turned into a *nō* play in the early fifteenth century, as well as being adapted for more popular stage entertainments. The story was represented in woodblock prints, but during the eighteenth century the depiction of the scantily clad divers, wearing only a red underskirt, became sexualized and provided suitable subject matter both for *ukiyo-e* designs of beauties (such as the opening image of the Utamaro's *Poem of the Pillow* album), and for explicit images of octopuses penetrating and sucking. Furthermore, *tako*, the word for octopus, was slang for vagina, for its ability to suck firmly, and this term is used in the dialogue here. Though the image lacks obvious references to the tale of the heroic diver, contemporary readers (or viewers) of the book would have been familiar with these links, and would have understood the visual play which Hokusai was deploying in his extraordinary design.[5]

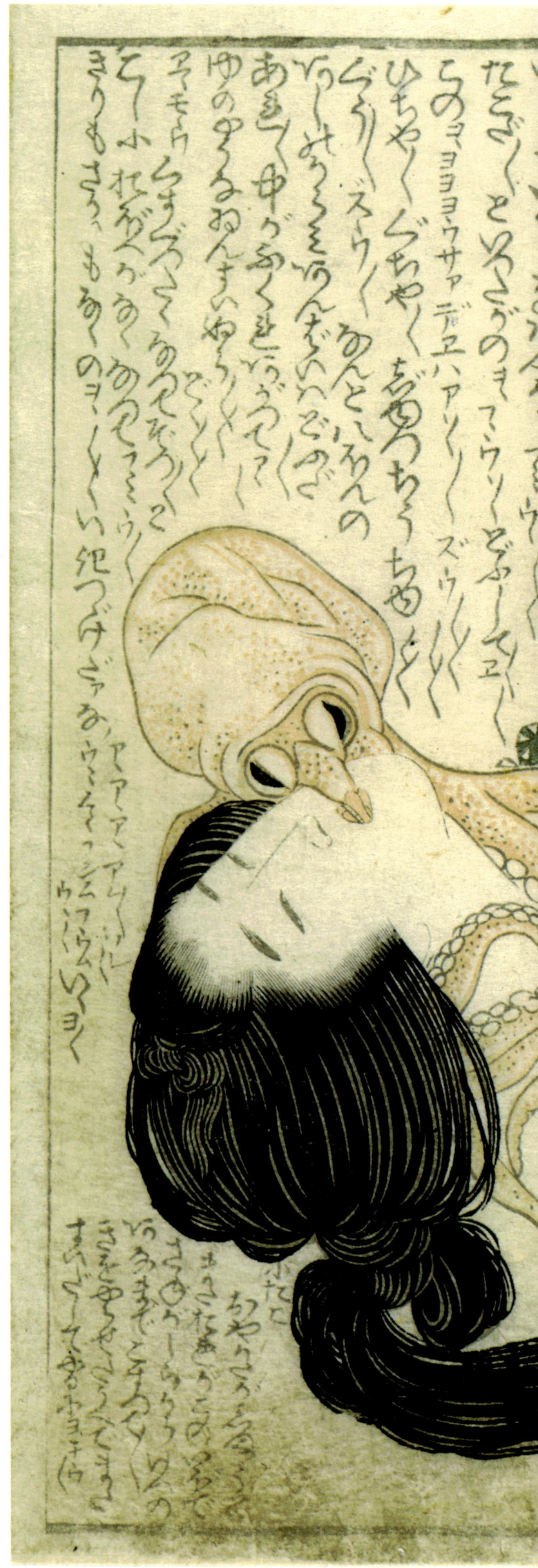

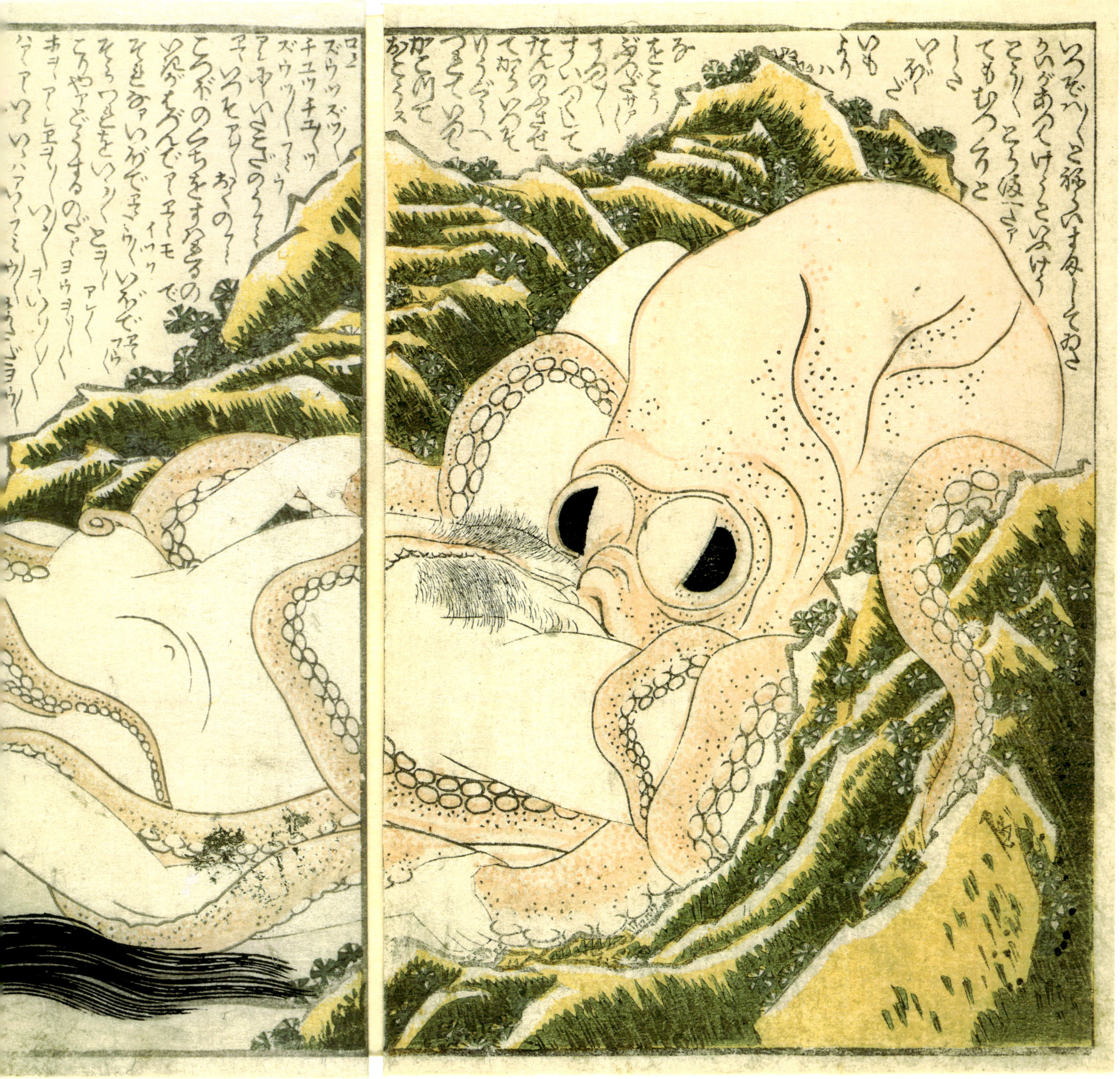

Hokusai's most significant illustrated erotic book was *The Gods of All Happiness and Intercourse* (*Manpuku wagōjin*), thought to have been published in 1821. It is unusual among erotic books as, rather than the customary collection of unrelated scenes, it presents a continuous story across three volumes, following the fates and sexual adventures of two women, Osane and Otsubi, from the age of thirteen to thirty.[6] The theme of the book is the intense, unending pleasure to be found in sexual activity, and the opening image shows the eponymous deities, whose faces take the form of a penis and a vulva. The next image presents an opulent display of sex toys, including dildos, penis enhancement cords, a substitute vagina, as well as incense and aphrodisiacs. The story begins with scenes of the conception of the two heroines: Osane's parents are well-off and benefit from many sex toys; Otsubi's are poor and their only pleasure is *bobo* (slang for vagina). As the two women grow up, their fortunes diverge: Otsubi gains sexual experience while working as a maid for several bawdy women, and then decides to increase her income by becoming a prostitute, at which she is very successful. From time to time she hires male prostitutes and she acquires a seventeen-year-old lover. Osane, meanwhile, has less luck in life. After terminating a pregnancy she marries, but her husband cannot satisfy her sexually, and when she runs off with her lover Saizō, she is disinherited. Raped by their landlord, she is abandoned by Saizō and goes to work in a brothel, eventually becoming a street-walker and gradually losing her health.

As with all *shunga*, we are in the realm of escapist fiction here: the message is not women's sexual empowerment, but rather a male fantasy of insatiable female desire. The women become prostitutes because they have such a hunger for *mara* (a slang term for 'cock' used originally by priests, and derived from Māra, a tempting demon in Buddhism who personifies the death of the spiritual life). They are always available for sex and, most disturbingly, even when violated against their will they end up enjoying the experience, as when Osane is gang-raped and the text describes her as 'sobbing with pleasure' at her repeated orgasms. Hokusai shows only the aftermath of this particular scene, and though horrific, it is in keeping with the tale's tenor of extravagant sexual excess.

Hokusai remained remarkably productive until the end of his life, but it seems he stopped producing erotica once more after 1822, with no such works confirmed from the remaining twenty-six years of his career.

Attr. Katsushika Hokusai
Picture-book: Patterns of Couples
(*Ehon tsuhi no hinagata*)
1817
Colour woodblock-printed album, each opening 25.3 × 18.5 cm

In the third opening from the album, the woman narrows her eyes and tenses at the point of climax, her hair in disarray as she grasps at the fallen headrest beside her.

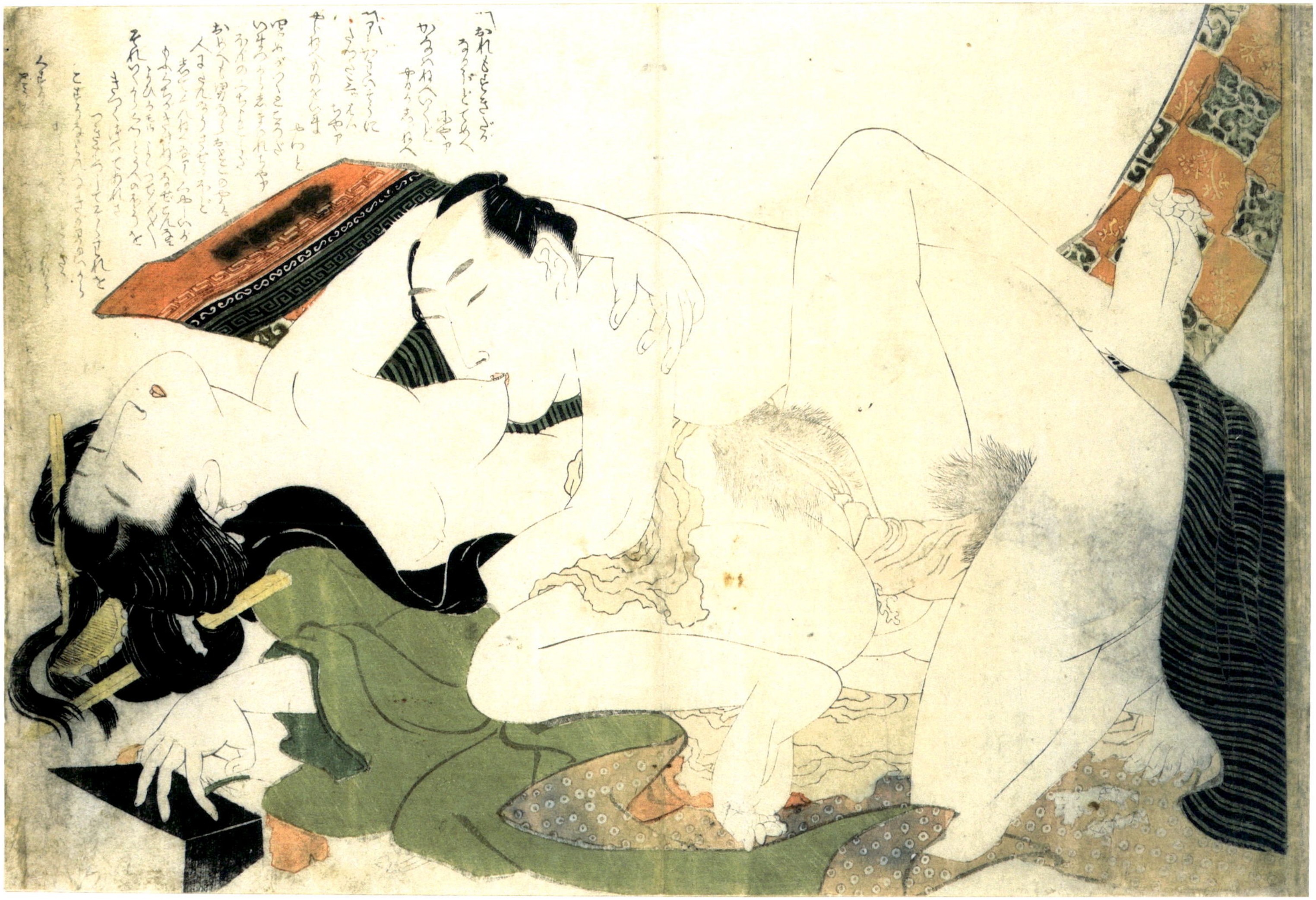

Attr. Katsushika Hokusai
Picture-book: Patterns of Couples
(*Ehon tsuhi no hinagata*)
1817
Colour woodblock-printed album,
each opening 25.3 × 18.5 cm

The pace slows in the next picture, with a scene of two lovers dozing on a summer's day. The woman has placed tissues in her vulva, and the closed eyes and limp hands suggest the bliss of relaxation after sexual passion. Her partner embraces her round the waist, and though she is turned away from him, she gently holds his penis. Two mice mating in the foreground provide a touch of humour, making the sounds, 'Chuu, chuu, chuu'. The commentary above belongs to the demure-looking kitten sitting to one side, who remarks on how entertaining the scene is. On the woman's fan is a comic verse reinforcing the couple's self-satisfaction. It reads 'Benkei and Komachi were fools, ha ha', referring to the legend that both the warrior Musashibō Benkei (1155–89) and the poetess Ono no Komachi (*c.* 825–900) rejected any sort of sexual relations throughout their lives.[7]

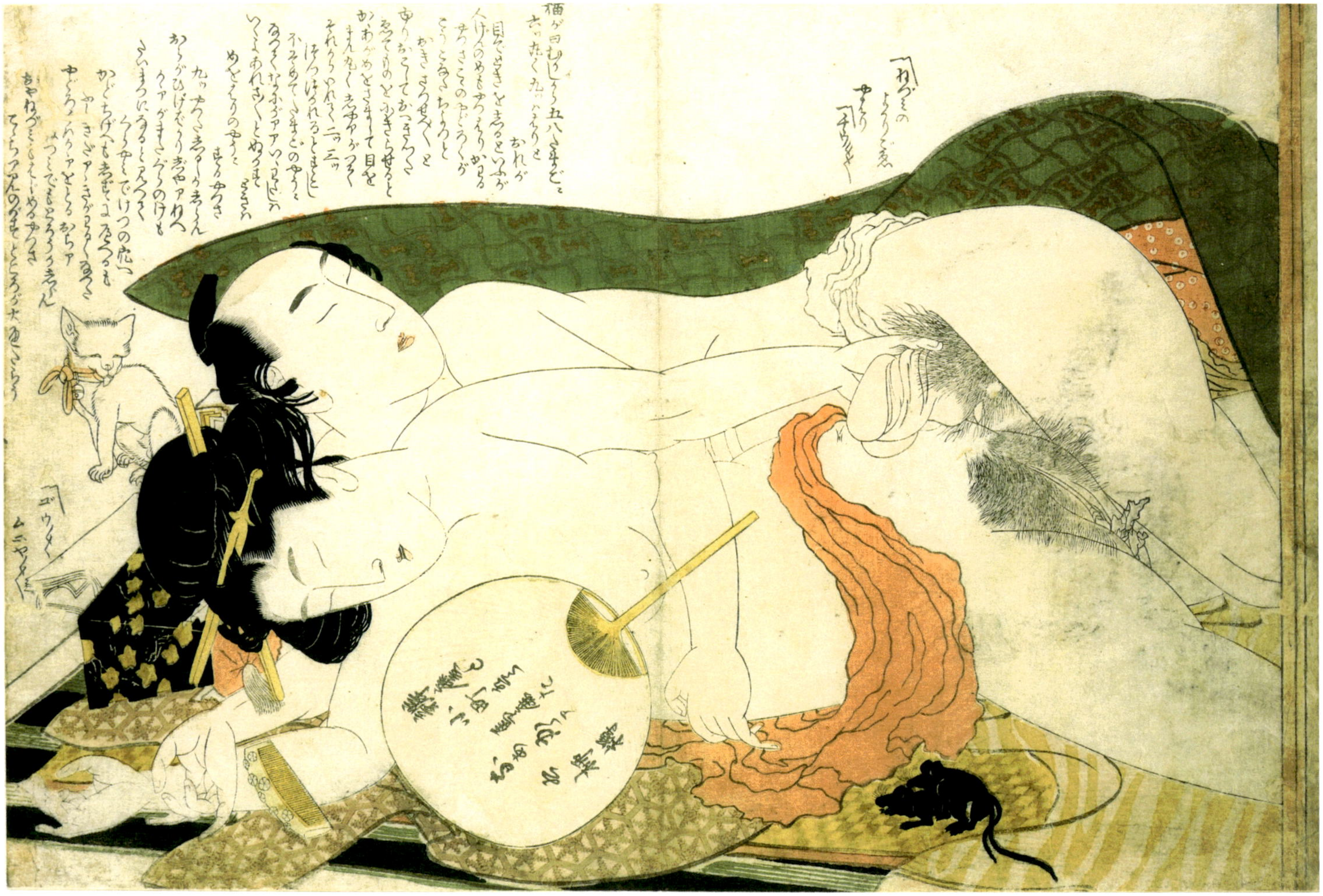

Attr. Katsushika Hokusai
Picture-book: Patterns of Couples
(*Ehon tsuhi no hinagata*)
1817
Colour woodblock-printed album, each opening 25.3 × 18.5 cm

In the seventh image of the album we find a married woman who has broken off from her sewing to entertain her young lover. He holds her shoulder as he mounts from behind, and she rests her head on her arms. A similar composition can be found several times in Hokusai's book illustrations, apparently favoured because it permitted a more naturalistic view of the genitals. Here a complex array of fabric patterns serves to frame the dramatically enlarged sexual organs at the centre of the picture.

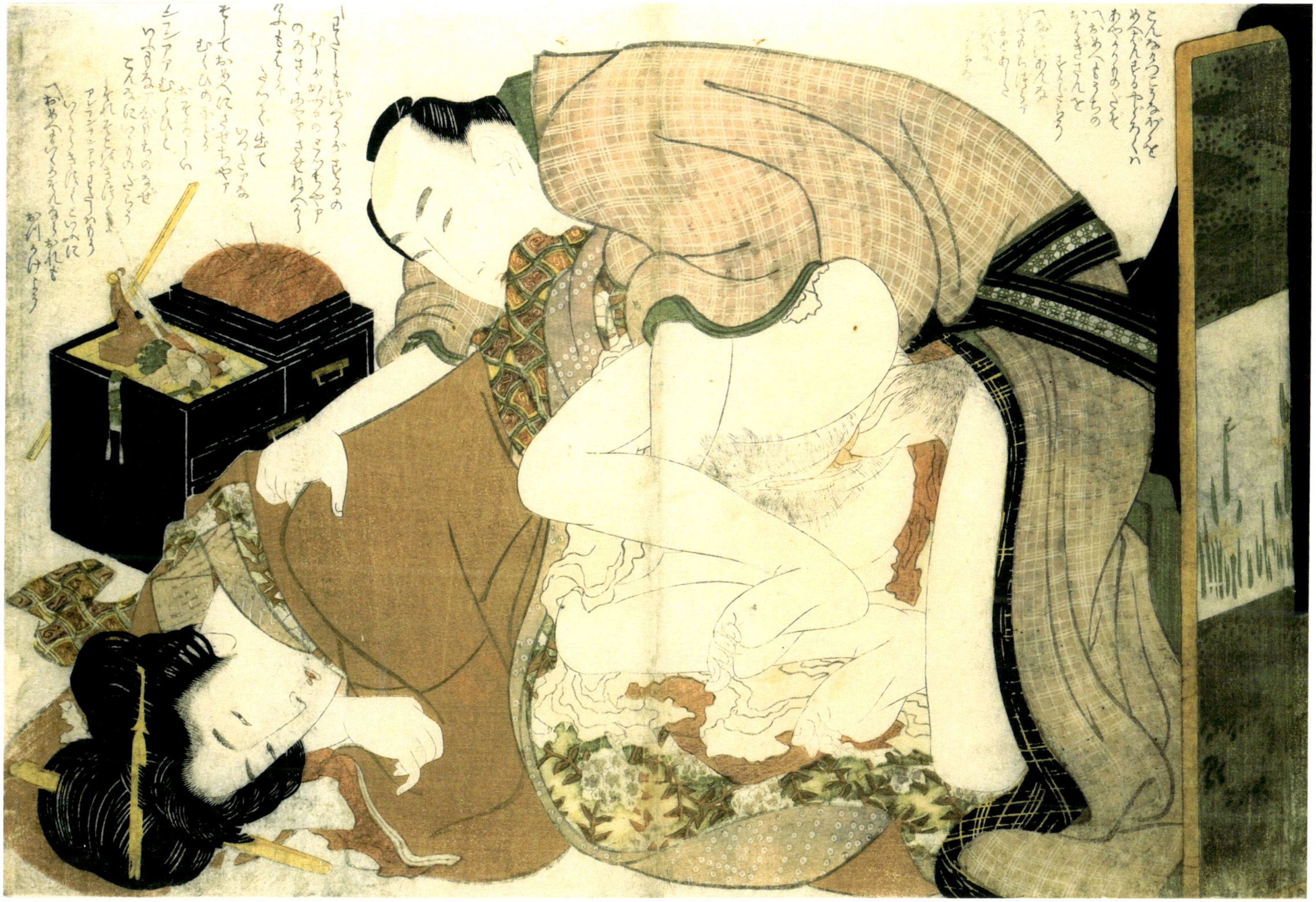

Katsushika Hokusai
***The Gods of All Happiness and Intercourse* (*Manpuku wagōjin*)**
1821
Colour woodblock-printed book, 22.5 × 15.7 cm (covers).
Private collection, Ritsumeikan ARC Database

Osane's parents, the text above tells us, spend hours engaged in love-making, making use of all manner of sex toys, a box of which we can see by their feet (with a jar of aphrodisiac ointment). Arisuke is wearing a penis enhancer, and his wife, Osuke, grabs the leg of an elegant Chinese lacquer table as she leans back in bliss. Even as Osane grew within her mother's womb, the story tells us, the couple's pace did not slacken and they became the 'model of conjugal love in their village'.

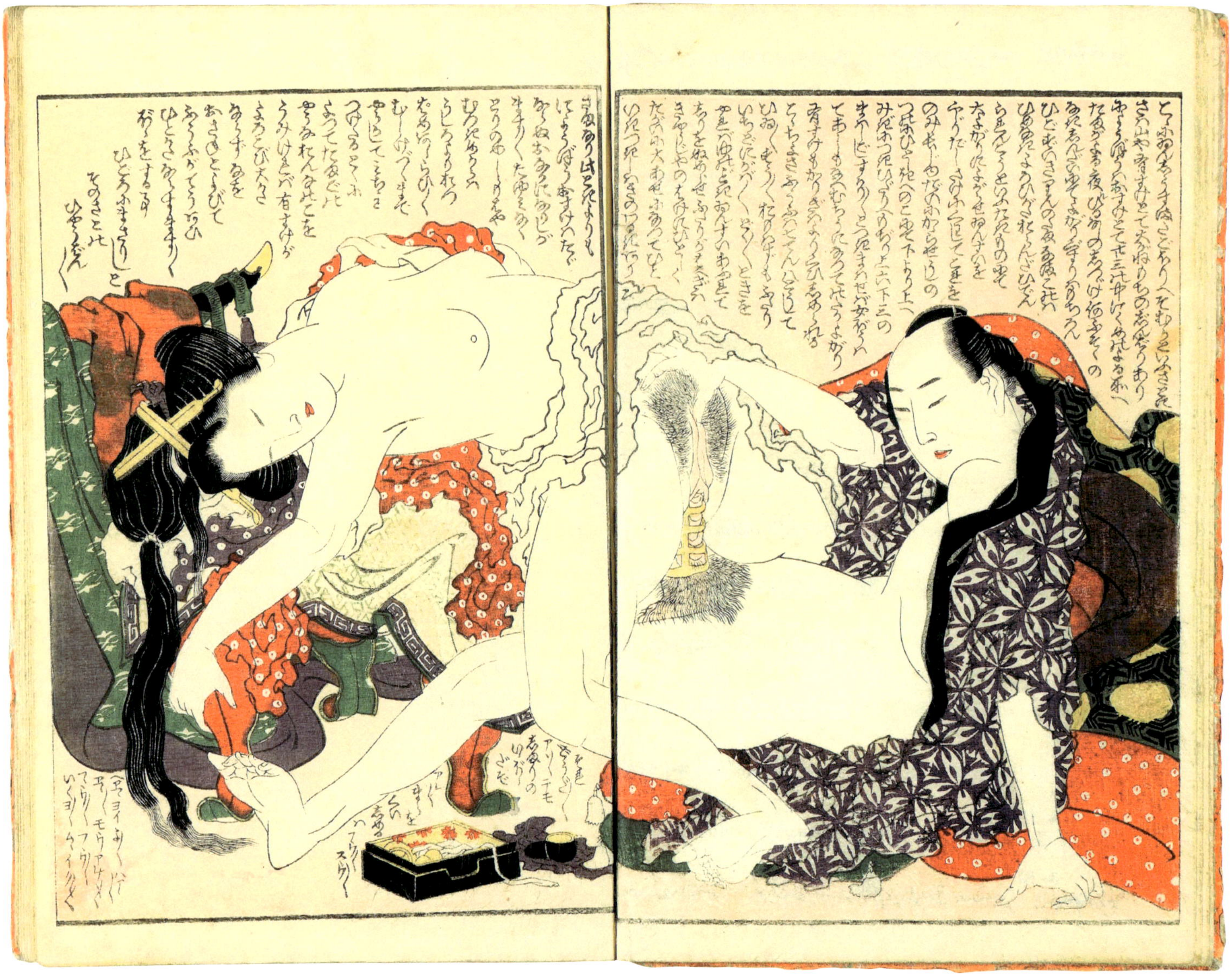

Katsushika Hokusai
***The Gods of All Happiness and Intercourse* (*Manpuku wagōjin*)**
1821
Colour woodblock-printed book,
22.5 × 15.7 cm (covers).
Private collection,
Ritsumeikan ARC Database

Otsubi starts a passionate relationship with Tonketsu, a Buddhist priest from the suggestively named Gyokumonji (Temple of the Jewelled Gate), who lives next door and who has been spying on her encounters with a male prostitute. The text tells us that she was dazzled at the sight of Tonketsu's marvellous *mara*, while he displayed 'mysterious techniques' in his love-making. Here they enjoy a tryst at a renowned lotus cuisine restaurant in Ueno; a dish of food sits on a tray to the left. Sadly, Tonketsu brings ruin on himself and his temple by throwing all his money at Otsubi, and after giving himself totally over to pleasuring her, he dies of exhaustion.

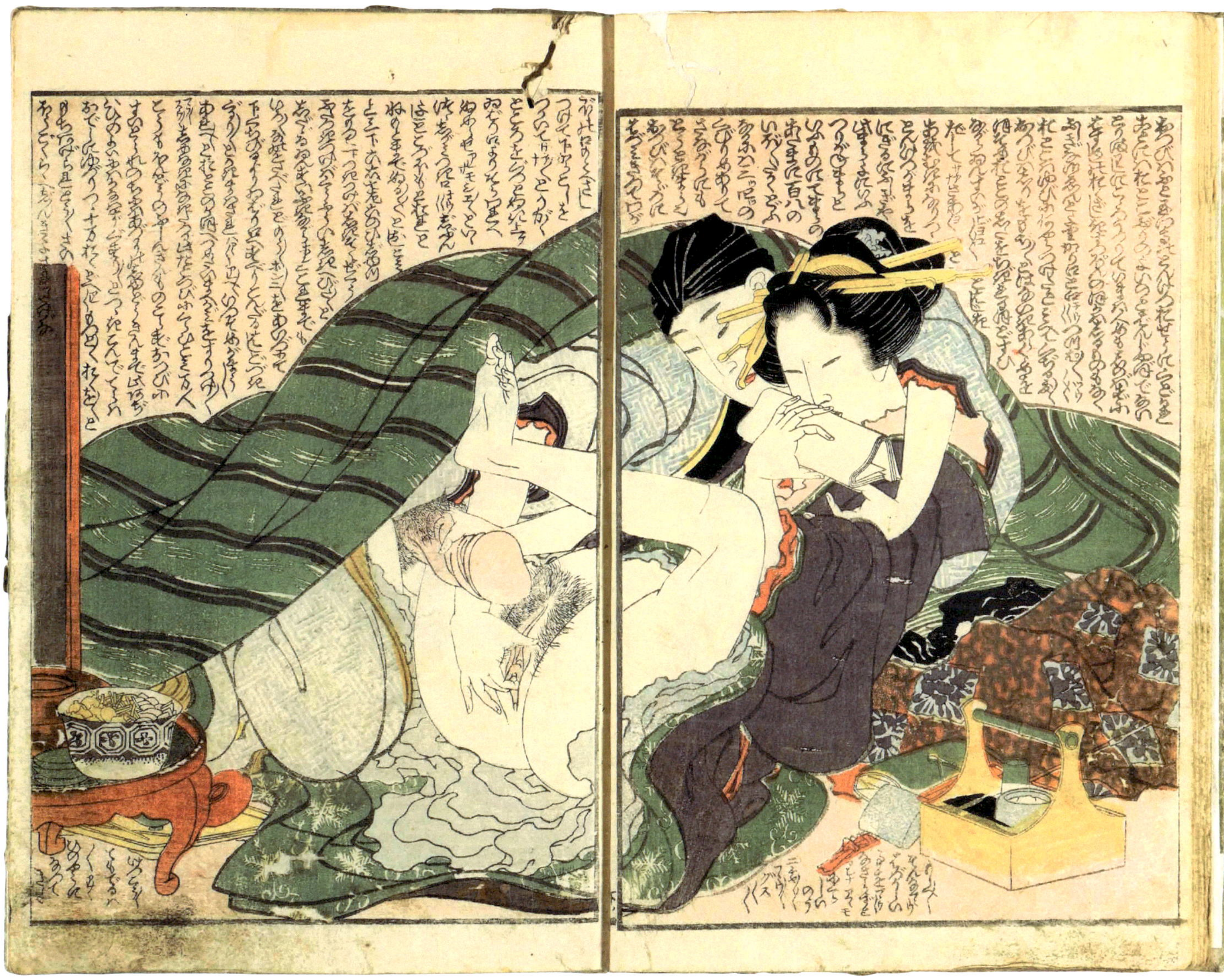

Keisai Eisen

The success of Keisai Eisen (1790–1848) came primarily from his *bijinga*, 'pictures of beautiful women', in single-sheet format. In keeping with the popular literary heroines of the day, the women he portrayed were more worldly and sensuous than the earlier elegant and idealized types. Eisen produced many illustrations for novels, and was himself a novelist and also a *kabuki* playwright. He authored a collection of biographies of *ukiyo-e* artists, in which he claimed to have formerly been a brothel owner. Eisen was by far the most prolific producer of illustrations for erotic books, providing images for a total of fifty-nine titles.

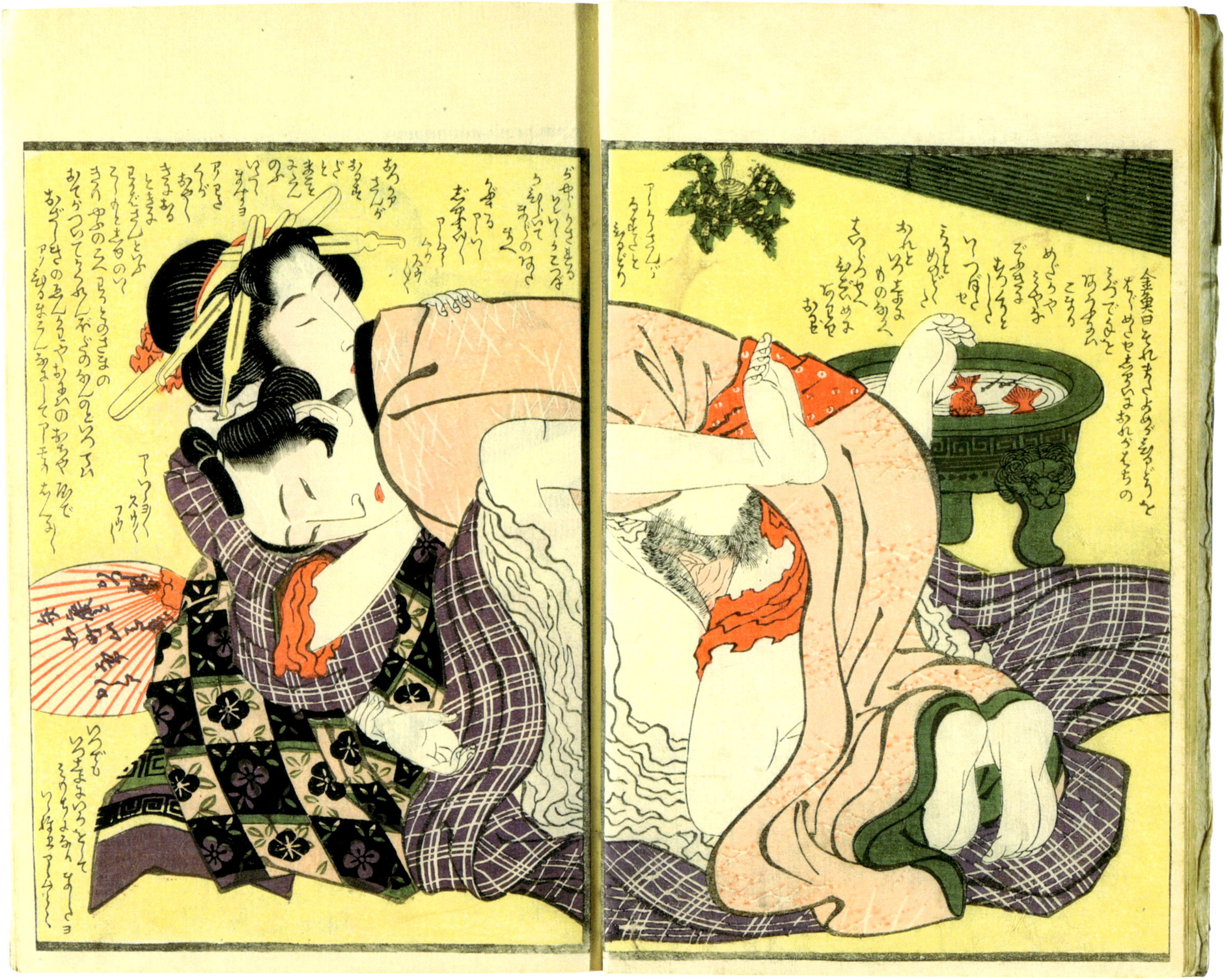

Opposite: Keisai Eisen
***Picture-book: Comparison of Beautiful Women* (*Ehon mime kurabe*), vol. 2**
1830–39
Colour woodblock-printed book, 22.4 × 15.7 cm (covers)

A scene on a summer's day, with the bamboo blind rolled up, a bundle of hare's-foot fern hanging from the eaves, and a fishbowl filled with cool water. The text begins with comments from the fish, who are concerned that the man, after having sex, will wash his hands in their water. The woman's dialogue provides a commentary in the past, saying that when Mother (or possibly the brothel madam) was out, she could rest and fool around with the nice young samurai Wakaba, playing hide-and-seek on the veranda or in the garden tea-house, and making love at any time.

This page: Style of Keisai Eisen
***Album of Piled-up Robes* (*Zōi-jō*)**
1810–20
Colour woodblock prints, each 9.6 × 13 cm

These two prints come from an album of small erotic *surimono*, privately produced luxury prints employing special pigments and texture effects. *Surimono* were usually issued at New Year, often as cryptic 'picture-calendars' (*egoyomi*). A playful aspect of picture-calendars was that information about the sequence of 'long' and 'short' lunar months for the coming year was concealed somewhere within the design.

Top: Here, the indication of which month will be long in 1826 is given by the six numerals in silver on the wad of tissues to the left. We know from the quantity of these crumpled tissues that the couple have already engaged in a long bout of love-making. Though the man may have wanted to rest, his partner pulls insistently on his arm, and he lifts a hand to plead for mercy.

Below: In a scene from *The Tale of Genji*, courtiers are playing kickball in the palace garden. As a pet cat escapes on to the veranda, the bamboo blind is lifted. Kashiwagi catches a glimpse of Genji's wife, Onna Sannomiya (the Third Princess), and falls in love with her. Any image of a woman in court costume accompanied by a pet cat with a red leash was easily identifiable with this well-known scene. The unknown artist has here taken the couple's mutual attraction to its logical conclusion.

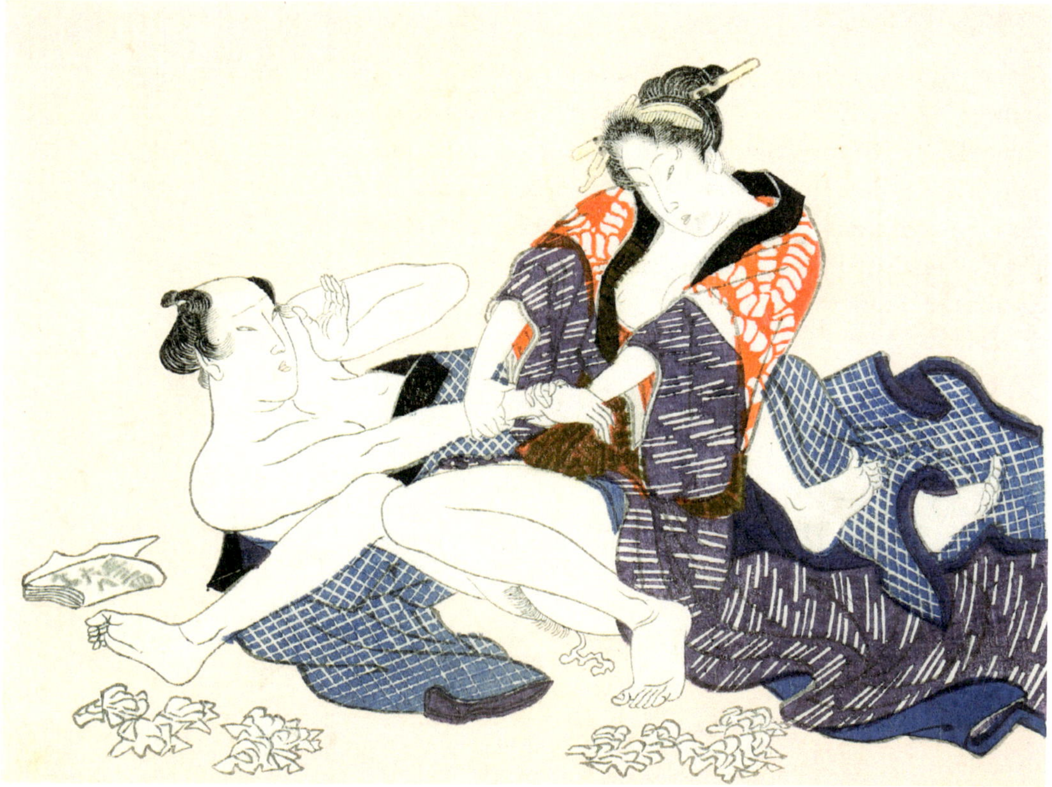

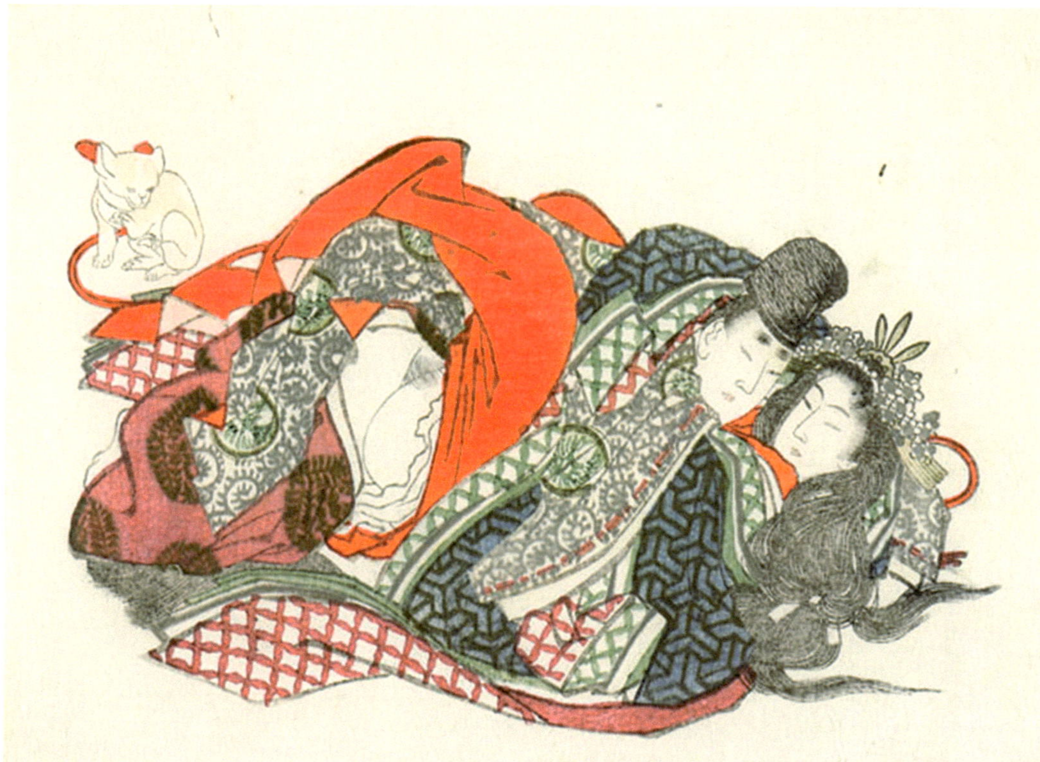

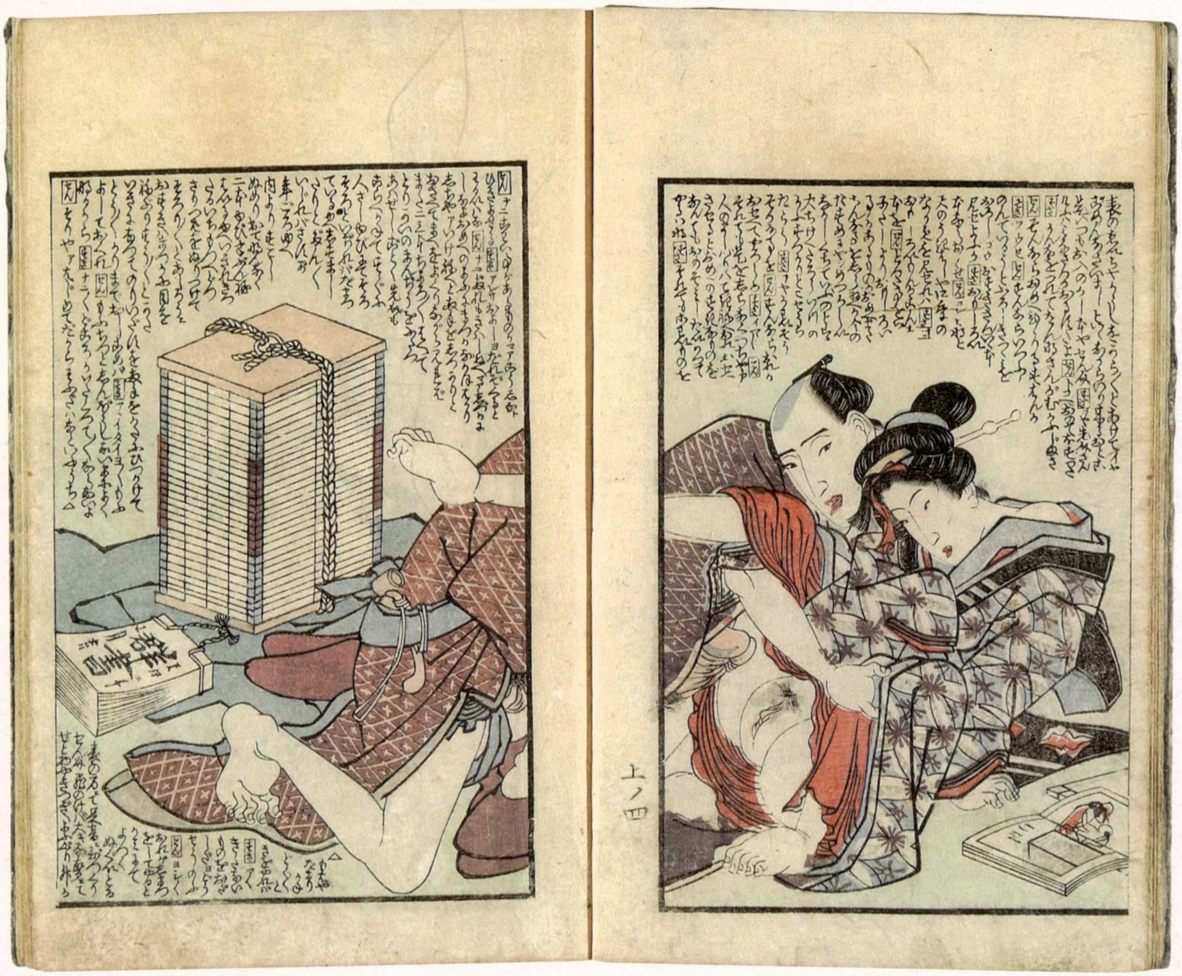

Book lenders

The popularity of printed books in general, as well as the high literacy rate, was facilitated by the phenomenon of book lenders (*kashihonya*). Itinerant salesmen would call house to house, carrying on their back a bundle of the latest stock to offer to interested customers. They would later return to collect the volumes and replace them with other titles. Lenders charged for new publications at a higher rate, then lowered the price as the book became worn and as other titles entered their catalogue. Erotic works were in high demand, and the *kashihonya* were able to charge a premium for them. For this reason, it has been suggested that they were potential sponsors for the expensive, deluxe *shunpon* (see p. 145), providing finance or committing themselves to purchase titles which they knew would be particularly popular.

Crucially, it was often the women of the household who selected the titles, meaning they had direct access to erotic books. An illustration from *Picture-book: Record of Waters of Passion* (*Ehon jōsuiki*) of 1831, by Utagawa Kunitora (fl. 1804–44), shows a female customer who has been browsing one of the titles recommended by the *kashihonya*. His stack of books can be seen unwrapped to the left, a catalogue lying beside it. The scene in the book open on the floor seems to be a couple making love beside a stack of books. Obviously inspired and aroused by this theme, the salesman makes an advance to the woman, hooking his arm under her leg and lifting her skirts. She seems fairly compliant, and leans back on one hand to steady herself.

Utagawa Kunitora
***Picture-book: Record of Waters of Passion* (*Ehon jōsuiki*)**
1831
Colour woodblock-printed book, 20 × 14 cm (covers).
Private collection, Ritsumeikan ARC Database

Luxury books

As well as the obvious appeal of their subject matter, erotic books (*shunpon*) were made more visually attractive by means of lavish printing techniques: a rich palette of colours, metallic pigments to give sheen and blind printing to create textured effects. From the 1820s some volumes had novelty devices known as *shikake*, hinged flaps of paper for a door or screen which could be lifted to reveal the sexual activity beneath. A design might have multiple flaps and even whole-page fold-outs, creating a dynamic and dramatic viewing experience. In fact, in terms of their technical finesse, *shunpon* were the most advanced type of book, and during the period 1804 to 1868 no other genre was given such deluxe treatment.[8] In a highly competitive market, they were among the most profitable commodities for publishers.

Such luxury production techniques made *shunpon* expensive items, often beyond the means of the average consumer. It has been speculated that wealthy townsmen may have acted as sponsors for these publication projects, perhaps even included by the artist as a character within the pages. Shops selling sex paraphernalia probably also provided financial backing, leading to a form of product placement. One of the most successful of these was Yotsumeya, which had branches in Edo, Kyoto and Osaka, and operated over many decades. Its merchandise appears frequently in *shunga*, sometimes accompanied by the shop's trademark of four diamonds.

Utagawa Kunisada

Utagawa Kunisada (1786–1864) was a towering figure in the world of later *ukiyo-e*, the most prolific print designer of his generation who dominated the market for actor prints, in particular. His output of erotic books was also prodigious, with an estimated total of some forty-two titles. *Spring, Summer, Autumn and Winter: Prospects for the Four Seasons* (*Shunka shūtō: Shiki no nagame*) is a fine example of the lavishly produced erotic books of this period. It is thought that the Spring and Summer volumes appeared at New Year 1827 and Autumn and Winter at New Year two years later. The work contained illustrations by Kunisada, together with a number of short stories and poems relating to the seasons by 'Enkōbō Tsukinari', a pseudonym of Utei Enba II (1792–1863). It has been suggested that Kunisada based his illustrations on drawings by his teacher, Utagawa Toyokuni I, which might explain why there is no signature, not even a concealed one.[9]

Each volume has seven or eight double-page images; in the earlier volumes these are gathered at the front – as was typical – but in the later ones they are interleaved with text passages, working more like a linked narrative. The images are characterized by a certain distance, or lack of emotional connection. There are relatively few scenes where the lovers are holding or looking at each other; their bodies are often drawn on different pages, meeting only at the sex organs. There are many furtive encounters where people look around fearing they will be caught – several take place outdoors – as well as depictions of forced sex.

Utagawa Kunisada
***Spring, Summer, Autumn and Winter: Prospects for the Four Seasons* (*Shunka shūtō: Shiki no nagame*), vol. 1**
1827
Colour woodblock-printed book,
25.5 × 18.5 cm (covers)

A brazier burns on the left, but the couple have cast their bedclothes aside on a spring evening. The crumpled tissues, fallen headrests and scattered hairpins indicate the energy and duration of their love-making. As they go at it once again, the woman lifts her legs on to her partner's shoulders and bites down on her robe. The screen in the background is pasted with a selection of prints, fans and poem-slips.

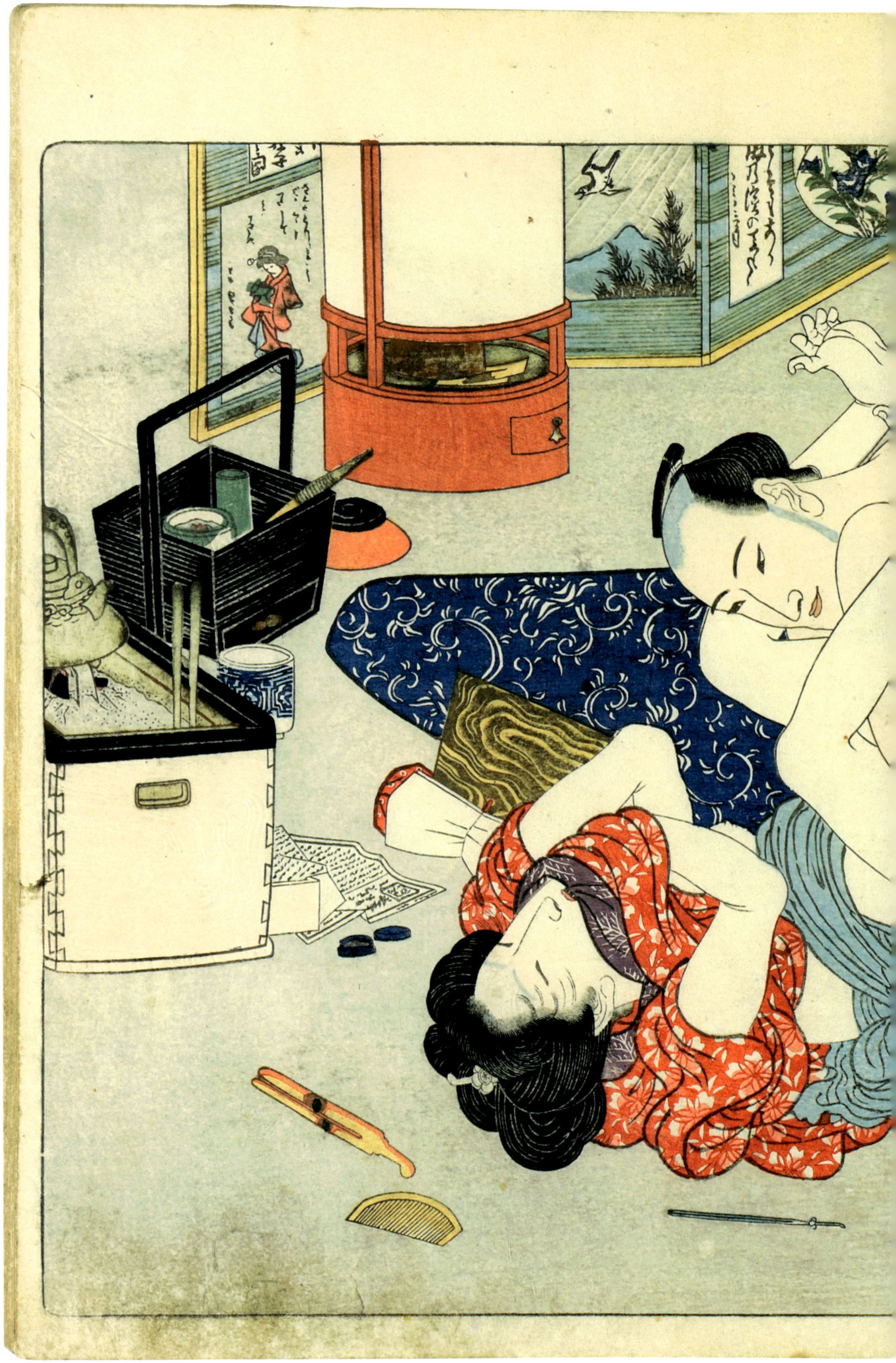

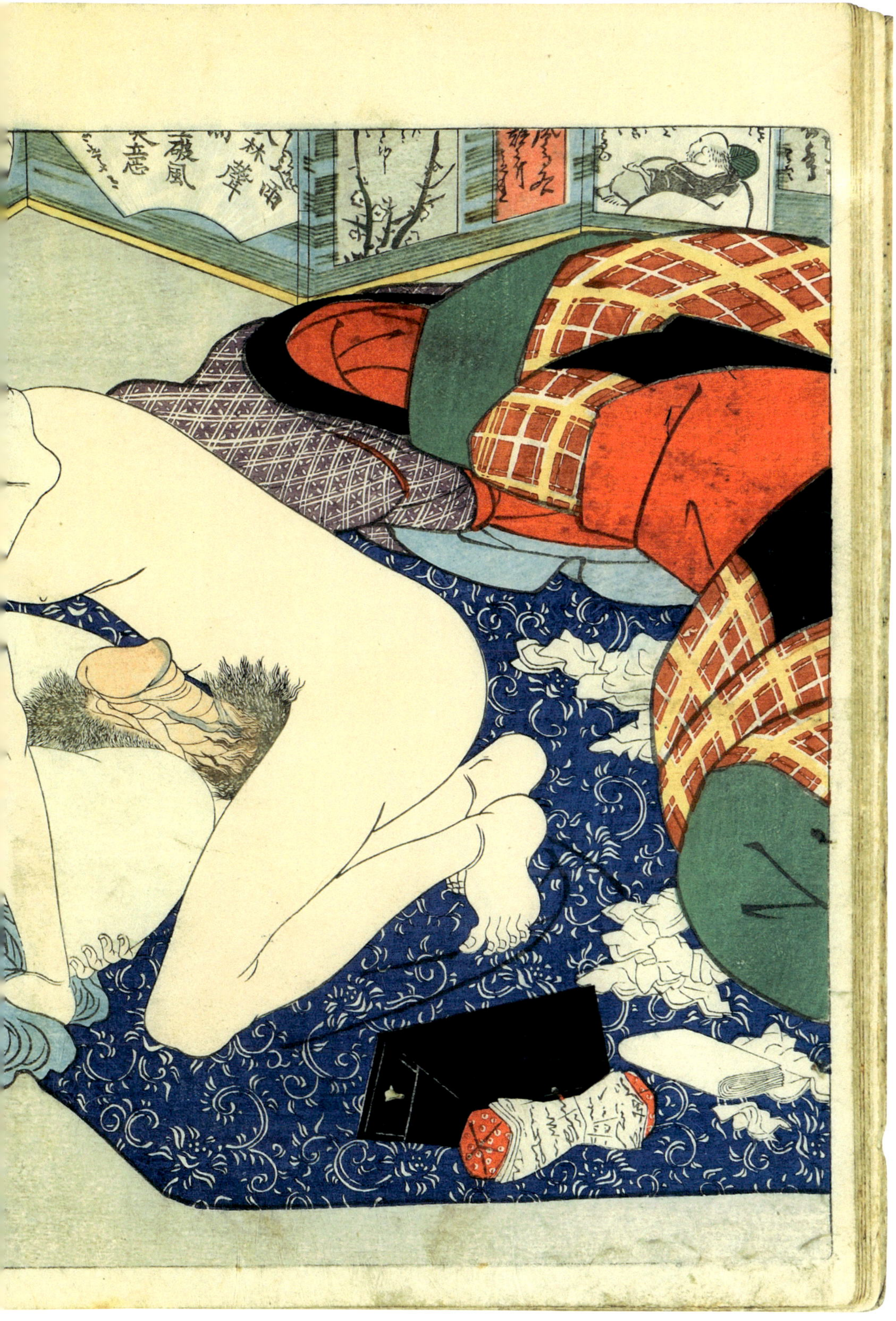

Utagawa Kunisada
Spring, Summer, Autumn and Winter: Prospects for the Four Seasons
(*Shunka shūtō: Shiki no nagame*), vol. 1
1827
Colour woodblock-printed book,
25.5 × 18.5 cm (covers)

In summer a *geisha* and her lover are enjoying an assignation in the upper floor of a tea-house. Attracted, and perhaps aroused, by the power of the thunderstorm outside, they have moved on to the balcony to enjoy passionate love-making. He grabs her tightly around the waist, and though his face is almost hidden, sexual desire can be read clearly in his intent gaze. A powerful dynamic is created by the criss-crossing vertical and diagonal lines of the composition.

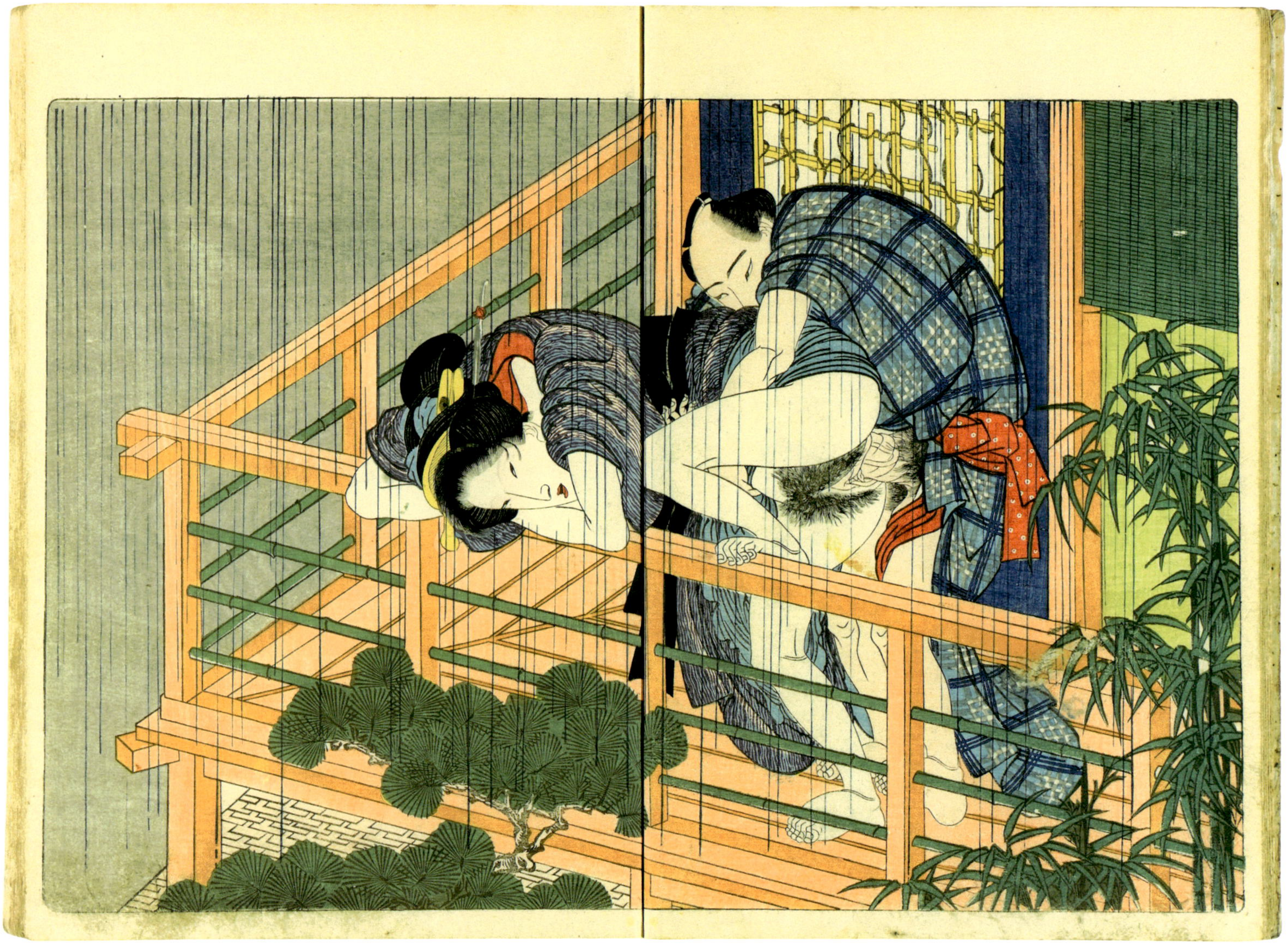

Many popular novels of the day received an erotic makeover, converting the relationships of the original story into explicitly sexual ones. These irreverent 'reworkings' were likely to find favour with the book-buying public, both those who had enjoyed the initial version and those who simply wanted erotica. One famous reworking was *Spring Love: Six Women of the First Birdsong (Shunshoku hatsune no ume)*, published in three volumes at the New Year 1842. 'Concealed' signatures on the folding screens reading 'Bukiyo Matahei' ('Clumsy Matahei') confirm that the work was illustrated by Kunisada. The original novel, *Spring Love: A Plum-Blossom Calendar (Shunshoku ume-goyomi)* written by Tamenaga Shunsui (1790–1843), had appeared in four volumes in 1832–3. It related the story of three women competing for the hand of the adopted son of a brothel owner. It was a highly acclaimed example of the new genre of 'books about human feelings' (*ninjōbon*), which featured affairs of the heart. The novel is set in Fukagawa unlicensed pleasure quarter, where the women were officially *geisha* entertainers rather than courtesans. In Fukagawa the atmosphere was more spontaneous and down to earth, and the working women were admired for their masculine qualities, in manners, speech, clothing and even names and hairstyles. Stock characters in the *ninjōbon* genre included 'female gallants', strong-minded women acting on their desires. Shunsui also supplied the text for the explicit spin-off, using the pseudonym Kyōkuntei Jinsui.[10] The book alternates text passages with lavishly coloured erotic scenes, each of which has a cartouche containing a poem, as well as the characters' dialogue.

Tenpō Reforms

Economic conditions worsened in the Tenpō era (1830–44), with bad weather causing crop failures and a severe famine which lasted from 1833 to 1836. There were riots in the cities due to high rice prices, and in some areas starvation occurred. Furthermore, for some years Western ships had been sighted off the coast of Japan, adding pressure on the government to respond to the threat. Reforms began after the death of the powerful retired shogun Ienari in 1841, led by Chief Senior Councillor Mizuno Tadakuni (1794–1851), and were consciously modelled after the earlier Kyōhō and Kansei Reforms. Exceeding these in severity, the programme was short-lived, however, as Tadakuni was ousted from power after only two years.

The government attempted to reform society by bringing the 'floating world' under stricter control. It clamped down on unlicensed prostitution by abolishing certain trades, curtailed the lavish lifestyles of the *kabuki* superstars, and punished authors and publishers associated with satirical and erotic books. The task of censorship was taken away from the publishers, and instead a rota of officials from the municipal government conducted inspections, though this lasted only until 1851. For prints, limits were placed on the number of sheets, the number of colour printing-blocks used and the price. Crucially, the two most important subjects, courtesans and actors, were forbidden, prompting artists – for a period of years – to find new and inventive ways to incorporate these perennial favourites into subsequent designs.[11]

Utagawa Kunisada
***Spring Love: Six Women of the First Birdsong* (*Shunshoku hatsune no ume*), vol. 2**
1842
Colour woodblock-printed book,
24.6 × 17.1 cm (covers)

This erotic novel depicts the adventures of *geisha* in the Fukagawa district. The cartouche explains that Jūbei is enjoying the pleasures of the 'twelve houses' (the main strip of restaurants and tea-houses in the district) with Adakichi. Beside the bed, wine-cups float in a blue-and-white porcelain basin of water, and a lacquered box of food stands beside. Adakichi throws her head back in abandon, holding tightly to Jūbei's arms and curling her toes in pleasure. She asks how it can be that he is so skilful, and he responds that he will be unable to forget something that 'tastes so good'. Metallic pigment is used to render the stripes of his robe. The signature on the screen is Kunisada's pseudonym for erotica, 'Matahei'. In the painting Daikoku, a god of good fortune and plenty, is standing on the customary rice-bales, but he has turned his back.

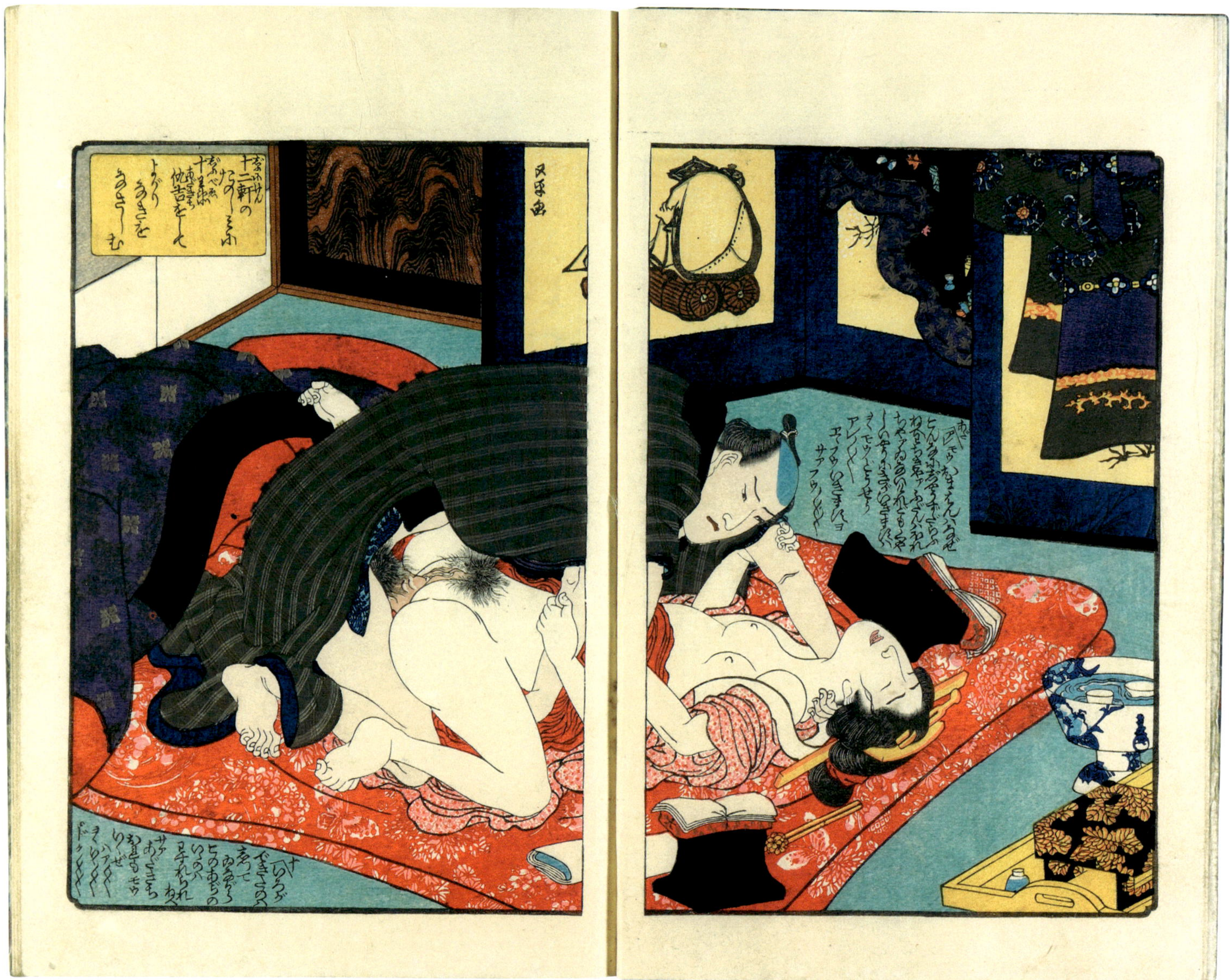

Utagawa Kunisada
The Eight Views of Ōmi Province (Ōmi hakkei)
1827
Colour woodblock-printed book, 20.5 × 13.4 cm (covers).
Private collection, Ritsumeikan ARC Database

As was seen in the previous chapter, the compositions of the painted handscrolls created in the early seventeenth century were reused and adapted by artists of a later generation. It appears, however, that the persistence of these motifs continued for as long as two hundred years. This book illustration uses the composition already seen on p. 62, of a man leaning down to perform cunnilingus, with the woman's leg wrapped around his head. The artist has placed this within a suitably furnished setting, with mat, bedding, tobacco pouch and pipe, a *shamisen* in its bag, a lantern and a folding screen. Kunisada could perhaps have seen a painted version of this scene, or a sketched memo in some painting instruction manual. He has corrected the anatomical inaccuracy of the woman's thumb seen in the earlier work, so that she grasps the padded headrest in a more naturalistic manner.

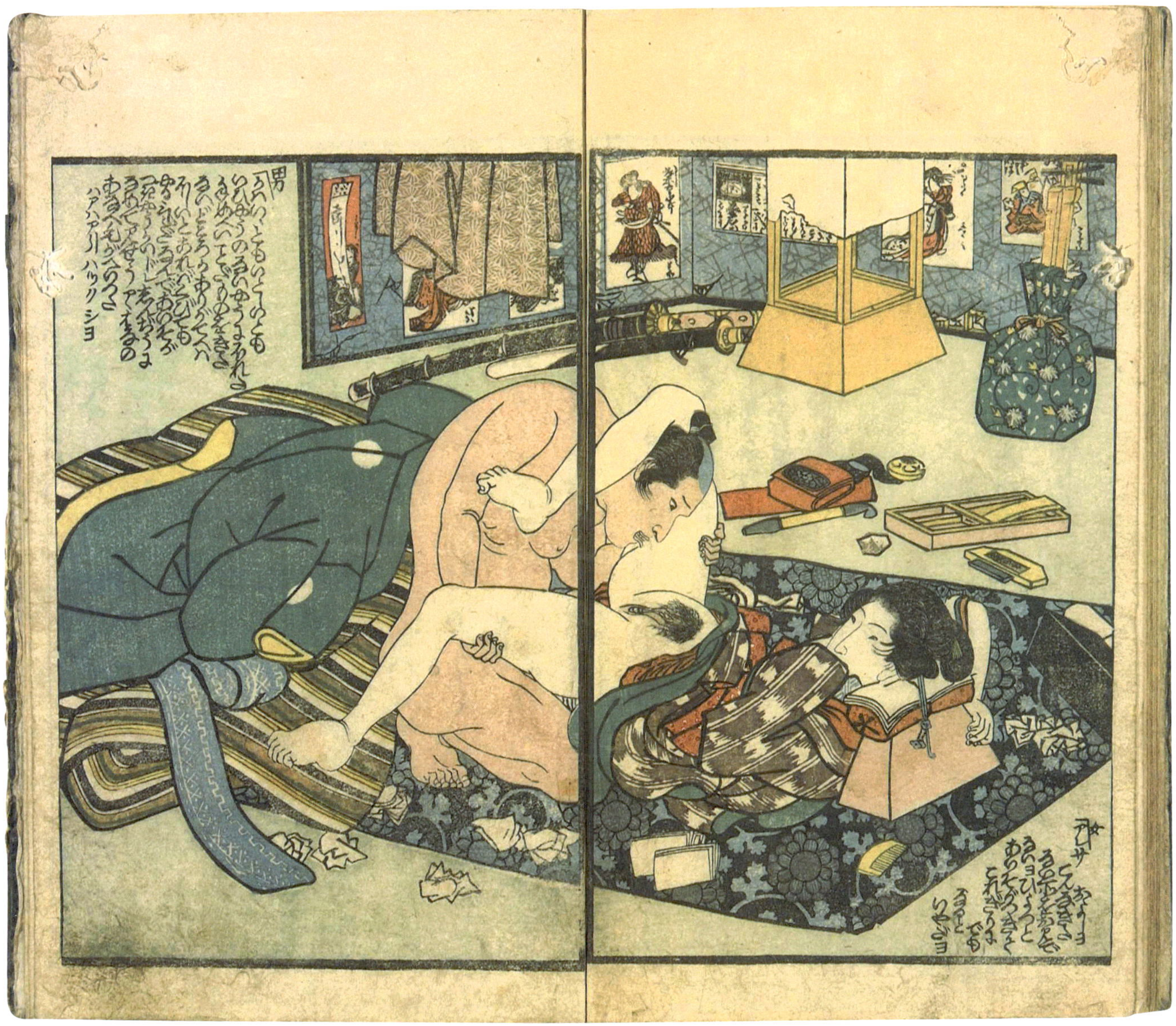

Utagawa Kunisada
Preparatory drawing
1830s
Ink on paper, 28.3 × 81 cm

This is one from a group of six drawings by Kunisada recently acquired by the British Museum, dating from the 1830s. They are thought to be preparatory drawings for a grand painted handscroll depicting *kabuki* actors in imagined scenes of love-making. This theme, although not presently known as a finished painting, indicates the status of *kabuki* stars within society, and the popular fascination with every aspect of their lives, extending to fantasy pictures of them in sexual situations. The theme of this drawing is a staple of *kabuki* theatre: the rivalry between Fuwa Banzaemon and Nagoya Sanzaburō for the love of Katsuragi, a high-ranking courtesan of the Shimabara quarter in Kyoto. On the right, Sanzaburō, played by Ichikawa Danjūrō VII (1791–1859), makes love to Katsuragi. He has disguised himself as Banzaemon by assuming the latter's distinctive robe with a design of swallows. On the left, the 'real' Banzaemon, played by Onoe Kikugorō III (1784–1849), hides behind a folding screen painted with the popular deities Daikoku and Ebisu. As he listens to the sounds of sex, he himself becomes impressively aroused. A concealed signature on the screen, 'Picture by Kokuteisai Hanabusa Ittai', gives a rare alternate name used by Kunisada at this time, indicating his affiliation to the painting line of Hanabusa Itchō (1652–1724).

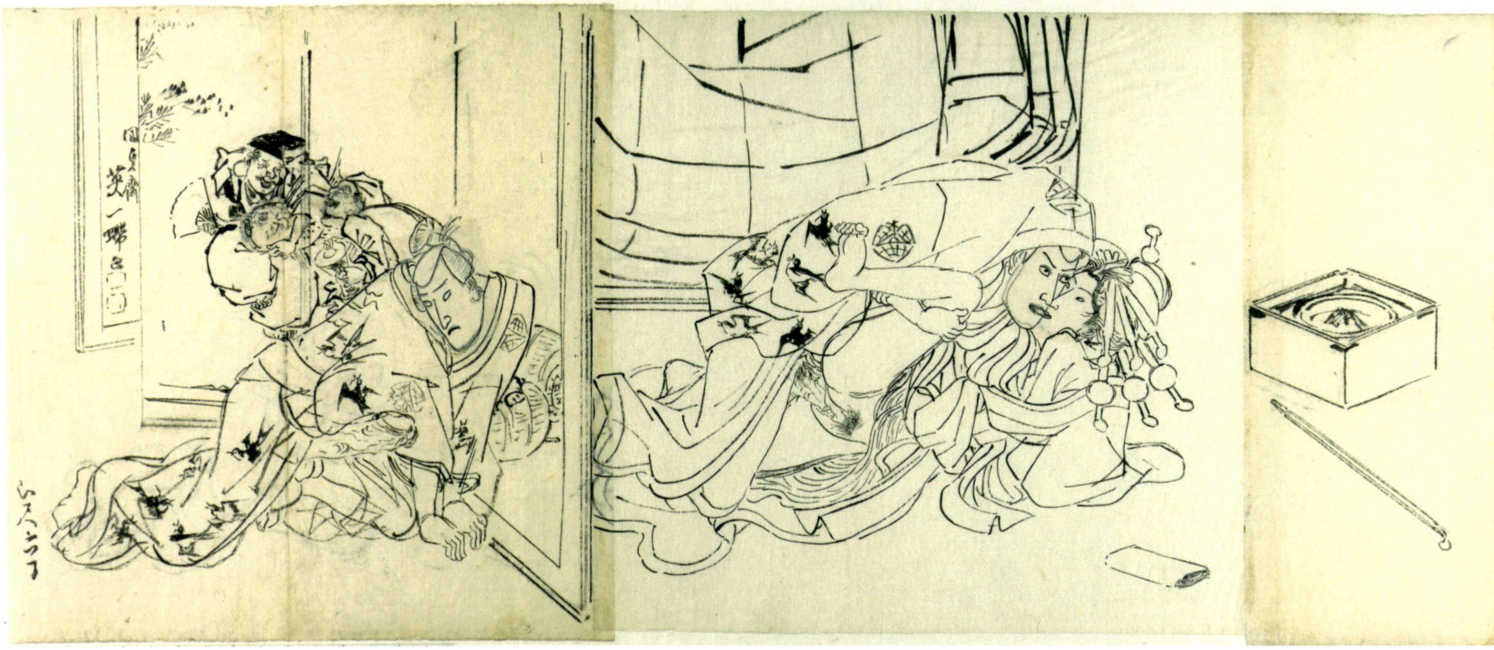

Utagawa Kuniyoshi

Utagawa Kuniyoshi (1797–1861) is regarded as one of the four leading *ukiyo-e* artists of the late Edo period, alongside Hokusai, Kunisada and Hiroshige (1797–1858). Whereas Kunisada and Hiroshige dominated the market for actor prints and landscapes respectively, Kuniyoshi was renowned for his powerful depictions of legendary warriors. He also produced numerous designs of comic subjects, and was adept at circumventing and even subverting the censorship regulations of the day. Like Kunisada (but not Hiroshige, it appears), Kuniyoshi was also prolific in his illustrations for erotic novels, designing an estimated total of some thirty-three books over three decades.

Well known as a cat-lover, Kuniyoshi produced many prints which feature cats or include them in the background. With erotica, too, he often included a cat washing or snoozing as its owners indulge in amorous pursuits, providing a sign of domesticity as well as a token of his own high regard for these animals. The cats so featured were most likely drawn from his own beloved pets. *Flowers with Abundant Benefits (Hana ikada)* was published in three volumes in 1836. The four-page text with which it opens and the commentaries within the pictures were supplied by Kōshoku Gaishi (also known as Hanagasa Bunkyō) and Adano Sanjin (an as yet unidentified author). The artist's name is not given explicitly, but signatures seen on screen paintings within the pictures read 'Ichimyōkai Nekoyoshi', one of Kuniyoshi's favoured pseudonyms for erotica. The name sounds like a genuine artist's nom de plume, but in fact means 'Feline-owning Cat-yoshi', attesting to his unbounded love for these animals. The illustrations are printed with opulent colours, and the settings are richly furnished. Much of the love-making is filled with energy and urgency, the bodies straining against each other. The printing illustrated here is a later one, employing slightly different colours from the original edition.[12]

The Pillowed Boudoir (Chinpen shinkeibai), published in three volumes in 1838 and with text again by Kōshoku Gaishi, was an erotic reworking of the hugely successful serialized novel *The New Jin ping mei (Shinpen kinpeibai)* by Takizawa Bakin (1767–1848), which ran to eighty parts over sixteen years (1831–47). This in turn was a Japanese reworking of the notorious Chinese novel, *The Plum in the Golden Vase (Jin ping mei)*, composed in the sixteenth century in one hundred parts by Lanling Xiaoxiao Sheng (a pseudonym). The novel related in explicit terms the exploits of an early twelfth-century merchant named Ximen Qing as he acquires a string of wives and concubines in his climb up the social ladder.[13] The illustrations by Kuniyoshi depict the passionate encounters of the heroes and brigands for which the artist was renowned. The sex scenes portray a variety of sexual permutations, with men and women, threesomes, and a man making love to a male actor who specialized in female roles. The sex is characterized by an intensity and immediacy, with bodies arched and contorted, often taking place in atmospheric night-time settings; also by a furtive, desperate quality, with many characters concealing their faces.

Utagawa Kuniyoshi
***Flowers with Abundant Benefits* (*Hana ikada*), vol. 3**
1836
Colour woodblock-printed book,
22.3 × 13.8 cm (covers).
International Research Center for Japanese Studies, Kyoto

As the man creeps up on the woman, he wonders aloud, 'Is Oriki really sleeping? She asked me to come, and yet she's already asleep. I bet she's just pretending [literally, 'racoon-dog sleeping']. We'll soon see which it is.' Oriki murmurs, 'He was so late turning up that I pretended to be asleep, but that hasn't stopped him.' They joke about how much he has to pay her, suggesting that she is a prostitute but that this is her secret lover rather than a client (erotic depictions of prostitutes are typically such scenarios). They end up exchanging a passionate kiss and the cat sleeps on peacefully despite their restlessness.

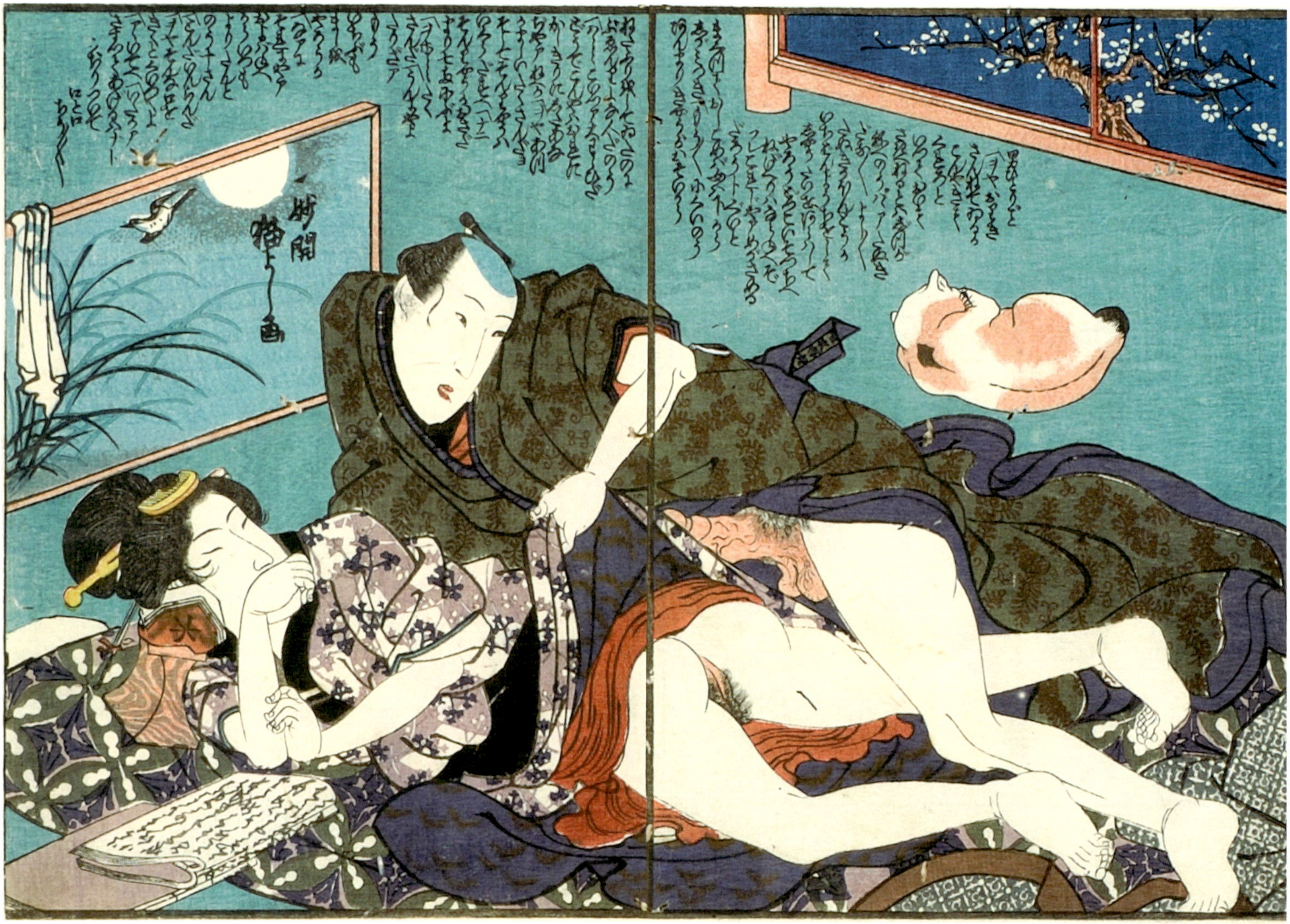

Utagawa Kuniyoshi
***The Pillowed Boudoir* (*Chinpen shinkeibai*), vol. 1**
1839
Colour woodblock-printed book, 22.2 × 15.6 cm (covers).
Private collection, Ritsumeikan ARC Database

In this scene from volume one, set in a kitchen, Taketarō, a vendor of 'osaragi' rice cakes, tells his wife Rakuyō he wants a quickie before he goes out on his rounds. The box of wares can be seen in the bottom right corner.

With her feet at different levels of the room, Rakuyō is trying to wash the rice, and she complains that the water is pouring out. In a humorous touch, Taketarō continues to stoke the fire in the stove by blowing through a bamboo tube. The water flowing from the pot conveys a sense of the jolt and sudden movement, but just behind the lovers a cat dozes unperturbed.

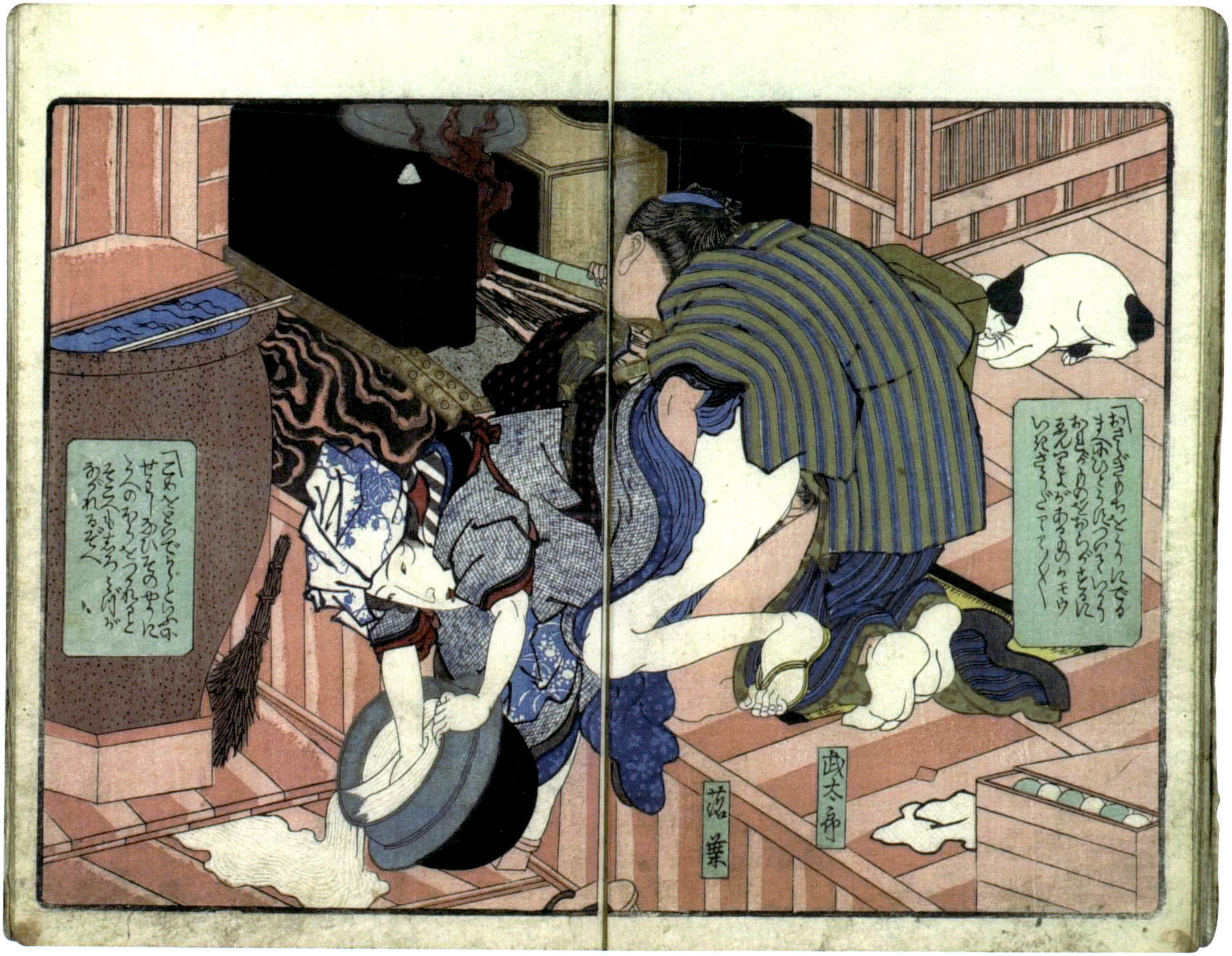

Attr. pupil of Utagawa Kuniyoshi
An Album of Fashionable Patterns
(*Tōsei komonchō*)
c. 1855
Colour woodblock-printed book,
23 × 15.8 cm (covers).
Private collection,
Ritsumeikan ARC Database

In a wonderfully tender scene we see a couple within the mosquito netting in their bedroom on a hot summer evening. While the woman lies in a state of complete physical relaxation after the height of sexual passion, the man has risen to pour a refreshing cup of tea. The used tissues scattered around them indicate their earlier exertions. The book was published in three volumes with an anonymous text, and the illustrations have been attributed to one of Kuniyoshi's pupils.[14]

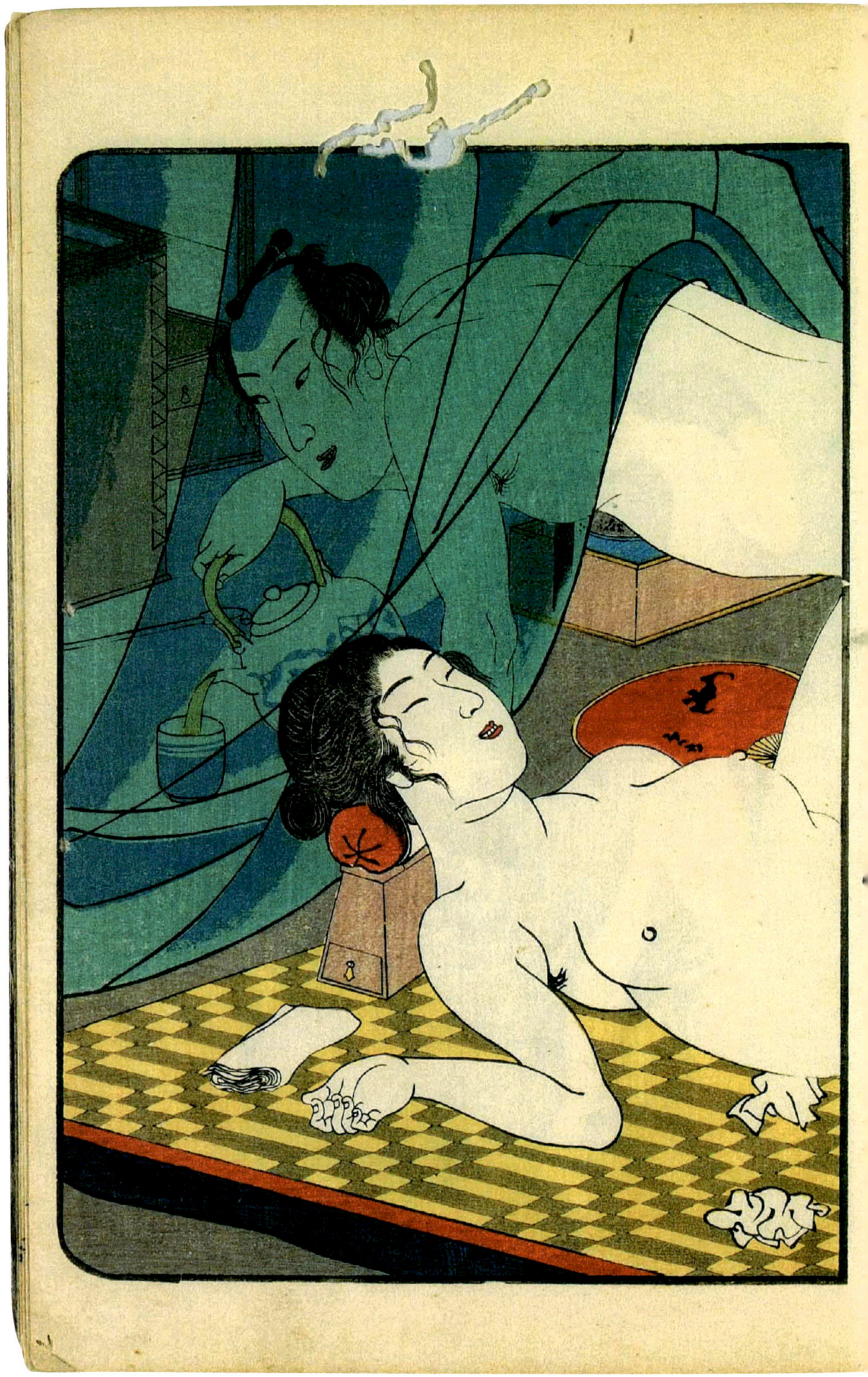

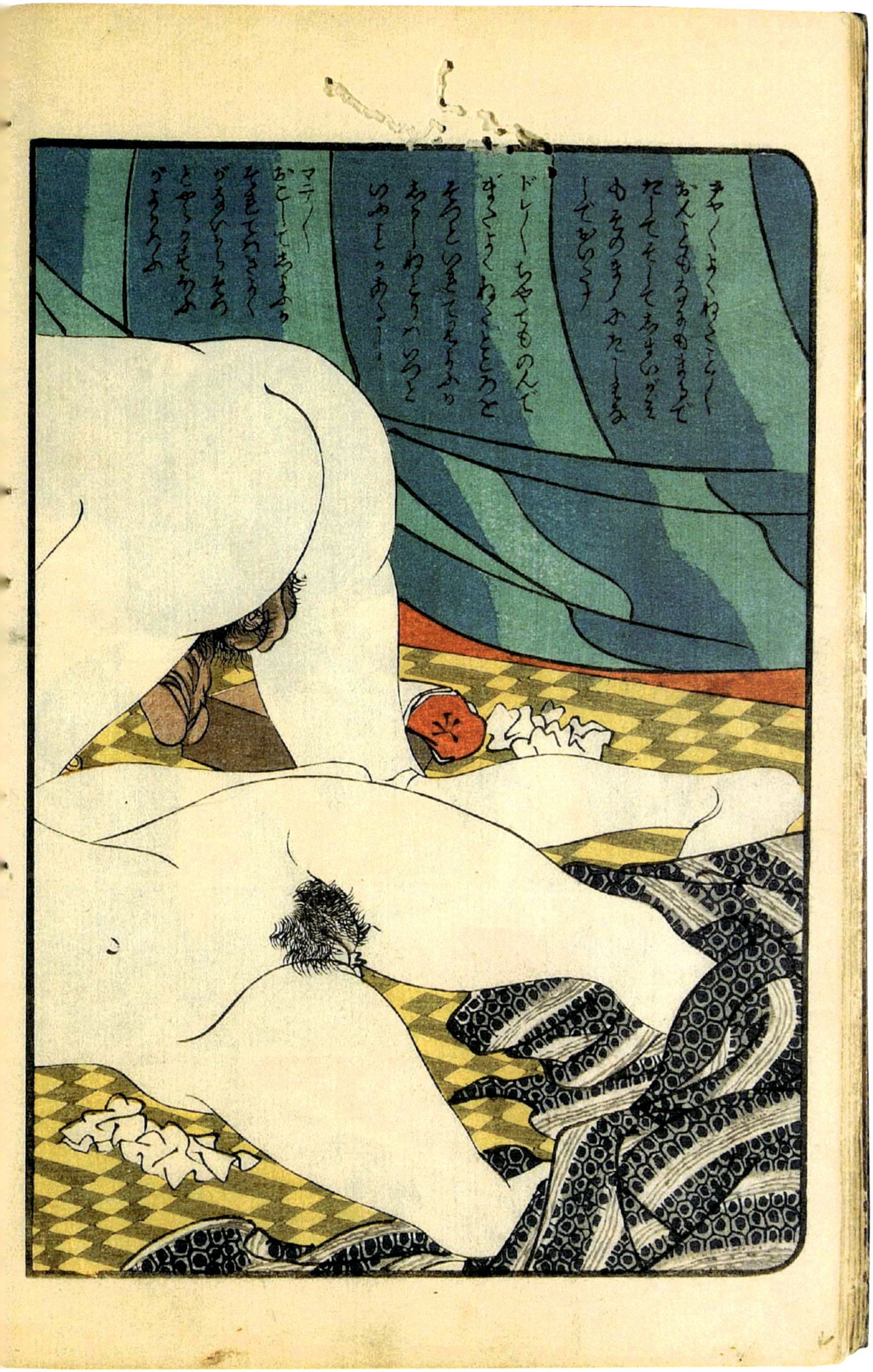

Meiji-era erotica

Under pressure from the Western powers, Japan signed a series of trade treaties in the late 1850s, greatly increasing the level of import of new goods and technologies. There was outright opposition among some samurai to the admittance of foreigners to Japan, which exacerbated the shogunate's inability to cope with the complex new diplomatic and trade situation. After several years of unrest and tension, in 1868 a 'restoration' of imperial power was declared, and a new administration was established in the name of the young Meiji emperor, inaugurating the Meiji era. The new government was determined to make Japan into an independent nation-state, and to this end set about remodelling society. A central tenet of the new government's programme of 'civilization and enlightenment' (*bunmei kaika*) was to demonstrate that Japan was a modern nation on a par with the Western powers. The ultimate aim was to achieve the revocation of unpopular 'unequal treaties', which granted foreigners tariff advantages and extraterritoriality. This reform, it was believed, required conformity with Western standards of morality and censorship. Long-established social practices, such as mixed bathing and the exposed bodies of labourers, brought critical comments from resident Westerners, and the government responded by outlawing such practices. The new morality naturally encompassed erotic material, with the publication of such items banned by a law enacted in 1872.[15]

Shunga had always depended in large part on representations of ordinary people's sex lives, and some Meiji-era erotica incorporated aspects of the changing society, including Western clothing and school uniforms, and men's short hairstyles (women took longer to adopt the Western styles). The Meiji era also offered new, more visible, roles for women, such as teachers, secretaries and nurses, and these figures entered the fantasy worlds of erotica as objects of desire.

Kawanabe Kyōsai

In the era of modernization, new expectations and standards were developing regarding appropriate subject matter for an 'artist'. Some may have produced erotic paintings on commission, but certain of the major artists produced very little erotic work: none is recorded by Tsukioka Yoshitoshi (1839–92), and Toyohara Kunichika (1835–1900) produced only a few book illustrations. The exception in the early years of the new Meiji era was the extremely prolific and inventive painter and print designer Kawanabe Kyōsai (1831–89), who produced numerous erotic printed works and paintings. As a young boy Kyōsai had trained briefly with Kuniyoshi, but he subsequently received a full apprenticeship in a branch of the official Kano school of painters to the samurai class. Although he painted many hanging scrolls depicting traditional subjects, his most memorable achievements were his humorous works, infused with his fertile imagination and comic genius. These works took conventional subject matter but gave it a novel twist, often poking fun at the new features of the age of 'civilization and enlightenment'. Kyōsai gained a reputation for his proficiency at producing extemporaneous works (*seki-e*) at public 'calligraphy and painting parties' (*shogakai*), and the spontaneity and speed of his brushwork is easily discernible here.

Kawanabe Kyōsai
Three erotic scenes
1880–89
Set of three hanging scrolls, ink and light colour on paper, each 115.4 × 18.9 cm
Israel Goldman Collection, London

This set of three scrolls exemplifies the spontaneous style of painting which Kyōsai so deftly brushed, often fuelled by his beloved *sake*. Having once prepared the inks and pigments, he would have needed only a few minutes to produce them. Notwithstanding the speed at which he worked, Kyōsai managed to imbue the images with both humour and expressiveness. On closer examination, we see that the scrolls depict three different classes of men: in the right-hand scroll, a young woman is seated on the lap of a priest (with shaved head); in the centre, a courtier wearing lacquered headgear (*eboshi*) grimaces as he pushes forward; and on the left, we see from behind a samurai with his distinctive top-knot, whose testicles receive some unwanted attention from an intrigued cat! The paintings do not explicitly represent the sexual act, but rather elicit a guffaw, in the true tradition of 'pictures to make you laugh' (*warai-e*; see p. 17). Beneath each signature Kyōsai used a seal appropriate to the subject matter, in the shape of a vulva.[16]

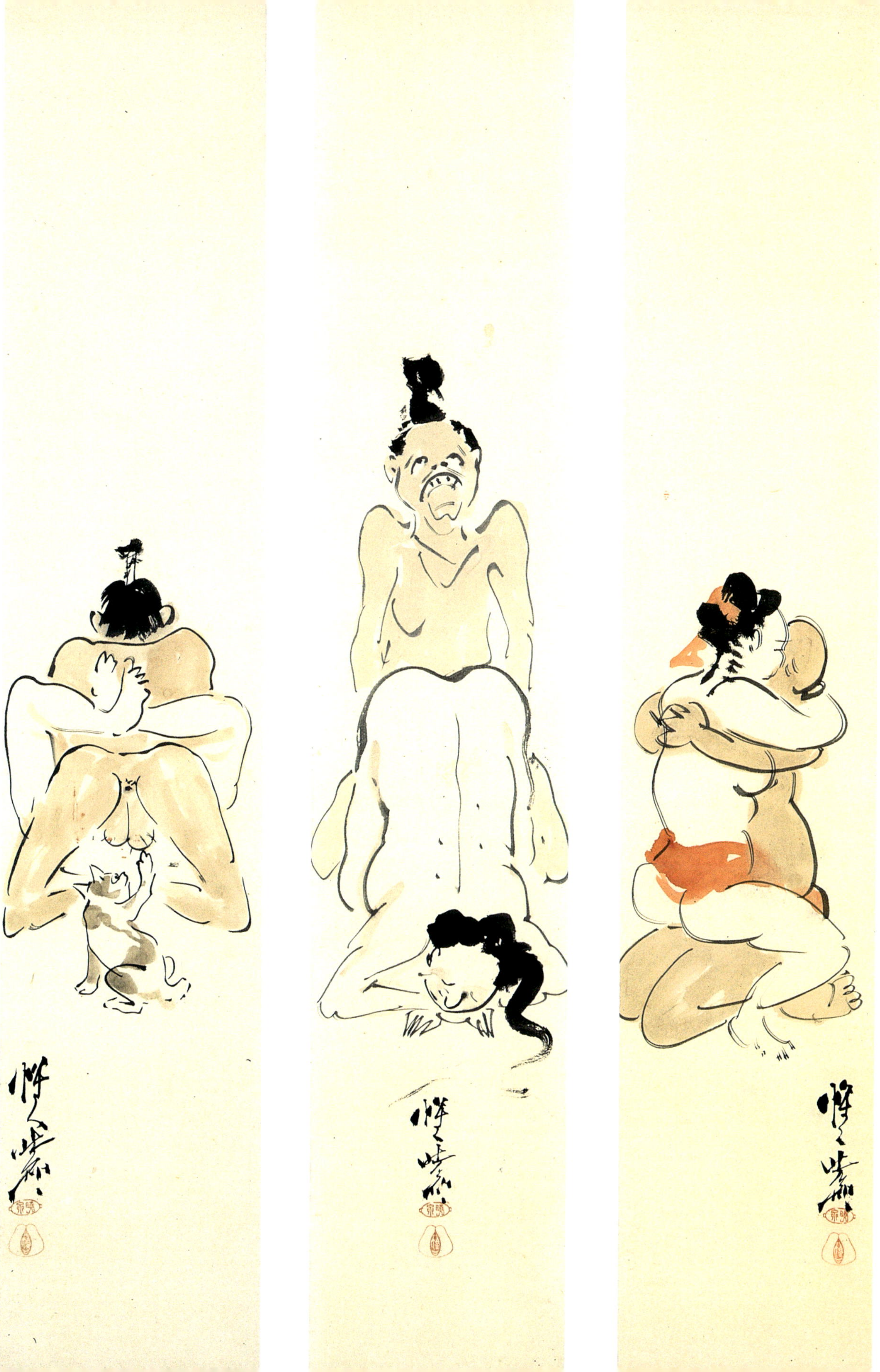

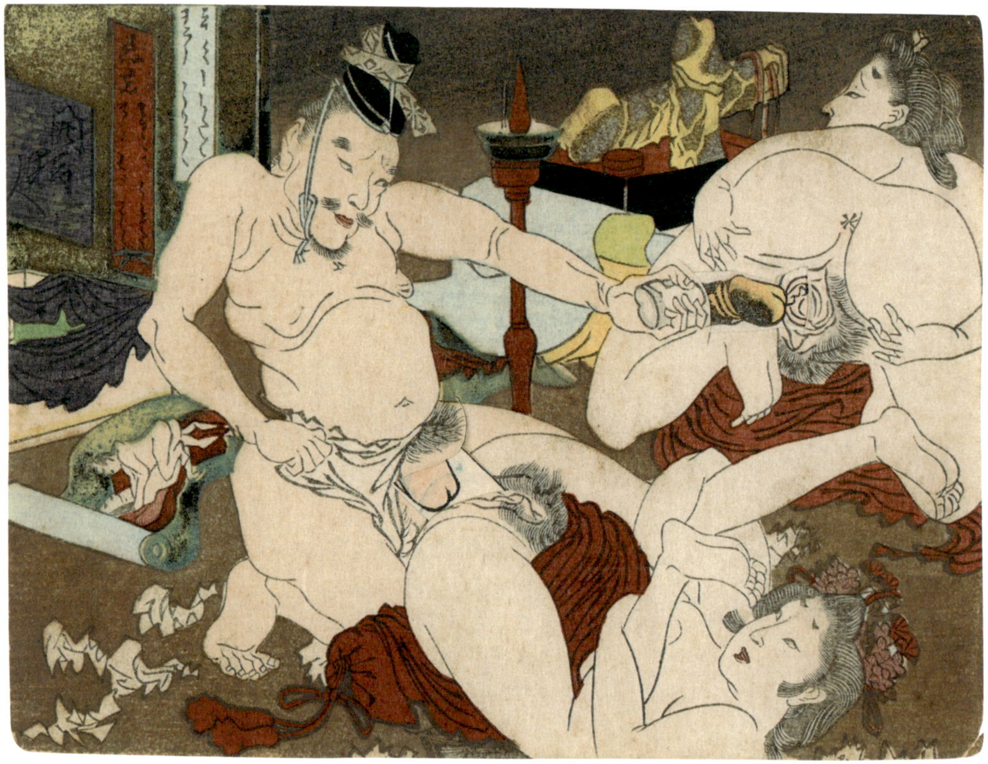

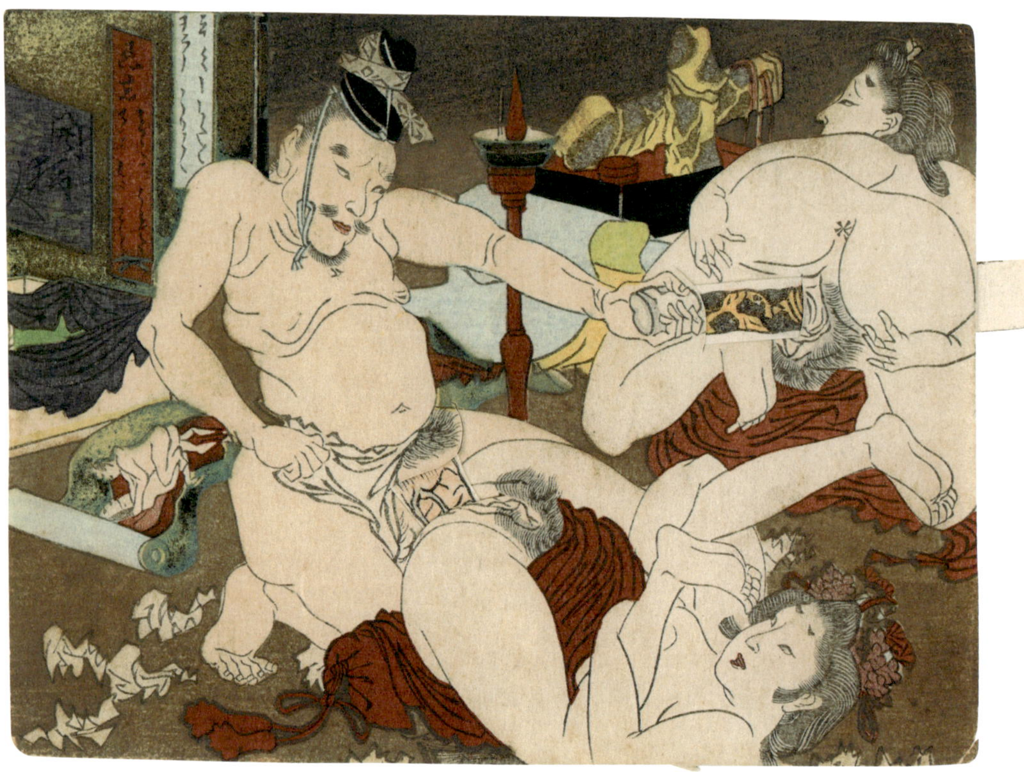

Kawanabe Kyōsai
Moveable erotic toy
Early 1870s
Colour woodblock print, 9.3 × 12.5 cm
Israel Goldman Collection, London

A night-time bedroom scene, in which a man is about to penetrate one woman while holding out a dildo towards another, who is obviously aroused and ready. The three have just been examining the painted scroll unrolled behind them – its box can be seen in the alcove – and more dildos and lubricant are on a tray in the corner. In a throwback to older erotic works, the man wears only a courtier's *eboshi* headgear. When the inserts are moved, the action gets well underway.

Kawanabe Kyōsai
Moveable erotic toy
Early 1870s
Colour woodblock print, 9.3 × 12.5 cm
Israel Goldman Collection, London

The design of this moveable print refers to an ancient belief about the shape-shifting abilities of certain animals, in the typical setting of a deserted house or temple. The samurai visiting a dilapidated mansion is impressively aroused in response to a beautiful young woman who invitingly lifts her skirts. However, when the insert is moved she is revealed to be a trickster fox, accompanied by its two cubs.

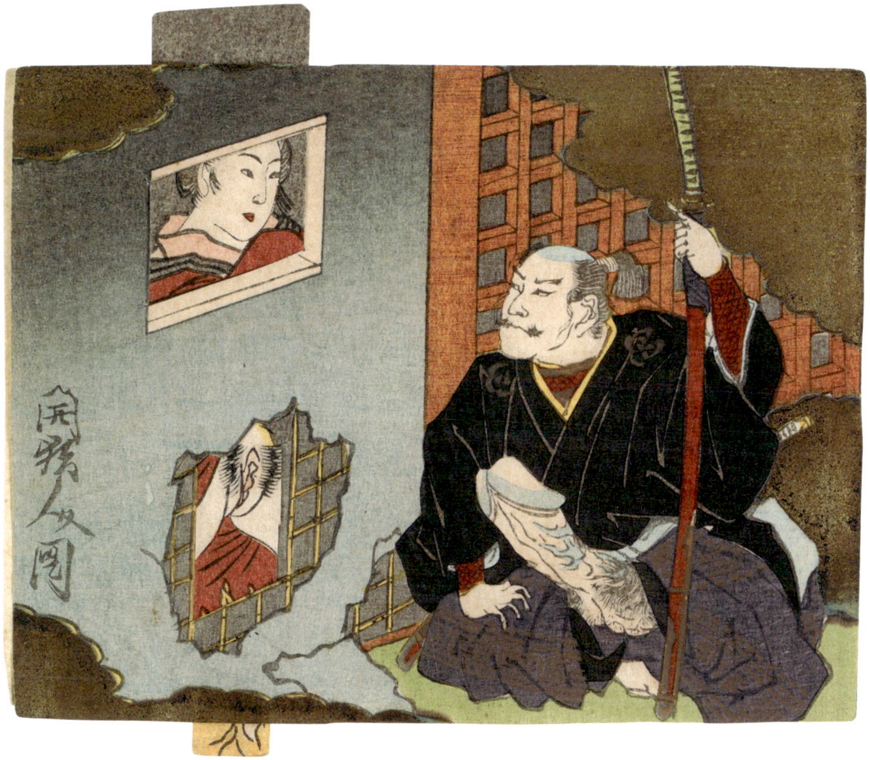

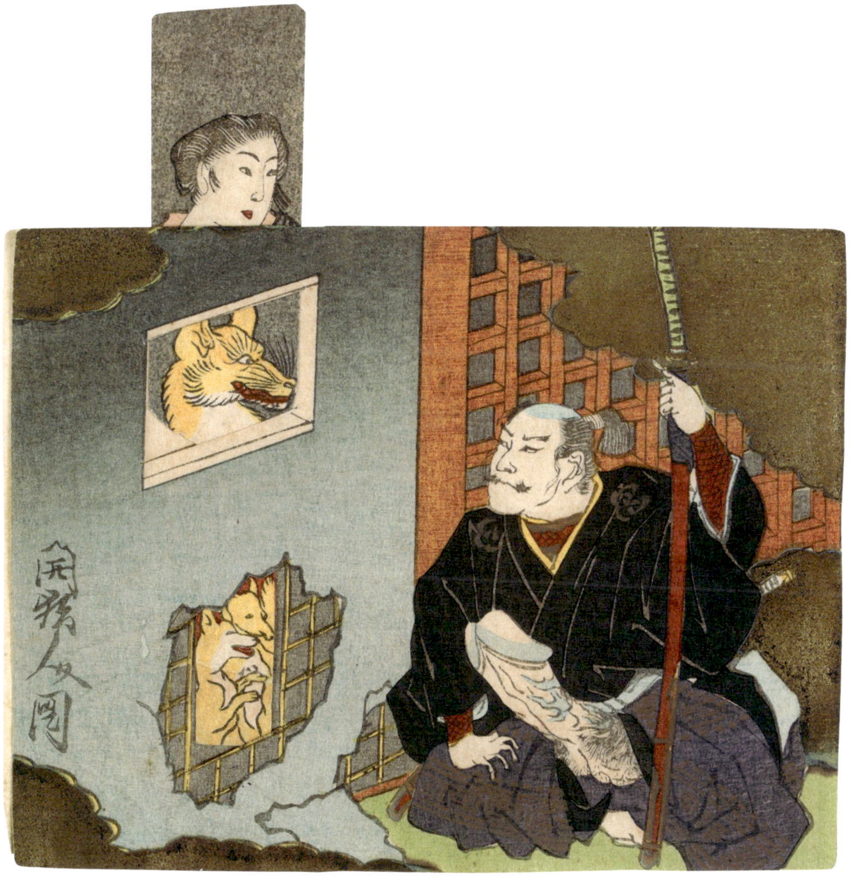

Kawanabe Kyōsai
***Crazy Pictures from the Brush of Seisei Kyōsai* (detail)**
1864
Handscroll, ink and colour on paper, 29.4 × 580.7 cm
Israel Goldman Collection, London

Kyōsai literally made a name for himself producing 'crazy pictures' (in the first part of his career he used the character for 'crazy' in his art-name). In this handscroll, the crazy pictures are humorous depictions of homosexual scenes, with characters customary for this theme of monks and acolytes. At the top right of this section, a monk kneels before a hanging scroll of a beautiful young man, masturbating into a bag with an intense expression on his face. Another young man tries to stop him (perhaps out of jealousy?), but is restrained. Below, the covers have fallen off a reclining pair of lovers. The somewhat manic quality of the scroll recalls the medieval pictorial traditions of the 'Farting Contest' (a theme also treated by Kyōsai; see p. 58) and the 'Phallus Competition'. The latter is depicted at left, overseen by a judge at a desk, and with two contestants using a rosary. Another man seems to be exhorting his reclining companion to take part.

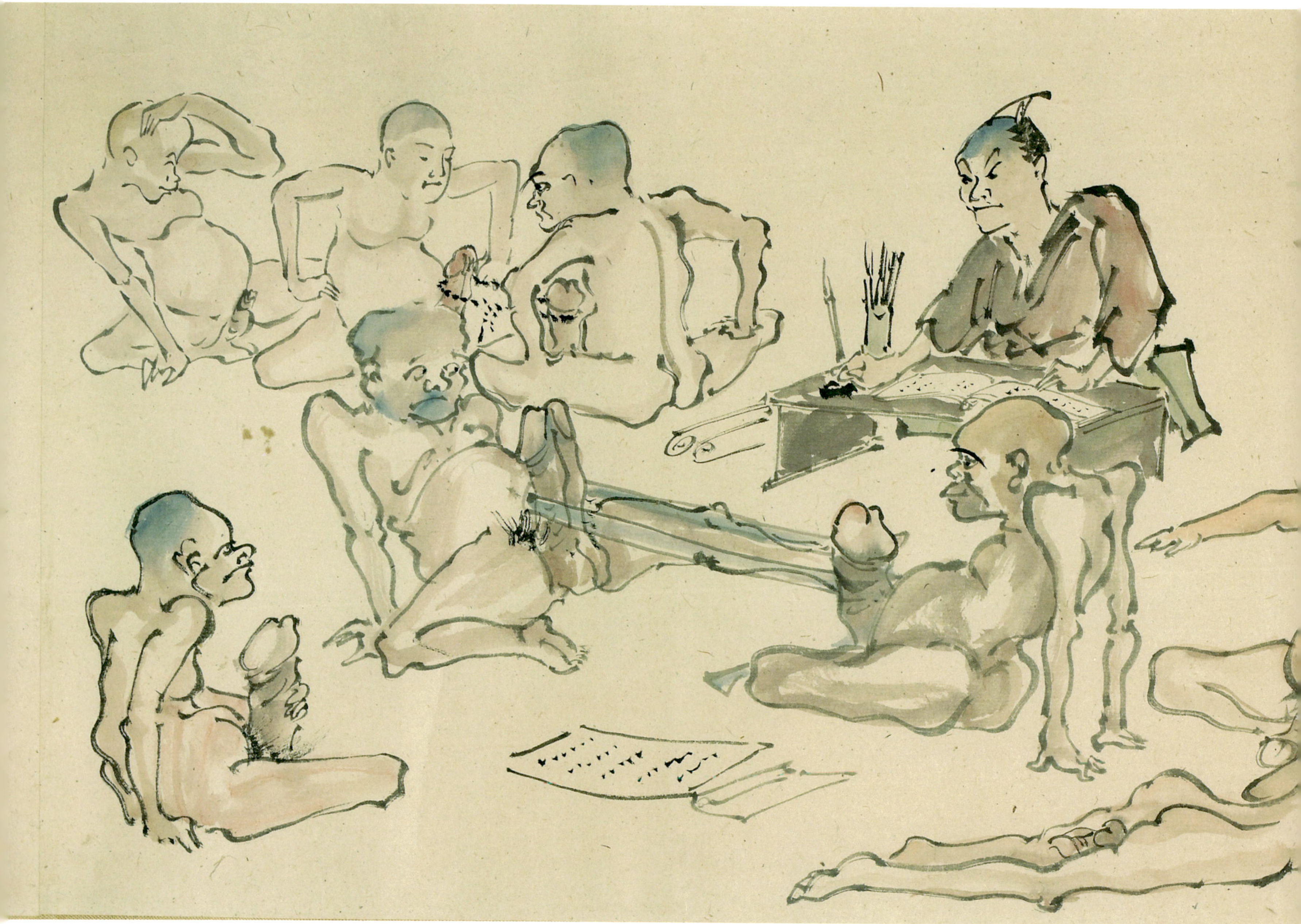

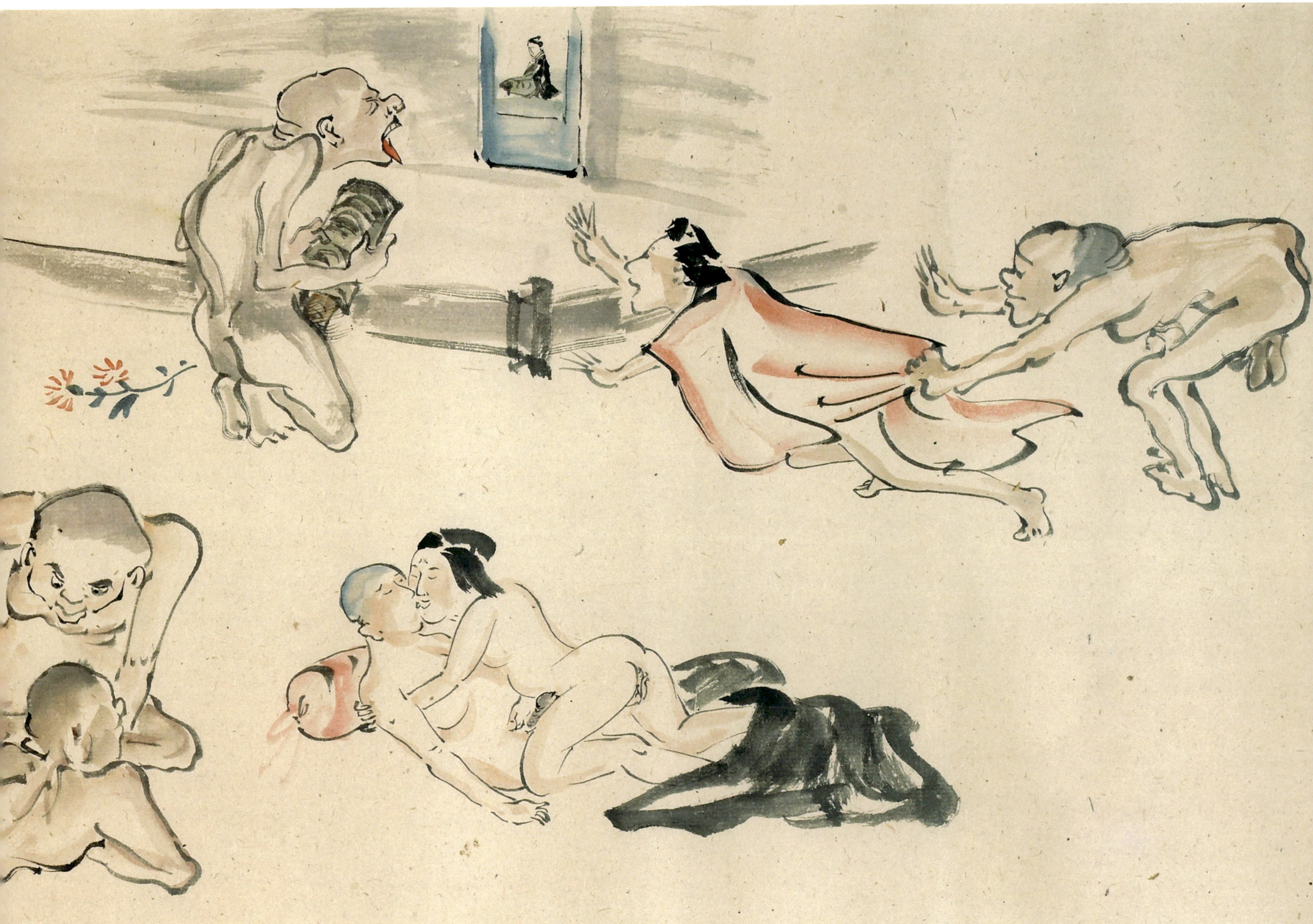

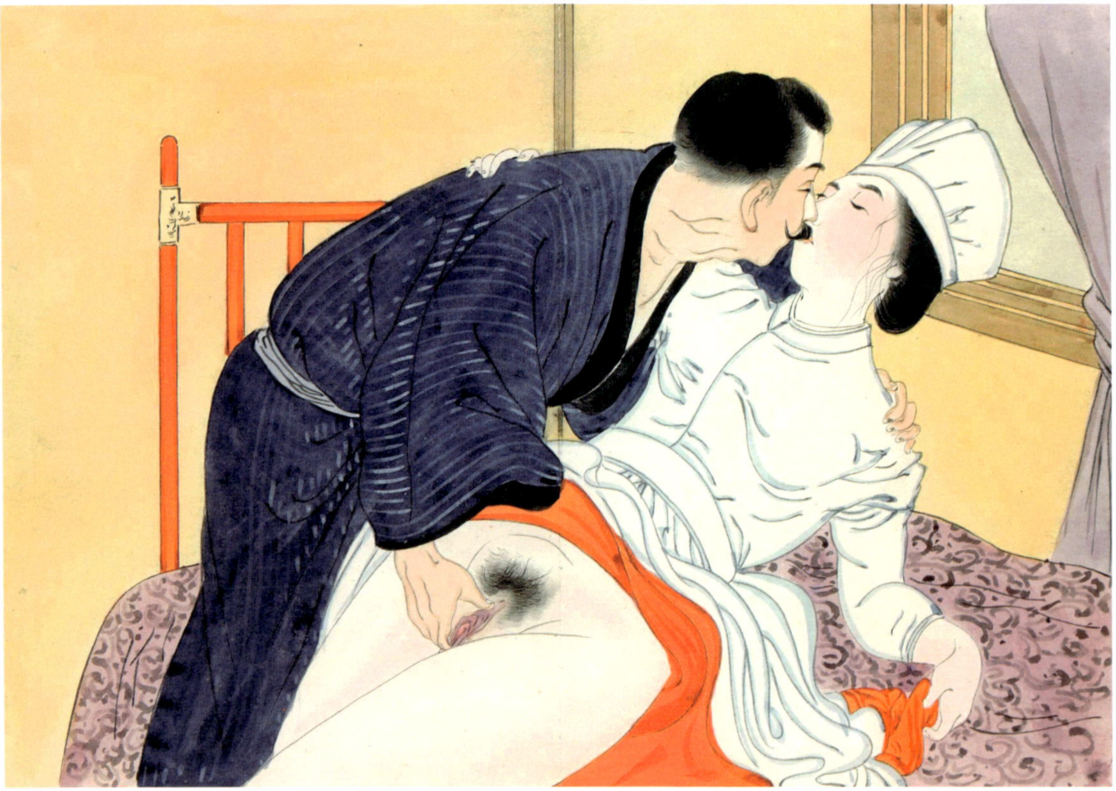

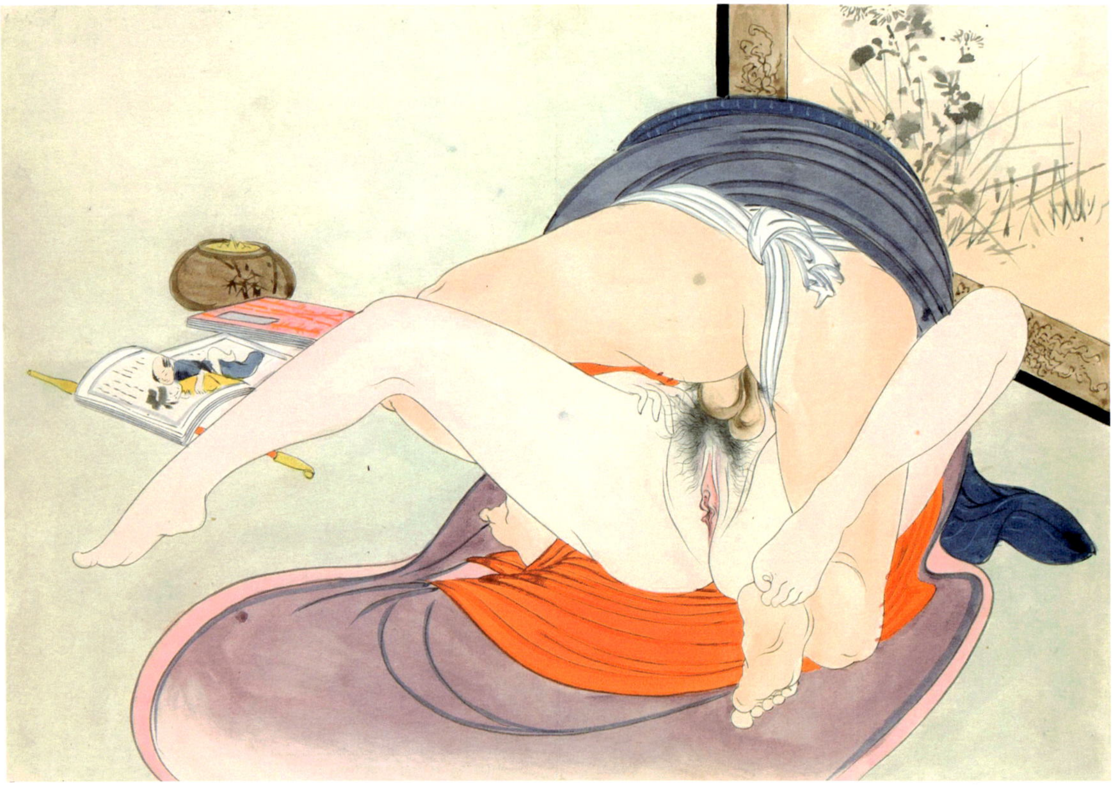

Attr. Tomioka Eisen
Album of erotic scenes
Late 19th century
Ink and colour on silk,
24 × 16.5 cm (covers).
Private collection,
Ritsumeikan ARC Database

Above: The first image in the album is set in a hospital, with a male patient seducing his young nurse. The fabrics are rendered with techniques of shading in the Westernized manner. Despite the woman's Western clothing, it serves the erotic purposes of the picture for her to continue the *shunga* tradition of wearing only a red underskirt beneath her uniform.

Below: In terms of setting, the ninth opening has little to distinguish it from a work of previous decades. Illustrated erotic books have obviously served to arouse the couple, with a tobacco pipe and ashtray lying beside them. The composition is unchanged from *Yakumo no chigiri*, and after the legal ban on erotica in 1872 images focusing on the sex organs became popular as the closing scene of albums.[19] Yet the depersonalization of the two bodies is a long way from the loving embraces depicted by earlier *ukiyo-e* artists, hinting at the shift towards something more like pornography as that category has been understood in the West.

An unusual and amusing type of *shunga* designed by Kyōsai was the articulated print. These were small prints (*koban*) in which the penis was printed on a moveable insert, operated by a tab. They were popular from the 1840s onwards, and many were designed by Utagawa Kunisada and his pupils. Kyōsai continued the format into the early 1870s, producing a number of sets of twelve prints, sold in illustrated wrappers. Characteristically for the work of this artist, the parts revealed are not always what one would expect. The theme was often embellished on the reverse of the print, with another perspective on the same scene, together with a humorous text.

Tomioka Eisen

Another of the few artists producing erotic imagery during the Meiji era was Tomioka Eisen (1864–1905). Born in Nagano Prefecture, he moved to Tokyo at a young age to study and soon after, in 1878, gained employment as a draughtsman with the Army Staff Office. He continued in this work until 1900, also producing numerous illustrations for newspapers, magazines and school textbooks, and frontispiece pictures for novels, as well as erotica. It was unofficial government policy to supply soldiers going to the front with stimulating erotic material, and Eisen may well have been supplying designs for distribution to soldiers in 'care packages' during the Sino-Japanese War of 1894–5. His *Poetic Intercourse* (*Yakumo no chigiri*, a title taken from the preface heading) is one of the best known erotic works of the Meiji era, and the last great *shunga* print album.[17] The album preserves the customary format of twelve pictures, and the settings and hairstyles suggest little of the modernization taking place at the time. In terms of style, however, Eisen drew on Western techniques of realism, particularly in the shading. Eisen's work was frequently copied, for example in a painted album which updates the scenes to include various aspects of modern life, such as uniforms and men's short haircuts. Five of the designs in this painted version overlap with *Yakumo no chigiri*, but even these alter the compositions. It is possible that Eisen, or perhaps his pupil Hamada Josen (1875–?), had a model-book containing multiple designs from which customers could select twelve for inclusion in a commissioned painting album.

Colour woodblock printing continued to be used for affordable prints containing both news and entertainment until the early years of the twentieth century, but increasingly it was competing with the new technologies of lithography and photography. After about 1885 a large number of reproductions were issued of *shunga* from the late eighteenth and early nineteenth centuries. Just as the physical traces of the old city of Edo were rapidly disappearing, so nostalgia grew for its past visual culture.[18]

Chronology

For further information, see 'Chronology of Japanese History', in *Japan – An Illustrated Encyclopaedia* (Kodansha, 1993)

1600
The forces of the warlord Tokugawa Ieyasu are victorious at the battle of Sekigahara.

1603
Tokugawa Ieyasu receives the title *sei-i taishōgun* (barbarian-quelling generalissimo) from the emperor; establishes the Tokugawa shogunate.

1610s–20s
Nationwide construction boom and stabilization of political situation.

1614
First measures to outlaw Christianity.

1615
'Laws Governing the Military Households' issued; final defeat by Tokugawa of rival Toyotomi clan in the Siege of Osaka.

1630s
Control of foreign relations: expelling Spanish and Portuguese, prohibiting overseas travel by Japanese, limiting trade to the Chinese and Dutch. Formalization of mandatory alternate attendance system for *daimyō*.

1657
Large conflagration in Edo ('Meireki fire'), prompting subsequent wide-scale urban regeneration.

1688–1704
Development of 'floating world' culture during Genroku era (*kabuki* and puppet theatre, novels, poetry, woodblock prints).

1716
Relaxation of laws against foreign learning.

1720s
Implementation of Kyōhō Reforms under shogun Tokugawa Yoshimune.

1720s–30s
Development of woodblock print technology, particularly by Okumura Masanobu.

1765–70
Development of full-colour woodblock printing, led by Suzuki Harunobu.

1780s
Period of creative blossoming during the Tenmei era; also 1782–7: serious famines and epidemics.

1787–93
Senior Councillor Matsudaira Sadanobu implements Kansei Reforms.

1808
Incident involving British warship *Phaeton* increases shogunate's fear of Western aggression.

1810s–20s
Poetic, literary and artistic activities flourish, centred around the cultural salons of Edo (Bunka and Bunsei eras).

1833–6
Severe famines and economic instability.

1841–3
Tenpō Reforms led by Senior Councillor Mizuno Tadakuni.

1840s
Number of foreign warships and whaling vessels in Japanese waters increases; shogunate learns of China's defeat in Opium War.

1850s
Growing dissatisfaction with shogunate, calls for restoration of imperial power.

1854–8
Series of treaties drawn up with Western nations (United States, Netherlands, Russia, Great Britain and France).

1860
Departure of shogunal mission to the United States.

1866–8
Alliance of Satsuma and Chōshū domains against the shogunate.

1868
Meiji Restoration proclaimed; series of defeats for shogunal loyalist forces.

1871
Abolition of domains and creation of prefectures.

1872
Establishment of modern school system.

1877
Satsuma Rebellion defeated by government forces.

1889
Meiji Constitution promulgated; Imperial Diet opens the following year.

1894–5
Sino-Japanese War; Taiwan becomes a Japanese colony.

Glossary

abuna-e	risky (i.e. risqué) pictures
aiban	medium-sized format
ama	female diver
bijinga	'pictures of beautiful women'
chōnin	townspeople
daimyō	lord of domain
eboshi	lacquered headgear worn by courtiers
egoyomi	calendar prints
geisha	entertainer
haniwa	clay figures placed on burial mounds c. 250–600 AD
harikata	dildo
harimise	display room for courtesans
hashira-e	vertical 'pillar print'
inrō	men's small medicine container suspended from sash
kabuki	popular form of theatre, with male-only casts
kashihonya	itinerant book lenders
kiwadoi	dangerous, risky
koban	small print
kōshokubon	amorous books
kyōka	humorous verses
mitate	irreverent reworking of traditional themes
netsuke	carved toggle for *inrō*
ninjōbon	books about human feelings
nishiki-e	'brocade pictures' (i.e. full-colour woodblock prints)
nō	classical form of theatre
ōban	large-sheet format
obi	sash
ōkubi-e	bust-portraits
ōraimono	conduct books
ōtsubi-e	close-up 'portrait' of woman's genitalia
sake	drink made from fermented rice
samurai	warrior
seki-e	extemporaneous works
shamisen	three-stringed musical instrument played with a plectrum
shikake	special devices used in book production, such as extra flaps of paper
Shintō	indigenous Japanese form of worship
shogakai	calligraphy and painting parties
shōgun	leader of the military government
shunpon	erotic books
surimono	privately produced luxury prints employing special pigments and texture effects
tako	octopus, also slang for 'vagina'
ukiyo-e	'pictures of the floating world', i.e. prints and paintings depicting the pleasures of urban life
wakashū	adolescent male, distinguished by hairstyle with the crown shaven and long forelock pinned on top
warai-e	pictures to make you laugh
warai-dōgu	'laughter tools' (i.e. dildos)

Notes

Picturing sex in Japan, 1600–1900

1. The manual entitled *Gasen* (*A Fish Weir of Painting*, 1721) by Hayashi Moriatsu was used as a textbook by painters of the Kano school until the late nineteenth century; Hayakawa Monta, *Shunga no mikata: 10 no pointo* (Heibonsha, Tokyo, 2008), p. 19.

2. It has been argued that this was their sole function, but this limited use seems unlikely. See Timon Screech, *Sex and the Floating World: Erotic Images in Japan, 1700–1820*, 2nd edn (Reaktion Books, London, 2009).

3. Henry Smith, 'Overcoming the Modern History of Edo "Shunga"', in Sumie Jones (ed.), *Imaging/Reading Eros: Sexuality and Edo Culture, 1750–1850* (The East Asian Studies Center, Indiana University, Bloomington, 1996), p. 27.

4. Hayakawa Monta, *Shunga no mikata: 10 no pointo* (Heibonsha, Tokyo, 2008), p. 28.

5. Roger S. Keyes, *Ehon: The Artist and the Book in Japan* (New York Public Library, 2006), pp. 46–7.

Features of *shunga*

1. Shirakura Yoshihiko, in *Shunga II: Iro moyō hyakutai*, Bessatsu Taiyō (Heibonsha, Tokyo, 2008), p. 2.

2. Haga Tōru, in Sumie Jones (ed.), *Imaging/Reading Eros: Sexuality and Edo Culture, 1750–1850* (The East Asian Studies Center, Indiana University, Bloomington, 1996), pp. 97–102.

3. Katharina Epprecht, in *Liebeskunst: Liebeslust und Liebesleid in der Weltkunst*, exh. cat. (Museum Rietberg, Zurich, 2002), p. 239.

4. Hayakawa Monta, *Shunga no mikata: 10 no pointo* (Heibonsha, Tokyo, 2008), p. 74.

5. '*Baka fūfu shunga o manete suji chigai*'; *ibid.*, p. 74.

Patterns of sensual pleasure: from luxury paintings to popular prints, 1600–1750

1. Richard Lane (1926–2002), the pioneering Western scholar of *shunga*, produced a comprehensive study of early painted handscrolls, *The Early Shunga Scroll – Ukiyo-e no shoki emaki* (Gabundō, Tokyo, 1979). Owing to Japanese publishing regulations, the reproductions were censored.

2. *Ibid.*, nos 15 and 45.

3. Margarita Winkel, in Chris Uhlenbeck and Margarita Winkel, *Japanese Erotic Fantasies: Sexual Imagery of the Edo Period* (Hotei Publishing, Amsterdam, 2005), pp. 200–201.

4. *Early Images from the Floating World*, exh. cat. (Sebastian Izzard, New York, 2008), p. 32.

5. The famed author and poet Ōta Nanpo (1749–1823) owned this particular copy and added his own handwritten preface (a not uncommon practice), dated 'Summer 1808'.

6. The novel has been translated by Paul Gordon Schalow, *The Great Mirror of Male Love* (Stanford University Press, 1990).

7. The work is reproduced in Richard Lane, *Genroku no Erosu* IV, Bessatsu (Gabundō, Tokyo, 1978), p. 36.

8. Ihara Saikaku, transl. Paul Gordon Schalow, *The Great Mirror of Male Love* (Stanford University Press, 1990), pp. 281–8.

9. Timothy Clark *et al.*, *The Dawn of the Floating World, 1650–1765*, exh. cat. (Royal Academy of Arts, London, 2001), p. 100.

10. Hayashi Yoshikazu, 'Sukenobu no kōshokubon', *Ukiyo-e Bessatsu: Tokushū Koga hiden* (February 1977), pp. 50–56.

11. Sarah E. Thompson and H.D. Harootunian, *Undercurrents in the Floating World: Censorship and Japanese Prints*, exh. cat. (Asia Society Galleries, New York, 1991), pp. 42–4.

12. Tom and Mary Anne Evans, *Shunga: The Art of Love in Japan* (Paddington Press Ltd, New York, 1975), p. 133.

Poem of the pillow: masterpieces of the late eighteenth century

1. C. Andrew Gerstle, *Great Pleasures for Women and Their Treasure Boxes and Love Letters and a River of Erect Precepts for Women by Tsukioka Settei*, episodic festschrift for Howard Hibbett (Highmoonoon, Hollywood, CA, 2009), p. 14.

2. Timothy Clark, '*Mitate-e*: some thoughts, and a summary of recent writings', *Impressions* 19 (1997), pp. 6–27.

3. The series had been preceded by Harunobu's non-erotic *Zashiki hakkei*. For further information on both these series, see Hayakawa Monta, *The shunga of Suzuki Harunobu: mitate-e and sexuality in Edo*, transl. Patricia J. Fister (International Research Center for Japanese Studies, Kyoto, 2001), ch. 4, *passim*, from which the translations used here have been taken.

4. *Ukiyo-e hizō meihin-shū: Komachi-biki* (Gakken, Tokyo, 1992), p. vii.

5. Translations by David Pollack and Timothy Clark respectively.

6. In the opening scene a woman seated about to compose a letter is surprised by a young man sliding open the door. In the earlier impression the door is decorated with *tachibana* (citrus-tree) motifs, but this was changed (as in the British Museum's copy) to a plain, two-colour design. For detailed discussion of this issue, see Naitō Masato in *Ukiyo-e hizō meihin-shū: Nami chidori* (Gakken, Tokyo, 1991), pp. 52–4.

7. Margarita Winkel, in Chris Uhlenbeck and Margarita Winkel, *Japanese Erotic Fantasies: Sexual Imagery of the Edo Period* (Hotei Publishing, Amsterdam, 2005), pp. 200–201.

8. Timothy Clark, *Ukiyo-e Paintings in the British Museum* (British Museum Press, London, 1992), p. 115.

9. These are listed in Hayashi Yoshikazu, *Kitagawa Utamaro. Edo makura-eshi shūsei* (Kawade Shobō Shinsha, Tokyo, 1990), pp. 36–9.

10. Shūgō Asano and Timothy Clark, *The Passionate Art of Kitagawa Utamaro* (British Museum Press, London, 1995), p. 281.

11. Shūgō Asano, 'Tenmei-ki no Utamaro', *Kokka* 1229 (March 1998), pp. 22–3.

12. Shūgō Asano and Timothy Clark, *The Passionate Art of Kitagawa Utamaro* (British Museum Press, London, 1995), p. 282.

13. *Ibid.*, p. 285. The dating of the book is based on a reference to the seventh instalment of *Ehon Taikō ki*. The book was banned in the fifth month of 1804 and *Ehon warai jōgo* was subsequently reissued with the reference removed.

14. See Sarah E. Thompson and H.D. Harootunian, *Undercurrents in the Floating World: Censorship and Japanese Prints*, exh. cat. (Asia Society Galleries, New York, 1991), p. 45, in which the print is reproduced.

15. Translations by Peter Dale; taken from Hayashi Yoshikazu, *Shunga geijutsu sensho: Kitagawa Utamaro: Ehon warai jōgo* (Beikoku Seiseidō, Tokyo, 1980).

Erotic adventures: heightened drama in the nineteenth century

1. Joshua S. Mostow, 'Utagawa Shunga, Kuki's "Chic" and the Construction of a National Erotics in Japan', in Doris Croissant, Catherine Vance Yeh and Joshua S. Mostow (eds), *Performing 'Nation': Gender Politics in Literature, Theater, and the Visual Arts of China and Japan, 1880–1940* (Brill, Leiden and Boston, 2008), pp. 383–424.

2. Jack Hillier, *The Art of Hokusai in Book Illustration* (Sotheby Parke Bernet Publications, London, 1980), p. 176.

3. Shūgō Asano, *Katsushika Hokusai: shunga no sekai* (Yōsensha, Tokyo, 2005), p. 17.

4. Danielle Talerico, 'Interpreting Sexual Imagery in Japanese Prints: A fresh approach to Hokusai's "Diver and Two Octopi"', *Impressions* 23 (2001), p. 37.

5. *Ibid.*, pp. 26–34.

6. Information and translations (by Peter Dale) are taken from Hayashi Yoshikazu, *Shunga geijutsu sensho: Manpuku wagōjin* (Beikoku Seiseidō, Tokyo, 1980).

7. Hayakawa Monta, *Shunga no mikata: 10 no pointo* (Heibonsha, Tokyo, 2008), p. 66.

8. I am indebted to Ellis Tinios for sharing with me the results of his preliminary survey of nineteenth-century *shunpon* and his ideas on their financial sponsorship (as yet unpublished).

9. Hayashi Yoshikazu, *Edo makura-eshi shūsei: Kunisada* (Kawade Shobō Shinsha, Tokyo, 1989), pp. 125–30. One illustration shows a marked similarity to a composition by Toyokuni in the book *Ōyogari no koe*.

10. *Ibid.*, pp. 154–6.

11. Sarah E. Thompson and H.D. Harootunian, *Undercurrents in the Floating World: Censorship and Japanese Prints*, exh. cat. (Asia Society Galleries, New York, 1991), pp. 76–9.

12. Robert Schaap, *Heroes and Ghosts: Japanese Prints by Kuniyoshi, 1797–1861*, exh. cat. (Van Gogh Museum, Amsterdam, and Philadelphia Museum of Art, 1998), p. 222. The book is also known by the title *Gyokueki chiwa hana ikada*.

13. *Ibid.*, p. 219. David Tod Roy, transl., *The Plum in the Golden Vase, or Chin P'ing Mei*, vols 1–3 (Princeton University Press, 1993–2006).

14. Robert Schaap, *Heroes and Ghosts: Japanese Prints by Kuniyoshi, 1797–1861*, exh. cat. (Van Gogh Museum, Amsterdam, and Philadelphia Museum of Art, 1998), p. 221. The book is also known under two other titles: *New Forms of Fashionable Patterns* (*Shinkei komonchō*) and *Smiling Face of Flowers* (*Hana no egao*).

15. Chris Uhlenbeck and Margarita Winkel, *Japanese Erotic Fantasies: Sexual Imagery of the Edo Period* (Hotei Publishing, Amsterdam, 2005), p. 235.

16. *Ibid.*, p. 225.

17. *Ibid.*, p. 236.

18. *Ibid.*, p. 217.

19. Higashiōji Taku, *Ukiyo-e Meiji no higa* (Gabundō, Tokyo, 1977), p. 43.

Further reading

Timothy Clark, *Ukiyoe-e Paintings in the British Museum*, British Museum Press, London, 1992

Tom and Mary Anne Evans, *Shunga: The Art of Love in Japan*, Paddington Press Ltd, New York, 1975

Sumie Jones (ed.), *Imaging/Reading Eros: Sexuality and Edo Culture, 1750–1850*, The East Asian Studies Center, Indiana University, Bloomington, 1996

Timon Screech, *Sex and the Floating World: Erotic Images in Japan, 1700–1820*, 2nd edn, Reaktion Books, London, 2009

Sarah E. Thompson and H.D. Harootunian, *Undercurrents in the Floating World: Censorship and Japanese Prints*, exh. cat., Asia Society Galleries, New York, 1991

Chris Uhlenbeck and Margarita Winkel, *Japanese Erotic Fantasies: Sexual Imagery of the Edo Period*, Hotei Publishing, Amsterdam, 2005

Illustration acknowledgements

Except where otherwise stated, photographs are © The Trustees of the British Museum, courtesy of the Department of Asia.

Page

2 Asia OA+,0.133.6

6 Asia OA+,0.140

8, 10 Asia OA+,0.133.5

9 Asia OA+,0.133.11

11 (*top*) Asia 1972,0724,0.4 (Given by Lady Jane Kelly)

11 (*bottom*) Asia OA+,0.86

12 Asia 1892,0523.11 (Given by Sir Augustus Wollaston Franks)

13 Asia 1981,0813,0.1.1–4

14–15 Asia 2008,3027.1

17 British Museum

18, 19 Private collection, Ritsumeikan ARC Database

20 Asia 1979,0305,0.30

22–3 Asia 1881,1210,0.1707–8

24 (1) Asia 1945,1017.434 (Bequeathed by Oscar Charles Raphael)

24 (2) Asia 1945,1017.675 (Bequeathed by Oscar Charles Raphael)

24 (3) Asia HG.147 (Given by Professor and Mrs Hull Grundy)

25 (4) Asia W.424 (Given by George Witt)

25 (5) Asia OA+,7134

26 Asia 1982,0701,0.2 (Given by Dr and Mrs Michael Harari)

27 Asia 1979,0305,0.146

28, 29 Asia 1979,0305,0.159

31 Asia 1881,1210,0.1710

32 Asia 1979,0305,0.70

35 Asia 1914,1012,0.3

36 Asia OA+,0.135.6

38 (*top*) Asia OA+,0.133.12

38 (*bottom*) Asia OA+,0.90

41 Asia OA+,0.133.4

43 Asia OA+,0.88

45 Asia 2008,3027.1

46 Asia OA+,0.97

47 Asia 1906,1220,0.41

48 Asia OA+,0.141.1–11

50–51 Asia OA+,0.135.6

52 Asia OA+,0.84

55 (*top*) Asia 1972,0724,0.4 (Given by Lady Jane Kelly)

55 (*bottom*) Asia 1906,1220,0.349–50

56 Asia OA+,0.434

57 Asia OA+,0.138

58 Israel Goldman Collection, London

60, 61 Asia 1980,0325,0.1

62 Asia 1986,0522,0.1

64 Asia OA+,0.434

66–7 (1–3) Private collection, Ritsumeikan ARC Database

67 Asia As1928,0609.1.1–9 (Given by M. Williams)

69 Asia 1948,0710,0.10

70 Asia 1972,0724,0.10 (Given by Lady Jane Kelly)

71, 72–3 Asia OA+,0.140

74 © The British Library Board; Or.75.g.27, fols 184v–185r

76 Asia OA+,0.65

77 Asia OA+,0.70

78–9 Private collection, Ritsumeikan ARC Database

81 Asia OA+,0.112

82 Asia 1980,0325,0.4

84 Asia 1996,1002,0.1

85 Private collection, Ritsumeikan ARC Database

87 Asia OA+,0.87

89 Asia 1937,0710,0.41 (Bequeathed by Charles Hazelwood Shannon)

90 Asia OA+,0.435

91 Asia OA+,0.83

92–3 Asia 2009,3024.1 (Purchased with funds from the Brooke Sewell Bequest)

95 Asia OA+,0.81

96, 97 Asia 1972,0724,0.6 (Given by Lady Jane Kelly)

98 Asia 1989,0603,0.1

100–101 (*top*) Asia OA+,0.135.5

100–101 (*middle*) Asia OA+,0.135.8

100–101 (*bottom*) Asia OA+,0.135.10

102–3, 104, 105 Asia 2008,3027.1

106 Asia OA+,0.133.9

107 Asia OA+,0.133.7

109 Asia OA+,0.133.6

110, 111, 112 Asia 1972,0724,0.3 (Given by Lady Jane Kelly)

114–115 (*top*) Asia OA+,0.135.13

114–115 (*below left*) Private collection, Ritsumeikan ARC Database

115 (*below right*) Asia 1972,0724,0.4 (Given by Lady Jane Kelly)

116, 117 Asia 1980,0325,0.4

118 Asia 1972,0724,0.15 (Given by Lady Jane Kelly)

119 Asia OA+,0.478

120 Asia OA+,0.122

121 Asia OA+,0.116

123 Asia OA+,0.117

124 Asia 1979,0305,0.173

125 Asia 1972,0724,0.7 (Given by Lady Jane Kelly)

126, 127 Asia 1972,0724,0.4 (Given by Lady Jane Kelly)

128 Asia 1981,0813,0.1.1–4

131, 132, 133 Private collection, Ritsumeikan ARC Database

135 Asia OA+,0.109

137, 138, 139 Asia OA+,0.141.1–11

140, 141 Private collection, Ritsumeikan ARC Database

142 Asia OA+,0.472.1–2

143 Asia 1973,0723,0.35

144 Private collection, Ritsumeikan ARC Database

146–7, 148 Asia 1981,0813,0.1.1–4

150 Asia OA+,0.463.1–3

151 Private collection, Ritsumeikan ARC Database

152 Asia 2006,0803,0.1

154 International Research Center for Japanese Studies, Kyoto

155 Private collection, Ritsumeikan ARC Database

156–7 Private collection, Ritsumeikan ARC Database

159, 160, 161, 162 Israel Goldman Collection, London

164 Private collection, Ritsumeikan ARC Database

Index

This index lists Japanese personal names as the user is most likely to search for them, e.g. Suzuki Harunobu is found under Harunobu. Page numbers printed in bold type refer to illustrations and their captions.